They forged a dynasty and embraced
THE SPIRIT OF AMERICA

Nathan—He built an empire from the raw earth with unstoppable courage and determination—and demanded nothing less from his children.

Martha—The proud matriarch. She offered her children the one thing her husband could never express—love.

Nathan—He carried his father's dauntless spirit to England to spur an industrial revolution—that eventually splintered his own family.

Stephen—He grew up in the shadows of his older brother, but his trailblazing journey with Lewis and Clark fired him with the ambition to lead the Stewart dynasty to undreamed of new heights.

Burl—His weaknesses could never satisfy the demands of being a Stewart and led him on a path to tragedy.

Maybelle—The only Stewart daughter. Her insatiable passions scandalized the family and victimized any man who tried to own her.

The Spirit of America ★ Book I

CHALLENGE

CHARLES WHITED

An Arthur Pine Associates Book

BANTAM BOOKS
TORONTO · NEW YORK · LONDON · SYDNEY

CHALLENGE

A Bantam Book / July 1982

ISBN 0-553-20181-6

Published simultaneously in the United States and Canada

Bantam Books are published by Bantam Books, Inc. Its trade-
mark, consisting of the words "Bantam Books" and the por-
trayal of a rooster, is Registered in U.S. Patent and Trademark
Office and in other countries. Marca Registrada. Bantam
Books, Inc., 666 Fifth Avenue, New York, New York 10103.

PRINTED IN THE UNITED STATES OF AMERICA

0 9 8 7 6 5 4 3 2 1

"A Stewart has a lust. The blood is a concoction of wild Scot and Englishman, spiked with other fiery brew and mixed, 'tis said, at fever heat."

—*Isaiah Stewart*

I

The track was quite fresh, pressed into loose earth. Nathan knelt and touched it with his fingers. He shifted the long rifle, inspected the loading, and squinted ahead into a leafy glade. Afternoon sunlight filtered down through autumn colors. The forest lay wrapped in primeval silence, so intense that he could sense his own breathing and heartbeat. His excitement freshened. He squatted, waiting.

A breeze came up out of the valley. But the sound he heard was solid, more than rustling grass and leaves. He scanned the downslope for movement. Brown sage grass rippled away toward a patch of hickory and ash. Late goldenrod nodded in dappling sunlight. From somewhere came the liquid chuckle of falling water. A bird called. And then the other sound came again. *Tap*. A hoof, knocking against rock. There was a soft tearing as invisible teeth foraged at low-hanging leaves.

He moved silently, duck walking down the slope, careful to remain upwind. Then he was on his knees in the brush at the edge of a tiny clearing by the creek, poking the snout of the long rifle ahead. A bee buzzed at his ear. He parted the tall grass.

1

There, not thirty yards away, stood the buck; a fine six-pointer intent on his afternoon meal.

Nathan brought the stock to his cheek, sighted down the slot and bead with both eyes open, breathed deeply, let it out. This was a rite to him, a supreme act of nature; hunter and quarry became, for a final instant of life, as one. His heartbeat quickened. Breathing again, concentrating on the bead and the target, a spot just behind the left ear, he squeezed the trigger . . . squeezed . . .

Ka-boom! The shot, as always, surprised him. The gunstock smashed against his shoulder. Ahead, as if in slow motion, the beautiful animal jerked, took a faltering step, dropped heavily to its knees, and toppled over. The left hind leg kicked twice and was still. Blood poured from the wound, making a pool in the dirt. Nathan lay quietly, watching over the gunsight. He breathed as if from physical exertion and sweat dampened his face. Blue smoke wreathed the gun, reeking of burnt powder. He stood up and walked to the deer. There was a stench of fresh blood. He was glad for the clean, quick kill.

It was a good hunt and the second deer of the day. Since dawn Nathan and his brothers had also bagged pheasant, wild turkey, squirrel, several fat rabbits, and quail. The exhilaration of it gave him a boundless energy that even trudging for many miles over these hills could not exhaust. After the last kill, he'd left Stephen and Burl behind and climbed swiftly, his long legs eating up the yards. Alone, he could relish the beauty of this day.

The autumn was stunning. Early frost had brushed the hills with flaming colors, and then the weather cleared. Indian summer brought endless days of bright sunlight, sweeping the hills from a crystalline blue sky. One's sight reached to infinity. Nathan stood over the deer and looked out from the height. The hunt had brought him to a kind of promontory. Far below, he glimpsed a slash of silver. A few paces more and the river came into his view, broad and shining as it meandered down its ancient course. A flatboat drifted with the current, a tiny blob in all that immensity. The Ohio. Born where the two lesser rivers joined near his father's doorstep, and his own birthplace, the river linked every Stewart's destiny. The thought brought a bittersweet nostalgia. He had grown up here. He hated to leave. This river, these hills, gave him a oneness with earth and sky. And now he was saying good-bye. This was his last hunt of youth. When he returned, if he ever returned, it would be as a man. He turned to the deer and propped the long rifle against a sweet gum tree. The gun was empty. He had forgotten to reload after the shot. But reloading was not on his mind.

Nathan drew a heavy hunting knife from its sheath and knelt to cut off the fine horned head. The cut began just under the right ear, slanted downward toward the upper breastbone, and brought a fresh gush of blood as it severed the jugular vein. The great brown eyes of the buck stared at the sun.

The heavy growl came from behind him, on the grassy slope. Nathan leaped to his feet, knife dripping blood. The bear was twenty feet away, no more, rising to its haunches with a bare-fanged snarl. Nathan lunged for the long rifle and cursed. Empty. He backed away. The bear, sniffing fresh blood, advanced at a lumbering trot. Nathan turned and ran, knife in hand. He ran along the contour of the hill. Then his pursuer roared. The sound put wings to his heels. Knees pumping, he bolted down the slope, crashing through underbrush. Massive footfalls were gaining at his back. He crashed through thickets and briars, stumbled, caught himself, ran on. His breath wheezed. From behind came panting breath and deep growls.

Abruptly, to his left, a man emerged, rifle in hand. The man stood, transfixed. Burl. It was his brother Burl! "Shoot!" he shouted. "For God's sake, man, shoot!" Burl seemed not to hear. Nathan, running, caught a vision of pale face and open mouth, the gun hanging slack. "Shoot him, Burl!" Ahead, at fifty paces, loomed a low-hanging oak tree. The great limbs dr ꭒed down to within a man's grasp, promising shelter, safety. "Please, God," he gasped. Nathan extended his stride, reaching.

It was not enough. The beast was at his heels. The powerful stench of him, sour and penetrating, seemed to envelope Nathan. Something grabbed at his foot, caught, held. He went down in an explosion of dry leaves. The foot came free and he rolled. The knife was still in his hand! He came to his feet, scrambling for balance, backing and facing the attack, knife extended. The bear reared again, roaring, and surged forward.

The shot was quite close, from just behind him and to the side. Nathan felt the muzzle blast and a soft nudging whisper of the ball in flight. It was the size of a man's thumbknuckle. It caught the bear in his yawning mouth and struck deep in the throat, to the brain. The rush continued of its own momentum, but the animal was dead in its stride. Nathan twisted aside as the heavy body plunged past him, a quarter of a ton of hair and stench, smashing into a hickory tree and sprawling headfirst into a bed of fern and ivy. Then it lay still.

From deep in the forest, a catbird cried.

"I think he was mad at you, Nathan."

Stephen Stewart stepped into the sunlight, cradling his smoking long rifle. His smile had the arrogance of a self-proud adolescent. Nathan felt a surge of relief and affection. "You were just in time," he said.

"Where's your rifle?"

Nathan's heart still hammered. "I left it back there, by the deer I shot. Dumb thing to do. I forgot to reload." He stepped to the side of the bear, impressed by the animal's size. "This fellow will give us a lot of meat."

"Burl and I heard your shot, so we knew which way to come. Serves you right for leaving us so far behind."

"I wasn't figuring on bear."

Stephen reloaded his own Pennsylvania long rifle, solidly tamping in wadding and shot. He checked his flint and replenished powder from a horn at his belt. As he worked, Burl Stewart came down the slope, rifle cradled on his arm. Burl's wretchedness was engraved in his face.

"I'm sorry, Nathan," he said.

Nathan and Stephen exchanged glances but said nothing. The discomfort of the moment bore down upon the three brothers.

"I was afraid I'd hit you," Burl said lamely.

Nathan forced a smile. "It's all right, Burl. There was nothing you could do." He looked over his shoulder at the slant of the sun. "Three hours of daylight left, maybe a little more. We'll have to work fast."

While Burl and Stephen knelt to skin and quarter the bear, Nathan returned to his dead buck. First, he reloaded the long rifle. Then he finished dismembering the kill. By sunset, the three were loaded up with the choicest cuts of bear and venison and had started the long homeward trek.

A hush fell over the hills. The hollows gathered purple darkness. They followed the gentle crests as much as possible, for the easier going. It was fully dark by the time they arrived back at the foot of a rocky drywash, where they had tethered a pack mule and stashed their earlier kills. A full moon rose to light their way now, bathing the forested land in ghostly silver light. They strode loosely, unspeaking and single file, in the manner of backwoodsmen. Nathan welcomed the chafing discomfort of pack straps and the sweat dampening his body. Amid the soft footfalls and creaks of leather, his mind picked out the night sounds: an owl, hooting from a towering sycamore; the bark of a fox. Not until past midnight did they finally cross the towering dark brow of Coal Hill, driving the pack mule, and descend along the beaten path into the river valley.

Now the moonlight turned smoky, and there was a familiar sharp odor of sulphur. Tumbled shapes of mine works and slag heaps loomed along the face of the hill, flanking the path. Below, the town lay cupped in its V-shaped plain formed by the joining rivers. The bluff dropped steeply into a sprawl of mills and smithies. The valley's customary smoke came partly from these, and partly from the factories and ironworks that proliferated on the other side. In the moonlight, Nathan could just make out the distant jagged presence of old Fort Pitt, crumbling in its desolation. And then they were down at last, stopping beside the black flow of the Monongahela. Around them rose the bulky silhouettes of keelboats, flatboats and scows, drawn up along the mudflats.

"I'll wake the ferryman," Nathan said. Moments later the ferryman stumbled from his riverside shanty, grumbling and pulling at his suspenders. He came fully awake when he saw the pack mule, and his eyes probed hungrily at the heavy, bloodstained sacks of fresh meat. "Good hunt, eh, Nathan? Ah, what I'd give for a nice chunk of venison to roast up on a chill night."

Nathan smiled, drew his knife, and cut loose a small sack. "Here then, Jack. Just for you."

The ferryman grabbed the sack as if it were treasure. "I'm much obliged, Nathan. By the way, your father's been down twice, calling across the river. 'Seen the boys? Seen the boys?'"

Nathan shrugged. They coaxed the reluctant mule aboard the ferry, a rude, log-and-plank flatboat secured to a cable that stretched across the river. Then all hands grabbed at the pull rope, to work the craft across the sluggish current of the Monongahela.

The compound of Stewart's Freightyard and Boatworks Co. dominated a broad stretch of riverfront. They passed through the wide gates into the main yard with its numerous parked wagons and large horse corral. At the big house overlooking the compound, a door slammed and someone emerged carrying a lantern.

"That will be him," Nathan said.

The bulky shape of Isaiah Stewart came out of the darkness. Tall, thick-bearded, he held the lantern high in a gnarled fist and peered. "Is that you, Nathan? It's about time you got back."

"A good hunt, Father. We went farther than we'd planned. Got two deer, pheasant, wild turkey, squirrels. A bear—"

"By daybreak I was going to send out a search party. I was thinking about Indians. You never know."

Stephen laughed. "Listen to him. Indians. Nothing like that, Father. A good hunt, that's all. And your son Nathan never knowing when to quit."

Nathan busied himself unpacking the mule. Bloody sacks of meat dropped into the dust as he cut the ropes. "We'll need some help here. Burl, better rouse up old Charlie and the stable hand."

"All right, Nathan."

Isaiah Stewart stood in the pool of lantern light watching his sons. The old man sensed a tension between them, but said nothing. There was no fathoming young people. Besides, they were back, and that was enough. "Yes, Burl," he said, "better rouse up old Charlie."

The morning dawned gray and cold. Smoke lay in heavy layers over the valley. Isaiah Stewart, a gray-thatched meatblock of a man, stepped onto his back porch and squinted somberly at the sky. Even at this hour, smoke gushed from half the chimneys of Pittsburgh—thick, roiling smoke, from burning coal. He wondered at times that the atmosphere of the valley could contain it all. Pittsburgh was a town of fires: fires to heat the houses and the smithies, fires to make crucible steel and to raise steam for the mills. From the hammering of his own blacksmith, forming pinbolts and iron strapping, to the hot pouring of molten torrents in the valley's biggest ironworks, the town thrived on its showering sparks. Even if he had to breathe its residue, Isaiah found an excitement to it all; excitement and, yes, power.

"Morning, Captain." The call came from a burly foreman, leading the first arrivals through the gate. The man was gloved and capped and muffled against the cold coming off the river. He carried his tools in a leather sack. "Turn of the weather today. Feel it in my bones."

Isaiah nodded. It was ritual, this. The master of Stewart's, fully dressed in shiny boots, woolen suit, and fresh linen, appeared at five minutes to six each morning to see his workmen in. Across his vested stomach hung a heavy gold watch chain. Deliberately, he drew from its pocket the massive casewatch, snapped it open, checked the time, snapped it shut, and returned it to the pocket.

"Aye," he replied. The voice was a low rumble that carried over distance. "A turn of the weather, for sure."

Passing men tipped their caps. Soon, the boatyard would come to life; the hammering, sawing, and shouting would commence, the chuff-chuff of steam winch and creak of tackle taking strain. And on the near side of the yard, the heart of Stewart's freight business, teamsters would worry their dray horses out of the corral, hitch up teams to the heavy Conestoga wagons, and— with whistles, shouts and whipcracks—begin the day's runs. Isaiah Stewart relished the restless energy at work. It was life and commerce, and growing every day. What more could a man ask?

But there was order to it all, order and method. He insisted on this, for order was his nature. It prevailed in the compound, in striking contrast to the shambles of many of his competitors' works. His compound was cobblestoned, against mud and dust. Wagons were parked in neat rows, axle-to-axle, each painted a distinctive green and white and bearing, on each side, the Stewart Line symbol, a triangle in a circle. Down at the river, even the jumble of the boatyard was marshaled: lumber neatly stacked and rope coiled, winches set square to the scaffolds and ways, block and tackle hung in its place and chain stored. Isaiah was an ordered man, fussy about details. He even insisted that the keel of a new vessel be laid either parallel or at ninety degrees to its neighboring craft, and the whole be aligned with the edge of the river.

"Morning, Isaiah."

"Morning, John Crafton."

He picked his men carefully, and there was a pride among them. No drunkards or loafers here. Good men. He thought of this now, looking down at ancient John Crafton, grown gnarled and bent in his service. A master carpenter, he had joined Isaiah in that hard first winter twenty years ago. All Isaiah could do then was promise to pay his wages. It was good enough for John Crafton, and he stayed. Isaiah saw now that he was amply rewarded for such loyalty.

Later in the day, he would stalk the works in greatcoat and with tall beaver hat set square on his head. Isaiah believed in high visibility and personal supervision. A looming figure of authority, he would be trailed by Dalton, his skittish male secretary who constantly scribbled notes. "We'll need a bit wider beam on this one, John Crafton. Put more rib in there . . . and there . . ." And he would point to the bearing beams with his walking stick while Dalton, sniffling and forever cold, dutifully scribbled at his back.

At one minute after six, the last boatwright came hurrying through the gate, lunchpail banging at his side. The man looked up sheepishly to the porch. Isaiah frowned but said nothing. Then he turned and went into the kitchen, where the warm odors of frying fatback and boiling coffee instantly brightened his mood.

"Are they all in?" She was at the stove, a plump, shapely figure still, her apron white and starched and tied neatly in the middle of her back. She did not turn. Her body moved rhythmically as she stirred porridge with a great wooden spoon.

"Yes," he said. "We'll finish the Johnson family's keelboat, if the weather holds." He let his eyes linger on her. The shiny black hair was done in a large bun, low on the back of her neck, and she wore a green cotton housedress. But the hair could loosen quickly and spill down to her waist, and the body beneath that housedress was firm and passionate, even though she was forty-five and had mothered four children, now grown. He felt a stirring of desire . . .

"Stop that," she said softly.

"Stop what?"

"You know very well what. Nathan will be down any minute now. Wash your hands."

Breakfast was uniquely hers. It was the custom of her life, to get Isaiah off to a proper start on the day. But more, this work was a throwback to the lean, hard times they'd had in early years; the time when their house was not this solid three-story manor of wood, but a rude shack trembling in the river wind. They froze, that first winter, and almost starved. Cholera stalked the town. Isaiah, a willful, tough-minded man, swore she would have a fine house and servants someday, and—yes—schooling for the children, if they wanted it. And so it had all come to pass, as he had promised. If he drove himself and the children too hard at times, so be it; this was his nature. But unlike his neighbors, and pioneers coming through on the way west, Isaiah Stewart had not seen his wife grow old and worn out and dying at forty. She could flourish as a woman now, with plenty of help to run the house; she could socialize and entertain well, and did. But fixing breakfast was still a deeply personal task, something between them.

"I don't want to be serving my son cold breakfast on his last day home," she said.

Chuckling, Isaiah went to the pump in the corner, removed his coat, hung it carefully on a peg, undid his stock, and rolled up his sleeves. The arms were thick, whipcorded with muscle and matted with curly black hair. He splashed his face from a bucket of cold water, shook his gray mane like a mastiff, and mopped his face with big, calloused hands. His beard was heavy and black, streaked with silver. The mirror reflected a broad face deeply ridged and weathered, with a high forehead and jutting cheekbones. Keen gray eyes nested in horizontal creases, separated by a meaty chunk of nose. The nose had been broken long ago by a Shawnee tomahawk and never properly set. The same blow had chopped off the ends of the little and ring fingers on his left hand. Scar tissue gauged the gray eyebrows, and the skin of the cheeks above the beard was grooved and pocked, the consistency of tanned leather. He brushed his long hair straight back, muttering to the reflection: "You're a real beauty, Isaiah. Indeed you are." As he drew on his coat again, Nathan's bulk filled the kitchen doorway.

"Good morning." Nathan leaned over to kiss his mother on the cheek. "Mother."

"You're just in time," she said.

The chairs scraped at the kitchen table. Martha had fixed a white tablecloth and good silver, as usual. Light filtered through leaded window panes in the breakfast nook, splashing the water goblets with pastel hues. Now one of the serving girls, Priscilla, came into the kitchen, and Martha took her place at the table. "Well, then," she said.

"You'll be seeing Mr. Palmer today, I suppose," Isaiah said to his son. "Please urge him to come to the party tonight. I know that he doesn't always enjoy such things, but urge him anyway."

"Yes, I'll do that."

There was a silence as they ate. Ordinarily, Isaiah and Martha took breakfast alone. Only on very special occasions did one of the young people join them for this meal. Even now, Stephen,

Burl, and Maybelle were together in the main dining room. If the custom seemed peculiar at times, it was nonetheless rigidly observed.

"I heard about the black bear," Isaiah said, spearing another slice of fatback. "You took a big chance, not reloading. Unusual for a black bear to attack like that, though. Nonaggressive animals, as a rule."

"There's always an exception," Nathan said. "Anyhow, Stephen stopped him with his long rifle."

"Stephen?"

"Yes."

"Where was Burl?"

Nathan paused. Then he recounted the adventure as precisely as he could. He did not amplify anything. Nor did he offer an opinion.

Isaiah frowned. "Why did he not shoot? Was he afraid to shoot?" There was an edge to his words.

"Isaiah—" Martha said.

"His own brother, and he did not shoot."

Nathan felt his father's rush of anger. He hated to see it, for this brought to the surface again the old schism of the family. Isaiah Stewart was an impatient, driving man, expecting excellence from his children. From Nathan and Stephen, he got it; from Burl and Maybelle, his pressures had generated deep resentments. If Burl was less than strong, and Maybelle less than innocent, Nathan felt that it was not their fault entirely. One had to make accommodations with human nature.

"Father, it wasn't what you're thinking. Burl did not want to risk hitting me, and so he didn't shoot. I'm glad he didn't."

Isaiah was unconvinced. He finished his breakfast without saying more. He pushed away from the table and put on his greatcoat. "I'll be bringing up the bourbon this afternoon," he said. Then he was gone.

Martha Stewart put her hand on her son's arm. "I'm sorry, Nathan," she said. "Your father is so . . . well, headstrong. It's his nature, and he can't help it. He loves all of you."

Nathan smiled. "I know that."

"And he's so very proud of you. Imagine! The first Stewart to go away to a university. In England! Do you know, he has talked incessantly about Oxford this past month. He's never even been there, of course, but all his life the university has stood for excellence, especially in philosophy. That's the attitude he always had about it, and that's why you're going."

She sipped coffee and stared thoughtfully at the leaded window with its multicolored prisms. Nathan saw the softness in her face and realized that his mother was still a beautiful woman. Time wears hard on some faces—most faces, indeed—but to hers, it brought a mellowness and strength of character. Her eyes were luminous and her skin finely lined but without blemish. "I know he drove all of you to excel. You've had to study since you were old enough to hold a book or write on a slate. But this is his way. These were things your father never had the leisure to enjoy. In his own childhood, as you know, he worked in the mines around Manchester; and then when his father brought him from England, with his older brother Bartholemew, life was equally harsh in the colonies..."

Martha looked into the eyes of this tall and handsome eldest son, seeking understanding. If any of them was capable of understanding, and perhaps of forgiving, then it was Nathan. Nathan and, yes, Stephen. They were of a parcel, these two sons, though Stephen—beautiful Stephen; almost too beautiful to be a man—was the more lighthearted and vivacious. There were so many things Martha wanted to tell him about his father, in order to grasp what she perceived as the greatness of Isaiah Stewart. A man who'd asked his bride, a schoolteacher, to teach him to read and write and cipher; a determined man who'd brought her west with little more than a dream to follow. Well...

"In many ways, Nathan, you're so like your father," she said. "I do hope you succeed in whatever you set your mind to do."

He laughed. "If only I could dance."

Martha was taking a sip of coffee and almost choked. She put down the cup sputtering with sudden laughter. "Impossible," she gasped. "Totally and absolutely impossible. And my fault, I fear. You're just like me there, completely and utterly tone deaf. You can't even hum a tune, much less dance to one."

He left her then, to go to his room and finish packing. She watched him pass through the doorway, ducking his head by habit to avoid bumping the frame. Suddenly, Martha Stewart's eyes brimmed. "Oh, Nathan, Nathan," she whispered. "I pray you find the woman who'll warm your life."

* * *

"Go, Star! Up, boy!" Stephen dug his heels into the flanks of the roan. With a scrambling jerk, the stallion topped the steep riverbank and clattered onto Water Street. Nathan was already ahead, tall and commanding on the big gray.

It was a slate-gray day with a cold wind knifing off the river. Ohio wind, Stephen thought, slashing from the north down the broad valley. Nathan reined to let him catch up. Then they put their backs to the wind, hunching in the saddles, and set out at a gallop, stirrup-to-stirrup.

By the time they reached Grant's Hill east of town, the horses were warmed and blowing. Sheep bells tinkled on the hillside. Slowing to a trot, Nathan turned upslope and the gray bent his great neck to the climb. At the crest they circled the Indian burial mound, a favorite summertime spot for picnickers and lovers, and dismounted. Below, Pittsburgh brooded under its smoke pall. The rivers converged in their giant V, and the broad Ohio flowed away on its sluggish course of muddy gray. Along the Monongahela, at their father's compound, they could see the ever-present line of flatboats, keelboats and an ungainly, arklike craft called a broadhorn. Ferry scows moved back and forth across the river like sluggish water bugs. Rising out of the boatyard, they could even make out the decking and masts of what would become a square-rigged sailing ship. Already named *Pittsburgh*, she would be floated on the spring floods down the Ohio and Mississippi to the Gulf of Mexico, laden with Pittsburgh bar iron, castings, flour, and pork for foreign trade.

Nathan shook his head. "Somehow I can't get used to the idea, building sailing ships this far from salt water."

"Water's water," Stephen said. "Father thinks it's a natural for Pittsburgh. Beside, you know what he says. 'Anticipate the need, and if there isn't one there—' "

"I know. 'If there isn't one there, create it.' Still, things can be carried too far. He's got a lot of money tied up in that square-rigger. We never know what lies ahead. If the Spaniards closed off New Orleans and the Mississippi, he'd have to sail her on Hogg's Pond."

Stephen's jaw twitched in irritation. This was Nathan's way, conservatism. It was a sore point between them. The younger brother was a risker, like his father; the elder took his mother's cautious approach to business. Stephen turned and looked eastward. From this point they could see a segment of the main road, feeding into Pittsburgh. Two wagons, hung with pots and pans, labored along the log-corduroy track, their white canopies jerking. One of the wagons led a tethered cow and a swaybacked horse. High on the wagon seat, a gaunt, leathery man worked the reins beside a woman in a sunbonnet. Two children poked their heads out from the canvas opening, giggling.

"There, Nathan, is what it's all about. All our lives we've watched them passing through Pittsburgh, heading west. Everybody's heading west. Sometimes I wonder why a man will risk everything he's got, including the lives of his family, to do this; to come to this roughneck town with a horse and wagon and every stitch he owns, and spend thirty-five dollars to buy a flatboat, and then push off down the Ohio for God knows where . . ."

Nathan was no longer listening. He caught Stephen's arm. "Look!" From Hogg's Pond, at the foot of the hill, a flight of quacking chattering canvasbacks took off, their wings raising tiny explosions of white water. As the fowl wheeled for altitude in the leaden sky, Nathan reached for the long rifle in his saddle. Quickly checking flintcock and flashpan, he knelt and took aim. The fine burled cherry wood and polished brass fittings gleamed dully in the light. Stephen stood still, watching. The flock made a banking turn to the north, caught the breeze and swung eastward again in a wide fluttering loop that would bring them across Grant's Hill. Nathan waited, tracking them over the long, octagonal gunbarrel. The flight smoothed, swooped lower, seemed to home on the Indian mound.

Nathan fired. The flintcock showered sparks into the flashpan. The boom of the gun sent echoes ricocheting off the surrounding hills. A bird faltered, showering feathers, and plummeted down. The flight wheeled sharply, flapping and quacking, and flew on. The canvasback thudded to earth not forty feet from where they stood.

"Good shot," Stephen said.

"A present for Zachary Palmer."

"It'll make him a nice dinner." Stephen went after the kill. "Don't forget to reload."

Nathan chuckled and stood the rifle on its buttplate. From ground up, the muzzle came almost to his chest. Uncapping a powder horn, he poured gunpowder down the barrel, then rammed home a greased buckskin patch and lead ball. Replenishing the flashpan powder, he then closed the pan by cocking the flintlock and slid the rifle back into its saddle sheath.

"Let's go to town," he said.

After a brief trot, they were engulfed in the narrow, teeming streets of Pittsburgh. The horses slowed, picking their way. Tall, soot-streaked houses, built by merchants and ironmongers, brooded along both sides of crowded thoroughfares. Ground-floor offices displayed the signs of varied enterprise—butchers and tanners, bakers, carpenters, chandlers and stonemasons, ironmongers and coppersmiths, gun dealers, blacksmiths and liverymen, makers of nails, wire, candlesticks, iron rims for wheels, even suspenders. Market day brought a flood of humanity. The streets were clogged in places with teams and wagons, rivermen, tradesmen, mill hands, ragtag Indians and drunks. Half-wild hogs rooted in the gutters. There was a mingled stench of coal smoke, animal urine, refuse, and rot. And everywhere, Stephen saw the emigrants. Weary, haggard folk, they seemed, trekking by horse, wagon, and afoot from the eastern seaboard and across the Alleghenies, to Pittsburgh and the river. The emigrants also spoke myriad foreign tongues, and some of them never got beyond this gateway river town. They settled, to work the mills and foundries and boatyards, or to become saloonkeepers, gamblers, and prostitutes, or simply to die, their dreams of western prosperity evaporated.

Stephen followed Nathan around a corner, drew rein briefly and looked down upon a clot of dirty-faced children beside a covered wagon. A girl, not ten years old, stared up at him with brown, frightened eyes. He smiled, touched his hat brim, and rode on. The smile lingered in his mind, hauntingly.

A saloon erupted in the clash and clatter of a fistfight.

Six blocks inland they came to the public square, The Diamond. Around the blocklike brick courthouse, with its whipping stocks and steeple, market day made a noisy swirl. Wagons and carts crowded the hitching racks. From market stalls, farmers and their wives hawked pumpkins, corn, potatoes, beeswax, tallow, jarred fruits and vegetables, maple sugar, and fresh bread. The brothers dismounted on Market Street, tethered the horses and—carrying the dead canvasback—entered a small shop, beneath a swinging sign that read: "Catechisms, Spelling Books, Bibles. Z. Palmer, Prop."

Zachary Palmer was delighted. He came bursting from the gloom in a flurry of hand-rubbing and spoke in French. "Ah, bonjour, *mon ami!* How nice to see you! Upon my *word.* Nathan, I thought you were going to be naughty and go away without stopping by for even so much as a fare-thee-well . . . Why, thank you, Stephen. What on earth is it? Heavens! Whatever it is, it's still bleeding. Well, I'll have Crumpton attend to it.''

A bustling soul, Zachary Palmer was bookish and timid, giving off the odor of musty bindings and dust. Pale and slight of build, he had ferretlike features and always wore untidy black suits, frayed and shiny at the sleeves. His linen, like his books, tended to yellow with age. In conversation, lapses seemed to make him uncomfortable. The handshakes over, there was a lapse now. He stammered nervously, then: "You're just in time for tea! Come on back. I've made a fresh pot."

Tea was more than a drink, of course. Tea was Zachary's passion. Tea represented, in this hellish, dreary town, civilization. And so, since their adolescence, Nathan and Stephen had endured the complex mechanisms of Zachary Palmer's tea: the brewing and steeping, the fussing with silver pots and silver tray and delicate bone-china cups, the numbing attention to sugar and milk and—if available—lemon. How often he had lectured them on the amenities, proprieties, and importance of tea. "My young friends, decisions that shake the *world* are made over tea. No gentleman can abide without it!" Now, in the unbelievable clutter of his small office in back of the shop—amid the books, pamphlets, and calendars, all piled helter-skelter around a great, dusty rolltop desk—tea was poured. Tea that steamed from dainty cups. Tea that exuded its exotic warm fragrance. Tea that calmed and soothed. Zachary Palmer lifted his cup, pinky finger poised, eyebrows lifting, eyes squinting, bladelike nose savoring. He hesitated. He sniffed. He sipped. "Ahhh!"

Then he was calmer. Then he could manage to converse. And as always, he insisted they speak French.

"So! So now it's off to England with you. And what do you think about that, Nathan? What do you really feel?"

As usual, Nathan felt oversized and clumsy in the presence of the little bookdealer in his cluttered office, the more so when balancing a teacup and a doily on his knee. No matter. He had acknowledged long ago that even these were necessary skills. Now, he put down his cup and admitted to Zachary Palmer that he had misgivings. Even Stephen seemed mildly surprised to hear it.

"Misgivings?" Zachary Palmer said. "Upon my word. In what way do you have misgivings?"

"Well, frankly, I'm afraid I might not be up to it academical-

ly. If I failed, you know, it would break my father's heart. Not
that I intend to do less than my very best, far from it; but the fact
is, I'll be trying to hold my own with young men who've
attended the very best public schools . . ."

"Yes, yes." With a napkin, Palmer flicked a nonexistent
crumb from his lap. "And I think you'll do quite well, Nathan.
Oh, quite well indeed. After all, both you and Stephen have been
tutored since you were five. Burl too, as far as he would take
tutoring. I myself taught you history, geography, and logic—and
if I do say so, I'm quite good in those subjects. And there was
that Frenchman your father hired from Gallipolis. What was his
name? Alexis DuBois, that was his name. He gave you, um, um,
French, Latin, and the Greek classics. Isn't that so?"

"Yes, that's so."

"Of course, that's so. You've also been well instructed in the
mathematics and basic sciences. And I doubt that there'll be
another student at Oxford who's skilled not only as a boatbuilder
but has worked as a surveyor as well. Those summers that you
and Stephen pulled the chains upriver, remember? So with some
possible exceptions, I'd say you have the makings of a renaissance education." The bookdealer liked the sound of that. He
said, "Um." He sipped tea. "Yes indeed, a renaissance education."

"Not to mention," Stephen interjected whimsically, "his
remarkable ability to run from bears."

Palmer was puzzled. "Bears?"

Nathan glowered. "Nothing, Mr. Palmer. Some little brothers
have got big mouths."

"I see."

Stephen's eyes roved innocently to the ceiling. The talk
droned. His mind wondered. He thought of Isaiah Stewart's
driving insistence that they not only be educated but learn a
variety of things. "You'll go only as far as your desire and
abilities in life," the burly boatbuilder would say, "but there's
no limit to opportunity." They had hated much of it, of course;
the never-ending lessons and recitals and memory games, the
poring over books in surveying and mechanics, and the constant working in the boatyard and driving freight wagons.
There was sense to it, Stephen had to admit. But all this
had worked its hardships as well. Burl was a slow learner and
intimidated by it all. Isaiah Stewart's ambition for his sons took
the fun out of life for the youngest. Burl seemed to lock inside,

and withdraw; and the more displeased his father became, the more he retreated from it. As for Maybelle—his sister, being female, felt herself ignored. She was probably the smartest of the lot, Stephen often thought, but was overlooked solely because of her sex. Her education consisted of the three Rs, to be sure; but also, it involved such domestic arts as cooking, which she hated, and sewing, which bored her to tears. Maybelle's frustration came out in temper tantrums and violent scenes with her father. Stephen remembered the shock of a year ago, when his teenage sister came storming from her father's office shouting, "I hate him! I hate him! I hate all men!" He wondered if this was what made her the way she was, aggressive with young men, forever flirting and teasing. There were knowing looks and whispers among the young teamsters and boatwrights. Once he had seen a man coming out of the barn looking disheveled and arranging his trousers, and Maybelle followed him out soon afterward. Nothing was ever said of the incident, but the hired man was abruptly fired by Isaiah Stewart.

"... and Father made a special point of asking you to come to my going-away party tonight," Nathan was saying. "His exact words were, 'Urge him to come.' So consider yourself urged."

Zachary Palmer could not conceal his pleasure. The bookdealer flushed, chuckled, and poured more tea.

The disturbance came from the front of the shop. Someone came rushing in, calling Zachary Palmer's name. "Mr. Palmer! Mr. Palmer!" It was Crumpton, the bookshop clerk. His bespectacled, moon-shaped face appeared at the office door. He was pale and perspiring. "Mr. Palmer, they're at it again. You said to let you know."

"Oh, dear." Zachary Palmer put down his teacup and dabbed his mouth with a napkin. "This is such a nuisance, absolutely barbaric. I'll just have to complain to the sheriff again." He bounded from his chair and through the shop. Nathan and Stephen followed.

"What is it, Crumpton?"

"Another whipping," the clerk gasped. "They've got a man in the whipping stocks again. It upsets Mr. Palmer no end—"

"Well, it always has bothered him. But he never tried to physically stop it before."

"He's doing it now."

A noisy mob had gathered around the stocks in front of the courthouse. Locked in the stocks, stripped to the waist in the chill, stood a heavy, flush-faced man with a wild tangle of red beard. His eyes were bloodshot and he bawled curses at the jeering crowd. Muscles rippled over his massive frame. Behind him, a burly jailer rolled up his sleeves and shook out the strands of a heavy black whip. Its multiple strands resembled a cat-o'-nine-tails, but without the knotted ends.

A sheriff's deputy stepped in front of the prisoner and opened an official paper. "Geoffrey Markowitz Faber, you have been tried and duly sentenced in the municipal court of the town of Pittsburgh for being drunk, disorderly and fighting in a public place, to-wit: the Three Moons Tavern. It is my duty as deputy constable to impose your punishment, which is to receive on your bare back the number of one hundred lashes. Do you have anything to say before sentence is administered?"

The miscreant scowled, belched, and spat. A group of rowdies yelled obscenities into his face, and several street urchins set up a chant, "The whip! The whip! The whip!" A slattern woman pranced before the prisoner in a torn and muddy gown. "Wanna dance, dearie? You ain't so high and mighty now."

The deputy nodded to the jailer, who stepped forward flicking the whip against his boot.

"Wait! Wait!" cried the prisoner. "I got somethin' to say, deputy. You ast me if I had somethin' to say, and I do, and that's fact—"

"The whip! The whip! The whip!"

"I'm dancin' now, dearie. See? Ain't I pretty? Don't it just fill you with desire to see me shakin' my body like this. Tah-tah-tah-tah-tah."

"Lissen. I got a right. I got a right to speak! The deputy said so. You said, deputy, I could say somethin'—"

"The whip! The whip! The whip!"

The deputy raised his hands. "All right, then, quiet in the crowd. Quiet."

"Yah, dearie, now you get yours . . ."

"Quiet, I said."

"The whip! The whip! The wh—"

"I said quiiiiet!"

Gradually the noise subsided. The deputy constable glared at the mob until silence was complete. Then he turned to the prisoner in the stock. "Well, then?"

"I can say it now?"

"You may."

"Whatever is on my mind?"

"Whatever is on your mind. It is your right."

"All right then." He paused, eying the constable, the crowd, the jailer with the whip. "All right then, here's what I got to say. Governor . . . Let me *out* of here!"

The mob broke into a cheer. The constable, flushing with anger, stepped back and said something to the jailer. The jailer, a massive man with huge arms, raised the whip and brought it whistling down.

Whop!

Zachary Palmer had observed all this from the crowd with growing agitation. Now the little bookdealer abruptly shoved forward, ran to the jailer, and grabbed his whip arm. "No, no. Stop it. Stop it, I say! You can't do that. It's uncivilized!"

The jailer, towering over him, seemed confused. Then, wrenching his arm free, he tried to push Palmer aside. "Get out of the way, you." But righteous wrath would not be denied and, like a pesky fly, the bookdealer came back.

In the crowd, angry voices began to shout. "Here, now, what's this? Get out of the way! Let the whipman do his work."

Palmer, undeterred, began to speak to the rabble. "You . . . Listen to me. Listen! . . You're the ones who suffer. No man should be beaten in public like a dog. It isn't right . . ."

"Get him out of there! Push him aside, jailer!"

"Listen to me! Hardly a day goes by when some poor wretch is not pilloried or whipped in front of this courthouse. And you, you who might be next on the flimsiest of offenses, stand and jeer . . ."

But the crowd grew angrier. The deputy constable, who had been shunted aside, cried, "Here now! Here now!" A group of loutish men moved in around Palmer, shaking their fists and cursing. "A dose of the knuckles will do for the little squirt . . ." The jailer paled and moved back a step, his whip hanging slack. A heavy fist thudded against the bookdealer's cheek, bringing blood. Palmer went down.

Nathan glanced at Stephen. "Well, here we go!" The brothers charged, shoving bodies aside and laying about with fists and elbows. A path opened through the crush. Stephen reached the bookdealer and snatched him to his feet while Nathan, behind him, turned to face the mob. The attack came on a wave of thuds and groans. A heavy boot aimed a kick at Stephen's groin; he sidestepped and struck the man full in the face, feeling the crunch of nose cartilage breaking. Then the brothers were shoulder to shoulder, flailing away with fists and feet, while behind them a distraught Zachary Palmer held the side of his bleeding face, muttering, "Oh dear, oh dear, oh dear..." From the stocks, the convicted offender bellowed obscenities. The deputy constable, meanwhile, started blowing his whistle. Now, the melee expanded as nearby saloons emptied, and idlers, loungers, and passersby gleefully joined in. Market stalls went crashing over, and the air suddenly filled with flying potatoes, apples, and canned goods. But even as fresh fights broke out between other rival factions on the fringe of the crowd, Nathan and Stephen began to tire and lose ground. Stephen took a glancing blow that sent him to his knees. As Nathan turned to pull him up, the mob made a fresh surge that threatened to engulf them in a murderous fury.

The reinforcements were totally unexpected. One minute, they were punching, kicking, and gouging for their very lives; the next, the pressure was easing dramatically as other fists and blows joined the conflict, on *their* side. From the corner of his eye, Stephen glimpsed a tall, hawk-faced man in buckskins and broadbrimmed leather hat, bashing heads with the butt of a formidable long rifle and bellowing in a voice like a thunderclap, "Make room, there! Clear out! Make way!" The newcomer was supported by a less towering, but no less vigorous, companion. As the wheezing, shouting mass fell back, yet another force made its appearance. Around the corner of the courthouse came a flying wedge of black-uniformed constables, swinging truncheons and blowing whistles. They struck the disintegrating crowd with such force that the square quickly cleared of all but the hardiest brawlers. Now, a florid-faced figure in uniform advanced authoritatively upon the group at the stocks.

"Mr. Palmer," he said, "you have caused a riot, sir. You interfered with an officer of the law executing his sworn duty. If you were a less substantial citizen, I should be forced to take you in. As it is, let this be a warning." He turned to Nathan and Stephen. "As for your young friends here..."

Zachary Palmer, though still in shock and nursing a rapidly swelling welt on the side of his face, found his tongue. "These are my former students, the Stewart brothers, Chief Constable."

"Yes, I know who they are."

"They were merely trying to save me from a very difficult situation."

"That's true, Constable." It was the tall frontiersman speaking now. He fixed the policeman with pale blue eyes, set in a face deeply tanned and weathered. "These young men undoubtedly saved his life and prevented you from having a murder right here in the street."

The chief constable pondered, slowly tapping the side of his boot with a long leather truncheon. In the course of his duties, he had learned long ago the value of prudence in his public dealings. It was one thing to manhandle a common tavern brawler into jail or the pillory; it was something else to deal rashly with the sons of rich and powerful men, or—however presumptuous his behavior—a bothersome merchant of Market Street. When in doubt, it was wise to be flexible. From the thoughtful exercise of such judgment, indeed, one managed to retain his position as chief constable. He stroked his chin and said to the frontiersman: "And who might you be, stranger?"

"I'm Mason Everett. Fur trader. Incidentally, chief constable, that's one of my men in your whipping post over there. Do you think we could get him loose?"

The constable studied the question. "Well, you'll have to go his bond. He doesn't have the money."

"I'll go his bond."

"Then I suppose it can be arranged." The officer turned to his deputy. "It might be a good idea to empty the pillory for the rest of the day. Let things quiet down. Take that man . . . What's his name?"

"Faber," the tall frontiersman said.

"Take that man, Faber, back to the holding cell and see if Mr. Everett here can arrange bail."

"Very well, sir."

"Good. Then that'll be that, I suppose. Mr. Palmer, you'll want to tend to that injury. And as for you Stewart boys . . ."

"Yes, sir?"

The chief constable eyed them gravely before turning away. "Please convey my respects to your father."

Mason Everett and his companion escorted them back to Zachary Palmer's shop. In the tiny office, the frontiersman selected some herbs from a leather pouch at his belt and quickly prepared a damp poultice for the wound. "This should take the swelling down very quickly, if there ain't no bones broken. It'll stave off infection, too."

"Herbs?" Stephen said.

Everett nodded. "Indian cures. Don't ask me how they work, but they work. Them Indians have got cures for most anything that ails you, except lead poisoning."

Stephen was fascinated. For all the learning the brothers had been exposed to, Indian skill was not among them. Their father's intense hatred of Indians forbade any association with "murdering savages." Now, he found himself mentioning this to the tall stranger, and telling him about Isaiah Stewart's war experiences, fighting Indians and the British with George Rogers Clark in the western campaign . . .

The frontiersman had stopped work on Zachary Palmer's facial dressing and was staring at Stephen, openmouthed. Abruptly, the words fairly exploded from him: "Did you say *Isaiah Stewart?*"

"Yes. Our father's name is Isaiah Stewart."

"Square-built fellow, strong as a bull? Got two fingers chopped off his left hand?"

"The same."

The blue eyes blazed. "Well, I'll be damned!"

A bourbon needs time to steep and gather itself into a smoky, mellow brew. Drunk too soon, its rawness warps a man's thoughts and inflames his temper; too late, and its quality is lessened. This one special cask was intended for perfection. For eight years its ten gallons of liquid treasure lay on end in the cool, dank cellar. Isaiah Stewart had seen personally to the sour mashing and distilling. With his own hands he'd hewn the staves and bound them in copper. Then he'd borne it, calked and full, down to its resting place amid the cobwebs, dust, and old apples. Here, in the cellar, a maturing cask was protected against extremes of heat and cold, isolated from noise and jostling, left to develop its distinctive flavor and magic for the ultimate heady pleasures of man.

And now it was time. The master of Stewart's, his anticipation rising delectably, descended the dark stairs, lit a heavy tallow candle and groped forward against the flowing shadows. The light danced off lowered beams and pearled in the damp of earthen walls. He moved past bins and shelves of things that Martha kept stored down here, the vital residues of a wife's domesticity—canned peaches and potatoes and beans, pickled beets and herring, dried raisins, peaches, and apples—and came

at last to the cask. It lay knee-high on sawhorses under a coating
of dust. Setting the candle down, he slapped at the dust with a
rag, coughed, blew his nose. Then, carefully, he inspected the
cask for telltale moisture that would indicate a leak. There was
none. The ash and hickory, nicked and gouged from his own
hand tools, had swollen into a perfect seal and stayed dry. "Ah,"
he muttered to the cask. "You'll make a lovely celebration
then." Stooping, he gathered the cask into his great arms and
backed out to the middle of the cellar. With a grunt, he sat it
down, retrieved his candle, and found a mallet, chisel, an
enameled cup, and a wooden spigot.

It was a precious moment, this, almost like a birth. Only the
maker of a fine bourbon should savor the first mouthful; for his
was the decision to swallow, or to spit. From the house overhead
came sounds of footfalls, voices, and a tinkling piano. Isaiah
tipped the cask on end and found the knock-bung. As he placed
the chisel and raised the mallet, someone above opened the cellar
door. Annoyance flicked at his mind. "Father, is that you?" It
was Nathan.

Isaiah did not reply. Nathan's heavy feet clattered down the
wooden stairs. "What are you doing down here?"

Nathan saw the cask in the pooling candlelight and laughed.
"Well!" Isaiah's annoyance vanished.

Together, then, they knocked open the bunghole and placed
the wooden spigot in its place. Isaiah turned the handle and
watched a stream of amber chuckle into the cup. He lifted the
cup and took a mouthful. Warm, it was, and musky, with a touch
of sweet. As Nathan watched, Isaiah swirled it around in his
mouth. He looked to the ceiling. He smiled. He swallowed.
"Good."

Nathan drank, too. The warmth flowed over them. Isaiah
looked fondly at his eldest son. Tall and strong, he was; well
proportioned, with a broad forehead and keen intelligence. A
handsome lad. "I made my first cask of sour mash twenty years
ago," Isaiah said. "Me and your mother, we'd only been here a
short while, from Baltimore. That was in eighty-four, the hard
winter, the winter she almost died. I told her that someday we'd
have fine sons. And I'd make up a very special cask and let it
mature, for a special occasion." He studied the cask, the
roughhewn wood and hammered copper bands, knowing intimately
each imperfection. "And I guess this is it."

The men stood in silence after that, feeling the warmth,

unaccustomed to such nearness to each other. Isaiah had never been a demonstrative man, and Nathan felt a surge of affection that he himself could not express. They drank and looked into the candle flame, while the light cast its deep and restless glow upon their faces. A man should say words of wisdom at a time like this, Isaiah thought; he should give some fatherly advice. The boy was going out into the great world, away from the Forks and family and all he'd known. Nathan was going to the Old Country, to England, and those halls of learning so unattainable to Isaiah. He'd have a chance to be an educated man. A father ought to say something, urge the lad to make the most of his opportunity, warn him of artful women and devious men. For was not the human predator more deadly than the silent serpent? Isaiah blinked, stirred, snapped his suspenders. "Well, then," he said, "Help me carry this up the stairs." Together, they grabbed hold of the cask.

Martha was waiting anxiously upstairs, to tell Isaiah about the fight.

The eyes watched her, boldly. They watched and probed and . . . knew. Brown eyes, they were; luminously brown and framed by dark, even brows in a strong young face. Maybelle Stewart shivered. She tossed her auburn curls and gave him a saucy glance, across the crowded room. The next musical number was a sprightly hoedown. Couples poured onto the floor, disrupting her view. Her blood raced to the rhythm of fiddles and banjos. No wonder some preachers disapproved of dancing, she mused; it was too exciting to be respectable. "Promenade and dosy doe . . ." But he made no move to come across. Maybelle nudged Jenny Carver, who was a year older than she. On Sundays they attended church together.

"Who is he, the one over there?"

"Which one?"

"The good-looking one with the black hair."

Jenny giggled. "I think they're all good-looking."

"He keeps staring at me," Maybelle said. "You'd think he never saw a female before. I wish he'd quit staring, it makes me nervous."

"Oh, *that* one. I wish he'd stare at me."

"He's probably been in the woods so long he's gone and lost his manners."

"Not him. If he's the one I think, his family came in from Baltimore. They've got two or three wagons. Your father is finishing their keelboat."

Maybelle patted the front of her gown. It was a pale green print, matching her eyes. Pale green also brought out her hair coloring to advantage. All afternoon she had toiled with a hot curling iron, so that the tight little rolls of hair would hang just so. A space opened on the dance floor, and she glanced across again, pouting. She tossed her hair so that it would catch the lamplight.

"You're positively disgraceful," Jenny said.

"Hush."

The distant brown eyes narrowed. Then Maybelle realized that someone was standing behind her, speaking. "M-Maybelle, can I . . . can we dance this here hoedown?" It was Maynard Self. Fat Maynard Self. He stood at her shoulder like a shy dog, ready to flee. His suit was too small for his belly. His hair was plastered down with bear grease. He had pimples on his chin that needed popping. He was disgusting.

"What did you say, Maynard?"

"Could we, um, dance?"

Maybelle patted back a tiny yawn. She looked across at Brown Eyes again. She made up her mind. "Well, I suppose so, Maynard."

Joy suffused the face of Maynard Self. They danced. He moved well, for a fat person. But soon he was puffing from the exertion. By the time the hoedown ended, sweat trickled down his florid cheeks and dampened his collar. He smelled of sweat. The fiddle-and-banjo band struck up a reel. Maybelle was warmed from the movement. The music played over her, and to Maynard's surprise she stayed with him.

Now, at the turns, she brushed closely against him. His eyes widened. Maybelle smiled inwardly. Her fingers lightly squeezed his, and he squeezed back. She let her right hand trail down his back. Softly, softly, her bosom brushed his arm. And then, as they came together, she let her body press closely against him and felt the rising presence at his groin. "Why, Maynard!" she whispered, breathlessly drawing away. "Whatever do you have in your pocket?"

He flushed, suddenly miserable, and stammered, "M-my p-pocket?" His face glistened, the color of fire.

Maybelle persisted. "Yes. I felt it just then, when we were

close. I pressed against you like this, and . . . Why Maynard, it's—"

"M-Maybelle, please. I—"

"Maynard, it's *you!* Well, I have never been so insulted in my whole life!" And with that, she released his hand and walked away, leaving him on the dance floor like a stricken blowfish. She rejoined Jenny, who seemed perplexed.

"What was *that* all about?"

"Oh, nothing. Maynard Self is such a bore." Her face set in innocent composure, she pretended to look around at the jostling, partying, dancing crowd. Within, she was aroused and uncomfortable. The quick presses against Maynard, even in tease, played upon her mind. She dabbed at her face with a hankie. Over near the punch bowl, a burst of heavy male laughter exploded from a group of men sipping from glass cups. Beyond them she could see her father near the doorway, talking with that tall frontiersman Mason Everett. Her brother Burl stood by himself against the wall, drinking punch and trying to look preoccupied. But she could tell that he was getting drunk. Nathan and Stephen were nearby, talking and laughing with a group of young people. As Nathan talked, that little brunette, Elizabeth Hanks, kept devouring him with her eyes. Forget it, dearie, Maybelle thought.

Now she looked back across the dance floor. The brown eyes were still watching. Quickly and deliberately, Maybelle stuck out her pink, wet tongue. The young face smiled, showing a blaze of even white teeth. Maybelle felt her stomach flutter. Oh, my goodness.

"My goodness," she said.

"What is it?"

"He's coming over. I think he's coming over. Yes, he is. I feel faint."

"Silly."

Then he was there, standing an arm's length away, still smiling, muttering something by way of introduction. The eyes were even bolder now. Maybelle flushed and said to Jenny Carver: "Well, did you ever? People nowadays just don't have any manners at all, coming right over and starting a conversation without even a proper introduction."

Jenny showed wide-eyed surprise. "Why Maybelle, you just . . ."

Maybelle smiled coquettishly at the young man. "But it's all right, I suppose. You are a guest in this house. Yes, I suppose it's all right. Do you think it's all right, Jenny?''

"I—"

"Very well then," she told him, "you may have this dance." She extended her gloved hand daintily and felt an electric intensity from his firm grasp as they swung onto the dance floor.

Isaiah Stewart was pleased with himself. It was turning into a damn fine party. He always half dreaded these things at first. But Nathan deserved a proper send-off for tomorrow; and besides, God knows they worked hard enough around here to earn a little fun once in a while. What an extraordinary coincidence it was for Mason Everett to turn up precisely on this day.

The older Isaiah became, the more he realized how complex was the fabric of his life. The past was part of him, a permanent and intimate phase, yet apart; once so compelling, or so dreadful, it ultimately passed like a breath of air and yet left its indelible marks. So it was with Mason, he supposed. Mason was the same man with whom he had endured so much—the fear, the misery, the pain—so long ago; still the tall, rawboned backwoodsman, calm and wise. About him there was that same air of authority that had won him command under George Rogers Clark, the steely blue eyes and quiet composure. But to all this were added the lines in his face, the gray streaks in the brown hair, and the even deeper certitude that time so often gives to a man.

Isaiah sipped his bourbon straight, unadorned by water. He was getting a little tipsy. "It's been a lot of years, Mason," he said. "A lot of years since Vincennes." The amber liquid was a warm fire, going down his gullet.

The room, the big carpentry hall where they turned out the intricate work for the boats, had been transformed as if by magic. All afternoon the women and the help had been preparing: pushing aside sawhorses and equipment, sprinkling sand on the floor for dancing, setting up tables to pile high with food and drink, hanging colored paper streamers and lanterns. And then the guests had poured in, all scrubbed and combed and coiffed. There were boat captains and top hands and master carpenters, a politician or two from town, merchants and suppliers, wagon masters and old, old friends; there were ironmongers and coal men and capitalists, with their wives and daughters and old maid aunts. The women wore their best gowns, and the men, their

Sunday suits. In the corner, the fiddle-and-banjo band kept it all going—that and the bourbon and the punch.

"You're a man of substance, Isaiah," Mason Everett said. "Never fancied you for a boatbuilder and man of business."

Isaiah told him, then, about his brother Bartholomew at Provincetown. A master craftsman, Bartholomew, building stout Yankee fishing boats and running his own fishing crews too, taking cod off the New England coast. "After the war, I went back there, still a boy. Bartholomew taught me what he knew. But I couldn't stand the stink of working a codfish boat. So I left. Went down to Baltimore. Met Martha there—she was a schoolmistress—and married her. She taught me to read and write. After Vincennes, and this"—he held up the left hand, where the two fingers were missing—"I vowed to get a little education if I could, make something of myself . . ."

Vincennes. Some memories never cease to be painful to the touch, and Vincennes was one of them. The word alone brought back to his mind the cold, the wet, the hunger; the two hundred-mile trek out of Kaskaskia in the dead of winter, the last of it sloshing waist-deep over the icy floodplain of the Wabash. Driven, they were; driven by the determination of a single man. Isaiah drained his glass of a final fiery gulp.

"How is he, the colonel?" he asked.

Mason shook his head. "Brooding, lonesome, in debt. I stopped off at Louisville on the way. He's got a place on the bluff, looking down on Corn Island. Remember Corn Island? We drilled there."

"We froze there," Isaiah corrected him.

"Truth, we did."

Brooding . . . lonesome . . . in debt . . . Isaiah had difficulty grasping such a dilemma. Some men seem beyond reach of mundane travails, immortal and indestructible. Such a man, in the mind of Isaiah Stewart, once private soldier of the western command, was Colonel George Rogers Clark.

"And his health?"

"Not good."

"I'm sorry to hear that."

Nathan worked his way through the crowd, accepting back-slaps and handshakes. He seemed to Isaiah even taller and more handsome than usual, and he was flushed and jovial from the drinks. Isaiah felt a quick surge of parental pride.

"What are you old-timers talking about?"

"Old wars," Mason Everett said. "Old campaigns."

Since afternoon a slight bruise had darkened beneath Nathan's right eye, and he had covered a nick under the ear with patching plaster. Stephen, who was now dancing with that pretty Hanks girl across the room, showed no visible wounds from the day's confrontation.

"Brawling in the streets," Isaiah muttered, "like common riffraff."

Mason Everett smiled. "Don't be too hard on the lads, Isaiah. They did a good job; saved your bookdealer friend from a mauling, or worse, and saved my man Faber from a whipping—although, God knows, he probably deserved it."

"Nevertheless . . ." Isaiah took another glass from a passing tray.

"So you're bound for Washington City, Mr. Everett?" Nathan said. "Will you be seeing Mr. Jefferson himself?"

"I intend to."

"Hope you brought along a pair of mud boots," Isaiah grumbled. "I hear that place is the end of Creation. Why they decided to put the capital there is beyond my understanding."

"We've got trouble brewing in the West," Everett continued. "There's folks in the territories, Tennessee, Caintuck, and Ohio, that's ready to split off from the United States and throw in their lot with Spain."

"That's treason!" Isaiah spat.

"Call it what you want to, it's a fact. And the shame of it is, the potential out there is so tremendous you can't believe it."

Several other men joined them now, and all were listening gravely to Mason Everett. Stephen left Elizabeth Hanks with some other females and came over. He listened in fascination, absorbing what the tall frontiersman had to say.

Mason Everett spoke with rapid intensity, the blue eyes flashing. "We don't even know what's out there, west of the Mississippi. Most of it's just a vast blank on the map. Oh, some of us have made some forays. My man Faber has done a lot of trapping. There's English and French trappers coming down from Canada, too. But their knowledge is limited—"

"But everything west of the Mississippi belongs to Spain," Stephen interjected.

"That's just the point. And that means they can control the Mississippi. The Spaniards ain't interested in furs, nor commerce. They've got a military post at St. Louis and they've got

New Orleans. They can shut down the river anytime they take a mind to.''

Several of the men murmured in angry agreement. Isaiah Stewart said: ''We can handle that with a few squirrel hunters with long rifles.'' Mason Everett shrugged.

''The way I see it, Isaiah, we can't take the chance. The fact is, this country of ours has got a peculiar geography west of the Alleghenies. Look at all these people and goods that's pouring through Pittsburgh today. They're all going the same way, right? Downriver. Down the Ohio to where there's land and space and a man can put down roots, or try. And the river only flows one way: down. It don't flow up. So when you build a flatboat for a family, or even a keelboat bound for New Orleans with trade goods, likely as not it's only going one way. And when they get to where they're going, they take the boat apart and sell it for kindling, or build a shanty with it. Your bargemen and keelboatmen float two thousand miles to New Orleans in fifty-five days; and to get back home, they either take a ship to go around to Baltimore on the east coast, or they walk back over the Natchez Trace, which ain't nothin' but an Indian trail infested with murderous thieves and outlaws.''

''Well, President Jefferson ain't going to change the way the rivers run,'' Isaiah said. ''And even if it was possible, that Congress would find a way to botch it up.''

Laughter coursed through the group.

''Yes, but don't you see what I'm driving at? Folks in Caintuck and Tennessee and Ohio territory are settin' out there on a limb. Their trade goods have got to go downriver. If a man's got a shipment bound for, say, Philadelphia or even some foreign country, he's got to float it down through New Orleans. There's no other way, because you can't manhandle a bargeload of hides or tobacco or cotton a thousand miles upriver. So to avoid the risk of being blocked if the Spaniards suddenly get mad at America, they're talking about splitting off, forming a government and making their own treaty.''

The prospect had a sobering effect upon Everett's listeners. These were men, after all, for whom the river trade was livelihood. A keelboater asked: ''Well, what can be done about it?''

Everett intended to take several ideas to the President. There was talk that the real power over the fate of the West was held not by Spain, but by Bonaparte. And so there should be strong

American representations not only with the Spaniards, but with the French as well. "I also think it would be a good idea to explore some of that territory in the Northwest. As far as I know, no white man has ever been all the way up the Missouri to its headwaters and then mapped a route on to the Pacific. We ought to find out, officially, just what in tarnation is up there. And then I think the government ought to start opening up the Ohio country by building a road, a national road, straight through from Cumberland to Pittsburgh or Wheeling, then across the river into Ohio. And finally, the United States ought to try to buy New Orleans . . ."

Eyebrows shot up. Some of the men, already amused by the frontiersman's audacious ideas, now laughed out loud. "Buy New Orleans? Sure. We could even buy Madrid."

Everett stood his ground. "Nothing ventured, nothing gained."

The group broke up amid amused chuckles. Hands reached for fresh drinks. The fiddles and banjos struck up a fresh Virginia reel. "This dance will be ladies' choice . . ."

One of the ironmongers, a corpulent dandy in a black silk costume complete with wig and pantaloons, plucked at Nathan's arm. "Your father's friend is an engaging fellow and an interesting conversationalist—"

"Yes," Nathan said.

"—but completely out of his mind."

Burl Stewart had watched them, heard scraps of the conversation, but did not take part. The whole idea of a party was an abomination anyhow, he reasoned; something for precious, precious Nathan. Precious Nathan, so smart, so good-looking. He drank, feeling quite alone. In this way the time went by, the drinks continued to flow, the merriment increased in intensity and volume. Even his father, now well into his cups, shared the frivolity. Isaiah Stewart had his arm around Burl's mother, Martha, in a circle of friends and was bellowing over the music some scrap of Shakespearian sonnet. "For thy sweet love remembered, such wealth brings, that then I'd scorn to change my state with kings!" Cheers, and down the hatch . . .

Burl's envy was intense, and his self-consciousness, acute. He despised parties. He could think of nothing to say. His brothers were both convivial sorts. Even Nathan, who could not dance a step for lack of any musical consciousness, was a devil with the girls. Everyone, it seemed, got along together, including loutish youths the likes of Maynard Self. Everyone, Burl brooded, except himself. The misfit. He could think of nothing to say, nothing witty or bright. He was dull, a dullard, and miserable for it. Neither males nor females sought his company, and so he stood on the fringe of the social swirl, unspeaking, unspoken to.

The liquor was getting deep into him, all right. He wanted to cry. My God, he thought, what's the matter with me? Oh, to be somebody else. To cast off this shell and be somebody else; somebody like Jimmy Lee James, glib and wisecracking and always showing off. Over in the corner, in that crowd of boys and girls, stood Jimmy Lee James. Only a workman from the boatyard, but the center of attention. What were they doing? Bobbing for apples, that's what they were doing.

"Woooooooooowh!" the crowd shouted joyously, and a beautiful red-haired female came up from the bobbing bowl, water streaming from the ends of her hair. Jenny, it was. Jenny Carver. Jenny Carver. JennyCarver. Jennycarverjennycarv . . . Burl was drunk. But he didn't show it. He never showed it. Only Burl knew when Burl was drunk. Hee hee hee. He knew it from the numbness in his face and the soft buzzing in his head. Zmmmmmmmmmmmmmm. Being drunk was good. Being drunk was being numb. Numb to their nonlooks, their nontalking.

The apples, red and ripe, floated in the big glass bowl. Each player bent over the bowl, hands behind the back, trying to get a tooth into an apple. Bob, bob, bob. Jenny Carver tried again. She almost succeeded. But the apple fell back into the bowl with a splash, bringing a burst of loud laughter . . .

The time had gone so fast. Where had the time gone? The dance floor was almost empty. The fiddlers sawed wearily at their fiddles. There was a litter of paper and felled streamers and dirty cups. Even his father had gone staggering off to bed, singing a Scottish ditty. His mother came into the room, looking around anxiously. "Burl, have you seen Maybelle anywhere?" No, ma'am. No, he had not seen Maybelle. His mother went away again. The apple bobbers shouted and laughed.

And suddenly Jimmy Lee James was there, talking to him. "Here, Burl. You show 'em how, eh? Try it, Burl." The others became aware of his presence. "Oh do, Burl. Do it, Burl!" It was a chorus and a babble. "Yeah, Burl! Bob for the old apple, Burl." All the eyes were looking at him for the first time, laughing eyes and open faces. He felt them, and an instant pleasure rose in him. He felt himself being drawn from the wall toward the punch bowl.

Jimmy Lee James loomed over him, tall and lean and laughing. "Burl, you'll show them how it's done. Lissen. Quiet! Lissen. Burl here, he is a master at apple bobbing. I tell you, there's no finer apple bobber in all of the Alleghenies. Ain't that right, Burl?" A large towel was tied around his neck. Jenny Carver hugged his arm and he could smell her sweet scent. He clasped his hands behind his back and bent over the bowl. Two apples bobbed under his nose, ripe and red. He bit at the smaller apple, but the slick surface slid away from his teeth. A chorus of groans went up, followed by shouts of encouragement. Suddenly it became very important to catch that apple. He snapped and bit, but it bobbed away again. Burl concentrated. Bite the apple. Bite it for Jenny. An edge of peeling had roughened in that last bite. His teeth found the rough spot this time, and caught, biting down . . .

Abruptly, his face was in the bowl, immersed in the bowl. From behind, somebody was pushing at his head, pushing his face powerfully into the bowl. He tried to shout, gulped water, thrashed. The hand, the cursed hand, held his head like a vice. Panic surged. He struggled, kicked, broke free, came up gasping and spewing, blinded.

The laughter swelled around him, gales of it. He mopped his eyes with the towel, opened them, and saw the open, laughing mouths, the wet teeth, the pointing fingers. Jenny Carver shrieked with laughter. Jimmy Lee James was laughing, wiping his hands on the towel.

"You!"

The shame, the mortification, rose in his throat like bile. A feeling almost of nausea swept over him. Snarling like an animal, he lunged for Jimmy Lee James. But the hated face disappeared, the hated body ducked to the side, and Burl went crashing on his face across the table. Punch bowl, table, cups, and apples flew everywhere. Someone screamed. Burl rolled clumsily to his feet, face still dripping, encircled by the crowd. Abruptly the laughter stopped and they were all staring at him, knowing as a group that the joke had gone too far. Burl whirled, saw James, took a step. There was murder in his heart. "Bastard . . ."

Someone grasped his arm in a steely grip. He looked up into the worried face of his brother Nathan. "Don't worry about the mess, Burl. Old Charlie'll clean it up. I need you to come with me." Confused, Burl let himself be led away. A blast of air struck him as they stepped into the frosty yard of the compound. "It's c-cold," he said, "I need my jacket..."

"It's Maybelle," Nathan said. "She's disappeared from the party, and Mother is worried. So let's just look around. Don't raise any fuss. I'll go this way, you go that."

Then Nathan was gone, into the shadows of the moonlit night.

Burl moved quietly, more by instinct than design. On the upper slope, the white-canopied freight wagons stood in line as silent sentinels, wheel-to-wheel, tongues outthrust to the ground and perfectly straight. He thought, Ten-shun!, and suppressed a giggle. Beyond the wagons, the big horse corral loomed in the silvery light. Horses stirred and clumped in their restless slumber. Then down the slope, at the river, spread the boatyard with its surreal silhouettes of masts, ropes, rigging. In Burl's hazy consciousness it seemed to float on a black and endless sea, steeped in utter silence. He glided along the wagon row, past the tool shed and the harness shed, past the cargo storage house. Maybelle, he thought, Maybelle, Maybelle, Maybelle. Where are you, little sister? My, my, my, my...

He stopped in midstride, one foot forward. He stopped and bent slightly and listened. There. There it was again. A sighing, moaning sound. The breeze? No, there was no breeze. This was something else, and it came from a wagon. That wagon. That large covered wagon. There.

Burl moved slowly, slowly around toward the back of the wagon, careful not to throw a shadow, careful not to bump a protruding hub. The sound stopped. It started again. There was a tiny little cry, like a bird cry, and breathing. Rhythmic movement and breathing. At the back of the wagon, where the canopy was open, he crouched for a moment to catch his balance. The darkness was deep here, covering him, but there was moonlight streaming down on the other end of the wagon and moonlight filtering down through the canvas. Gently, gently Burl straightened up. At one heartbeat his eyes were still looking at the wooden tailgate; at the next, they were clear of the tailgate and focusing upon the rhythmic moving shapes inside. He saw the white blobs of a man's naked buttocks moving up and down, bracketed by moon-white female legs. Each thrust had a stronger urgency and power, bringing more small, mewing sounds, cat sounds. Then a frenzied whisper: "Oh, I'm going to...I'm going to...Oh..."

"Yes. Yes." The male voice was deep and husky. "Take it in deep, deep..."

Burl felt frozen, hypnotized. His eyes were two shining, focused stones. A wild excitement surged in his stomach and groin. His mouth was dry and his breathing hard.

"Oh," she moaned. "Oh, oh, oh. Oh! Oh!"

"Now," he said. "Now. Now. Now . . ."

A shadow flicked across the front of the canopy. The wagon bed creaked as suddenly an extra weight stepped on the tongue. Burl ducked and scurried deeper into the shadow. From inside the wagon came frantic sounds of bumping and disengagement, a desperate snatching for cloth. "What? What? My, God . . . My *God!*"

Nathan's voice spoke then, low and firm.

"Maybelle, get into the house."

"Nathan, I . . ."

"Pull your clothes on and get into the house."

Scurry, scurry, bump. "Nathan, listen to me. Please, Nathan . . ."

"Move!"

Burl listened, numbed. He could sense Maybelle's shock and fear. He heard more clutching and clothes, more tugging and pulling and bumping. Then there was the scramble of a body hurrying to climb out from the front of the wagon, over the driver's seat, and dropping down. He saw her feet hit the ground, the party shoes, the dropping hem of the pale green print gown. Then the feet were running, running.

Behind her flight, Maybelle left a deepening stillness. A door slammed. For an agony of time, then, nothing moved. Burl lay in the dust behind the wagon, in the blackness of the shadow, and tried to curl into a fetal ball. Finally, Nathan spoke again.

"I ought to kill you right here."

The other man said nothing.

Nathan stood for a long time. Then he said, "Don't ever let me set eyes on you again." And he left the wagon and walked away.

Clutching his boots and trousers, and naked from the waist down, the man leaped from the wagon and hit the ground running. He raced for the gates in the moonlight and was swallowed up by the night.

Burl lay in the dust panting for breath. His heart hammered in his chest. Nausea swept over him like a tide. And then, somewhere in his foggy brain, the enormity of it struck him like a blinding light. His sister. His own sister. And he had not done a thing to stop it!

He rolled over in the dirt and vomited.

* * *

The next morning, an hour after sunup, Stephen Stewart put
the last of Nathan's suitcases into the buckboard and drove him
to Market Square. Nathan seemed moody and withdrawn and
said little on the way. Stephen himself had difficulty grasping the
fact that they were separating for the first time in their lives, for
years and perhaps for all time. The big, lumbering coach to
Baltimore made up on time. Stephen shook Nathan's hand as he
climbed aboard.

With a whipcrack, thudding hooves, and a jingle of harness,
the coach was on its way. Stephen watched until it was out of
sight and felt a sudden, crushing weight of loneliness.

But the sky overhead was clear. The warm Indian summer was
back. It was going to be a beautiful day.

II

The Conestoga wagon labored against steep grade. A shout
coursed thinly across the afternoon. Topping the crest at last, the
six horses steamed and blew, streaked with lather. But there was
no stopping. Angry clouds boiled on the horizon. The air was
heavy, threatening. John Colby was anxious to be off the
hill. With a whistle and a whipcrack, he made the wheels
rumble on.

On the high seat of the Conestoga, the burly teamster mopped
his face with a red bandana. Since morning, when he and Jamie
had left the swampy encampment by the river, he had hurried the
horses under a sense of dread. Even bullying the team failed to
dispel the mood. A thick-muscled man with massive arms and
shoulders, he blinked his eyes, brooding. Nonsense, he told
himself. The gathering storm worried him, nothing more. The
lead horse, Bigfoot, was skittish and trying to kick his traces,
that was part of it. And besides, he was in another of those blue

funks. Colby had suffered them recurrently these two years since Maggie died. He stuffed the bandana into his back pocket and thought: Oh, God. But nothing would shake this thing. Colby had a cloying premonition that he was about to die.

"Yaaah, Bigfoot! Steady, ye damned good for nothin' . . ."

"Father." It was Jamie's voice, beside him. Slenderly built and quiet, Jamie shared the Conestoga driver's seat. Colby heeded, swallowed, tightened rein slightly. Jamie, he thought: Almost twelve years old and wise as Solomon, with those gentle reproaches.

"Sorry, young un'," the teamster muttered.

Well, it was too good a day to be out of sorts. Colby was sensitive to nature in all her moods, splendid and awful. From the seat of a big wagon, a man gets to be one with nature. For a decade he'd driven on Isaiah Stewart's line; a decade hauling trade goods and supplies in the distinctive Stewart Conestogas with their green and white coloring and the Stewart mark, a circled sail, painted on the sideboard. He wondered, sometimes, where all that cargo ended up. Salt, hides, and silica went eastward from the Ohio country; plows, tools, weapons, whisky, and yard goods went westward, for people on the frontier. Once he'd even hauled an entire wagonload of Bibles. Who the hell, he thought, would need all those Bibles?

The wagon rounded a curve. Abruptly, the valley opened wide below them. The ragged sky overhead seemed soaring and immense and, for all its menace, achingly beautiful. A beam of sunlight stabbed down through a hole in the clouds, splashing the road ahead with molten gold. Around them the Pennsylvania hills blazed in autumn dress of blood scarlet, russet, and gold. In the distance, the river was a brilliant silver ribbon twisting through this rugged land. And beyond the river, Colby could see the heavy purplish masses, rising and restless and flickering. The damned storms this time of year could be fierce. Raking out of the northwest, they spawned thunder and lightning and torrents of cold rain.

"Easy, now. Steady, now. Steady."

He was weary and musclesore and knew that Jamie must be the same. The youngster never complained, but sat placidly rocking with the wagon's motion. It was no life, Colby thought, for the likes of Jamie. But a man did what he could. There was no place to leave Jamie for proper schooling and learning the better things of life. Of what worth was the ability to snap flies at ten feet with a bullwhip, a deadly accuracy with the long rifle, and a knack for handling horses that would be the envy of many grown men? Such were the benefits of sharing the life of a teamster father; these, and the arts of survival. For this, mainly, is what it was on the wagon road. One survived the tedium of bone-jarring days, the perils of washouts, robbers, drunken Indians, and runaway teams. One trusted to luck, or to God; and since John Colby had his unanswerable questions about the existence of God, it was luck that mattered. Luck.

He thought, on occasion, of leaving Jamie in the Stewart compound at Pittsburgh, but he never brought himself to broach the subject with his employer. It would mean letting the secret out, letting everyone know about Jamie. This would happen soon enough, but he didn't think they were quite ready, just yet. Give it time, a little time. Even as he reflected on this, however, John Colby knew he was being selfish. The truth was, he loved the company of this youngster, had grown accustomed these two years to having someone to talk to besides the rump of a horse, and dreaded the day when he would be alone again.

"How much farther to the Forks?" Jamie said.

Colby spat tobacco juice and squinted at the sky. The clouds were spreading and thickening fast, and had blotted out the sun. Even the air was heavy with expectation. Thunder rolled out of the hills and hollows. "Three days," he said. "Maybe four."

They were descending the hill now, lurching in deep ruts. The horses were nervous, tossing manes and harness, stepping gingerly over rock outcroppings. "We'll stop tonight at Ragland's Inn, across the river. Give you a chance for a bath and a hot meal that somebody cooked besides your daddy. How does that sound?"

Jamie smiled. "Good."

Colby was not prepared for the rush. The lead horse, Bigfoot, shied at a bolt of lightning and tried to rear in harness. The teamster reined sharply, too sharply. "Whoa! Easy, now. Settle down, now!" But fear ran in a spasm through the team, disrupting the rhythm of the gait. It was the sudden shift in weight that broke control; the sudden weight of the wagon pushing the team from behind, on a sharp inside curve. The slope steepened abruptly here, and a rough section of exposed rock caused hooves to slip. Colby jammed his boot against the brake lever. Brake shoes clamped down hard on the ironbound wheel, grinding sparks. Grabbing up reins in both hands, Colby half stood, drew back with the full force of arms and shoulders, and fought to bring the animals straight again. The curve of road was too sharp, the slope too severe. The wagon yawed violently, jack-knifing. The horse called Bigfoot went down in a tangle of harness, pulling the others with him. Animals plunged and screamed. The Conestoga pitched over slowly.

"Pa!"

Colby felt himself going, felt his arms entangled in leather reins, heard Jamie's shout of warning. Then he was falling headfirst over the footboard. His last conscious impression was of being catapulted into a screaming mass of huge bodies and slashing hooves. One of the hooves crushed his skull.

An upended wagon wheel was still turning as the first heavy drops of rain began to fall.

Dusk gathered as the men came. The rain had settled into a light drizzle. Mist crept up from the river valley, enveloping trees, rocks, and road in its smoky wisps. Sounds dampened. From the gulley where Jamie lay, the wreckage of wagon and spilled cargo appeared in darkening relief against the milky swirl. The men came from the west. Jamie heard their footfalls and muffled metallic clankings on the road, then saw the dark forms emerge one by one. There were three of them, driving a pack mule. The lead man was tall, very tall, and cradled a long rifle on his arm. From the woods one of the loose team horses nickered softly. The men slowed their pace and stopped.

"What is it, Mister Everett?"

The tall man motioned for silence, shifted the long rifle, stooped, and peered into the mist. Then he lowered his body to a half-crouch and waited, listening. A hoof thudded and the invisible horse blew. In the gulley, heart hammering, Jamie slowly drew John Colby's long rifle into position, cheek pressed against the heavy stock. The tall man, rising slowly to advance, now lined up perfectly in the V-notch of Jamie's gunsight, chest high. The man hesitated as the wreckage came into view, moved cautiously to one side and then the other. Finally he saw John Colby's body, ducked down again, waited, crept forward, felt for a pulse.

Jamie's right foot cramped. Worse was the torment of indecision. What to do? Shoot? No—the long rifle had one ball, and there were three men. Shout from the gulley and order them to leave? That would not do, either. Jamie could only pray that they were honest travelers and not highwaymen. At all costs, the wagon, cargo, and surviving horses must be protected. That was John Colby's code. The property of Isaiah Stewart's customers was entrusted to the teamster's care. Now it fell to his survivor. Jamie watched and waited.

Night fell. The men left Colby's body where it lay, tangled in harness alongside those of two dead horses. Jamie hoped they did not notice that four animals had been cut loose to wander in the woods and that one dead horse had been shot. But they would know soon enough. In darkness they moved to a small clearing across the road and made camp, raising a crude half shelter against the rain. A small fire was kindled, and soon the smell of fatback bacon wafted through the woods. Jamie's hunger became excruciating. The sight of creature comforts magnified the awareness of being cold, wet and lying on open ground. After a long time the men stopped moving about, talk subsided, and the fire died down. Night descended in total blackness. The grief took hold of Jamie then, wracking to the core. Not twenty feet away lay the body of the strong, gruff teamster who'd been father, protector, teacher, and companion. No more. John Colby was as silent and remote now as the night, and one with it. "Now I lay me down to sleep," Jamie whispered, "and pray the Lord my soul to keep. If I should die before I wake . . ." And finally, sleep came; the total, all-consuming sleep of exhaustion.

Jamie was still sleeping an hour after daybreak, when the tall man with the long rifle stepped into the gulley and said, "Well, what have we got here?"

The inn of Thomas Ragland was modest even by standards of the western hill country. It was not your clean bed and board, the likes of Boston or New York or Baltimore. Ragland's Inn served a rough and ready clientele traveling over the Alleghenies by team and afoot, bound for Ohio, Caintuck, Tennessee, and beyond. It was a two-story structure of whitewashed sideboard, expanding with the trade, set in a grassless yard with corral and barn. Travelers choked in summer's dust, sloshed in the mud of fall and spring, and cursed the rough ice underfoot in winter. The inn's only attraction was its location at the conjunction of two busy dirt roads. One road bore northward to the town of Pittsburgh; the other lay generally east and west, the route linking Cumberland, Maryland, and Wheeling. There was talk of building a National Road on this westward stretch, a broad pike with stone bridges extending ultimately into Ohio country. But Thomas Ragland was skeptical, and in no mood to spend money improving his establishment against such doubtful future windfall.

Among travelers stopping at Ragland's, as many chose to sleep outdoors as in, the better to keep an eye on their wagons and worldly goods. A road, any road, drew its measure of thieves and ruffians. The journeyman could be none too careful. So the innkeeper provided, at modest charge, a fenced corral for cattle and sheep, water for horses and lean-to sheds in which outdoor patrons could also spend the night. Those who did prefer the indoors were served on a first-come, first-served basis. If things were crowded, one could expect to be bedded down with a stranger, perhaps even two strangers. There were three double beds to the room, and none of them especially clean. A night at Ragland's was likely to afflict the unwary with lice and fleas, if he did not already harbor them on his person. The innkeeper did not concern himself with such matters; take it or leave it, he reasoned, for demand was always greater than supply—especially when the weather turned cold.

Thomas Ragland was a gruff, unpleasant man whose crosses to bear included a nagging wife and frequent attacks of sour stomach. Instinctively, he disliked people, and the feeling was mutual. Molly, his wife, swore that a meaner man never drew breath and wondered aloud why the Good Lord had so accursed her with marital travail. They had two motley sons, Tommy and Barth. The latter was none too bright; the former was a loud-mouthed bully who led a small band of footloose urchins who camped about the place. They were adept at petty theft and swindles. Molly Ragland despised them all, but her husband saw no point in driving them away. He maintained an authority of sorts by beating Tommy occasionally with a razor strop. The boy was twelve, large for his age, and lived for the day when he could return the punishment in kind. "Someday, Pa," Tommy Ragland whispered after absorbing a particularly severe strapping, "you'll get yours."

An all-day rain set in, turning the roads to mud the consistency of porridge. The frontiersmen arrived at Ragland's inn soaked through. There were only two of them, riding heavy dray horses and accompanied by a youngster who wore oversized clothes and a broadbrimmed hat pressing down around the ears. Something long and heavy, wrapped in blanket, was slung over a third horse. The tall frontiersman reined in at the porch and looked down at Thomas Ragland. "Innkeeper, there's been an accident on the road. This here"—he jerked his thumb—"is Jamie Colby. His daddy's dead. That's him, John Colby, in the blanket. Their wagon ran off the road on the hill. One of my men is back there guarding the goods. We'll need to get some people together, go up there and salvage what we can."

There was no shortage of volunteers. In the face of tragedy, western hill people found a common willingness to do what was necessary. Thomas Ragland, motivated by the opportunity of turning a few dollars, gave the word to a passing teamster bound for Pittsburgh: "You tell Isaiah Stewart one of his drivers, John Colby, is dead. There's a damaged wagon, some freight, and Colby's boy to attend to. Tell him I said to send somebody." The teamster touched his hat brim with a whip handle and, flicking the reins, set his team in motion.

Men returned to the wreck with wagons. The Conestoga was capable of repair. They fitted it temporarily with a mismatched wheel and makeshift axle, salvaged the cargo, and buried the two dead horses. The four surviving drays pulled the crippled Conestoga and its lightened load back to the inn.

Mason Everett and his men saw to it that Jamie was provided bedding and a place to sleep in one of the lean-tos at the corral. The clink of coins from the frontiersman's purse gladdened the innkeeper's heart. Everett also arranged to bury John Colby on a hillside overlooking the road, with a wooden marker for the grave. "That's about the best we can do for him, son," he said. "It ain't much, but it's better than nothing."

A small group gathered in the rain around the raw open hole and the rough board coffin. Everett, lean and lank in buckskins, dug a worn Bible from his pack and spoke quietly. Rain dripped off the broad brim of his hat. His face was long and thin, dominated by an axblade of a nose and deeply creased from weather. "The Lord giveth and the Lord taketh away," he said. "Blessed be the name of the Lord."

Jamie stood, only half-listening. John Colby had never put much stock in praying and would prefer not to have it done over his grave. All this, then, was in the interest of custom. Jamie looked at the rain-sodden hills. So this is how it happens; first Mother, and now Pa. Jamie remembered the happiness they'd had, the three of them, in the cabin John Colby built with his own hands at Cumberland. The big teamster would saw away at a fiddle, and they would join him in singing. Colby's voice had deep, rich timbre, and Jamie could almost hear it now, in the sighing of the rain: "Here's a home for us at last Molly, for you and me and this child. I'm going to build a fence for you to grow roses on, lass. A fence..." But he never did, because Molly Colby sickened and died, as abruptly as if you'd blow out a candle. That was the end of any notions the teamster had about God. In the darkness of his grief, John Colby had rolled on the cabin floor and moaned that a God wo'd do such a thing must be evil, and he could not believe in an evil God, so there must be none at all. Then one day they walked out of the cabin for the last time, and the man said, "We're leaving for good, child. There's just you and me, and we'll be together on the road. In time, I'll get my mind steady again." He was never the same after that. He never played the fiddle again, never really laughed out loud. And never again, ever, did they sing.

"...This here is John Colby, Lord, a man I never met in life, but I'm sure you knew well. A good man, from what I hear." Mason Everett paused, groping for another thought. He shut his eyes. The thin nostrils flared. "Look over his boy Jamie, Lord. We commend this soul to you and your everlasting grace. Amen."

The rain pelted down hard as they lowered the body of John Colby into the grave and two men with shovels threw the first clods of earth.

Mason Everett drew a clay pipe from his pocket and filled it with strong tobacco, shredded from a twist. The aroma filled the air. "You can go with us if you like," he said. "We're going to Washington City and then back to Louisiana Territory. I'm opening up my fur company. Figure to get rich in a few seasons." Smoke wreathed his head. He leaned forward and poked at the fire. They had chosen an outdoor lean-to—Everett disliked sleeping indoors among strangers—and Jamie felt warm and secure. Their bellies were filled with beans and coffee. Everett's companions, including a red-bearded giant named Faber, picked their teeth with wood slivers. The frontiersman spoke of his friendship with Isaiah Stewart and his trip east to see President Jefferson. He talked passionately of the western territory, untapped and unexplored. He vowed to carve out a personal empire in the fur trade, upriver along the Missouri, then to the Canadian border and beyond. "I'll tell you, son, the beaver's thick as flies on a hog's back. Come spring, we'll load the pelts on rafts, float 'em down the Missouri to St. Louis, and get top dollar for our labors. There's competition, lots of it; Astor's men and the Hudson Bay boys and plenty of Frenchies who'll cut your throat for a farthing. But it's worth it, by God. It's all there, ripe for the plucking."

Jamie lay back on a pile of blankets, weary but strangely at peace. Such a feeling could not endure, of course; the loss of John Colby, when the shock wore off, would override everything. For the moment, however, it was enough not to think. "I've got to look after my father's goods, Mr. Everett," Jamie said. "He would expect for me to see that everything got back to Isaiah Stewart. And then there's schooling. Pa said I needed more education. I've only been to fourth grade."

Mason Everett nodded, staring into the fire. "Schooling's something every young feller ought to have. Without it, he's not going to amount to much." The frontiersman yawned, knocked out his pipe against a stone. "Yep, Jamie Colby, I like that."

They rolled in their blankets and slept.

It was at least six days' journey to the Forks at Pittsburgh and back. Jamie settled into a lean-to in the corral to await the arrival of another teamster from Stewart's freight line. The frontiersmen had left with their pack mule, and for the first time an acute loneliness bore down upon Jamie Colby. The weather did not help, for the days continued to be gray and chill, with intermittent rains. Inactivity was broken only by the few necessary chores, consisting of feeding and caring for the horses. The damaged Conestoga and the pile of cargo, covered against weather, remained in Thomas Ragland's corral. From this spot, too, Jamie could see the fresh mound of earth on the slope beyond the road. The grave was marked by a rude wooden cross, on which Mason Everett had carved: "J. Colby, Tmstr. R. I. P." Grief lay under Jamie's heart like a stone. And to make matters worse, there was trouble in the air.

A friendly wagoner, familiar to this parts, warned Jamie to be alert. "You've got a lot of goods there, young un'. It wouldn't do to let 'em out of your sight, day or night. Things got a way of disappearing quick around here. They'll steal anything; wood or gold, it don't matter. It's them boys that does it, Tommy Ragland and his bunch. Mean as rattlesnakes, they are." Jamie thanked the man.

The taunting began on the fourth day. Tommy Ragland came around the corner of the barn, trailed by three smaller boys. Ragland had the loutish features of his father, augmented by a pugnacious manner. If the boy possessed any redeeming qualities, they were well concealed. But beneath the ugly surface, Jamie sensed a deep and lurking fear. Ragland stood, fists on hips, and smirked. "What you got under that there canvas, boy?" When Jamie ignored the question, idly picking up a bullwhip, the bully's face reddened. "Hey, blond-head, I'm talkin' to you."

"Freight cargo," Jamie replied quietly. "It belongs to the Stewart freight company." The bullwhip hung in a loose coil, from the right hand. "It'll be delivered to Pittsburgh."

Ragland poked at the pile with the toe of his boot, pushing up the edge of the canvas. "Interesting." Then he sat down on the cargo, groped in his pocket, and brought out a twist of tobacco. Biting off a plug, he chewed thoughtfully and squinted at Jamie. "You and me, boy, we're going to have us a tussle." He snickered and turned to his companions. "Got to get straightened out who's boss around here. Eh, fellers? Hah, hah, hah." He spat a glob that splashed on Jamie's shoe.

Jamie turned away, took four easy strides, and whirled. The bullwhip lashed like a striking snake. Ragland had his mouth open, half-rising, when the popper cracked an inch from his right ear with the sound of a rifle shot. Four more cracks in rapid succession burst around his head, *Kapow! Kapow! Kapow! Kapow!* Ragland and his followers beat a hasty retreat, yowling and covering their heads.

"You there, Tommy Ragland!" It was the innkeeper, storming out from the house. "You boys get away from there, leave them goods alone. Let that young fella be." Thomas Ragland watched the last running foot disappear around the corner of the barn and bustled down to where Jamie calmly recoiled the whip. Thomas Ragland picked his way over the muddy ground and spoke now with an oily smile. "Good enough fer 'em. Serves 'em right, I say. Don't let them boys bother you, young Jamie. We'll look after them goods. And when you get to Pittsburgh, you tell

Isaiah Stewart that Thomas Ragland is an honest man. You'll do that, won't you?'' He rubbed his dirty hands briskly, and his breath exuded the odor of whiskey. The eyes had an unhealthy glitter, bulging and rheumy. They shifted quickly to the bullwhip. ''I'd say you're mighty good with that there weapon, for a shaver. Yes, indeed, I would.''

Jamie did not reply.

The weather cleared on the fifth day, bringing a warming trend. Late the following afternoon, as sunlight spilled down through tall sycamore trees along the road, Jamie saw a green-and-white Conestoga wagon approaching. From the easy gait of the four-horse team, the wagon bore a light load or was empty. The driver was a lean, black-haired youth, tall and well muscled. Jamie strolled toward the Conestoga as it turned into the corral. The driver finally reined in and looked down with a friendly smile. The face was extraordinarily handsome. ''I'm looking for Jamie Colby. Would that be you?''

''Yes.''

''Stephen Stewart. I came to give you a hand.''

''Boy,'' Jamie said, ''am I glad to see you!''

Despite his three-day journey, Stewart quickly began getting things in order. By the next morning, he had managed to find a full-size replacement wheel for the damaged freight wagon and to hire men to replace the axle, using a jerry-rigged block and tackle. A knot of onlookers gathered to watch the work, including several of Tommy Ragland's urchin band. Jamie looked around for the bully but did not see him. The most time-consuming task was the repair of the broken linchpin, requiring the use of a bellows and forge from the back of the Stewart wagon. Stephen worked the glowing iron expertly, the blows of his hammer ringing across the afternoon. Jamie was astonished to discover that he was only sixteen years old and the youngest of Isaiah Stewart's three sons. By the following afternoon, the new axle and wagon tongue had been bolted into place, the wheel installed, and the work—by Stephen Stewart's critical inspection—pronounced satisfactory. ''Now all we need's a driver.''

''I can drive,'' Jamie said.

Stephen surveyed the light build and slender frame. Even the hands seemed smallish. And he had not noticed until now, but the features of the face were wide-eyed and delicate. Almost . . .

"Nonsense," he said. "That's heavy cargo. We'll need an experienced hand."

Jamie persisted. Grudgingly, Stephen agreed to a trial. His misgivings lessened somewhat as young Colby quickly brought the four horses together, put each into harness, and hitched up the Conestoga. Jamie then climbed into the high wagon seat, unwrapped the reins from the brake handle, released the brake, and whistled the horses into motion. A week of idleness had made the animals skittish; but as they attempted to shy, Jamie worked them down with a strong and steady rein, speaking softly. "Whoa, now. Easy, now." The team settled, made a circuit of the corral and was brought back to an easy stop. Stephen laughed. "All right, then. We'll try it your way."

Dusk settled over the valley. The air was misty and cool. Both wagons were fully loaded for an early start the next morning. Jamie walked alone to John Colby's grave and stood in the heavy silence. Beyond the grave, the hills had a bluish, smoky cast. "Well, Pa, I'll be leaving in the morning. Ain't no telling what'll happen next. But I'll try to do like you always said, and be honest and not afraid. I—I'm sorry, Pa, it had to happen like this." The grief tried to well up inside, as Jamie knew it would. So there was no lingering at the grave. Jamie turned away and walked toward the barn, deep in thought, to retrieve a section of harness.

A figure detached itself from the gathering shadows, followed by three more. Tommy Ragland advanced slowly, arms slightly spread. "You ain't got that there whip with you now, Colby," he said. "And your friend ain't around neither. So you and me, we're going to have it out. I want you to lick my boot. If you don't kneel down and lick my boot, I'm going to break both of your arms."

Jamie stood quite still. The younger boys hung back in a cluster watching. Tommy, relishing his advantage now in the presence of his audience, growled softly and came at a rush. Jamie, timing the move, abruptly sidstepped and kicked, tripping the heavy attacker. Ragland tumbled noisily into a pile of empty cans and buckets. Scrambling to his feet with a look of mingled surprise and wrath, he crouched into a wrestler's stance, circling. This time his rush found its mark. Bulling forward, Ragland's arms enveloped Jamie, and the two of them went down in a kicking, grunting melee. Jamie wrenched one hand free and jabbed at Ragland's eyes, but the bully tightened his grip and dug his chin into Jamie's shoulder, squeezing the breath out. "Now, you're going to find out what a bear hug's like." The vicelike hands loosened, groping for a better grip; the tightening arms moved upward toward the chest...

Tommy Ragland's body suddenly stiffened, as if frozen. His eyes widened in surprise. "Well, I'll be—" Abruptly he released his grip and scrambled, panting, to his feet. Jamie was up like a shot, shouting. "Don't you say anything, Tommy Ragland. Don't you say a word! You say anything, and I'll fetch that bullwhip and split your head wide open!" Ragland blinked his eyes stupidly and shook his head. The urchins merely ogled the scene, dumbstruck.

Jamie retrieved the fallen floppy hat and went back down to the wagons. In the rapidly deepening twilight, Stephen came out of the inn with a lighted lantern and quickly busied himself checking out the lashings on the load and filling the water barrels slung to the back of each Conestoga. Jamie knelt over a horse trough, washing mud from the fight off of face and hands.

"Are you all right, Colby?" Stephen said.

"Yes. I'm all right."

At first light, innkeeper Ragland saw to their departure. The man was simpering and obsequious. Stephen dropped a generous tip into his dirty palm. Ragland fairly quivered with pleasure. The wagons rumbled away, taking the north road toward Pittsburgh.

Later, Ragland rewarded his own enterprise with a few drinks from his favorite cask. Then, flush-faced and out of sorts, he confronted his loutish son. Tommy Ragland recognized his father's mood, but was surprised when the innkeeper took off his belt. "Boy, I'm goin' to teach you about startin' a fight you can't finish. You jumped on that young feller Jamie Colby again, didn't you? And you let him whup you!"

Tommy eyed the belt and backed away suddenly, wailing in protest. "It weren't that way, Pappy. Honest..."

The boy's fear inflamed Ragland's wrath. "Don't you lie to me, boy," he shouted, advancing with the heavy belt. "You'll get double!"

"Pappy, please!" Tommy pleaded. "It weren't like you thought. Listen. That Jamie Colby ain't...He ain't what he appears to be."

"What do you mean, he ain't what he appears? What are you talkin' about, boy?" The belt slapped in Ragland's hand.

"Pappy, Jamie wears feller's clothes and all, but he's—he's—"

"He's what?"

"Pappy, Jamie Colby's a *girl!*"

Winter spread its cold over the Forks. Soon after Jamie Colby arrived at the Stewart compound, the cold rains turned to sleet. By Christmas, snow blanketed the town and surrounding hills. New Year's brought fresh snowfall, a quick thaw, and a hard freeze. Icicles drooped down the sooty face of Coal Hill and hung ponderously from the eaves of Isaiah Stewart's house and outbuildings. The woods were leafless and stark, silhouetted darkly against white slopes. The rivers made broad, black curves through the Alleghenies, crusting with ice near their shores. Frost cut lacy patterns on windows.

Jamie rolled reluctantly from her bunk and dressed quickly in the cold. Daylight was a wash of gray over the bunkhouse behind the horse corral. In the next room old Charlie was already up, poking kindling into the stove and rattling pots and pans. By the time she finished lacing her boots and had shrugged into heavy work clothing, the cookstove gave off warm odors of breakfast. She found the ancient black man busily frying fatback in a battered iron skillet. "Child, you need somethin' in yore stomach to start a day's work," he muttered without looking up. "It ain't fit for man nor beast out there, especially hongry."

"Thank you, Charlie." As she sat down at the table, he put a steaming mug of coffee and a chunk of bread beside her plate. "It is cold, and that's a fact."

Jamie wondered how much old Charlie suspected. Nothing had been said between them, and no questions asked. But soon after she moved into the bunkhouse three months before, still in the guise of a boy, Charlie abandoned the sleeping quarters for a cot in the kitchen. "I likes to be here by the stove," he explained. And that's where it lay between them from then on, an unspoken understanding. When other men, teamsters or transients, stayed the night, Charlie saw to it that Jamie had privacy. Once she heard him tell an itinerant bargeman, "I sure wouldn't want to share a room with that young fella, Jamie. He snores worse than a herd of buffalo. Must be his adenoids. Once

he gets started, he rattles the windows and doors." Flimsy as it
was, the warning sufficed.

Old Charlie hummed and mumbled to himself in the manner
of those who've spent long years in solitude. He served her
fatback and fried eggs and, as usual, took his own breakfast at
the stove. "Charlie, how can you enjoy a meal standing at the
stove?" But he shrugged, smiling a whimsical smile that displayed a two-tooth gap in his upper gums. Now she finished her
breakfast quickly, pushed back the chair and said, "Well, here
we go."

"You need any help out there, child, call me."

"I won't need any. It's a light day."

"Don't you go shoeing no horses. Shoein' a dray horse is a
man's work, and we'll get some of the help to do it. Mind what I
tell you."

"All right, Charlie."

She stepped out into a shock of numbing cold. The wind cut
sharply off the river, blowing snow. Leaning against it, she
hurried through the white world to the barn. Inside, she was
quickly enveloped in the close, familiar odors of horses, clumping
in their stalls against the cold. Jamie fired two lanterns and went
to work filling the feed bins with grain shoveled from heavy
sacks.

Old Charlie must know, she thought. He had to know. But the
others, the Stewarts and the workmen, apparently did not suspect. So the wizened Negro handyman with his kinky gray hair
and toothless grin respected her secret. It made them kindred
spirits, in a way; a part of the world around them, and yet
detached from it. She wondered how long this could continue.
Certainly not indefinitely. Soon she would be filling out the
loose-fitting, hand-me-down shirts that her father had provided.
Already her hips and thighs were straining the boy's work
trousers that she wore. Some men had begun to look at her
lingeringly now, almost with a hunger. One teamster, taking in
the flawless skin, cropped blond hair and luminous blue eyes,
wagged his head and muttered: "Damned if you ain't nearly too
pretty to be a boy." Such incidents made her uncomfortable. She
slept with her father's huge flintlock pistol, loaded and primed,
under the pillow.

The thoughts of John Colby stole over her at odd times, often
overwhelmingly so, and she wept with great, shuddering gasps.
Then Jamie would spill out all her ache and sorrow to the horses,

who listened with their big, dumb eyes seeming to heed and sympathize.

It had been three months since her father's death, and three months since young Stephen Stewart entered her life and her thoughts. On the journey from Ragland's Inn to Pittsburgh, driving the two heavy wagons, they had slept in the wilds and shot small game for their suppers. Stephen was impressed with Jamie's sharpshooting and ability to handle a team. Over the campfire he had talked of his own father, who meant to build a fortune in western Pennsylvania, and about his mother, brothers, and sister. Jamie gathered that Maybelle was headstrong and rebellious. She also sensed Stephen's intense loneliness for his older brother. "Nathan has gone to college in England," he said wistfully. "And he's the smartest of the lot."

She felt welcome at the Stewarts'. Stephen's father, Isaiah, wanted to do what he could for John Colby's orphan. "Your father was a fine man, son. You would do well to follow in his footsteps. I appreciate the way you looked after the goods. Chip off the old block. Stephen here says you've got a way with animals. I like that. We need a stablehand. So for now I reckon that's what you can do. You'll live in the bunkhouse with old Charlie." After that, Jamie rarely spoke with Isaiah Stewart; there was, after all, a yawning gulf between a stablehand and the master of Stewart's.

Work became a refuge and a pleasure. The days passed quickly, filled with the constant demands to feed, groom, and tend to an endless succession of animals arriving and departing. There were day workers from town to help, too, as well as teamsters, a blacksmith, and transient wagoners. Life responded to the demands of mules, oxen, saddle horses, and heavy drays. Some animals were mean, sick, or half-wild. But as Stephen had noticed, Jamie could gentle down the most cantankerous brute with a few soft words, a handful of snack, and a scratch behind the ear.

"Colby, you're daydreaming on the job again."

Jamie spun around, pitchfork poised over a pile of manure-filled straw. It was Stephen, leaning quietly against a post, chewing on a straw. "You startled me. I didn't hear you come in."

"Sneaked in the back door." He smiled, showing those strong, even teeth in a darkly handsome face. His presence warmed her, as always. "I came to give Star a rubdown."

Jamie smiled. "I already did."

"So I noticed. You're going to spoil that horse, Colby. But I don't mind. Anyhow, I'll take him out for a run with the little sleigh. He needs the exercise." Stephen took down a handful of harness from a wooden peg. "Might even drop over to Jenny Carver's for a bit." A conspiratorial wink. "I'd take you along, boy, but you're a mite young yet."

"No thank you." Jamie's voice was suddenly frosty.

Stephen harnessed the roan and backed him into the light-runnered sleigh. He attached small bells to the harness, which would jingle as the horse trotted. He drew on a heavy fur coat and gloves. Then he climbed onto the padded seat, flicked the reins, and the sleigh lurched away in a burst of bells and flying snow.

Jamie watched from the open barn door until he was out of sight. She thought of Jenny Carver and felt a stirring of jealousy.

The calamity came in midafternoon. She did not feel well—a tiredness and a tight feeling in the abdomen. "I must be coming down with something," she thought. This probably explained her feelings toward Stephen. What did it matter to her if he visited Jenny Carver? A Stewart could do as he pleased. And certainly she had no cause to be jealous. She finished spreading fresh straw in Star's stable. Putting down the pitchfork, she hurried to the privy behind the bunkhouse and slipped down the heavy work pants. Her underwear was spotted with blood! It came from her private parts.

Confused and fearful, she returned to the barn. But more work was impossible. What had she done to herself? Frantically she picked at her memory. A fall? No. A strain of muscles? Not really. After half an hour she examined herself again. It had not stopped. This was terrible, and embarrassing, and . . .

She left the barn and hurried through the snow to the back door of the main house and knocked timidly. A hired servant girl opened the door a crack, one eye peering through. "What is it?"

"Mrs. Stewart, please. Is she here?"

"Miz Stewart? What do you want to see her about?"

"I just want to see her, please. Mrs. Stewart, please."

"You mean Miz Martha?"

"That's right. Miz Martha."

"Now what would a stableboy want with Miz Martha? Get on out of here, stableboy—"

"What is it, Nell?" The voice was Maybelle's, from the kitchen. "Who is it at the door?"

"It's the stableboy, Jimmy—"

"Jamie," Jamie said.

"He wants to see Miz Martha about something."

Maybelle stepped to the door and opened it wider. "If it's something about the horses, he ought to talk to Stephen or Father. Is it about the horses, Jamie?"

"No. I—I—" Jamie looked up into the soft oval face with its mass of auburn curls and groped for words. "It's an emergency, about me."

Maybelle saw the terror in the eyes, heard the entreaty, and dismissed the servant girl. "Wait right here. I'll get her."

Martha Stewart came out in a flurry of taffeta. She was a tall woman with gentle brown eyes full of concern. Ignoring the cold, she stepped onto the porch and shut the door behind her. "What is it, Jamie? What's wrong?"

"Miz Martha, I'm scared. I must have hurt myself something awful. I'm . . . I'm bleeding from my p-private parts."

The brown eyes widened. Martha turned, to go for Isaiah. Jamie plucked at her sleeve. "Please. I've got to confess something to you. I'm not"—the words seemed to stick, and Jamie swallowed hard to clear them—"I'm not a boy, like you think. My father, he just dressed me in boy's clothes because he thought it would be safer, traveling and all. I'm a girl, Miz Martha. I'm thirteen years old and scared to death . . ."

Martha Stewart's mouth opened as if to speak, shut again, then broadened into a smile. Abruptly, she gathered her stablehand into a strong embrace. "Why of course you're scared. Tell me, what's your real name, child?"

"It's Catherine. Jamie Catherine."

"I understand that your mother died several years before your father, is that right?"

"Yes, ma'am."

Martha grew thoughtful. She looked deeply into the pretty young face, as if searching for something. And, she seemed to find it. "Well," she said, with an air of decision, "you come right into the house and upstairs with me, Catherine. First we'll get your little, er, problem attended to, and then I've got a few things to tell you about being a girl."

Three hours later, surprise swept around the Stewart family dinner table.

Isaiah Stewart banged his fist so hard the plates jumped. "A girl! He can't be no girl!"

Stephen looked stricken. Maybelle giggled. Burl pursed his lips and mumbled, "Well, well, well . . .''

Martha Stewart smiled her warmest smile. "Yes, and a very pretty girl she is, too—as you're all about to find out." She left the room and returned leading a shy Jamie Catherine Colby by the hand. The rough work clothes had been replaced by one of Maybelle's outgrown party frocks. A green ribbon adorned the cropped blond hair, which now had been washed and fluffed until it shone like spun gold. "I want you all to welcome the newest member of our family," Martha said.

Stephen seemed thunderstruck. Maybelle's eyes widened in frank admiration. Isaiah crumpled his napkin, his jaw opening and closing and nothing coming out.

Martha eyed her husband with amusement.

"Don't work your mouth like that, Isaiah. You look like a frog . . ."

III

Spring came grudgingly to Birmingham. Already it was late April, and still the cold rains swept off the midlands onto the town. The misty chill seeped into a man's soul, and even the heaviest wool sweater could not block it out entirely. This, Nathan reasoned, must explain why so many people here suffered from hacking coughs; the weather, aggravated by a pervasive and cloying coal smoke that reminded him so much of Pittsburgh. He was glad he'd brought along a few bottles of good Scotch whiskey, to slake his thirst and warm his bones.

A turn of weather was coming, though. The warmth was distinct now, bringing a greening to slopes and valleys. He walked with springy step and loose stride, having grown accustomed to people's constant staring at his height. The women had bold glances. Someone had said that the women of Britain were cold, but Nathan knew better. Cold in appearance perhaps, he mused, but likely as not, cauldrons inside. But hold. He was letting his instincts play again, and this would not do at all. "Let's keep it clean, old sport," he said aloud, and lengthened his stride.

Nathan had filled out in the two years since leaving Pittsburgh; filled out and added another quarter-inch to his height. Lord, he thought, will I never stop growing? He had gained immeasurably in confidence. His elation at the moment knew no bounds, and he had to repeat the fact over and over in order to affirm its truth. Honors. My lad, you've made honors for the spring term! The proof, of course, was here and now: his trip to Birmingham as reward for excellent performance at Oxford. Just yesterday he had arrived by the great swaying coach—a hair-raising ride, that, thundering along the high road as if chased by Satan himself—and found rooms at a modestly priced inn. He was up at dawn, writing a quick letter home and taking it down for posting. Now he was on his way to attend a special honors lecture in steam mechanics. But first, he stopped for breakfast in a pub. As usual, his accent was quickly recognized and someone said, "You're from the colonies, ain't you, mate?" Someone else stood him for an ale. Finally, after an hour's backslapping and noisy good cheer, he had to push his way out onto the cobblestoned street with its crowds and heady odors of fish and horse manure and garbage. People were no cleaner here than in Pittsburgh, he saw, and even less so in their careless manner of dumping human refuse. One had to step carefully to avoid soiling one's boots.

The street twisted between closely set brick buildings that gave off an air of age and decay. Finally it opened into a kind of square with a fountain in the middle. At a corner, a large crowd had gathered, and people were peering down a side street. Nathan joined them in time to hear a mechanical shriek and a rumbling, chuffing noise that rapidly increased in volume. He nudged an elderly man with a long, mournful face.

"What is it? What's going on?"

"Hell's own contraption, that's what it is," came the reply. "Aye, a metal monster of eternal damnation!" The man's eyes glittered strangely. Nathan recognized the look of religious fanaticism. "Even to look upon it, thou risketh an evil incantation . . ."

In proof of his dire warning, there burst from the narrow street
a huge, smoke-belching machine disgorging sparks and infernal
noise. So mighty was the rumble of its iron wheels that it shook
the very cobblestones beneath Nathan's feet. Pitching and swaying
on the high driver's seat perched an angular figure, more
apparition than man, operating a set of levers. Beside him,
clutching a three-cornered hat and wearing a frock coat of forest
green, was a smallish man, thickset, with muttonchop whiskers
and narrow spectacles. He had the fastidious expression of a
worried clerk.

"Push back, there. Make way!" A babble of warning shouts
rose up around Nathan as the mechanical monster rushed past on
its demoniacal course. Nathan grasped his hat and turned away
against a shower of sparks, belching smoke and fumes. Looking
up, he saw a team of heavy horses, hitched to an ale wagon,
begin to rear nervously in their traces. Abruptly the brutes surged
forward, their massive iron shoes striking sparks on the pavement. In their path stood a tall, well-dressed old man, peering
after the steam car. Nathan caught his breath. The man was
about to be run over!

"Look out!" His shout was drowned in crowd noise. Nathan
elbowing people aside, started running. The huge horses were
bearing down on both of them now. The old man, sensing peril,
turned and saw the onrushing juggernaut. His eyes widened and
his face worked in silent protest. Nathan left his feet. His body
hurtled forward and caught the other's midsection. He felt the
wind go out of the old man as he caved in like a sack, hurled
backward. A great hoof flew past, an inch from Nathan's skull,
followed by the heavy rumble of an ironshod wagon wheel. The
two men tumbled in a heap over the hard cobblestones and lay
there, wheezing for breath.

People came rushing toward them. Hands reached to pluck and
tug. Voices murmured sympathy. Nathan shrugged off a hand and
looked to the target of his assault. The old man sat half upright,
wobbling like a broken stick. Recognition burst upon Nathan.
"Professor Watt!" Rolling to his feet, he helped the other to a
firm sitting position. "Professor, I didn't dream it was you. Are
you all right? Are you hurt?"

"No, I don't think so." The face was long and scholarly, the
white hair disheveled. Professor Watt was still trying to catch his
breath. "The alternative (puff, puff), I'm afraid, would have
been (puff) untidy." A cane lay nearby, and a bystander retrieved

it, along with the old man's hat. His silvery hair stirred in the breeze as they brought him shakily to his feet. "No broken bones, I suppose." From beneath shaggy white brows a pair of searching blue eyes now fixed on Nathan. "That was quite a stupendous block, young man. Play rugby, do you?"

"Only a bit."

"I see. American, are you? Tell by the accent."

"Yes. I've heard you lecture, at the university."

"Indeed."

They were both standing now, dusting off their clothes. Professor Watt had a lengthy rip in the side of his black coat. The fabric was stained with mud and dirt. A slight bruise darkened his right cheekbone. Nathan's own new suit was a mess, and he felt a bad scrape on his left knee. But there were no serious injuries, luckily.

"I'm sorry, sir. It's all I could do—"

Professor Watt seemed to have dismissed the incident from mind. "The university you say? Then you must be an honors student."

"—the team was a runaway. They were frightened by the machine."

"My compliments, young man. Young fellows from the colonies seldom make honors. Some of 'em do well to pass. You must be bright. Yes. Very bright indeed."

"The machine was so noisy . . ."

"Ah, the machine! Yes. Monstrous, isn't it?" James Watt smiled and took Nathan's arm. They walked slowly through the crowd, which murmured its recognition of the old inventor and automatically opened a path. ("It's Professor Watt . . . That's 'im, Professor Watt . . . Almost got run over by the ale wagon.") James Watt nodded and raised his stick. "Still haven't made up my mind if it's appropriate use for steam. A road-running machine, indeed. Ponderous, I'll admit, and plays hob with the roads. But it's better than that madness some fellows are talking about nowadays. Locomotives! Building them to run on iron tracks and that sort of nonsense." His lean face reflected an inner disgust. "No, no, that will never do. Too expensive. Too cumbersome. Quite."

The professor broke his stride and stopped, staring at someone approaching in the distance. "Robert," he said. Then he called: "Robert. Over here!"

To Nathan's surprise, it was the smallish man in the green

frock coat who had been riding on the steam car. Now he was on foot and seeming quite displeased. He voiced this displeasure without even saying hello. "You were right, Professor. It just won't do. We blew another gasket and lost steam pressure shortly after passing you. It's going to take a different boiler, and perhaps—I say, what happened to you?"

"Allow me to introduce one of your countrymen, Robert. This young man here saved my life. His name is—I say, I quite forgot to ask your name."

"Stewart. Nathan Stewart."

But the man in the frock coat was preoccupied. "The infernal machine is too heavy anyway. I don't see why a steam boiler must have such weight. Couldn't we reduce pressure even more, and allow for less metal?"

"His name is Nathan Stewart. And let me tell you, Robert, if it had not been—"

"Perhaps even a smaller boiler would do? What do you think, Professor? A smaller boiler, smaller car, revamp the piping a bit to require less heat . . ." He stopped speaking and stared at the professor. "Saved your life, you say?"

"Yes. That infernal steam car frightened a team back there, and I almost got run down by an ale wagon. If it had not been for Mr., er, Mr.—"

"Stewart."

"—Mr. Stewart, here, I'm quite certain I should have been done for. I'm much obliged to you, Mr. Stewart."

"Yes, we all are," said the man in the green frock coat. "My word, it's lucky you happened to be on hand, isn't it?" He removed a glove of soft gray kid and extended a pale hand. "Allow me. Robert Fulton. I'm an associate, so to speak, of Professor Watt."

"Mr. Stewart is a student at Oxford, Robert. He's done quite well for himself. Honors, and all that. Says he's heard my lectures."

"You talked about the principles of steam mechanics," Nathan said.

The old man sighed. "Not one of my best efforts, I'm sorry to say."

"Posh," Fulton said. "All of your lectures are brilliant." He turned to Nathan. "A fellow American, eh? I don't suppose you're interested in engineering. Probably reading economics or somesuch. Everybody from America nowadays wants to get rich.''

Nathan chuckled. "Well, I'd like to get rich, all right. But it so happens I'm keenest on engineering."

Fulton's eyes widened. "Do tell? How interesting. Professor, isn't that interesting? An American honors student in engineering. Extraordinary.''

"Hear, hear," Professor Watt said.

They had strolled for the better part of two blocks. They came to a waiting carriage with a driver. Fulton extended his hand. "Well, here we are." He shook Nathan's hand and then helped the professor climb up.

"Mr. Stewart," Watt said, "perhaps you would be so kind as to join us for dinner. I have a house on the outskirts of town. A few friends will be dropping in this evening. What say?''

"Delighted," Nathan replied.

"Good. Around six o'clock then. Just ask any hackie for James Watt's place. He'll know the way."

Fulton climbed in beside the professor and nodded to the driver. Then they were off, rocking and swaying over the cobbled pavement.

It was a large, rambling house set back from the road. Lamplight glowed from every window. A clopping and clatter sounded in the driveway as carriages arrived to deposit guests. Nathan alighted from his hired hack and paid off the driver. Some of the carriages, he noticed, bore crests and were attended by liveried footmen. As new arrivals hurried into the house, he caught glimpses of silken gowns and jewels. Suddenly, he was conscious of the drabness of his remaining good suit.

A doorman took Nathan's hat and cloak, and he stepped into the subdued elegance of James Watt's house. By inquiry he had learned that the inventor actually was in retirement now, to the serenity of home and hearth. But it was far beyond what Nathan expected of the old man. Rich carpets and furnishings filled the foyer and parlor, where guests already congregated in conversational clots. Oil paintings adorned oak-paneled walls. In a dining room beyond the parlor he could see gleaming silver and wine goblets set for dinner, lit by a crystal chandelier. On a side pedestal stood a small bust of Julius Caesar that appeared to be newly sculpted from well-veined marble. He was engrossed in examining the bust when a pleasant female voice said: "Do ye fancy it? My husband finished it just last week."

She was a handsome, elderly woman wearing a velvet evening gown and with a small diamond-studded tiara in upswept gray hair. Her accent bore a heavy Scottish burr. "I'm Anne Watt," she said. "This Julius Caesar is the result of his latest invention. It's a machine that copies sculpture." She smiled. "Ye must be the young American I've been hearing about."

"Nathan Stewart, ma'am."

"Ah, yes. I didn't dream that ye'd be such a handsome lad. You'll set some hearts a fluttering, I fear. What a pity I've got to postpone the ladies' pleasure. But James and Mr. Fulton asked that you come down and join them the moment ye arrived." She lifted her hand and gave him a coquettish smile. "Shall we?"

Flustered, Nathan shifted from one foot to the other. "Ma'am?"

"Your arm?"

"Oh. Oh, yes!" He offered her his arm.

Anne Watt led him through the gathering, ignoring the admiring female glances, and through a paneled side door. "As usual, they're in the workshop," she said. "James thought ye'd be more comfortable there for the moment. Worse luck."

They followed corridors and descended stairs, passed through an outdoor courtyard, and came to a square, brick outbuilding that brooded behind massive oak doors. These doors swung open, and Nathan stepped into a large, high-ceilinged room crammed with machinery of every type and description. They walked past wheels and cylinders, rocking arms and pistons, fireboxes and boilers. Several work benches bore the clutter of unfinished projects. In one corner stood a strange sort of cutting device, built into a frame and surrounded by a great litter of broken marble and fine white dust. "The bust copier," Anne Watt said. "It will make..."

Unexpectedly her words were engulfed in a mighty blast of steam erupting from a far corner. The blast set off a clanking and chuffing. As they hurried toward it, Nathan saw the massive silhouette of a huge rocker arm, immobile in the gloom. Two men in shirtsleeves stood by a large gearbox, grasping wrenches. Their shadows made giant silhouettes against high stone walls.

James Watt mopped sweat from his brow with a soiled rag, leaving a grease smear. Sweat dampened his white dress shirt. Seeing Nathan, he sprang down from a low iron platform and offered a greasy handshake. His words of greeting struggled to be heard over the hissing and clanking. "... just in time ... need your help ... design for smaller ... coat off ..."

Anne Watt cupped her hand into her husband's ear and shouted something. He nodded vigorously. "... won't be long ... soon as mechanism ... hungry as a horse ..." The inventor's wife turned back to Nathan, shrugged, and retreated the way she had come.

Nathan found himself shaking hands with Robert Fulton. The American was no longer the figure of sartorial impeccability he'd met that afternoon. Fulton's ruffled shirt bore oil stains, his sleeves were rolled to his elbows and sweat beaded his face. "Thought you'd be interested in this," he shouted. "New design for a marine engine. I ordered it from Boulton and Watt. Steamboat. But the gear mechanism here"—he pointed to the gearbox—"has sprung loose. Can't drive the rocker arm. Need a good strong muscle for the pry bar ..."

Moments later Nathan had his coat off and stood in the bowels of the great machine, engulfed in clouds of steam, as he threw his weight against a massive iron bar. James Watt waved his arms excitedly. Robert Fulton nodded and pushed a heavy lever projecting from the works. There was a clank and a shudder in the huge framework of the steam engine. A hidden piston slid into action. A fresh blast of steam poured over Nathan. The rocker arm above him groaned to life, rising and falling in ponderous sweeps like a gigantic pump, two stories high.

Both Watt and Fulton were cheering soundlessly as Nathan disengaged his pry bar and stepped free of the engine. "Good show!" Watt shouted through cupped hands. "Couldn't have done it without you!" Fulton watched his gearbox, flushed with something resembling ecstacy.

Anne Watt sent her message down three times before they ascended from the Watt workshop, talking animatedly of gears and levers and pressures. A servant bearing an armload of towels escorted Nathan, Watt, and Fulton to a washroom and held an oil lamp while they soaped and scrubbed. To Nathan's dismay, his clothing now bore fresh stains and smudges. "Professor," he said ruefully, "I'm not very presentable."

"Nonsense, my boy. Think nothing of it."

Fulton grinned. "Stewart, I'm afraid we're costing you money. That's the second suit you've managed to ruin today."

"Oh, well. It's worth it."

As they joined the guests upstairs, Nathan became uncomfortably aware that he now gave off a distinct odor of lubricating grease. Eyebrows lifted in amusement as Professor Watt and Fulton introduced him to guests whose grooming bespoke wealth and social bearing.

One man refused to take Nathan's hand as the professor murmured introductions. "Lord Malvern, may I present Mr. Nathan Stewart?" The man's face was long and dour, the left eye encased in a white patch. An angry scar descended from the hairline to the patch. Nathan also noticed that the left hand seemed shriveled and was hidden in a black glove. Lord Malvern returned a crooked smile of unconcealed malice. "Another colonist, eh? How amusing."

Fulton drew Nathan away. "Don't mind Lord Malvern," he said quietly. "He's still bitter about the war. He was shot up at Yorktown as a very young lieutenant."

Nathan understood. "I've managed to run into a few men like him from time to time. There's even some animosity at the university."

"He's an accomplished duelist," Fulton went on. "I don't know how you feel about such things . . ."

"It's not my idea of a favorite sport." Nathan made it sound lighthearted. But the implied warning in Fulton's tone made him ill at ease.

The dinner table was set with fine English china. Candlelight gleamed in silver and crystal. There were vases filled with Anne Watt's own hothouse flowers. Nathan's place was toward midtable, diagonally across from Robert Fulton. Opposite him, and next to Fulton, sat a vivacious brunette in a wine velvet gown. She inspected him with startling green eyes. "I must confess, Professor Watt, that I'm quite taken with your rescuer," she said, sipping from a glass of Chablis. "But then, I have an inordinate weakness for beautiful young men."

"You have a weakness, my dear," a sharp-faced woman said icily, "for *all* men."

The brunette shrugged. "At least some of us make no pretense."

Nathan was enthralled. He thought he had never seen a more beautiful woman in his life. He returned her smile and forked at a flaky sole in cream sauce. The delicate aroma of the fish wafted to his nostrils; but he was not really hungry. He could think of nothing to say, nothing clever nor witty. He kept his silence.

"I believe, Marian, that you have the fellow's tongue." It was Lord Malvern again, speaking from the foot of the table. Challenge continued to glint from his one good eye. Nathan looked levelly at the nobleman. Lord Malvern had been drinking steadily before dinner and now was into his second glass of table claret. "It takes a certain wit to function in polite society, a quality that I fear is lacking in the typical American temperament." He nodded toward Robert Fulton. "With certain exceptions, of course."

The green eyes persisted in their warm inspection of Nathan. He felt them flicking over his chin, his hair, his shoulders. The awareness brought a tightness to his stomach. "Pay no attention to my husband, Mr. Stewart," she said. "He is a bore when he drinks."

Other guests hastened to change the subject. "And what on earth are you inventing now, Mr. Fulton? Still tinkering with that underwater vessel of yours? What is it you call the thing?"

"The *Nautilus*, Mrs. Finch," Fulton replied, beckoning to a waiter for a slice of rare beef off the standing rib. "It's a submarine, actually."

"A submarine, of course. How quaint. And what do you intend to do with it, pray tell?"

"Mr. Fulton believes that the submarine will be the ultimate weapon of war," Lord Malvern interjected. "Isn't that right, Robert? He has the notion that a torpedo-armed submarine will be so horrible that nations will simply give up fighting one another." He patted down a belch with his fingertips and took a slice of beef. "Personally, I think there's more money to be made in his canal patents, the digging machine and the double-inclined plane . . ."

"A double-inclined *what?*"

"It's a device, Marian, for moving canal boats over stretches that can't be navigated by water," Fulton said. "We take the boats out of the water and transport them overland by rail. That way, you avoid the huge construction costs in certain terrain."

"Robert believes canals are the way of the future," Professor Watt said. "Lord knows we've got enough of them in England now. He even gave up his London residence a few years ago to work on the Duke of Bridgewater's canals for barging coal . . ."

"Must we prattle on about all these technical things," Anne Watt said. "Frankly, I haven't the foggiest notion what you're talking about."

"Tell me, Mr. Stewart," Marian Finch said, "do you have canals in the new world?"

"Not really. We're dependent on rivers for inland trade. But I think it's only a question of time."

"No need for improvements there," Lord Malvern said. "Nothing west of Boston except savages. Bloody barbaric country, I wouldn't give a quid for the lot of it."

"The world lost a fine portrait painter when it gained an inventor," Anne Watt said. "When we first met Robert, he had a very promising career in London. A pity, if you ask me."

Nathan was surprised. "You're a painter?"

"Originally, yes. I came over here to study with Benjamin West. It was . . ."

"He did an excellent portrait of your Mr. Benjamin Franklin," the professor said. "Quite professional, I'd say."

The wine was mellowing Nathan and loosening his tongue. He was pleased with the wit and charm of James Watt. The old man obviously relished the company of people. Nathan was so at ease he could have exchanged pleasantries with Lord Malvern, had the latter offered an opening. He did not. As dinner wore on, Lord Malvern drank more and more and ate less and less, until finally he slouched in a half stupor in his chair, barely acknowledging anyone's presence.

The condition of her husband did not trouble Lady Malvern. She now stared recklessly at Nathan and, on the pretext of getting his attention, reached across to grasp his hand. The green eyes turned smokey. Nathan's excitement turned to discomfort. Occasionally, he also sensed the eyes of Lord Malvern upon him. He looked to Robert Fulton for help, but the inventor was engaged in conversations of his own. Finally, Nathan blurted out: "Mr. Fulton, do you think I could go down in your submarine?"

He had spoken more loudly than he intended. Heads turned and table talk subsided. Lady Malvern regarded him strangely.

"I beg your pardon, Nathan?" Fulton said.

"Your submarine, the *Nautilus*; do you think I could make a descent with you?"

"Well, I . . ."

"Now that's what I call nerve."

"Nerve? Foolishness is more like it."

"The young are irrepressible."

"Imagine anyone wanting to go, I say, actually wanting to go down into the depths in a device like that."

"Do you mean you're actually interested?" Fulton said. "Most people are more disbelieving than they are interested. Most people don't..."

"Of course, he's interested," Professor Watt said. "Why the idea stirs the blood. Robert, you've got a convert! I'd make a descent myself if I weren't a thousand years old."

"Rubbish," Anne Watt said.

"It isn't rubbish at all. Robert is quite serious about his submarine, aren't you Robert?"

"But how on earth does one *breathe* down there?"

"Compressed air..." The voice slurred. Lord Malvern eyed them through the fog of drink like a one-eyed owl. He lifted a finger and repeated the words in the manner of solemn benediction. "Compressed air... Lets you breeth... lets you breeth... four hours. Four hours. Ain't that right, Mister Inventor?"

"That's right," Fulton said.

"An' I don't think..." Lord Malvern swayed in his chair, frowned, focused his eye half the length of the table and fixed it upon Nathan. "I don't think a bloody savage from the bloody colonies is entitled—entitled to go down in a vessel that by rights should be a British ship of war."

There were gasps around the table. Eyes turned to Nathan. He felt his face flush with indignation. The insult was direct and pointed. Professor Watt blanched, and his wife's face contorted with embarrassment. Robert Fulton shot Nathan a warning glance. Lady Malvern's lips parted as she waited for the response that her drunken husband richly deserved.

Nathan suppressed an urge to stand and confront his heckler. He masked his resentment, deliberately made his facial expression sublime, took a sip of water, smiled. "Perhaps Lord Malvern is right. I'm a landsman, after all, from Pittsburgh. Not cut out for the sea." He looked to Professor Watt and let his smile broaden. The tension around the table eased as if wind had gone out of a sail.

Someone murmured, "Good show."

But three hours later, as Nathan stepped down from Fulton's carriage in front of his inn in a dark and misting rain, the inventor combined his farewell with a warning. "Be on your guard, my young friend. I doubt that you've yet heard the last of this."

Nathan did not expect his request to be taken seriously, and certainly not so promptly. Nor did he anticipate the distances involved. Two days later, however, a note arrived at his rooms. "Nathan: Forgot to mention that the diving boat is docked at Le Havre, France. I have booked passage for us on a Channel packet that will get through the blockade. She sails next Monday morning. We leave here on the London coach day after tomorrow. Y'r Mst Obdn't Srvnt. R.F." It barely gave him time to attend to finances and pack his things.

The journey was a misery. First, the London coach barreled eastward at breakneck speed, lurching heavily and tossing them about like dried beans in a jar. Then, for the Channel crossing, the weather turned blustery and cold. Barely had they cleared the Thames Estuary when Robert Fulton, muffled in greatcoat and beaver hat, flopped over the rail and lost his breakfast.

The doughty square-rigger was smelly and old, her scuppers clogged with filth and sails a mass of patching. But she tacked to the wind like a terrier with a bone in her teeth, roughly breasting the swells and standing, quivering, on each crest. Fulton clung groaning to the rail, face the color of ashes. Not until well past midnight, when they were spirited ashore in a dinghy and deposited, bag and baggage, Nathan knew not where, did the suffering inventor begin to rally. He swayed in the misting rain and croaked: "My God, this infernal curse of mine. I get seasick in a bathtub . . ." And he wretched once more for good measure.

Leaving their baggage on the beach, Fulton led the way on a two-mile walk into town. Waking the keeper of an inn, he hired a trap to fetch their things and arranged for rooms. Nathan fell into a sleep of utter exhaustion and did not awaken until late afternoon. To his surprise, sunlight streamed into his open window and songbirds played in a greenbud tree just outside. The weather was quite balmy, and beyond the town the sea was a sweep of blue. A servant knocked softly at his door, bringing a washbasin, soap, and towels. Nathan's boots had been shined and a suit laid out. In French, the servant announced that Monsieur Fulton hoped he had slept well and would meet him downstairs for dinner in an hour. "Delightful," Nathan said.

He found the inventor in the lively company of several men. They gathered around a white-clothed dinner table, laughing and making noisy conversation in French. Nathan's arrival brought them to their feet for introductions. He caught the name of Joel Barlow, an American living in Paris. The others were old friends or business associates and a minister for naval affairs. The minister bowed and greeted Nathan in English. "A pleasure, Mr. Stewart. Robert has been telling us about you. He is quite impressed with your scholarship and grasp of engineering."

"Thank you very much."

They settled again. The rotund innkeeper fawned over his important guests, bringing table wine in large wickered bottles. Nathan ordered a chicken dish, asparagus tips, and small new potatoes. Fulton, he noted, selected a filet of haddock in wine sauce and nothing more.

"And how are you feeling, Robert?" he asked quietly.

The inventor sighed and patted his stomach. "Tolerable, Nathan. Just tolerable."

As they finished the meal, darkness had fallen outside, and the inn glowed warmly in lamplight. A rich odor of cigar smoke permeated the air. Joel Barlow was speaking now of the diving boat.

"Good news, Robert. Monsieur Povey here"—he nodded toward the minister for naval affairs—"tells me the government has renewed its interest. He has a proposition to offer."

"A proposition?" Fulton lowered his brandy glass.

"It involves both the *Nautilus* and your self-moving torpedo."

"But they rejected them before."

"Quite so. However, Robert, you are not exactly unknown in France. Your canal projects, your patents, and that panorama you painted in Paris that's become so popular . . . Um, what's it called?"

"*l'Incendie de Moscow.*"

"Yes. All of this has given you considerable prestige. Some of your friends have brought it to the ear of the emperor."

"The emperor?"

"What Monsieur Barlow is leading up to," said the minister for naval affairs, "is the fact that the emperor is prepared to appoint a commission to examine your plans for the diving boat as a weapon of war. If it shows real promise, an agreement will be drawn up providing, uh, a means by which you can secure remuneration. How does that sound?"

Fulton looked to Barlow. "What do you say, Joel? After all, it's your money we're playing with."

"I like it, *mon ami*. At least it's something more definite than we've ever had before."

Fulton smiled and nodded to the minister. "Then we'll do it. In the meantime, I'm taking Nathan here out tomorrow on the *Nautilus*. You gentlemen are welcome to observe if you like."

The response was enthusiastic. Talk surged with renewed vigor. Brandy glasses clinked. Nathan happily snipped the end of a cigar and leaned into a candleflame. As he settled back again, blowing smoke, a disquieting thought flicked across his mind: What am I getting myself into?

He dismissed it and refilled his wine glass.

A brisk sea breeze raised a light chop in the narrow river. Nathan turned up his collar, back to the wind, and eyed the strange craft at the foot of the dock. The grandness of her name defied reality, for the *Nautilus* was a squat, ugly thing of rounded ends and dark protrusions, floating on the oily surface. An ancient mechanic with a face the texture of old leather fussed at a stubborn bolt amidships, muttering to himself in countryman's French. Nathan's misgivings heightened as he sensed the impatience of Robert Fulton, pacing the decrepit dock to which his creation was moored. Two other mechanics, younger and stronger men, labored nearby at an ungainly pumping apparatus, pumping air into two steel tanks.

"For God's sake, Ekland, won't ye hurry? We'll lose the tide!"

"We're doing our best, Monsieur Robert. I've had to replace this bolt, after all. The old one would have sheared for certain when we tried to make her watertight." The old man spoke in the querulous tone of one accustomed to back talking authority. Skill, after all, deserved certain prerogatives. "We wouldn't want to spring a leak down there, would we?"

"Oh, very well. Do your best."

"It won't be long now."

"I hope not."

Fulton took Nathan's arm and drew him closer to the vessel, looking down with the pride of creation. "This is history in the making, my friend. History. Napoleon will buy her, I'm certain of that: The English''—he grimaced with the pain of a rejected suitor—''simply can't grasp the significance of this weapon. That's what it is, you know. The ultimate weapon. With an armed torpedo, capable of being catapulted forward bearing a fused powder charge, the *Nautilus* will be able to sink a man-o'-war. There will be no defense against her. None.''

Nathan was dubious. The black hull rose from the water like the hump of a whale. Wooden planes and fins stuck out from the sides and stern. The round hatch on top was fitted with glass portholes. A stubby mast jutted up amidship, on which to hoist a sail for movement on the surface. Nathan started to ask questions, but was interrupted by the arrival of several carriages. Their dinner companions of the previous evening arrived, accompanied by several women whose conversation and laughter quickly brightened the morning. Even old Ekland smiled, and the younger men made haste to finish their pumping and stowing of the air tanks. Nathan was busily shaking hands when the minister for naval affairs tapped his shoulder and said, ''Mr. Stewart, may I present my niece, Yvette Marchand?'' Nathan looked down into a pair of large brown eyes set in a soft oval face that reminded him of a cameo. He stammered something and bent over her hand. There was a wafting scent of French perfume. She wore a blue gown and matching cloak, with a small bonnet.

He stumbled on a coil of rope and recovered. He lost her hand. Damn! His mind was racing, and suddenly blank. This accursed discomfort in the presence of women! The brown eyes were amused. ''Something wrong, monsieur?''

''No. That is, I—I'm charmed to meet you, Ahem.''

Then her back was to him, and she was moving on her uncle's arm toward the *Nautilus*. Her words drifted back. ''What an odd-looking craft. Somehow I thought it would be, well, larger.''

Fulton trotted along behind them. ''Oh, it's large enough, mademoiselle. Yes, quite. She'll accommodate a crew of four. Including myself, of course . . .''

''How interesting,'' one of the other women was saying. ''And when you get down there, in the water, what do you manage to use for light?''

The question was directed to Nathan. ''Light?'' He was nonplussed. A gruff male voice beside him offered a reply.

''Well, we ain't rightly figured that out yet,'' Old Ekland said.

"Some daylight filters down through the portholes in the hatchway there. But you can't light a lamp, or nothing like that. You'd suffocate."

"Oh."

Ekland still bore his wrench in hand. The ancient face was impassive. He tugged at his leather cap and called out to Fulton. "We're ready, monsieur. You wanted the tide."

"Yes, yes," the inventor replied. He was engrossed in explaining the workings of the vessel to Yvette Marchand, who listened politely. Nathan listened, too, but could not take his eyes off the soft oval face.

"The movement of the diving boat is up and down, and also forward," Fulton was saying. "To accomplish this we have two systems. The one is what I call the water ballast system. We can fill those cylinders in the side of the boat with water, using manually operated plungers that work rather like a butter churn. Fill those cylinders and the craft descends; push the water out again, and the boat comes to the surface again . . ."

"Monsieur, the tide . . ."

"To move forward on the surface, we simply rig that sail there. But underwater, we move by turning a large hand crank at the stern. The crank turns a screw-type propeller that pushes us right along. And we steer by means of levers inside the boat that control these fins and vanes . . ."

"Monsieur?"

"Yes, Ekland. Very well. Let's get on board, then. Nathan, just step down there, if you will."

Nathan smiled at Yvette Marchand, but she seemed bored and looked away. As he stepped onto the black hull, it gave slightly beneath his weight. Again, he had to struggle ungracefully for balance. Finally, he was descending a wooden ladder down the hatchway, aware of the sudden constriction of tight quarters. There was an odor of stale air and bilgewater. Gloom enveloped him, filled with metallic echoes. The sloping interior of the hull was damp and slippery to the touch. There was not enough room for him to stand erect. In an instant of unreasoned panic, he stifled a desire to climb back up the ladder and escape. Now, the old man, Ekland, clambered stiffly down, muttering to himself, followed by Fulton.

"Do we have enough air in the tanks, Ekland?"

"Yes, monsieur."

"And the bolt. Did you fix the bolt?"

"I think so, monsieur."

"You *think* so?"

"Well, you were in a rush, monsieur. You can't rush machinery. A machine has a mind and soul of its own."

Fulton frowned and moved about briskly, inspecting the craft. A large compass was mounted in the center, beneath the hatchway. He tapped the glass and seemed satisfied. Then he motioned Nathan toward the stern and indicated a large wooden crank. "This will be your job after we've made our descent, Nathan. This is the crank that operates the screw propeller. It takes a strong arm, but moves us along nicely."

"Very well, Robert."

"All right, then." The inventor moved back to beneath the hatchway and shouted up through cupped hands. "Cast off the line, LaFarge. Then rig sail and take us out."

"Oui, monsieur."

Fulton was in his element for the moment. His eyes seemed to flash in the gloom, and his moustaches bristled. Nathan felt a bumping and scraping as LaFarge pushed the *Nautilus* away from the dock. A pulley creaked as the sail was hauled up the stubby mast. Slowly the craft got under way, wallowing as it went. Soon light drops of spray came down from the open hatch, and he knew they were moving out of the mouth of the river into open water. The wallowing motion grew more pronounced as they progressed, and Fulton's face—even in the half light of the submarine—took on a familiar pallor.

"Oh, dear," he said.

"Is there anything I can do, Robert?"

"Yes. P-please instruct LaFarge to take in sail and come below. Maybe if we descend, we can stop this infernal rocking."

The assistant's big feet clumped down the ladder. The hatch cover clanged shut, and its bolts were tightened, closing off both light and air. In the deepened gloom, old Ekland opened a pitcock, bringing a hiss of air from one of the steel tanks. Nathan had the vague sensation of being buried alive. Sweat beaded his face and his throat constricted. Involuntarily, he began gulping for air.

Fulton manipulated values, and water gurgled into the ballast cylinders. "Relax," he said. "Try to breathe naturally." With a watery sigh, the strange craft began to sink. The interior light weakened even more as seawater engulfed the portholes around the hatch. Fulton scrutinized the face of a large dial and drew

Nathan to his side. "Barometer," he said. "It measures our descent. We'll go down to twenty feet. Your ears might pop a bit. Just swallow and they'll clear. See that pipelike device right beside you?"

"Yes."

"That's a lookscope. Shove it upward, look through the eyepiece there, and tell me what you see."

Nathan raised the lookscope and scanned the upper world of daylight and open water. From this vantage point, it was like peering into another world, all sparkling and clean. Turning, he looked back toward the dock. The small crowd of friends seemed forlorn, watching the spot where the *Nautilus* had slid beneath the surface. The face of Yvette Marchand swam into his view.

"Lovely," he said.

"Eh? Yes, it's pretty, especially when viewed from down here."

They were moving slowly away from the dock. Nathan became conscious of the creak of the great wooden handle being turned at the stern. LaFarge, unbidden, had taken up the chore of turning the screw propeller. Descent indeed had smoothed the submarine's progress, as Fulton expected. The pitching and yawing stopped. But the air was rapidly turning fetid and warm. Fulton mopped his face with a handkerchief. In a weak voice, he instructed Nathan in the operation of hand levers for manipulating the external rudder and diving planes. Nathan then started back to replace LaFarge at the hand crank. But without warning, the inventor sat down, holding his stomach.

"Shall we go back to the surface, monsieur?"

"No. You take over the steering here, Ekland. And I want Nathan to get the hang of this vessel. I—I apologize, Nathan." The voice was suddenly filled with dismay. "Every time I get aboard any kind of boat, this infernal sickness..."

"Monsieur Fulton, we have a leak." Old Ekland's words seemed unnaturally loud.

"A leak?"

"That hatch bolt, it ain't holding. Up there, see?"

Over their heads, water was oozing in around the hatch cover. Even as they watched, the flow strengthened into a dribble.

"Nathan, check it, will you?"

Nathan climbed two rungs of the ladder and put his hand to the spot. The bolt obviously had been cross-threaded under pressure partway and now slipped, so that it loosened a portion of the hatch cover. The leak worsened steadily.

Fulton said to Ekland, "Can you fix it?"

"Can't tighten her any more, monsieur. She'll pop, I'm afraid, and then we'll have trouble for sure."

"Damn," Fulton said.

Nathan was surprised at the old man's intransigence. In his father's boatyard, no handyman or mechanic would give up so easily. He could almost hear again the rumble of Isaiah Stewart's big voice: "If it's got to be fixed, then find a way!" Now Nathan descended the ladder and groped for tools and loose materials he had seen in a corner. He found an iron wedge and several other pieces with which to fashion a clamp. Fulton watched in the gloom, saying nothing. LaFarge kept his crank turning, with the *Nautilus* barely under way. Ekland, too, seemed to retreat into a petulant silence.

"This might work," Nathan said. "I'll give it a try."

For ten minutes he labored in a cramped position beneath the hatch cover. His arms grew heavy and muscles strained. The cascading water slopped over him, saturating his clothes. His labored breathing sounded in the gloom. Below him, the others watched without offering to help.

"We're flooding," Ekland said at one point. "Shall I—?"

"No," Fulton replied.

Nathan attempted to wedge the iron piece against the loose bolt, thus adding pressure to secure the hatch cover. But it kept breaking loose again. Finally, however, he managed to fashion a jerry-rigged vice to hold the wedge in place. Then he loosened the stripped bolt into the remaining portion of its undamaged thread, slid the wedge into place, and tightened the bolt again. The flow slowed. Arms aching from laboring in such cramped position, he gave the wrench one more turn. The leak stopped. Exhausted, he descended the ladder and stood catching his breath. "Whew!"

"Good job," Fulton said. "Now we'll take her back to shore and surface. A little more speed please, LaFarge." The inventor raised the lookscope, peered, dropped it down again. "Nathan, would you please help LaFarge with the crank?"

Two hours after she had sunk beneath the surface, the *Nautilus* emerged again, her glistening hulk rising from the depths like a sea monster. The hatch opened, and LaFarge climbed out, rigged the sail again and guided the craft back to the dock.

Nathan ascended the ladder into a watery midday sunlight, sucking in great mouthfuls of fresh air. He looked to the dock. Only Joel Barlow and the other mechanic remained. The others, including Yvette Marchand, were gone. He felt a twinge of disappointment.

"Well, Nathan,"—Fulton was still pale, but reviving with the fresh air—"how did you like your first voyage aboard the diving boat?"

"Fascinating. But I was thinking, Robert. Do you suppose that hatch cover could be redesigned? I've got a few ideas..."

"Certainly, my friend. Go right ahead. Get something on paper and let's take a look at it."

Nathan climbed the path to the carriage, deep in thought.

Fulton watched him go. Then he turned to Ekland. "Well, what do you think?"

The ancient mechanic lit a gnarled stub of pipe and blew tobacco smoke. "Not bad. I've seen journeymen do worse. I'd call it a fair job in a pinch."

"I thought so too."

"He'll do nicely, monsieur."

Fulton smiled, rubbed his hands briskly and looked out at a ragged bank of clouds advancing from the northwest. "That settles it, then. I'd suggest you put the regular hatch cover back on. It looks like we're in for heavy weather."

Life seemed to take a gigantic leap forward. The world was broader, fuller, more exhilarating. He returned to the university reluctantly, as one stepping backward. Academia was small by comparison, petty and constricting to the spirit. Out there beyond these cloistered stones and musty classrooms spread new worlds to conquer. Oh, to be free of this humdrum college life!

Nathan settled into the droning lectures, his thoughts drifting elsewhere. He pored over Homeric classics in the Latin and Greek, bent his mind to mathematics and logic, observed the protocols and the schedules. His grade averages held, but by dent of extra effort. When possible, he took long weekend trips to Birmingham to visit with Professor Watt. The old man was delighted with Nathan's company, for the young American was constantly picking his brains on technical subjects. Nathan chafed for lack of adequate research materials on canal building, engineering, and steam power. Although the steam engine had been around for a century in one form or another, there was little that one could read about it. Technical doers and builders, worse luck, did not write; and writers did not do.

James Watt recognized the dilemma, having suffered it himself, and therefore invited to his house men of like mind, including surveyors, diggers of canals, and builders of viaducts. Among these was the young Camden Willoughby, the fifth Earl of Somerset. A lighthearted youth of twenty-two, Willoughby already had designed a huge viaduct that could be cast from iron, for use in transporting coal by barge from the mines of his uncle, Lord Blalock. He was delighted to meet an American at Oxford, having graduated there himself, and invited Nathan to visit him in London. "You really should spend some time in London, you know. I'll help you find digs. It's a jolly good place to go on spring holiday, what with the night life and all." They played tennis together in Birmingham—Nathan lost badly—and shared a common zeal for the company of Professor Watt. Over dinner, he told them: "Steam, my young friends, will be the next technical revolution. Mark my words, the steam-powered boat will free man from the whims of river current and ocean winds. It will change dramatically our concepts of time and distance."

"But if the steam engine will work with boats, Professor, then why wouldn't it also power a locomotive? Same principle, after all."

"Bosh, Camden. You know what I think about those infernal things. First you've got to prepare a level roadbed and put down permanent rails—wood or iron or somesuch—and then your locomotive is simply tied to the rails and can't go anywhere else. There's no freedom of movement. No, the locomotive will never be a success. A steam car, now; that's something else again. A steam car will move on any decent roadbed and give you great mobility . . ."

On one such weekend, Nathan and the young earl shared a strange conversation. Much later, it would play heavily upon Nathan's mind. They were having a sherry in Camden Willoughby's room. The handsome young nobleman had enjoyed another evening of playful verbal joust with the professor. They laughed at the old man's stubborn mind.

Willoughby lit a pipe, loosed a smoke ring at the ceiling and abruptly changed the subject. "I say, there's a little personal matter I've been meaning to discuss with you. I hear you had a little run-in with Peter Finch at the professor's dinner party."

Nathan wondered how on earth Willoughby had found out about that or why it seemed pertinent. "Not really," he said. "Lord Malvern was a little out of sorts, that's all."

Camden smiled. "Unfortunately, he didn't take it that way. He can be quite an unpleasant man, you know."

"So I've been told."

"Really I shouldn't bring up the thing at all. It's none of my business. But you'd be surprised at the gossip going round about the big, handsome American student who bested Lord Malvern at his own game. It seems that you totally ignored his barbs, which is something the man absolutely can't stand. Put him in his place, so to speak."

"I wasn't aware that . . ."

"Know anything about his wife?"

"Marian Finch? Only what I've seen of her."

"Pretty little package, what?"

"Beautiful."

"She was an actress, you know, and a live-in mistress for several wealthy and powerful men. Would you believe that?"

"Of course not."

"Well, it's true. Some of the more malicious tongues speak of her as a high-class strumpet."

Nathan remembered the frank green eyes, the stunningly beautiful face framed in a mass of soft, dark hair. He said nothing.

"Apparently she was quite taken with the young Nathan Stewart. Not that that's anything extraordinary; she flirts shamelessly, and quite deliberately. The point is, this time it really got under Peter Finch's skin. I understand Fulton took you off to France to get you out of his way."

"I didn't know that."

Willoughby shrugged. "Figured you might not. It never hurts to be aware."

"True."

"Nobody understands why Lord Malvern married her at all. A kind of self-punishment, I suppose. He was really quite brilliant in his youth, but duty in the colonies turned him sour; that, and the terrible wounds. He never came to terms with being imperfect. Anyhow, Professor Watt and Lord Malvern's late father were the closest of friends. And so the professor has maintained that standing—or tried to, anyway—with the son."

"Not an easy task."

The Earl of Somerset blew another smoke ring. "Quite so."

There were letters from Robert Fulton in France. The mechanics were making steady improvements to the *Nautilus*, with better air tanks and more reliable controls. Fulton was vexed by the lack of a strong propulsion system for the torpedo and despaired of the unreliability of its explosive mechanism. As for the emperor's commission, he suspected that the whole thing was more political than practical. "No one has even come to inspect the diving boat. Ah, well, such is the hard lot of the technical pathfinder." Finally, as the spring term at college neared completion, Fulton sent the question Nathan had been hoping for: Would he like to join them in France for the summer?

Would he!

And so as June began, he was again rocking toward London in the great public coach with its blaring horn and thundering horses. Camden Willoughby had been as good as his word and indeed found him excellent rooms in the heart of the city. Nathan took a long-term lease, knowing he would be back in the fall. He spent a happy week with the bright young Earl of Somerset and his friends, seeing the highlights of London. At last they escorted him, not quite sober, to the Channel packet for Le Havre. This time it was Nathan's turn to be seasick, and he did not recover until French soil lay firmly beneath his foot. Then it was on to Paris, where Fulton awaited his arrival.

Paris! The city did not just warm with the spring, it glowed. Nathan drank in the sights and sounds of it all, strolling the boulevards or sipping afternoon wine with Fulton and his friends in a sidewalk cafe. Paris was light and boisterous and filled with pleasures. The French professed a kinship with Americans. "Ah, Nathan, we are spirits alike; our revolutions have the same ideals!"

And then one day there came a summons by Monsieur Povey, the minister for naval affairs, to meet with Robert Fulton. "This could be it, Nathan. I'd like for you to come along." At the ministry, they pushed through ornate double glass doors and were ushered into the office of Monsieur Povey, who greeted them warmly and beckoned a servant to pour cognac. When the preliminaries were completed, the minister came down to business.

"Monsieur Fulton, I am empowered to offer you a proposition in the name of the commission for the study of underwater warfare."

"Underwater warfare?"

"Your diving boat."

"Ah, yes."

"It is the commission's desire that you prove the effectiveness of the device by carrying out attacks on British vessels."

Fulton's eyes widened. He did not speak.

"By this, I mean that you would attempt to sink English ships of war with the *Nautilus* and her torpedo. You will be entitled to payment for every such sinking, according to the size of the vessel. A thirty-gun frigate, for example, will be worth four hundred thousand francs."

The inventor blinked. But his face was troubled. "Monsieur Povey," he said, "I am not a military man. I would not wish to harm another human being, or cause his death."

The minister fiddled with a paperweight. His mouth lifted slightly at the corners. "Monsieur Fulton, those are the terms of the proposition. Is it not true that in America you were once apprenticed to a gunsmith?"

"Why, yes. But..."

"And is it not true that you are highly indignant over English practices of stopping ships of various nations on the high seas, including your own?"

"That's true."

"Well, then, I think it's purely academic who commands the diving boat and fires the torpedo. We certainly have no officer in the French navy with the slightest ability to do that." The minister let his words sink in. Then he adopted a more conciliatory tone. "As a personal matter, my friend, I suspect that if the emperor had been a naval man, rather than an artillerist, things would have gone differently."

Fulton nodded. "I suppose that's true."

The minister stood up. "Think about it. I shall be awaiting your decision."

Nathan had arrived with a question burning in his mind, but he found no tactical way to ask it. Not until they were at the door did he sense an opening. He made it sound casual. "And your niece, Mademoiselle Marchand, she is well?"

The minister smiled. "Quite well, thank you. She is out of the city, visiting in Florence."

Nathan felt strangely deflated.

They left Paris the following morning for Le Havre. The journey was interminable, as the coach jolted and rocked and heat enveloped them in its moist embrace. Fulton alternately brooded and agonized, searching his soul. His mood gyrated from loquacious self-torment to black despair. "I cannot do it, Nathan. I just cannot do it. They're asking us to take human life. It's too much, too much." And yet if he did not at least make the attempt, the *Nautilus* project was doomed. He would have to face his backers and his creditors with empty hands. Nathan watched the countryside hurtle past and thought of Yvette Marchand. By the time they arrived at Le Havre, however, Fulton's mood was brightening somewhat. It was as if the throes of decision making had been a palliative to conscience. "I have no choice," he announced.

He sent off his acceptance of the terms by return coach to Paris.

The diving boat was quickly made ready. On a morning of pristine calm and glassy water, they pushed off from the dock with a dinghy in tow. Nathan and the young mechanic LaFarge took turns manning a sweep at the stern until they encountered a slight breeze offshore. Then they hoisted the single sail, and the strange craft moved slowly out from land. Robert Fulton trained his spyglass over an empty sea. "Now," he breathed, "to find our target."

The days passed with sunshine and calm waters. Seagulls wheeled overhead. A sultry heat beat down on the metal hull of the *Nautilus*, making life below quite uncomfortable. An occasional sail appeared on the horizon and then passed from view. Then the weather took a turn for the worse. Clouds gathered to blot out the sun. A wind sprang up, bringing a heavy, running sea. The *Nautilus* pitched on the crests and wallowed in troughs, her hatch shut to prevent swamping. Fulton's face turned from chalk color to a grayish green. The seasickness wracked him without relief. At last, as drinking water ran low, they turned back into Le Havre for supplies. He sat on the rickety dock, moaning, "Oh, God . . ."

July brought hot days and breathless nights, with intermittent thunderstorms to break the monotony. August came, with more of the same. And still no ship passed near their various stalking grounds. "Not a ship even near enough to hail," grumbled old Ekland, "much less torpedo." They returned to Le Havre periodically for rest and supplies, and now each arrival attracted a small crowd of curious townspeople to the dock. One day the mayor himself arrived, bustling and officious, sporting his heavy silver medallion of office. "Monsieur Fulton, if I may be so bold, what on earth are you doing? The talk is everywhere. You are not fishing. You do not go on a journey. Please. The people are driving me crazy..."

Fulton was ingratiating. He smiled through a sunburned face. He clapped the mayor on the shoulder. "Ah, I would love to tell you, monsieur. In time it will be known. All I can say now is that we are on a mission of the highest importance, on orders from Bonaparte himself. You understand." He gave the mayor a conspiratorial wink. The mayor rolled his eyes, nodded, and waddled away, speaking rapidly to the crowd that now trailed in his wake. After that, the townsfolk stayed clear of the *Nautilus* and her strange crew.

September came. The weather could not last. Already the chop ran heavier, and occasional light squalls drove them close to shore. But the climactic day was sparkling, filled with the glories of autumn. Nathan was in a buoyant mood. Fishing boats drifted in the distance. The Channel was an easy wash, lapping the sides of the submarine. The dinghy danced at its mooring line. Ekland had taken his turn on watch, sweeping the horizon with the spyglass.

The glass stopped sweeping. Ekland stood up, focusing. "Monsieur," he called. "A ship! I see a ship!"

Fulton scrambled up the ladder, almost losing his footing as he stepped free of the hatch. "A ship, you say? Where?"

"Dead ahead. And not far. How did she get so close?"

"I can see her."

"Frigate. By God, she's a frigate!"

Nathan needed no glass. She came on under full sail, no more than two leagues away and on a slight starboard tack. Even at this distance he could see that she raised a slight froth at the bow.

"Down!" shouted Fulton. "We go down!"

Ekland jumped into the dinghy, cast off and began rowing free. Nathan and LaFarge scrambled down the hatchway, followed by Fulton. The hatch cover clanged, and he jerked down the spring clamps—Nathan's invention—to lock it shut. Already Nathan was opening the sluice valves to flood the ballast cylinders. LaFarge manned the stern crank. The *Nautilus* settled easily, pitching them into underwater gloom.

Fulton pushed up the lookscope and waited for it to clear. Peering intently, he muttered, "Come a bit to port, Nathan. A bit more. That's good." Nathan manipulated the steering controls gently in response to the commands. The tension was excruciating. He realized that his fists were white-knuckled, grasping the levers. Sweat streamed down his face. He was having trouble breathing. It was as if a heavy weight pressed against his chest. Breathing was...

Breathing! The air. "Robert, we forgot to turn on the air!" Nathan grabbed for the nearest air tank and wrenched open a pitcock. Air gushed out loudly. But it was some moments before his breathing was comfortable.

Fulton stepped back from the lookscope and moved to the bow to adjust the torpedo mechanism. Nathan put his eye to the glass. The frigate was still coming on. He half expected her to turn aside and show her gunwales, but the vessel held steady on course. "Robert, she's going to come right past us on this heading. We can't miss."

Distances are deceiving. This distance closed with maddening slowness. Nathan gave LaFarge a hand at the stern crank, but still the minutes dragged by. But finally:

"Nathan, she's almost here. She's coming across our bow, Nathan. Get ready at the torpedo..."

Nathan reached for the lever that would trip the powerful spring catapult. He pictured the torpedo, poised on the snout of the *Nautilus*, armed with a waterproofed charge of gunpowder and a flintlock that would trip on impact to explode it.

"I can see people on deck. Seamen, they are; and officers on the poop deck. She's coming on—coming on..."

Nathan's grip tightened on the firing lever.

"Release the torpedo!"

He jerked the lever down, heard the spring mechanism let go. The action would propel the missile free of the *Nautilus* and also trigger a second, smaller spring assembly in the torpedo itself, activating a flywheel and propeller.

They waited.

Fulton stood in a half-crouch, eye glued to the glass. LaFarge was frozen at the stern crank, barely breathing. Nathan could hear his own heartbeat and the gentle lapping of water in the ballast cylinders.

"It's too *slow*," Fulton muttered. "The thing is just too..."

The words froze in his throat. He seemed to lean into the lookscope itself. "Oh, my God."

"What is it, Robert? What's wrong."

"The flag. I see the flag. She's flying the tricolor."

"The *what?*"

"Nathan, she's *French!*"

Another heartbeat went by. And another. Nothing happened. They waited. And waited.

"Nathan, a seaman has come over to the side of the ship. He's looking down and gesturing. Here's an officer coming over. The officer is abusing the man. He's ordering him away from there, and back to work. I think it hit but didn't explode. Yes, that's what's happened." Fulton's voice cracked. "She's moving right on past us, Nathan. Oh, what a lovely, lovely sight! It was another dud. Another wonderful, wonderful dud . . ."

"A dud!" Nathan shouted.

"God be praised!" LaFarge said.

Fulton snickered. The snicker became a chuckle. The chuckle grew into a laugh. The laughter exploded, consuming him, doubling him over. And as Fulton laughed, Nathan laughed. LaFarge snorted twice, gurgled, and laughed. They were all laughing, then. Nathan doubled over and held his stomach. The tears streamed down his face.

"A—A—" Fulton gasped between convulsions, choked, sputtered. "A *dud!*" And he was off again, lost in gales of laughter.

They waited another hour before coming up. Finally, the *Nautilus* surfaced as sunset spread its rose tint over miles of empty, slate-calm sea. The three men emerged from the hatch and settled on the sloping black hull, breathing in cool fresh air. The last gulls of evening made wheeling silhouettes. Nathan knew that never again would he experience a moment more compellingly beautiful.

Fulton sighed and ran a hand through his thick brown hair. "I'll never be a warrior," he said. The words had a tone of finality.

Nathan smiled. "It's just as well. The world has got too many warriors already."

It was almost dark when they heard the rhythmic creak of oars. The shadow of the dinghy emerged out of a silvery gloom. Old Ekland was back.

* * *

Nightfall swallowed London. Carriages rattled over wet cobblestoned streets, the conveyances of nobility preceded by footmen bearing lighted torches. The air grew heavy, a mix of fog and coal smoke. Nathan took an early supper at a public house and walked back to his apartment, enjoying the solitary exercise. A solid week with Camden Willoughby and his many varied acquaintances both revitalized and wearied him. He did not divulge to the young earl how he spent his summer, and the other—in his graceful way—did not ask. Nathan suspected that Willoughby knew; and he had to admit to himself that it was a paradox indeed. Oh, yes, Nathan spent the summer trying to sink a British ship with Robert Fulton's submarine. What jolly good fun! Still, he felt no sense of duplicity or painful conscience. Wars were monstrous games played by nations, in which the individual was a pawn. So be it.

The apartment was immaculate, as usual, thanks to his dour jewel of a housekeeper, Mrs. Norman. She had gone off at five leaving him a plum pudding in the oven and tea to warm for a late snack. Nathan lit a fire in the grate and put on his smoking jacket. Then, with a glass of sherry and an after-dinner pipe, he relaxed in his fireside chair and picked up a periodical. He was skimming an article of theater criticism when the knock came at his door. Slightly irritated, he went to answer it.

She stood in a shadow of the landing, muffled in a hooded cloak. Lamplight reflected off beads of moisture on the dark fabric. "Mr. Stewart?" The voice was just above a whisper. "May I come in?"

"Well, madame, I really don't . . ."

But the woman pushed past him, rustling taffeta and trailing a costly scent. Something about the scent seemed vaguely familiar. She drew back the hood. Nathan caught his breath. Marian Finch, the Lady Malvern, was a mess, the green eyes puffed and red-rimmed and the shiny black hair badly disheveled. A dark welt mottled her cheek. The skin was broken, with a trickle of dried blood. A heavy swelling disfigured her lower lip.

"What on earth!"

"Forgive me for bothering you. I know it's late, and I should not have come here. But there was nowhere else to turn. Oh, Nathan, he's—he's a madman."

"Who?"

"My husband. Dear God, it was terrible, terrible. He's so insanely jealous, so unpredictable in his tempers."

Nathan, befuddled, took her cloak. She leaned heavily against him. He said, "But your friends..."

"Friends?" She smiled ruefully. "There aren't many left, I'm afraid. I could think of nowhere else to turn. You seemed so self-assured, so gentle." Tears welled up and spilled over. "There was no one else whom I could trust. None of them would dare take me in, they're all so fearful of him."

Nathan led her to the divan, saying, "Yes, yes. I understand. It's all right." But he did not understand, and it was not all right. He sat her down and fetched a glass of sherry. She drank and seemed to feel better. He said: "Shall I go for a doctor?"

"I'll be all right. Just let me rest a bit."

"Your injuries, that bruise on your face..."

"It's all right." She drained her glass. "This is not the first time. Life with Lord Malvern can be, shall we say, difficult."

Nathan bit his lip and sat quietly, his mind racing. Stupid clod, he hadn't the foggiest notion of what to do. Instinct told him not to be drawn into the lady's problems—God knows, he'd had warning enough. And yet here she was, and here he was. He rebuked himself. Unfeeling churl. "Here, let me fix you another sherry."

She wore a sleeveless gown of pale blue. Again, it was a color to set off her strange eyes. The eyes were clearing now, and she ran a comb through her hair. The gown, he noticed, was slightly torn near the bodice, and her arms bore purplish bruises, as if someone had grabbed them in a fit of rage. He gave her the sherry and brought a bowl of water and a washcloth. She dabbed at her face with the wet cloth. Oddly, the face seemed even more beautiful for its wounds.

"Nathan, what would you think of a man who deliberately flaunts his wife to other men, and then flies into a jealous rage when they become interested?"

"I wouldn't know what to think," he said.

She looked into his face thoughtfully. "No, I suppose you wouldn't."

"I mean, it's quite beyond my experience." Blundering idiot, he thought. "You see, I—"

"Tell me something, Nathan." The voice was soft now, caressing. "Have you ever been with a woman?"

"No. That is . . ." He looked away, suddenly miserable. "I have not been with a woman," he said.

"Enchanting."

"What?"

The green eyes seemed to glow with an inner fire. "You are a magnificent specimen of young manhood, Nathan Stewart. And all the more so for your innocence. I don't doubt that women are fawning all over you. But you're totally unconscious of that, aren't you? I don't think it ever crosses your mind to have conceit." She placed her hand on his cheek. "If only the world could stand still for a little while, just for you; if only the stars would hold still in their courses, or even if time could go backwards in its flight . . ."

He was uncomfortable. But her nearness also gave him a powerful sense of longing. The mouth, injured though it was, had drawn so near to his own. The scent of her worked a subtle magic upon him and was richer now than mere perfume. Then, abruptly, she withdrew her hand. He sensed, too, a withdrawal of her self. The green eyes looked away. "No," she whispered, "it's too late."

"Marian—"

"The man is quite insane at times, I fear." She found a handkerchief and dabbed at her eyes, suddenly preoccupied. Her quick change, a sudden aloofness and deliberate return to the subject of Peter Finch, the Lord Malvern, struck like an invisible blow. "His rages are quite unreasonable, quite beyond belief."

"Was it the war? He was badly wounded, after all."

Her laughter had a cutting edge. "Ah, yes, the war and the colonies. Those are his big fixations. Everything that goes wrong is the fault of the war. It is never his fault; never due to his drunken, twisted . . ."

"Do you love him?"

His own question took him by surprise. It was more instinctive than contrived. She seemed startled. The green eyes widened. "Why do you ask that? Nobody ever asked that before."

"It just crossed my mind, I can't tell you why."

She looked away, at the wall. Then: "Yes. Yes, I suppose in a curious way that I do love him. He took me out of the gutter, after all. You didn't know that either, I suppose. Everybody else knows. He took me out of the gutter and gave me a title." Then she was silent, thinking.

"What will you do now?"

"Do? What can I do?" She sighed. "I have no place to go tonight, except to the streets. He drove me from the house, called me a slut and a harlot. He said the streets were good enough for me . . ."

"Poor fellow," Nathan said.

She blinked. "What did you say?"

"I merely said, 'Poor fellow.' It's tragic, a bright man losing control of himself."

"Upon my word, Nathan Stewart, but you are full of surprises. And what a switch. Pity, for Peter Finch! He would really despise you for that. No, my young friend. Lord Malvern is not deserving of pity. There is too much blood on his hands for that."

"Blood?"

"My husband is one of the most notorious duelists in England. He has shot dead three opponents and grievously wounded half-a-dozen others. Only his connections and title have kept him out of gaol."

Nathan could not keep her there, alone. When Marian seemed to have fully regained her composure, he took a cab to the home of his housekeeper, Mrs. Norman, and persuaded her—with the promise of ample reward—to come back and spend the night in his apartment. Then he himself went to the lodgings of Camden Willoughby.

The earl was aghast. "Nathan, you can't let her stay in your rooms. It wouldn't do at all!"

"I have no choice. She has no money and no place to go."

"Peter Finch will find her. He is a resourceful man."

Nathan nodded. "I know. But that's just a chance I shall have to take."

He slept soundly on Willoughby's couch, however, and awoke refreshed and well rested. Willoughby was still asleep at nine when Nathan returned to his own apartment. Along the way, he stopped at the office of a neighborhood physician, who agreed to examine the Lady Malvern's injuries. They arrived to find Nathan's houseguest finishing breakfast and Mrs. Norman fussing over her like a motherly hen. "She's feeling much better this morning, poor dear." The old woman pursed her lips in disapproval. "Imagine, a lady like her being treated in such brutal fashion."

"Did she tell you what happened?"

"No. But I got a fair enough notion, having had a brute for a husband myself once. Believe me, Mr. Stewart, if I were a man . . ."

The physician took the patient into Nathan's bedroom and examined her quickly. He came out shutting his medical kit. "No broken bones, thank goodness. She ought to rest today. I'll give her something to put on those bruises. If you need me, just send word." Then he was gone.

Marian Finch emerged with her hair done and spirits brightened. The bruises were artfully covered with powder and the gown mended. "Well, what do you think?" she said.

"You look ravishing," Nathan said. It came from his heart.

At eleven o'clock, Camden Willoughby arrived in the company of a lady friend. At his suggestion, the four of them went out to lunch and for a stroll. When they returned at midafternoon, a heavy carriage with brass fittings stood at Nathan's door.

Marian Finch turned pale.

"It's his carriage."

A flustered Mrs. Norman met them at the door. "He insisted on waiting for you, Mr. Stewart. There was nothing I could do. He barged in and sat down. He's been in there for an hour, drinking your sherry."

The Lord Malvern sat brooding at the fireplace, glass in hand. The bottle that had been three-fourths full last night now stood empty. The hawklike face that turned to him bore the flush of wine. The one eye seemed to burn in its socket.

"Well, well, well, what have we here? The colonist, I see. And Camden Willoughby, too. How nice. Birds of a feather, taking the afternoon air?" From the edge of the eye patch, the facial scar stood out lividly against pale flesh. The face itself was drawn downward, as if from the weight of ill humour. "And might I remind you, sir," he said to Nathan, "that you are in the company of another man's wife?"

"Peter, for heaven's sake!"

"Ah, my dear. So now it's heaven, is it? Last evening it was hell, if I recollect. Yes, quite so. Are you familiar with hell, Mr. Stewart?"

"I believe, Lord Malvern, that hell is something we create for ourselves."

"How interesting. Then you're not a strong believer in Holy Writ, I gather. Nor, perhaps, in the commandments contained therein, having to do with a man's exclusive right to cleave unto his own wife—"

"Peter!"

"You did spend the night here, my dear?"

Camden Willoughby stepped forward. "Mr. Stewart came to my lodgings and remained there all night. You have my word as a gentleman."

"A gentleman?" Lord Malvern rose from the chair. To Nathan's surprise, they were of equal height. He had not noticed before that the man was so tall. The single eye focused upon him its naked hatred. "So now we're gentlemen, are we? Well, then, gentleman—"

The lean hand came up with the speed of a striking snake. Before Nathan could move, the slap stung his cheek. He clenched his fists and grabbed for the man's collar, but Lord Malvern nimbly backed away. "Tut, tut, my man." The thin lips twisted. "Gentlemen don't brawl like street thugs. There are better ways to settle our differences."

Willoughby said, "Careful, Nathan."

"I fear it's much too late for caution." Lord Malvern glared, nostrils flaring. "My second will be in communication with you, to arrange our meeting." With a swooping motion, he caught up his discarded cloak and cane. "Come, Marian."

She looked into Nathan's face, silently beseeching. He said, "You don't have to go with him." But she shook her head, blinking back tears.

"I won't let this happen," she whispered. And then she followed her husband out.

Nathan stared at the sunny, leaded panes of his parlor window glass. The striking sunlight gave it a rainbow effect. It reminded him of the kitchen nook at home in Pittsburgh, where he had eaten that farewell breakfast with his parents so long ago. He wondered what his father was doing at this moment, and his mother, and Stephen. How would Stephen handle this situation?

Camden Willoughby was the first to speak. "Old chap, we're in a hell of a mess."

Nathan smiled grimly. "Correction. *I'm* in a hell of a mess."

The dread was like bile in his mouth. Nothing like it had ever come to him before, no feeling so palpable and inescapable. He sat in the dark carriage waiting for dawn, and hating it. Ordinarily the light spreading over the forest clearing would have seemed beautiful beyond expression. Already the songbirds were rustling in those great gnarled oaks over there. One could see the mist gathered in a marshy copse beyond the clearing and a line of cattails standing motionless in silhouette. It had a subtle, silvery sheen, this first light of morning.

Steam rose from the warm flanks of the horses. Restless, they stamped the grassy earth and tossed their heads. In a gray wash, the men were still standing like cardboard cutouts, their tall hats and black cloaks in somber keeping with the spirit of this place. Nathan shivered. A deadly place. It is not, he thought, a good morning to die.

At last, one of the cardboard figures separated from the others and turned toward his carriage, growing ever larger as he advanced. By the swinging gait and slender figure he recognized Camden Willoughby. His friend bore a box, held solemnly in both hands as if in offering to propitiate the gods of terrible mornings. The black shadow took form, and Nathan picked out the handsome face of his noble second. Willoughby opened the box, and Nathan looked down at the gleaming pistol, nested in red velvet.

"One ball, no more," Willoughby said. "Loaded and primed. I've inspected the weapon. It's in good order. The balance is nice. Fine workmanship. Do you want to get the feel of it?"

Nathan nodded wordlessly. He removed the black glove from his right hand—it seemed odd to be so somberly and completely dressed at this hour, as if for a funeral—and lifted the dueling pistol. The polished metal was cool to the touch, and there was a certain delicacy to the finely worked bone handle. He drew down on a distant tree, sighting with both eyes open, turned the weapon over in his hands, checked the works, returned it to the case. "Very well," he said.

"You can still choose sabers. He's a crack shot with these things."

"I can do better with a pistol than a saber," Nathan said. He could do best of all with the Kentucky long rifle, of course, but made no mention of that. He thought of the canvasback wheeling over a leaden Pittsburgh sky long ago, the rifle up, his eye down the sight, the shot, the bird falling. Would the same instincts serve him now?

Several more carriages and coaches arrived, drawing up under the black trees to wait. A surgeon emerged from one, carrying his kit, and joined the other men. Gradually the light strengthened. It seemed an eternity. At last a gaunt scarecrow of a man stepped to the center of the clearing, drew out a pocket watch, and snapped open the case. "Gentlemen, it's time."

Things happened so swiftly, then, that the impressions went hazy in Nathan's mind. Suddenly coatless in the chill, they were grouped in the center of the clearing and someone was mumbling instructions. " . . . ten paces, turn and fire." Ten paces? He had thought it was five. Or was it fifteen? He wanted to laugh and ask Lord Malvern. But then the lean face came at him out of the gloom, dour and pale as death, the eye patch a splotch of wrath. The face vanished as they turned to stand back to back. Ten paces, the man said. "Now!" One, two, three . . . His feet and legs were lead. His mind refused to grasp any of it. For God's sake! Eight . . . nine . . . ten . . .

He turned. His eyes sought Lord Malvern, flicked over the group of spectators, the brooding trees, caught shadows of the carriages and standing horses—all in a twinkling—and settled, at last, on the tall, thin figure in shirt sleeves standing in the distance. So far. Could he really be so far away? The weapon in Nathan's hand was an iron bar held aloft. Slowly he brought it down, and saw that the other man was doing the same. The other pistol came to the level of Nathan's head and stopped its descent. The muzzle seemed to enlarge, focused between his eyes. Nathan's arm continued its fall. He heard a loud report and was stupefied. His own weapon had gone off, the ball plowing into the ground at Lord Malvern's feet! Nathan stood, frozen, watching the muzzle, sensing the single eye searching for the spot that would send the ball into his brain, sensing the tightening trigger finger . . .

"Stop!"

She had come out of the carriage, a shadow in bulky dress and cloak, hair streaming as she ran. "No, Peter! I won't let you!" The lean face jerked, the eye was distracted. Then the eye came back, the pistol adjusted its level.

Nathan did not move. His mind was numb.

The finger tightened again.

But the rushing shadow would not be ignored. She was upon him now, fist upraised. "*I told you no!*" Hand and arm came down, plunging the dagger into his side. The pistol wavered and went off, its ball ricocheting into a tree. The eye widened in surprise. The dagger struck again, again, again. Lord Malvern fell slowly, like an emptying sack, the air rushing from his chest. He began to speak, but the words were lost in a red froth. They locked together in mortal struggle, and the arm kept plunging, her voice keening across the morning, *"No! No! No! No! No!"*

She was still screaming when they came in a rush to wrench her away.

Nathan loved this room in James Watt's house. It was part study and part parlor, but without frills. The room gave an aura of rich woods, carpets, old paintings, a massive sideboard topped by a silver tea service, books. He poured himself another sherry from the crystal decanter.

"Well, it could have been worse, I suppose," Professor Watt was saying. "She could have been hanged, poor dear."

"He treated her too shabbily," Camden Willoughby said. "There was ample testimony to that. And then, of course, the intimation of a love affair between Marian and Nathan was simply overwhelmed."

"Oh, yes, yes, I daresay. Most unfortunate. And I feel so responsible, Nathan." The old man's expression was gravely remorseful. "I really do. You met them at my house."

Nathan smiled. "Please, Professor. It was nobody's fault. This would have happened sooner or later anyhow, I suspect."

"I think Nathan is probably correct." Robert Fulton entered the conversation for the first time. Seated primly in a high-backed chair, the inventor had gained weight in the year since their *Nautilus* adventure. "It was an unhappy situation between them. One simply cannot account for human nature at times. But you've handled yourself admirably through all of this, Nathan."

"Hear, hear."

Nathan welcomed the tribute. It was difficult for him to shed the memories of Marian Finch's trial and murder conviction. For days the austere, lofted courtroom with its bewigged judges and lawyers had dominated his life and thoughts. The sentence of thirty years imprisonment had struck him like a blow. It was his own life, after all, that she had saved. And the court found this only a mitigating circumstance, considering that dueling of itself was an unlawful act. In light of Lord Malvern's bloody reputation, and Nathan's youth and inexperience, the crown had seen fit not to press any charges against him. And so he watched her being led away, the beauty now rendered plain and lifeless in prison dress, the sorrow deep within him akin to physical pain. Afterward, she refused to accept his visit in prison. Through all that, and more, these friends—Robert Fulton, Camden Willoughby, Professor Watt and a few others—had remained steadfast. His gratitude could not be put into words.

Fulton looked stocky and prosperous. His thick brown hair was carefully brushed. He wore a broadcloth coat and pure white neck linen. His hands, free of grease and callouses, were again the immaculate hands of the artist. He seemed to divine Nathan's thoughts. "The submarine is a total failure, I'm afraid," Fulton said. "Even the English won't buy it."

Professor Watt chuckled. "Fate plays tricks."

"After our dismal experience with the submarine, I went back to Paris." Fulton sighed. "I was miserable. But there I met a countryman of ours, Nathan. Robert Livingston. Lovely man. He is our minister to France and is said to be trying to talk Bonaparte into selling us the city of New Orleans. He also has an interest in steamboats."

"Why on earth would the colonies want New Orleans?"

Nathan broke in. "It's rather vital to us, really." Quickly, he explained the problems of the landlocked western territories, drawing on what the frontiersman Mason Everett had talked about in Pittsburgh four years earlier. As Nathan described the dilemma of trade and transportation on one-way rivers, the Ohio and Mississippi, Robert Fulton leaned forward listening intently. When Nathan finished, Fulton was deep in thought.

"But what is Mr. Livingston's interest in steamboats?" Camden Willoughby asked.

Fulton came back from his reverie. "Back in New York, Robert Livingston has a contract with a Colonel Stevens—his brother-in-law, I think—to develop a steamboat to haul freight and passengers on the Hudson River. Mr. Livingston has great political influence, even though he is a Federalist. Already the New York Legislature has granted him a monopoly to run such boats between New York City and Albany."

Nathan was puzzled. "What on earth for? There aren't that many people living upstate, to my knowledge."

"I daresay," Fulton replied. "But there has been talk—only talk, you understand—of digging a canal that would run from Albany all the way across to Lake Erie. Even President Jefferson thinks the plan unworkable, and there is a lot of political resistance. And yet such a canal, if it were built successfully, would open up the entire region of northern Ohio and the western territory. If that happens, a monopoly of Hudson River steam boats would be lucrative indeed.''

James Watt nodded. '' 'If' is a very big word, Robert. If you're really going to build steamboats, remember that they have taken the measure of men before. You had a fellow countryman named John Fitch who devoted years to the thing. A clockmaker, he was. Should have stuck to clocks. Mr. Fitch did contrive a workable paddleboat. Trouble is, it was too slow even to compete with stagecoaches. He became an alcoholic, poor wretch, and died a broken man. Suicide, some say. Somewhere in all that travail, he wrote: 'I know of nothing so perplexing and vexatious to a man of feelings as a turbulent wife and steamboat building.' ''

Their laughter filled the room. Fulton said, ''I've heard of Fitch. Terribly obnoxious man. Managed to alienate all of his financial backers.''

''True.''

Fulton turned to Nathan. ''I hope you can join me again. I've been working with different hull shapes and paddle designs in a test tank in Paris. I've concluded that side paddles probably will be best. I do need a good assistant, preferably an American named Stewart.''

Nathan chuckled. ''Robert, you're incorrigible.''

''Absolutely.''

''I'd be delighted.''

''Good. Then that's settled.'' He jumped to his feet, suddenly ebullient. ''And now, Professor, shall we go to the workshop?''

They left their sherry glasses and descended the stairs.

And so the working association was formed. Nathan had intended to go home to Pittsburgh at the completion of his studies. Now all thoughts of Pittsburgh were put behind. Letters from home expressed the family's disappointment that he might remain in Europe for another year. Stephen wrote of the rising prosperity of their father's enterprise. ''More and more settlers are coming west every month, it seems.'' Like Nathan, however, Stephen was anxious to make his own way. But there was also another element in Stephen's life, more implied than stated. From many written references, Nathan could discern that his younger brother was captivated by their parents' ward, Catherine Colby. ''She is a delight to everyone and is growing into a beautiful young woman,'' Stephen wrote. ''I can't believe this is the same freckled roughneck I brought home, thinking she was a boy!''

Nathan felt a twinge of envy. For all the variety of things that filled his own letters home, his life was empty of love. He looked in the mirror and acknowledged that he was not all that bad-looking. Certainly Marian Finch had found him attractive enough. ''Your trouble, Nathan Stewart,'' he grumbled, ''is that you're a stick-in-the-mud.'' A stick-in-the-mud, forever tinkering with springs and chains and sprockets, forever pondering not the beauty of a hillside but ways to cut a canal through it. At Oxford, of course, he had been engrossed in four years of study, spurred by old fears of failure. ''Workhorse,'' sniffed his classmates. ''Bit of a stick.'' In the process he had missed out on a great deal of college life, belonged to no clubs, and had made his friendships elsewhere. The Lord Malvern duel, with its spicy overtones of possible hanky-panky between the tall American and the ravishing Marian Finch, had dropped on the college like a bomb. Suddenly he was besieged with invitations. But he accepted none, and he had no qualms at leaving for good.

Robert Fulton returned to Paris. Six weeks later, Nathan and Camden Willoughby joined him there. At a dinner party Nathan met Robert Livingston and his family. The American minister was indeed polished and charming. ''Oxford, you say? Well, well, well, I'm indeed impressed. A toast to you, sir, and may your future be crowned with success.'' Glasses clinked. They drank. Livingston dabbed at his mouth with a napkin. ''Ah, to be your age again. There is a splendid future ahead for young men of spirit.'' The Finch affair was not mentioned.

With James Watt in Birmingham, Nathan had expressed misgivings about the weight of the new steam engine. The firebox was lined with brick, the boiler seemed excessively heavy, and the superstructure for the driving gear—while certainly functional enough to power the paddlewheels—could easily have been scaled down. Fulton, however, was intent now on assembling the entire vessel as quickly as possible. Livingston suggested that a successful run might mean a sale to the French government. ''Bonaparte may not be in the market for your submarine, Robert, but I'll wager he'll buy an operational steamboat. Let's christen it on the River Seine, and give all Paris something to shout about.''

Fulton, Nathan, and the ancient mechanic Ekland scoured boatyards for a suitable vessel on which to mount the engine.

Fulton reasoned that for operations on the Seine, the draft should be shallow and the craft itself rather light.

"We still don't have the engine, Robert," Nathan reminded him. "Shouldn't we have the engine and machinery *before* we decide on a vessel?"

"There's no time. Livingston is getting impatient and so am I. Besides, the equipment should arrive any day now. Boulton and Watt promised the shipment would be here by now."

"Yes, but they did not take the blockade into consideration. They might have to ship it through Lisbon . . ."

"Posh," Fulton said.

Finally, he found a river craft to his liking. Nathan's doubts increased. It did seem smallish for the task ahead, more of a light barge than a heavy duty riverboat. They went to work installing reinforcement timbers belowdecks, to support the heavy equipment. At Fulton's specifications, boatwrights bolted together massive beams to serve as superstructures for the side wheels. The scheduled date for the demonstration drew nearer and still no machinery arrived. Not until one week before launching did it come trundling into Paris aboard heavy wagons. "Sorry monsieur," the wagon master shrugged. "It came by way of Lisbon." They worked day and night installing it all to the last bolt and fitting.

The vessel rode strangely heavy in the water, reminding Nathan of some ponderous beetle. "Robert, the barge is just too frail. Why don't you postpone the demonstration until we can find a stronger vessel?"

"No, no, Nathan. This one is fine."

Nathan and old Ekland exchanged glances. Ekland spat.

Launch day came on fine. Paris basked in April sunshine. Balmy spring breezes stirred flags and the green-budding trees along the Seine. By midmorning a festive crowd was gathering. Women brought picnic baskets for lunch, while children gamboled on the grassy slopes. Wine flowed. By noon there were people as far as the eye could see. A uniformed band appeared, its brass instruments gleaming in the sunshine, and struck up a medley of martial airs. The ever-present sidewalk artists set up their easels to record the scene. Elegantly dressed deputies and merchants rubbed shoulders with street people. A group of hussars appeared, resplendent in uniform, shining tassels, and polished accoutrements. At last, a ponderous carriage arrived, drawn by half-a-dozen milk-white horses and bearing the Imperial Crest. Its occupants did not emerge, but remained inside.

At the launching dock, Fulton was a restless dynamo, shouting orders and attending to last-minute details. He wore dove-gray breeches, boots of soft English leather, a wine-colored waistcoat, a handsome coat of dark blue trimmed in satin, a white lace neckcloth, and a magnificent tall gray hat with a golden buckle in the front.

Nathan's worry was now a nagging premonition. The craft awaiting its maiden voyage looked like nothing that had ever floated before. Heavy paddle wheels rose on each side, blades glistening in the sunlight. At angles from the wheels there jutted moveable iron beams, soaring skyward to a great steel joint and then plunging into the bowels of the vessel like the legs of a gigantic grasshopper. A smokestack brooded amidships, belching black smoke and sparks. The whole was gaily bedecked in ribbons and flags. But it was the hidden heart of the vessel that gave Nathan his dread; all firebrick and steel, steam boiler and condensers, pistons and driving rods. Tons of it.

"Robert," he said, "don't you think . . ."

Fulton seemed not to hear. He beckoned to a group of waiting dignitaries who moved hesitantly up the gangplank and onto the deck. Nathan recognized Monsieur Povey, the minister for naval affairs. Along with the dignitaries came workmen who were to see the equipment at the launching.

"Robert, I really think . . ."

"Not now, Nathan. For God's sake, man, can't you see I'm busy?"

Doffing his hat, Fulton beamed a smile to the crowd and bowed. The band struck up a sprightly air. Massed onlookers waved back. Fulton walked the gangplank and stepped onto the deck. A ceremonial ribbon stretched between the boat and a stanchion, waiting to be snipped. Fulton stood by the ribbon, shears in hand, and made a lengthy speech in French. The breeze whipped part of it away, so that from where Nathan stood only scraps could be heard. " . . . Auspicious occasion . . . glory of the French people . . . day in history of water navigation . . . distinguished visitors . . ." At last he knelt, snipped, saw the ribbon fall, stepped back, smiled, waved. The crowd roared. Workmen threw off the mooring line.

Robert Fulton, all smiles, adjusted his top hat and stepped back with the dignitaries amidships. The band played lustily. The vessel drifted into the stream, blowing smoke and sparks. The paddle wheels stood immobile. Fulton shoved a lever. Slowly, the wheels began to turn. More cheers erupted along the riverbank.

Abruptly, the boat began to shake. There was a popping, grinding noise. The cheering became ragged. Fresh billows of smoke belched from the stack, heavier than before. There was a groaning and cracking. The crowd fell silent.

The boat seemed to sag in the middle.

An excited murmur spread across both sides of the Seine, increasing in volume.

The boat broke apart. A geyser of steam shot up. On board, alarmed dignitaries scurred for the railings. Slowly, majestically, the whole began to disintegrate.

Robert Fulton stood quite still, clutching at his magnificent top hat, his face without expression . . .

And thus, he sank into the Seine.

Dressing had been an ordeal. It was his first formal affair, and the business of struggling into proper attire left him frustrated and out of sorts. Dubiously, Nathan surveyed the result in a full-length mirror: ruffled shirt with onyx studs, winged collar and neckpiece, white ruffled cuffs, black satin knee breeches and matching tailcoat, waistcoat and cummerbund, black hose (his legs were much too bulging and muscular), and patent leather evening shoes with silver buckles. "My word," he said to his reflection, "you look like a mortician." To complete the preparations, he combed out his tangle of long black hair and tied it in the back with a black ribbon. Feeling foolishly conspicuous, he walked the hall of the residence hotel to Robert Fulton's apartment and rapped at the door.

"Ah, Nathan, don't you look elegant!" Fulton himself stood framed in the doorway, a study in velveted splendor. His evening suit was a spectacle in burgundy velvet, his linen and stockings snowy white, his hair carefully coiffed—by a hairdresser—and his left hand displaying a single massive finger ring of precious stones. Fulton took a pinch of snuff from a silver box, sniffed delicately, sneezed against the back of his hand. "Quite so."

Guests were already present, taking cognac. They included Joel Barlow and Robert Livingston. The American minister greeted Nathan cordially and complimented his costume, then resumed his conversation.

"Frankly, I'm quite certain that Napoleon's whole purpose in staging this affair is to announce his willingness to sell us New Orleans. In our talks with the ministers there has been every suggestion of willingness to do so, even enthusiasm. Our special envoy, Mr. Monroe, is very optimistic."

"If you ask me, Bonaparte is rather over a barrel," one of the other men remarked. "It's either sell the city to the colonies or perhaps lose it to the British. And he wouldn't fancy that at all, would he?"

"Not hardly."

Fulton touched Livingston's elbow. "I hate to interrupt, Robert, but it's time. The carriages are waiting downstairs."

Moments later, Nathan sat back in a large, open carriage with Livingston, Fulton, and Barlow watching the passing sights of nocturnal Paris. The rhythmic clop-clop of a spirited matched team bore them down the broad, tree-lined Avenue des Champs-Élysée, past gaily lit apartment houses and hotels and bistros. "Paris!" he said happily. "Paris is music and beauty and excitement and—"

"Ah, we have the makings of a poet," said Barlow.

"I share your elation, Nathan," said Livingston. "Paris is all that and more. And love, too. Don't forget love. That's important for a young man. It is what radiates from this city's soul and makes it unique. I could indeed spend my life here, middle-aged as I am, were it not for the press of business back home. I think every young man should have a taste of Paris, in order to have a standard of life's elegance. Do you agree, Robert?"

"Yes, yes." Fulton was emphatic. "A glorious city. I've lived here for a good many years, off and on, and never get my fill of it. It's the artist in me, I suppose. There is something about the light . . ."

At last the carriages made a final turn and drew up before a vast columned structure bathed in lamplight. Massed before the building and spilled across the broad boulevard were the people of Paris, taking in the splendors of a grand ball of Napoleon. Carriages of every description filled the driveway waiting to deposit their passengers. Nathan absorbed the glittering panoply of magnificently gowned women, handsome men in full dress and uniform, shining coaches and sleek horses, footmen and lackies. "I didn't dream it would be like this. I thought, since the revolution . . ."

"Yes. This is tame compared to the old days," Livingston

said. "*That* was a sight to behold. Royalty knew no limit to its conspicuous display. This"—he waved a white-gloved hand casually—"is plebian by comparison."

They alighted from the carriage and mounted sweeping flights of stone steps. Nathan found himself ogling like a schoolboy, unable to resist the impulse to throw his head back and stare up at those soaring columns with their ornate capitals. Everywhere he looked there stood a statue, a fountain, or an imperial bas relief in bronze.

They passed through enormous double doors, Fulton leading the way into crowded lobbies and anterooms. Finally they came to the grand ballroom itself, a blaze of worked gold and tapestries, polished marbles and crystal chandeliers. From his height, Nathan easily could see over the heads of the crowd to a great stage at the far end of the room, where a full orchestra played. He watched the dancers, dipping and pirouetting, and devoutly wished that the music made sense to him. It did not. The tune was noise to his ear, a distraction, and the timing incomprehensible. Born with a tin ear! If only . . .

". . . and this, my dear, is Mr. Nathan Stewart."

"Yes, I believe I have met Mr. Stewart."

The voice was as familiar as a caress. A scent of perfume struck some buried chord of memory. Nathan came back to reality with a jerk. He looked down into the oval face and large dark eyes of Yvette Marchand. The eyes regarded him with humorous detachment. The brown hair was a cascade of loose curls, caught on the side with an ivory comb. Her gown was a shimmer of blue, plunging at the neck to accentuate a high, firm bosom. Diamonds splashed cold fire across white flesh.

"M-Mademoiselle." He bent clumsily over her hand.

Her smile stabbed at his soul. "It seems that I'm always taking Monsieur Stewart by surprise."

"Mademoiselle, you take any man by surprise," Fulton said.

Nathan mumbled something. And then she was gone, moving lightly through the crowd on Robert Livingston's arm, nodding greetings to all sides as a path parted before them.

Behind Nathan, someone sneezed. He turned to see the miserable countenance of Monsieur Povey, the minister for naval affairs. "Ah, Monsieur Povey, your niece is radiant as usual. But you look a bit under the weather."

"I hab a miserable code," Povey said.

"Sir?"

"This code in by head. I—I—Achoo! Forgib me."

"Certainly."

"Poor fellow," Fulton said.

"Id was the river, and your boat sinking like that. I got—I got—"

"Soaking wet," Fulton said.

"Yeb." Povey's watery eyes blinked. "Soakig wet."

"I didn't know Mr. Livingston knew Yvette Marchand," Nathan said.

"Her father was one of Robert's best friends," Fulton said. "He died, tragically, in a carriage accident. The Livingstons regard Yvette somewhat as a foster daughter."

Livingston soon rejoined them. Nathan saw that Yvette Marchand was now seated with a lively group of friends near the orchestra. As he watched her, Livingston spoke to Fulton. "I believe Madamoiselle Marchand would be pleased to dance with your young friend here. See seems quite taken with Nathan."

Nathan froze. Livingston, smiling, moved away. Of course, he had meant to be overheard. But the idea left Nathan in acute distress. He spoke quietly to Fulton. "Robert, this is terrible."

"What's terrible?"

"I don't know how to dance."

"Posh. Everybody knows how to dance."

"I don't, Robert. I can't dance a step."

Fulton rolled his eyes in dismay. "Of *course*, you can dance. Anybody can dance. It's as simple as one-two-three."

"I can't dance."

Fulton thought for a moment. Then: "I'll just have to teach you. Come along with me, Nathan. There's really nothing to it."

They pushed through the crowd and found an alcove leading to an empty balcony. With difficulty, Fulton explained the rudiments of properly holding a woman and of the dance itself. "Uh, one-two-three, one-two-three. Really, Nathan, you should try to relax . . . No, no, don't count out loud . . . Ouch! . . . You're a trifle off the measure, there. One-two-three, one-two-three . . ." Two French couples came out through the double doors, saw the struggling men, and laughed. "Strange, these Americans, *n'est-ce pas?*" Fulton threw up his hands in disgust. "It's hopeless, hopeless! I never saw anybody so clumsy. Nathan, I'm sorry, old man. You'll just have to do your best without me. No offense, understand, but it's just—just—"

A servant came to the double doorway. "Monsieurs, the emperor!"

They hurried back inside. A hush had fallen over the vast ballroom. Livingston was waiting. "Where have you been?" he whispered. "The emperor wishes to greet all the Americans. Come along quickly, please." They followed him through the crowd toward the stage. Over the heads, Nathan now saw Napoleon himself, resplendent in blue and white uniform and reflecting medallions. As they drew near, assorted dignitaries were being introduced. Men bowed and women curtsied before the emperor's great gilded chair. Nathan sensed the aura of power about the man, a phenomenon intensified by the classic dark Corsican features, sensuous mouth, and brooding eyes. Bonaparte's French came to his ear, slightly accented and spoken in a quiet, rapid delivery. The intense magnetism of the imperial presence seemed to mesmerize the crowd. The ballroom, indeed, had become transfixed in all its splendor, around a single being larger than life. Small wonder, Nathan thought, that men would rush to their deaths in his name.

The American minister, Livingston, was now making introductions. Nathan heard the name of James Monroe, special emissary, and Napoleon's word of recognition. Fulton bowed lightly as his name was spoken, and the dark eyes widened. "You are a persistent man, Monsieur Fulton. An admirable quality. I demand persistence of my commanders in the field; sometimes it can win the day when all else fails. Don't you agree?"

"Absolutely, your excellency."

Nathan now heard his own name spoken. The eyes seemed to measure his height and strength as he offered a slight bow. "*Mon Dieu,* you young Americans are growing tall. Monsieur, you would make a formidable imperial guard." Nathan responded with a broad smile of pleasure.

When the introductions were completed, an imperial major-domo placed a beribboned document in Napoleon's hand. Livingston and Monroe exchanged expectant glances. Napoleon untied the document and began to speak. "We do hereby decree that the land in western America known as the Louisiana Territory, including the City of New Orleans . . ." A murmur went through the audience. Nathan's instinct told him that something quite unexpected was unfolding. Livingston's patrician features were a study in dawning surprise. Monroe seemed incredulous, a half-smile playing at his mouth. With stunning clarity, the details were being spelled out. The government of France offered for sale to the United States the entire western half of the Mississippi-Missouri Rivers drainage basin, along with a vast reach of territory following the Sabine and Red Rivers northward from the Gulf of Mexico, and westward to the great Stony Mountains all the way to the Canadian border. This sale was conditioned on the payment by the U.S. to France the sum of eighty million francs, or about fifteen million in American dollars . . .

The Americans broke into spontaneous applause. Quickly it spread through the ballroom, interrupting the emperor's speech. He looked up from the document, nodding and waving to the crowd.

At Nathan's elbow, Fulton declared: "It's a windfall! My God, he's talking about the entire French holdings in America. That's a million square miles, maybe more!"

Napoleon soon left the ballroom with his retinue. Jubilation gripped the Americans. While Livingston accepted congratulations from a swarm of well-wishers, Monroe hurried away to draft a message to President Jefferson. The fastest sailing ship would take about eight weeks to reach the New World. To further insure that the word reached Washington, it was sent on two separate ships.

The orchestra returned to the stage and struck up a sprightly dance tune. A young aide of Minister Povey presented his compliments to Nathan Stewart. "I believe, monsieur, that you have the honor of the first dance with Mademoiselle Marchand." The aide, a handsome youth in the uniform of the naval service, did not bother to mask his envy.

On leaden feet, Nathan made his way across the dance floor, shouldering through the crowd. His mind was a wild jumble of elation and dread. He sensed that all eyes were upon him. Then the lovely oval face was turning up to him, the eyebrows arched in silent question.

"Mademoiselle?" he said.

She smiled, placed a gloved hand lightly on his arm, and came to her feet. Almost immediately they were on the polished dance floor. Music poured over them, to the swirling accompaniment of dancing couples. Nathan hoped in his heart for a miracle; that suddenly, in a burst of inspiration, the music would become measured and clear, the melody a thing of sweet and pulsing clarity. It did not.

Awkwardly, he placed a meaty hand at her tiny waist. Desperately he fixed his eye upon a point on the distant wall and counted in his mind. "Uh, one-two-three, one-two-three . . ." They stepped off. He lost the rhythm. He lost his balance. He recovered, moved along with halting steps out of rhythm to hers.

The luminous eyes widened in confusion. Nearby, someone tittered. Madamoiselle Marchand seemed distressed. "Please, monsieur . . ."

He stepped on her foot.

"Sorry."

Anger flared in her eyes. "You're making a joke." Again, the foot. "Ouch!"

He lurched into another couple, received their withering glances, apologized, tried a turn.

There was a ripping sound.

"My dress! You oaf, you've torn my gown!"

Nathan offered a terrified chuckle. He attempted to cover the tear at her waist with his left hand. "I don't dance," he said through a frozen smile.

"That," she hissed, "is evident."

It was an agony. The music seemed never to end. But finally, blessedly, it did. He escorted her back to where Livingston was seated. The minister looked at him curiously. Madamoiselle Marchand sat down in a red-faced pout.

Nathan murmured, *"Merci,* madamoiselle."

She tossed her lovely head. "Really, monsieur, if America is made up of such louts as yourself, I will be pleased never to go there. And especially, I shall endeavor never again to encounter the likes of you. On or off a dance floor!"

He bowed and walked away, in an agony of embarrassment.

Suddenly, Nathan Stewart could hardly wait to leave Paris and return to America.

IV

It was a sweltering July, the hottest in memory. One's clothing stuck, and sweat put a constant dampness to the skin. Pittsburgh steeped in odors and noises. Tempers were short. In the saloons catering to millhands and rivermen, minor disagreements erupted into brawls. From her upstairs window in the great, rambling Stewart House, Catherine could view the fork of the rivers, the water low and murky and still as glass. A new seagoing square-rigged sailing ship stood at anchor off Isaiah Stewart's boatyard, her jutting masts newly cut from Allegheny pine. Catherine wondered where such a vessel would be bound from this odd birthplace so many miles from saltwater.

The Stewart enterprises swarmed with activity. Along the riverbank, workmen sweated and cursed, rushing to construct barges, keelboats, and scows for waiting customers. In the freightyard frenzied wagon traffic raised a constant haze of dust and smell of horses. Over all, there was the noise; a hammering, yammering, whinnying, cursing, shouting, whistling, creaking, sawing barrage of noise.

Catherine found excitement in it all, excitement and wonder. The marvel was she was a part of it. She worked now in the cluttered office of Isaiah Stewart, keeping books and ledger accounts, jotting in tight, neat figures the interminable listings of rope and wood, iron fittings and nails, eyebolts, wagon tongues, boards and beams, yards of canvas and quantities of paint, pitch, oakem, oats, straw, harness, and twine that went into such a complex as Stewart's Freightyard and Boatworks Co.

She was sixteen now, rapidly bloomed into womanhood, trim-figured with rounded hips and high breasts that even practical, everyday dresses could not subdue. Her skin was creamy and unblemished, her eyes as blue as the July sky. And her hair tumbled down in soft waves the color of spun gold. Stephen was forever telling her how beautiful she was, but Catherine lacked consciousness of it. She was happy, and that was the important thing; happy to be so warmly accepted into this family of Stewarts, one of the household. Isaiah and Martha Stewart regarded her as a daughter. Even Maybelle, for all her temper and difficulties with a domineering father, did not resent her. "Oh, Catherine," Maybelle would say, "how I wish I could be more like you, pretty and smart and, well, serene." And, of course, Maybelle was a beauty in her own right.

At heart, however, Catherine was not serene. Far from it, she suffered a deep hunger, and that hunger was growing. Its name was Stephen. He seemed forever to fill her conscious mind, waking or sleeping: a constant, thrilling presence. It troubled her to feel such stirrings for Stephen. Was he not, after all, practically a brother? The only thing they lacked was kinship of blood. Martha Stewart herself would say aloud, "They're like brother and sister, those two." How could she, Catherine Colby, betray that trust? And as for Stephen, if he felt anything beyond loving friendship—as one would love a member of the family—he never let it be shown. Never. Tall, strikingly handsome, friendly, he seemed hesitant even to look her directly in the eyes. Besides, he was much too busy helping his father in the thriving business, overseeing boatbuilders and teamsters, dealing directly with customers. Frightened strangers, most of them, with no knowledge of boats or the perilous moods of wild rivers, they looked to Stephen with instinctive trust.

In ever-increasing numbers they came to Pittsburgh, men, women, and children, speaking many tongues. On the crowded streets one heard German, Dutch, Finnish, Gaelic, dialects of Scotland and Wales; there were Frenchmen, Spaniards, even an occasional Chinese. Their wagons came lurching over the Alleghenies, rattling pots and pans, from Boston, New York, and Cumberland, from Philadelphia and Northern Virginia. They brought their oxen, horses and mules, chickens and sheep, dogs, cats, pigs. The children were of a breed, wide-eyed and wondrous. The men tended to be tight-lipped, already worn from the trail. And the women had a common expression that Catherine quickly recognized as fear of the unknown. She often pitied them, knowing they ventured into a dark and hostile world, a westward country of river hazard and trackless forest, natural calamity and assault by red Indians or white brigands. She looked into the faces and thought to herself: Will you survive?

"There's just me and the wife there and the young'uns, and we need us a boat. Nothin' too costly, mind, but something safe enough for us and the animals. Can you sell us a boat like that, mister?"

"Yes, sir. That's our business, boats. We got a flatboat here, with sheds to shelter your family and the animals. When you get to where you're going, you can take it apart and use the timber for building. That's what a lot of folks do. There's Stewart sheds all down the Ohio and the Mississippi, too. Thirty-five dollars. Where are you bound?"

"Uh, Ohio country. Near a place called Fort Washington, at Cincinnati. We got a claim there, land grant from the war."

"The war?"

"Yes. The land grant's my pappy's here. He was with General Washington at Monmouth. Four hundred acres of river bottom. Leastways, I hope it's river bottom."

"A flatboat is what you need, then. When you get there, you've got something to live in for a few months, till you can build something better. A word of advice, though. It's best to travel with somebody else, another family or two. That's always best, if you've never been on a river before."

"Thank you, young fella. What's your name again?"

"Stewart. Stephen Stewart. My father owns this boatyard. We're pleased to have your business."

"Much obliged, Mr. Stewart."

"Nothing to it."

"Mr. Stewart?"

"Yes, ma'am?"

"We heard there was wild Indians in the Ohio country. Is that right? Is there danger?"

"There's always danger, ma'am. The Indians in that country still go on a warpath from time to time. But you never can tell about an Indian. He can be your best friend or worst enemy. It all depends."

"Depends on what?"

"On luck, ma'am. Luck . . . and the good Lord."

Luck and the good Lord. He spoke so authoritatively and knew so little. Stephen winced inwardly at the thought of his ignorance of the West, of anything beyond Pittsburgh. All his life he had been in the clutch of this river, these forks. Oh, he had talked with rivermen, listened to their tall tales, thrilled to the adventures of men like Simon Kenton, George Rogers Clark, and Daniel Boone. But it was all secondhand, nothing of personal experience. A greenhorn he was, not even dry behind the ears. And so he looked into their faces, eager faces or wary faces or frightened faces, and envied them. Yes. Envied what lay ahead of them, beyond these forks, down the big Ohio, down the Mississippi itself, or maybe even onto that wild, turgid river they called the Missouri, Big Muddy. That was the river Mason Everett had talked about; the river that thrust northward and west, twisting and thundering, they said, into Indian country and God knows where else, for two thousand miles.

Wonderlust. He suffered it, in the humdrum routine of business and town. He bent his back to a crosscut saw, cutting another beam, another mast, another bowsprit, and thought of the river, the forest, and the high mountains peaked with ice—mountains that from a distance shown like jewels. He had seen drawings of them in a book that Zachary Palmer once gave him as a child. The book was written in French, and the mountains were in Europe, but no matter; mountains were mountains. A man could dream of them, having never even seen one. A man? A lad, not yet nineteen.

And so he worked and he daydreamed. But there was more. Damn, why did life have to be so complicated? There was more, and the more was Jamie Catherine Colby. The touch of her hand could take his breath away. She'd grown too beautiful to be real, and he loved her. Stephen knew that he lóved her; he wanted to speak of it aloud, but could not. For she was too beautiful, too fine, for the likes of him. Someday she would have a prince, no doubt. Maybelle said as much. Even Burl—quiet, stolid, mulish Burl—saw Catherine as, well, different from the rest of them. "I see them guys, how they look at Catherine, and I get real angry inside, Stephen," Burl would say. "It's like they was looking at someone who's much too good for the likes of them."

"You make her sound not even human, Burl. Catherine's beautiful, but she's human."

"I don't like them looking the way they do. She's an orphan and ain't got no folks to speak for her, except us." Burl stammered and became red-faced in an attempt to express himself. He could never pick the right words to say. His mouth puckered, in stubborn reflection. "Anyhow, you know what I mean." He darted a shrewd glance at Stephen. "You know exactly what I mean."

But then, with no warning at all, the life of Stephen Stewart changed.

The man rode into the compound at midmorning on a big chestnut mare, dismounted, tossed the reins to old Charlie and asked for Isaiah Stewart. Instinctively, the servant touched his forehead. Tethering the mare, he went off in search of his employer. The visitor took a seat in the shade of the broad front porch of Stewart House. Tall and slightly bowlegged, he had dark hair combed forward over a broad forehead. His nose was a trifle long for the face, the eyes were reflective and heavy-lidded. He wore the clothing of a city man, set off by expensive English boots. He was accompanied by a large black Newfoundland dog.

It was Stephen who answered the summons. Mounting the porch, he glanced at the boots and clothes and felt the softness of the hand. "Stephen Stewart," he said. "My father is not here at the moment. He had to go into the city."

"Meriwether Lewis," the man said. "I'm having some difficulty and was told that your father would be the man to see. People hereabouts say he's the best boatbuilder in Pittsburgh. And my problem involves a boat."

"A boat?"

"A keelboat." There was a momentary lapse. The visitor seemed hesitant to speak further. Or perhaps it was a quirk of shyness. Stephen waited, saying nothing. "I'm, uh, on government business," Lewis said. "An expedition to the West. We ordered a keelboat by letter from one of your competitors. It was supposed to be completed and ready for launching by now. Unfortunately, the work was barely begun. Our boatbuilder, it seems, has a fondness for the bottle."

Stephen beckoned for old Charlie to bring cold drinks. He offered Lewis a cigar. "I'm sorry you are having difficulty, Mr. Lewis..."

"It's Captain Lewis." The visitor drew on the cigar and acknowledged its quality with a nod. He settled back in a rocking chair and surveyed the busy freight compound and boatyard. "You have quite an operation here."

They small-talked for nearly an hour. Each instinctively liked the other. Stephen sensed in Captain Lewis an air of hesitancy and solitude. The conversation drifted to books, and he learned that his visitor had a penchant for poetry. Stephen also surmised that more than a keelboat would be needed. Meriwether Lewis would require a freight wagon and temporary storage as well. He had accumulated a large quantity of supplies in Pittsburgh, and more was on the way, from army quartermaster depots in Philadelphia, New York, and Harpers Ferry, Virginia.

Stephen looked out over the river. Prolonged summer drought was causing the water level to drop badly. Rivermen talked of shallows and sunken snags already causing problems down the Ohio. Without rain, things would get worse. "Who is your boatbuilder, Captain Lewis?"

"Fellow named Gary. Buford Gary."

Stephen nodded. Buford Gary was a good craftsman when sober, but unreliable in the extreme otherwise. The man had a temper and was not the kind to abide interference. "We'll have to talk to Father."

Isaiah Stewart arrived just before noon with a load of supplies from town. The proprietor of Stewart's climbed down stiffly from the wagon and mopped his face with a bandana. As usual, he wore a business suit even in the heat of the day. He listened to Lewis with a mournful expression and asked to see the plans from his saddlebag and they spread them on the porch. Isaiah's eyebrows lifted.

"Don't believe I've seen anything quite like it, Captain. Your own design?"

"Partly, yes. We have special needs. She's fifty-five feet long and ten wide. I figured those ten-foot decks fore and aft will serve for our manpower and supplies. As you see, I've added a forecastle and aftercabin."

"And what's this amidships?"

"Those are regular gunwales, but I've got 'em backed up with these wooden lockers that can be raised higher in case of Indian attack from either shore. We'll mount a small gun in there, maybe two. And I want to be able to fasten a big tarpaulin in place over the waist area here"—his forefinger traced the area on the plans—"for protection against rough water."

"Where do you intend to take this here boat, Captain?"

"Up the Missouri river."

"How far up?"

"As far as she'll go."

Isaiah stepped back, stroking his jaw with a thumb. He drew out a stubby pipe and stuffed it with tobacco. "Mind if I make a suggestion?"

"Be my guest."

"I see you're planning a vessel that you can either pole or row. Very sensible. Poling's fine in shallow water. But if it was my keelboat, I'd mount me a short mast too, for a square-rigged sail. Come in handy, you know. On open river, you can sometimes pick up quite a breeze."

"Good idea."

Isaiah studied the plans some more, humming softly to himself. Then: "And you'll need ringbolts and cleats down here along the bow. That's so's your men—or mules, if you've got any—can haul her across the riffles and wood islands."

"Riffles and wood islands?"

"Shallows. I guess Stephen here told you, the Ohio's falling every day. If we don't get rain pretty soon . . ."

"Yes, he mentioned it. So you can see, Mr. Stewart, that I'm in a bit of a hurry."

Isaiah sniffed. Everybody was in a hurry. Rarely did he talk to a westbound traveler who didn't want his boat ready yesterday. Captain Meriwether Lewis was no exception. The boatbuilder sucked on his pipe and blew a wreath of smoke. "We'll see what can be done," he said. "How much would ye say Buford Gary's got done on this job?"

"Not even half of it, and we're almost through July."

The captain folded his blueprint and went his way, with an invitation to dinner at Stewart House that evening. Then Isaiah and Stephen saddled horses and rode three miles upriver to the boatyard of Buford Gary.

The place was in a sad state of disrepair. Despite the inpouring of travelers and business, Buford Gary's establishment suffered from inattention. Weeds grew in the stocks and ways of the boatyard. Half-finished keelboats tilted on the mud flats, rotting. Iron scaffolding and rollers were covered in rust. Rats scuttled through the debris. There was a mingled odor of decay and dead fish. The proprietor of all this sat on his front porch, bulgy-eyed and unshaven, a half-empty bottle of rum at his side. A fly stood on his nose, undisturbed. The man was staring at the river. There were no workmen about, anywhere. Isaiah and Stephen rode into the dusty yard and dismounted. A screen door banged and a small, pinch-faced woman walked onto the shady porch and peered into the sunblast. "Who is that? Is that you, Isaiah Stewart? Upon my word, Buford, it's Isaiah Stewart and his boy Stephen."

"Well, well, well," Buford Gary said. The eyes groped and focused. He belched softly. "Well, well, well."

Isaiah mounted the rickety steps and took a chair. Stephen sat down on the edge of the porch, nodding to Mrs. Gary.

"Just happened to be passing by, Buford," Isaiah said amiably. "Thought I'd drop in, cadge a drink of your whiskey."

Gary snickered. "You came to the right place, Isaiah." He shoved the bottle over with the edge of his boot. "It ain't whiskey, but it'll do." Isaiah took a deep, thoughtful pull, wiped his mouth, blinked his eyes, handed the bottle to Stephen. The rum was like a swallow of liquid fire. Stephen, unprepared, erupted in a coughing fit, spewing rum and wiping tears. The two men laughed.

"Don't believe that boy is up to a man-size drink yet, Isaiah. I figured you'd raised up your young'uns better than that."

Isaiah chuckled. "Stephen's a bourbon man. Likes his daddy's home brew."

Harriet Gary vanished into the house and soon returned with a plateful of sandwiches. Stephen wolfed down two of them, suddenly aware that he had not eaten lunch. The men ignored the plate and engaged in idle talk.

Finally: "What brings you out here Isaiah, away from that gold mine of your'n? I know you've got better things to do than sit and chew the fat with Buford Gary in the middle of a busy afternoon."

"I can't think of a better way to spend an afternoon, Buford, and that's a fact. How long have we been friends, would you say?"

Buford Gary thought about it, tilting his head slightly. From the angle of his jaw, Stephen could see that the man had lost a great deal of weight. There was a pallor of skin that hinted at a deeper sickness than the bottle.

"Twenty years, best I can figure," Gary said. "Yep. I'd put it at around twenty years. Maybe more."

"That's right," Isaiah said. "And do you remember when we first came here, me and Martha, and the hard time we had getting started? You and Harriet helped us out. I had that shack on the river, and one day you came down there with a big sack of food. Remember that, Buford? You said you didn't need it and was just fixing to throw it away, but maybe I knew somebody who could use it. There was smoked meat and canned vegetables, jerkie and hard bread, enough for two people to feed on for a month. Well, we fed on it, Martha and me, and we were much obliged. Remember that, Buford?''

Gary stirred in his chair and smiled wistfully. "Yes," he said quietly, "I remember, Isaiah."

Stephen watched and listened, spellbound. Buford Gary was a proud man and quick to take offense. When drunk, he was known as a fighter. His hostility had lost him friends and workmen. And yet here, in the presence of an old friend, a different man emerged.

Isaiah chuckled and slapped his thigh. "We sure as hell fooled you, Buford Gary. Martha and me, we might have starved without that food.''

Gary laughed too, and took another swig at the bottle. "You ain't answered my question, Isaiah," he said.

Isaiah sighed. "That's a fact, Buford. Sometimes I think you're too smart for your own good. I did come down here for something. There's no use trying to fool Buford Gary. I came down here to ask a favor.''

"A favor?" Gary guffawed and swept his arm at the empty boatyard. "What the hell kind of a favor? I ain't got nothin' to offer a man as rich as you.''

"There's a project you're working on, a government project." Isaiah's voice dropped to a conspiratorial murmur, as if others might overhear. "Keelboat. It's for an officer named Captain Lewis.''

Buford Gary straightened slightly in his chair. The bloodshot eyes grew foxy. "I'm listening.''

"Well, see, I never had a government contract of any kind and never worked on a government boat job. This one seems kind of different. From what I hear it's got some special features. Ten-foot decks, built-up gunwales amidships, forecastle and aftercabin. I want Stephen here to get experience working on different kinds of boats, and especially on government contract boats. We'd like to get that kind of business too, in the future.'' Isaiah spread his hands and studied them. "Hell, I might as well speak plain, Buford. It's strictly a selfish motive I've got. From working on this boat, I'd know better how to bid for some federal jobs in the future. That's the only thing we ain't got. I knew, see, that you had this contract, that your health wasn't too good, and your men had walked out on you . . ."

"That's a fact," Gary said. "The sons of bitches just up and walked out."

"So I figured I'd come and take a chance. No harm in asking, I always say."

Isaiah fell silent. Buford Gary stared at the river. Stephen studied the boatyard and finally located what he thought would be the Lewis keelboat, a large hull half completed and surrounded by stacks of fresh lumber.

"What have you got in mind?" Gary said. "I mean, what kind of terms?"

"Well, I was thinking that Stephen here could bring over a crew of men, do the job, and you pay them wages and take ten per cent. How does that sound?"

"Ten per cent!" Gary sputtered. "You're out of your mind. Damn it, Isaiah, I never took you for a robber!" He clinched his fists and leaned forward in his chair.

"Now hold on, Buford. Don't get riled. That's just what I was thinking. It don't mean that's what I would settle for."

Gary settled back, a gleam of avarice in his eyes. "Well, I should think not. Taking advantage of a sick man."

"No. As I got to thinking more on it, I thought that twelve per cent would be more like—"

"Not on your life. You're not even close, Isaiah. But I tell you what I would do. I'd let you pay the men's wages, I'd take my entire profit and let you have the blueprints . . ."

And so they haggled. It was friendly barter. Stephen could see that both men enjoyed the joust. Finally, they struck an agreement satisfactory to both, but with Isaiah giving more than he ever would in a normal business agreement. Buford Gary signaled his acceptance by breaking wind and saying, "Somehow, Isaiah, I think you're cheating me. But what choice have I got?"

Isaiah said, "Now that's what I call a Christian attitude, Buford."

"All right, you've got a deal."

"Do you want it in writing?"

"Since when do we need to put things in writing?"

Isaiah extended his hand. "I appreciate your putting your faith in me, Buford. And that's a fact."

They left him sprawled in the chair, swigging from the bottle. When they had mounted the horses, Harriet Gary came to Isaiah's side and looked up. "Thank you, Isaiah," she said. "May the Lord be good to you." She took his hand and kissed it. Then she stood and waved until they had passed through the broken-down gate.

Isaiah and Stephen rode in silence until they were almost at the compound. Isaiah said, "He was a good man once, that Buford. I didn't know he was this sick. He's got the stamp of death on him, I'm afraid. I'm glad we can do this for him, Stephen. I know you'll build a proper boat, and we don't have to tell anybody how it came about. I've owed the man a lot for all these years and never had a chance to repay. I'm glad to get that chance."

"I understand," Stephen said.

He felt a surge of affection for the old man.

And so the work began, a wild rush against time. Stephen took the best three boatwrights in the yard with him to Buford Gary's place. Within a week, they had the keelboat hull ready for floating downriver with the lumber loaded aboard. Then, stripped to their waists in broiling heat, the crew hammered and warped, sawed and glued. Sawdust filled their nostrils and caked their flesh. Caulking pitch mottled hands and blackened fingernails. The workday began at first light and continued until dark, when Stephen staggered off to bed exhausted. Even their best was not fast enough for Meriwether Lewis. Stalking the dried mudflat in his English boots, trailed by the big Newfoundland dog, the captain seemed possessed by demons. "Stephen, can't you work any faster, lad? The river's falling. We'll never get started at this rate."

Isaiah Stewart had a liking for the man. At his invitation, Lewis moved into Stewart House bag and baggage. And the baggage was something to behold. The expedition would carry enough rifles, powder, and ammunition for a small army. There were knives and tomahawks, a small swivel gun for the deck of the keelboat, and assorted pistols. He had accumulated twenty-one bales of gifts for Indians—beads, curtain rings, coins, mirrors, women's clothing. He carried provisions and clothing for forty men, including cold weather garb, plus an ample supply of kegged whisky and rum. There were cartons of blank notebooks and writing supplies, extra spyglasses, magnifying glasses, tools for drawing, an iron framework for a portable boat, and a quantity of powdered "portable soup."

The captain spoke little about his plans, keeping a manner of quiet reserve. If it was to be a civilian exploration or military, he did not say. In the Stewart compound, however, curiosity quickened one day when five army soldiers arrived under command of a corporal to take billets in the barn. Captain Lewis told Isaiah, "I also need to hire some boatmen and a pilot. Would you say ten men would be enough to get us to Louisville? You will be compensated, of course, for their food and lodgings."

"Whatever you require, Captain. Happy to oblige."

Occasionally, a courier would arrive from the East bearing a letter for Captain Lewis in a leather pouch. The messenger would then depart at a gallop, carrying the captain's written reply. One day a letter arrived from Louisville. Lewis tore it open and uttered a joyous whoop. "By God, Isaiah, I've got my fellow captain. William Clark has agreed to accompany the expedition. We'll pick him up in Louisville," He glanced at the unfinished keelboat and frowned. "That is, if we ever get to Louisville."

The subject of Stephen accompanying the expedition came up unexpectedly on the night the keelboat finally was completed. Over dinner, Captain Lewis remarked, "I understand that you've done some surveying and map making in the past, Stephen. Is that so?"

"A few years ago, my brother Nathan and I mapped some of the homestead ranges downriver a little way. Nothing of any importance."

"Surveyor, boatbuilder. Crack shot, too, I'm told."

Stephen smiled self-consciously. "Everybody hunts around here. It's our way of life."

"Ah, yes. Have you ever thought of going west?"

"Yes. I intend to do that someday."

It was a family dinner with several visitors. The others carried on desultory conversation. Catherine was speaking with Martha Stewart about knitting. Isaiah Stewart chatted to a guest. It all made a low murmur, interspersed with the sounds of clinking dinnerware.

"How would you like to come with us?"

The murmur ceased. Heads turned. Stephen was taken by surprise, and for an instant he could not think of a reply. "Go with you?"

"We could use a strong young fellow with your talents. I think this is going to be quite an adventure, unlike anything that's been done before in this country."

"Well..." Stephen glanced at his father. Isaiah Stewart smiled, a forkful of food suspended over his plate.

"We discussed the possibility," Isaiah said. "I told the captain it was strictly up to you."

Martha said, "Stephen..." Isaiah lifted his hand, and she fell silent. Catherine's face was a conflict of expressions. At the foot of the table, Maybelle and Burl merely stared at Stephen, saying nothing.

"I don't know," he said. "The business...I have to think about it."

"Of course."

The captain sipped wine. The conversation turned to other matters. Not until after dinner, when Lewis, Isaiah, and Stephen moved out to the front porch for cigars, did the subject come up again.

Meriwether Lewis lit his cigar and leaned back in obvious enjoyment. From the darkness came the summer sounds of frogs and crickets. A full moon stood above Coal Hill, casting the slope and the river in its ghostly glow.

"You've done a fine job on the keelboat, Stephen," Lewis said. "My compliments. It's finally completed and we'll be loaded by tomorrow night."

Isaiah Stewart grunted. "Old-timers can't remember when the river's been this low, Captain. They say it's impossible to navigate downriver right now with a load of cargo. Tricky river, the Ohio. In places, your deepest water right now is six inches."

Lewis grimaced in vexation. "We can't wait any longer."

"It'll be easier, once you get below Wheeling. That's a few days of travel. I'd suggest you haul part of your cargo to Wheeling by wagon, then load it on board."

"Good idea."

"I'll arrange it for you."

Stephen said, "What more can you tell me about the expedition?"

Lewis grew thoughtful. "I'm calling it the voyage of discovery," he said. "As of right now, I don't feel disposed to let many of the details be widely known. It never hurts to be cautious. But you ask a fair question and deserve a fair answer. The fact is, of course, I don't have many answers myself. We're going places where a white man's never been. Our objective is to explore."

His voice took on an edge of excitement.

"The United States has just made a remarkable land acquisition. Bonaparte sold us one million square miles of Louisiana Territory. It's a huge land mass, spreading northward from the Mexican border clear to Canada and encompassing an enormous unexplored mountain range. It cost us fifteen million dollars, and as of this moment we don't even know what we've bought! Deserts, mountains, Indians, great rivers, animals, and plant life of which we're totally ignorant, huge uncharted wastes. Our mission is to take a company of men and go up the Missouri River as far as we can go. There's always been a theory that if somebody looked hard enough he'd find a northwest passage, a river route all the way to the Pacific Ocean. I don't put much stock in it, from what little we do know, but there's always the possibility. This expedition, at any rate, is under orders from President Jefferson himself, to seek and find and report back. That includes some map making, descriptions of wildlife and plants, and trading with the Indians."

Lewis pondered. The glow of cigar lit his dark brows and jutting nose. His face brooded. "There are dangers out there that we haven't even dreamed of. God knows what terrors await us. I can't even guarantee that any of us will get back alive. You need to know that, Stephen. You need to weigh the risks in your mind."

Stephen already had done so. His earlier indecision was behind now, replaced by a rising anticipation that he felt barely able to contain. The shining mountains beckoned. He did not intend to let this opportunity pass.

"I'm going with you," he said.

There would be times in the months to come when he would look back on these words as insane.

Two mornings later, on the last day of August, 1803, the strange-looking keelboat rode the shallows off the great mudflat left by falling waters in front of Stewart's boatyard. Isaiah Stewart had dispatched two wagons the previous day loaded with expedition goods and bound for rendezvous at Wheeling. A hot morning sun already blasted the hills, promising another sweltering day. On board the keelboat, muscular bargemen stood ready at poles along the gunwales, five on each side. The soldiers were gathered on the foredeck with their corporal.

On shore, there were hugs and handshakes all around. Even the boatyard workmen had gathered to see Stephen off. Old Charlie brought down a box of fried chicken, handed it to him, and wept. Isaiah Stewart shuffled from one foot to the other, telling him to be careful and keep his long rifle dry. Catherine stood aside with the workmen and Maybelle. She had not spoken. Finally, everything was said and, with a last disappointed glance at Catherine, Stephen turned to follow Captain Lewis to the boat.

"Stephen!"

She came running down the mudflat, her shoes sinking. Behind her, the tracks were small blobs of shadow in the soft bottom soil. He stood foolishly, not knowing what to do, his hands filled with a duffel of clothes, long rifle and the greasy box of chicken. Catherine flung her arms around his neck and kissed his cheek. "I'll be waiting," she said. "I love you."

Before he could reply, she hurried back up the mudflat, petticoats flying.

The kiss was a warm, lingering presence on his face.

For a river that wants to go west, the Ohio has a hard time making up its mind. It is as if during the primeval glacial upheavals that shaped and reshaped its destiny, Fate was in a capricious mood. And so from birth at the Forks, the river swings northwestward for twenty miles to Beaver Creek. Then it jogs properly southwestward for a similar distance. But then, abruptly changing again, it plunges south. And repeatedly along the shore, the verdant hills drop down to the water's edge, offering to mortals scenes of riotous beauty.

This time, however, the Ohio was sickly from drought. The river seemed to be filling up on its own bottom. From sluggish shallows, masses of brush, gnarled treetops, and floating logs reached out as if to grasp the keelboat and hold it. The farther they progressed, the more numerous these wooden islands became. In places, the water was barely deep enough to clear the keel. Finally, after only five hours of poling, they encountered a combined wood barrier and shallows offering no channel through. The only way across was to be dragged. An enterprising farmer, seeing the keelboat's difficulties from ashore, brought his two-horse team and shouted, "Two dollars!" The price sent Meriwether Lewis into a fit of temper. The farmer shrugged, spat, and prepared to lead his horses away. "All right, all right!" the captain fumed. "Two dollars." But his mood darkened and remained that way. And the first barrier was merely a taste of things to come.

The polers worked five to a side, moving rhythmically along narrow walkways. As each man came to the limit of his walk, he shouldered his pole and returned to the prow. At the rear, another boatman steered by means of an oar-sweep. As they worked, their voices poured out across the quiet water, singing a chanty song. At midafternoon, a breathless humid heat bore down. Gnats and flies bedeviled the men. Corporal John Floyd, in command of the soldiers, slapped at his neck and cursed. "By God, we need rain and that's a fact. This heat won't let you live."

Stephen took a voluntary turn at the poles to allow a boatman to rest. Half an hour of the labor left him musclesore and drenched in sweat. He sipped at a dipper of tepid water from the deck barrel, but it offered no coolness. Stephen had taken an instant liking to John Floyd. The corporal was a tall, rangy young man, not yet twenty-one, with an easy smile and quiet ways. Returning the dipper to its peg, he said to Floyd, "Well, they said we'd never get through, that the river's impassable. Now we'll find out."

At the prow of the keelboat stood the pilot, a squat, gray-bearded man named Harry Slade. Silent Harry, they called him back in Pittsburgh; a dour loner with little gift for talk and less, it seemed, for friendship. For all that, he knew the river—knew it as intimately as a lover—in all its twists and moods. Silent Harry was one of the best pilots in the business and was said to have a sixth sense for danger. Now, he gave a signal for the polers to stop their work. As the keelboat drifted, Slade squinted ahead with an ominous frown. Captain Lewis, who had been writing in one of his journals, looked inquisitively to the pilot.

"I was afraid of this," Slade grumbled.

"What's wrong, Pilot?" Lewis put down his work and went to Slade's side.

The pilot pointed a stubby finger. Spread across the river was a tangle of tree branches and logs that extended downstream as far as they could see. A channel snaked its way through, in places twice the width of the vessel. But the channel held only still pockets of shallow water, and in places it was no more than wet gravel. "There ain't been no boat through there in a week," Slade muttered, "and we ain't going through neither."

Captain Lewis said, "What do you mean, we're not going through? Of course we're going through."

The pilot shrugged. The keelboat drifted slowly toward the barrier. Finally its keel slid softly into the gravel bottom and stopped. Ahead, the deepest water pockets were only six inches. Lewis glanced hopefully toward the shore. "Maybe we can hire another of those bandit farmers to help us." He cupped his hands and shouted, "Hallooo!" His voice trailed off across the stifling afternoon. There was no reply.

Slade scratched his head. "No use anyhow, Captain. A herd of oxen couldn't drag us through that."

"How far ahead would you say it's like this?"

The pilot squinted against the sunny glare. Reflection from the water pockets bathed his face in rippling light. "Hard to tell. Fifty yards, maybe. A hundred, maybe."

"All right, then." Lewis turned to Corporal Floyd. "Corporal, I want you to take two men and reconnoiter ahead. Tell me how far this gravel bar goes."

"You mean get off the boat and walk in the river, sir?"

"That's exactly what I mean."

"Yessir."

The men clambered clumsily over the side and onto the gravel bar, sinking ankle deep into the sucking mixture of gravel, mud, and water. "Keep a distance between you," Lewis commanded. "Watch for quicksand." Grunting and sweating, they sloshed away and soon were out of sight. The others settled down on the keelboat deck, assailed by gnats. Stephen fidgeted in inactivity, half-wishing he had joined the others. Half an hour went by before they came floundering wearily back. Corporal Floyd looked up from the side of the keelboat, catching his breath. "About sixty yards, Captain," he said. "Then we hit a narrow channel that's deep enough to float us. But there's a bend in the river, and I can't tell what's beyond that."

Lewis jumped up, rubbing his hands with enthusiasm. "Capital! Capital! All right, men. You and you and you, go aft. There's shovels in the tool locker. Bring up what you find. We're going to dig our own damn river and go through!"

It was an exhausting business. A dozen men moved out ahead of the keelboat, thrust their shovels into the muck, scooped up a load, and flung it to the side. To open enough channel, they had to dig down at least three feet along a center trough, sloping gradually upward along each side along an eight-foot swath. They dug by turns, until the whole company was either digging or resting. Stephen jumped down to take his turn. After a quarter of an hour of labor, his muscles ached and his body was saturated with sweat and slime. Gnats attacked in clouds, filling ears and nostrils, impervious to curses. The worst of it quickly passed, however, and with a few inches of water depth the going became somewhat easier. Still, it took them an hour and a quarter to channel through a distance of sixty yards. Not until almost sunset did they finally break through. As the keelboat floated past the last shallow and into six-foot water, they raised a ragged cheer.

The men clambored back aboard, exhausted. Captain Lewis ordered the whiskey barrel opened and a hearty drink for every hand. "Good lads!" he said, with a kind of giggling snort. "Good lads!" Stephen took his turn at the dipper of Monongahela whiskey. As the fiery brew went down his throat and warmed his blood, he thought he had never tasted anything so fine. They made camp on a point of sandy beach flanked by towering sycamore trees. The gnats were replaced by swarms of voracious mosquitoes that even the smoke from wet leaves tossed on the campfire failed to discourage. Slapping and scratching ("Pesky buggers, they'll bite clean through buckskin!"), the company wolfed down a supper of boiled meat and steaming beans and fell into their blankets, totally worn out.

Lewis had them up at dawn, shouting and prodding. Heedless of groaning protest, he harangued them through a fast breakfast— fried fatback, hard bread, and scalding black coffee—and back to the river. Twice more that day they repeated the channel-digging process. When the second ditch was cleared, the mud-caked apparitions threw their shovels onto the deck, and a burly, bewhiskered Irishman named Flannery grumbled, "Blast my eyes if we ain't a'goin' to dig clean to Louisville!" Silent Harry chuckled for the first time in living memory and replied, "Clean to St. Louis, if I know this captain." On another occasion, Lewis hired a team of oxen to drag the keelboat through a wood island of tree limbs and brush. And this time, to everyone's surprise, he did not protest the two-dollar fee. A few miles farther, the prow of the boat scraped bottom again. But now the dauntless captain surveyed the shallow depth ahead, ordered cargo removed, and floated the keelboat through while the men lugged barrels and bales by hand, stumbling and splashing. In this manner they passed the village of Steubenville, Ohio, where a group of ragged children and tattered Indians silently watched their struggles. "Next thing you know," muttered one of the hired crew, "he'll have us carrying the boat."

Not until the thirteenth day did they arrive at the rickety wharf in Wheeling, a town of a hundred houses spread back from the riverbank. Stephen's weary spirits leaped as he spotted the familiar green and white Conestoga wagons of the Stewart line. He jumped from the keelboat and wrung the rock-hard hands of the teamsters who had brought the cargo down. "Boss boy, you look a sight," said one of the men. "What'd you do, wallow down the river?" Stephen looked down at his mud-caked trousers and shirtless, sunblasted body and laughed. "You won't believe this, but we dug halfway from Pittsburgh." They believed it.

The wagon cargo included some of the heaviest supplies for the expedition, such as surveying instruments, guns and ammunition, extra axes, tarpaulin, rope, sail, replacement parts for the boat, and the bulky boxes of Indian gifts. Meriwether Lewis stood looking at the huge pile of it and worried. "Mr. Stewart," he said, "how do you figure we're going to put all this stuff on board and make any progress at all on that river?"

Stephen reflected for a moment. "Well, Captain, if it was me, I'd find me a way *not* to put it on board. From what these Wheeling folks say, there's not much more water downstream than up, at least for the next forty miles. After that, you've got several tributary streams feeding in that will give us more water depth. Fishing Creek comes in about forty miles downstream, and then there are a few more small streams before we come to the Little Kanawha."

"That doesn't answer my question."

"Captain, why don't you hire a couple of heavy duty canoes, load 'em up with the surplus gear, and bring them down with the keelboat. Might even bring an extra canoe, just to be on the safe side."

And so it was done. In the process of shifting the loads, they not only accommodated the new cargo but also managed to lighten the keelboat itself. As they set off again downriver, Meriwether Lewis seemed in brighter spirits. But Stephen stood at the stern watching the retreating Conestoga wagons with a heavy heart.

At his side, Corporal Floyd asked, "First time away from home, Mr. Stewart?"

Stephen nodded. "Except for a few surveying trips with my older brother."

"Well, it's never easy breaking away, not for anybody. And however many times you do it, leaving home is something a man never gets used to. I know. It's the same with me every time."

Stephen looked out at the hills flanking the river, rolling away in their blue-green immensity. A light breeze had sprung up and there seemed to be more life and sparkle to the river now. A great cumulus cloud coasted overhead. A fish jumped, leaving a spreading ripple that multiplied itself in diminishing circles. The day was turning into one of aching beauty. But the larger ache was inside him. He thought of home, and of Catherine's farewell. In his mind, he tried to create it, just as it was; to relive her touch and sweet scent and the urgent warmth of her voice. "I love you. I'll be waiting." What a fool he was to leave now, on this wild goose journey to the end of the earth. There was nothing for him on this river. Everything that mattered was back there, back in Pittsburgh. He groaned and put his head down on the bulwark.

Captain Lewis summoned Corporal Floyd for a brief conference aft. The corporal returned and detailed men to take turns on guard through the night. After picking three of the soldiers, he nodded to Stephen. "You're to stand duty too, I'm afraid. Captain Lewis says every man will share the responsibilities." Stephen nodded his assent, glad for the additional activity.

Navigation became somewhat less arduous the farther they went below Wheeling, but not much less. There was still the intermittent shoals and gravel bars, the clatter of shovels and ache of protesting muscle as they climbed down into the heat and muck to dig again. They could open fifty yards of channel in an hour, working at top speed; but the worst stretch required nearly two hours at the shovels, and the worst day found them either digging or carrying or being hauled past five obstacles. And still the heat and the drought wore on, still the river fell. A stretch that would have been navigable yesterday was impassable today; and unless the rain came, tomorrow would be worse.

After a seemingly endless succession of toiling days and mosquito-infested nights, they came to the river town of Marietta. This was a community of neat Yankee homes and businesses, with shops, tradesmen, artisans. From the river, Stephen could see evidence of a grist mill and sawmill, wagon works, a barrel factory, a boatyard. The Marietta landing was piled high with trade goods waiting for shipment downriver when the water rose again. Captain Lewis sent a party ashore for fresh provisions. There they met half-a-dozen stranded families with their barges, flatboats, and scows. Some lived miserably under rude canvas shelters on ten-foot scows; others had roomy houseboats furnished with chairs, beds, and stoves. Young and old, masters and servants, they shared their lot in adversity along with their cattle, hogs, sheep, horses, barnyard fowl, and domestic pets. They were astonished that the expedition had come this far. The shore party brought back a supply of fresh vegetables and meat, and Captain Lewis resumed the journey.

Gradually the crew was forming the roughhewn acquaintances typical of rivermen, built on common experience and discomforts. While the keelboaters were simply hired muscle, and not regarded as permanent members of the expedition, they now included in their circle of easy camaraderie those who had not been hired to push poles—the soldiers, the pilot, and Stephen. The process was made easier for their shared hardships.

As the miles wore on, the river had undergone subtle changes in width and terrain. Sometimes the subtle shoreline gentled back along a broad floodplain. To Stephen, it hinted of rich bottom soil and fine crops. From time to time along this stretch, they also passed a flatboat moving by sheer human muscle power in the opposite direction. Men toiled along steep bushy banks hauling at tow ropes or simply grabbing onto tree branches and shrubs, a method called bushwhacking. There were hailings and halloos, and occasionally the melodic tootling of a horn, as travelers acknowledged the presence of others in the immense spaces of time and river.

"Where ye bound, keelboat? Louisville?"

"To Louisville," Captain Lewis shouted, "and beyond!"

"Beware the falls. They're rocky as hell."

Stephen even managed to break through the shell of Silent Harry Slade, a matter of sheer persistence combined with their common hardships. "It's changing, all right," the pilot said, shading his eyes to observe another flatboat in the distance. "I seen the time when you'd go downriver for days and never pass nothing but an Indian canoe. Now the Ohio's getting downright crowded."

Like so many quiet men, Slade—once he'd found voice and a willing ear—proved to be a storehouse of fact and whimsy. It was Slade who explained the sudden appearance, fourteen miles downriver from Marietta, of a large, well-cultivated island in midstream, an island on which there stood a newly built white mansion surrounded by formal gardens, bridle paths, and standing cattle in the fields. The house commanded a broad grassy slope that swept down to a stone wharf. The astonished keelboaters watched a woman moving along a shore trail on horseback. She wore a scarlet cape, gold-laced riding habit, and a hat with a large white plume. Trailing her was a man who appeared to be a groom. "That's Margaret Blennerhasset," Slade said. "She's the wife of the island's master, Harman Blennerhasset. He would be indoors, more than likely, playing his cello or fiddling with his scientific gadgets."

"Glory be," said the Irishman, Flannery. "What fancy diggings, out here in the middle of nowhere."

"The man is a countryman of yours, Flannery," the pilot went on. "A real aristocrat. Strange fellow. Rumor is his wife's actually his niece, the daughter of his own sister. She's fifteen years younger than him. Their marriage so upset folks back in Ireland that they came to the New World and settled here on this island." He grimaced. "Godforsaken place, if you ask me, for all its beauty. They keep pretty much to themselves."

Stephen watched, enraptured, as the island plantation slid past. It gave him an unearthly feeling, as if he had glimpsed a fable come to life. The experience left a new dimension of mystery to the river, and the memory of the woman in the scarlet cape haunted him for the rest of that day.

Silent Harry chanted their progress, as if by rote. Day followed day in the tedious routine of keelboat life. When they were not struggling past another shallow, the time dragged in unrelieved idleness. Captain Lewis put in at Cincinnati for several days of rest and went off in the company of his black dog, Scammon, and friends from ashore. Stephen walked about the town and its army fort accompanied by John Floyd. The captain returned and they were off again, for Louisville.

September slipped away. Finally, the last day of the month brought rain. It came in muttering, flickering thunderheads that broke at last in the late afternoon. Rain pounded the river in sheets and drummed on the roof of the keelboat cabins, where they sheltered and cheered. October dawned with more heavy showers that then settled into a two-day downpour, bringing the first hint of cold.

The river filled and broadened now. There were flatboats, keelboats, and scows drifting along within sight, some of them lashed together as several families shared their lot.

"She's a hundred and sixty-two miles from Pittsburgh to the mouth of the Little Kanawha," mused Silent Harry, perched on the prow with an eye for sandbars and snags. "The Little Kanawha, that's in Delaware country, heading for Shawnee country. And then you've got the Hocking River, and the palisades country, and forty-five miles of bends and rapids to the falls . . ."

And then came the morning when the water grew swifter under the keel. Two men climbed atop the aftcabin to bend their weight against a great steering sweep. By this time, they had brought all of their cargo and equipment on board and lashed the freight canoes on the sides. Meriwether Lewis ordered extra lookouts all around for rocks, and he announced to the pilot: "We'll be taking the falls now, Mr. Slade."

"Very well, Captain."

Ahead of them the river seemed to be dropping away in front of the prow. Stephen sat close to the pilot, sensing the rapidly increasing surge of water. "These falls is a chute, actually," Silent Harry said. "This river drops twenty-two feet in just two miles. You got three channels ahead through the rapids. I figure Indian Chute is the best, even though there's plenty rock on both sides. Like dragon's teeth, they are. I've seen craft get their guts ripped out . . ."

They were in the full grip of the current now and swinging slightly off center. The men at the sweeps strained to bring the vessel straight again, and the Irishman Flannery hurled his weight with theirs. Slowly, the keelboat leveled again. At both sides, more men manned long oars to shove against jutting rocks and steady the descent. The roar of water rose to a tumult. Flannery bellowed, "Jesus Christ!" The keelboat swayed again.

Downward they swept, swaying and lurching. Stephen grabbed at a stanchion, heart pounding. Then they seemed to vault through a churning frenzy of white water, down and down. But at last, with a final half-turn of the keelboat, the roar subsided and they coasted into calm eddies. The crew seemed to give a spontaneous sigh of relief as Captain Lewis ordered the vessel maneuvered toward a wharf. When the boat was secured at last and the guard list posted, the captain summoned Stephen to the afterdeck.

"Mr. Stewart, I'd like for you to accompany me, if you will. We're going to meet the co-commander of this expedition, and also pay a visit to someone who was very special to your father."

"Yes, sir.'"

They found William Clark at an inn overlooking the river. A red-haired, outgoing man, he sprang from his chair and rushed to give Lewis a joyous welcome and a wringing handshake. "By God, only you could have gotten down that river, Meriwether," he thundered. "Stubbornest bastard on earth. What a fantastic surprise!"

Lewis smiled gravely. "There are a few more channels on the Ohio these days, William. We dug them by hand." The captain then turned and introduced Stephen. "Mr. Stewart is a civilian from Pittsburgh. He saw to the completion of our keelboat and is experienced at surveying and map making. I think he can help us with the armament and in writing the journals."

"Excellent," said Clark. He took Stephen's hand in a vicelike grip and fixed him with laughing blue eyes. "Glad to make your acquaintance, Stewart. We've got some high old times ahead."

The two commanders quickly settled down to a serious discussion of equipment and personnel. Clark had recruited more men in Louisville and expressed hope they could form a strong force of about forty men by the time they reached St. Louis. Several of the new recruits joined them at the inn. They gave Stephen the same iron handshakes and seemed to share with Clark a spirit of limitless enthusiasm. They were also, to a man, young and strong. The common characteristics, Stephen noticed, seemed to be self-assurance and physical prowess.

The talk went on until late afternoon. Then, with a scraping of chairs and more hearty handshakes, Lewis and Clark left the table, taking Stephen with them. They hired horses at a stable and rode northward through the town. As the animals picked their way along a path skirting the woods, Stephen drank in the

panoramic scene below: the town and rolling hills splotched with
the dappled colors of early autumn. Beyond lay the great sweep
of the Ohio, broad and blue in the distance, then sparkling as it
churned down the rapids, raising white froth. At last they
climbed a hill to a log house overlooking the river. They
dismounted and went in without knocking, into the presence of
George Rogers Clark.

Stephen was awed. The revolutionary hero of the western
campaigns—the man who, with a ragtag force, took Vincennes
from the British after a forced march through flooded country in
bitter weather—stood up shakily to welcome them. He seemed,
to Stephen's eye of the mind, immense and constricted in this
humble house. But the face was wizened and weathered, the hair
prematurely gray. A shawl fell away from his shoulders, and the
hand Stephen shook seemed palsied and empty of life. "Mr.
Stewart? You'd be Isaiah's boy, then." It was a flat statement,
spoken with deep strength. "Yes, I can see it in your bearing.
Proud man, Isaiah. He served with me at Kaskaskia." The
seamed face lifted, but only on one side. The realization then
came to Stephen like a blow. George Rogers Clark, the commander whom Isaiah Stewart worshipped like no mortal man,
was broken and sick, half paralyzed.

They settled down around him. An Indian woman brought
whiskey in a jug. They filled pipes and lit them, blowing smoke.
"So you're going up the Missouri, are ye, brother? How I envy
that."

"You'll go too, in time, General," Meriwether Lewis said.

The gray head wagged. "No, no, I've seen my last sunset
from a saddle, I'm afraid. And my last shining mountain, too.
I'm sick and broke and not worth a bullet in the brain. But, hell,
I can still drink whiskey, and that's bound to be worth something." Strangely, this was said without bitterness, as one would
recite a known fact. The voice retained its tone of command.
"I'm glad the President saw fit to push this, Meriwether. By
God, we've needed a real exploration of that territory, and from
what William here tells me you are the man to see it through."

"It's a joint command, General; your brother and me. I can
think of no man alive with whom I'd rather serve."

"Yes, yes, I know that. You're two old friends, and you'll get
along. That's the important thing, to get along. Don't let personal differences come between you, lads. That will break a com-

mand quicker than anything I know. Jealousy is corrosive to the human spirit, after all.''

"We won't let it happen.''

"You're in frequent contact with the President, Meriwether?''

"Yes, sir. He asked for regular reports by courier, and I'm sending them back. We'll be collecting specimens of flowers, plants, and wildlife. I shall try to send them by boat through New Orleans.''

"Good.'' The general chuckled. "I like to think I had a hand in inspiring this expedition. I urged Mr. Jefferson to make such an effort. A former member of my command, Mason Everett, went to Washington to speak with him about it.''

"He met with Mr. Everett,'' Lewis said. "I was the President's secretary at the time, and he asked me to take notes of their conversations. The visit certainly influenced Mr. Jefferson's thinking.''

George Rogers Clark grew thoughtful. "There's Indians up the Missouri that few white men have ever seen,'' he said. "There's Sioux and Mandan and Flathead. You got plains Indians and mountain tribes. And God knows what you'll find on the Pacific coast . . .''

Abruptly, he stopped speaking and was seized by a fit of deep, rattling coughing. They sat in embarrassed silence until he recovered. The general then drank off another whiskey and slapped his knee. "Imagine. The far Pacific! By God, it's history in the making, my lads. History in the making. I think you ought to give your expedition a name. Call it the Corps of Discovery. What do you think of that, eh? Yes, that would make a fine name, indeed.''

It was dark when they left him. They rode back down the hill in silence, each engrossed in his own thoughts.

The following morning the newly christened Corps of Discovery pushed off downriver for St. Louis. The chill winds of October sent dry leaves swirling down in showers of gold and scarlet on the hillsides, and the Indian summer was a thing of nostalgic beauty, aching in its splendor.

A cold wind moaned out of the northwest to slash at the gray, leafless woods. Stephen Stewart trudged along the riverbank, head down, cradling the heavy rifle on his arm. Behind him the other men of the party struggled along, cursing beneath their loads of animal carcasses killed on the morning hunt. Stephen rounded the last bend and saw the encampment ahead, its log huts huddled under a constant haze of blue smoke. A dog barked—Scammon, Captain Lewis' Newfoundland—and from a clearing he heard the measured shouted cadence of the daily drill. "Hup! Hup! Hup! Right turn . . . march! Hup two-three-four, hup two . . ."

He led the huntsmen around the edge of the clearing to the big mess hall, a structure of raw timbers and canvas built well back from the river. He then left them there under supervision of a corporal to finish skinning the meat. Still carrying the new rifle, he went in search of Captain Clark and found the red-haired commander in the headquarters tent, writing in a journal.

Clark looked up with a smile. "Well, did you have a good day's shooting? What do you think of it?" He nodded at the rifle on Stephen's arm.

"Damn fine gun," Stephen said. "To tell the truth, I had misgivings about loading a fifty-two caliber ball with a hundred grains of powder. I half expected her to blow up in my face." He hefted the weapon with admiration. "She's got real hitting power and shoots true."

"Good. Army ordnance made up three of 'em for Captain Lewis at Harper's Ferry before he left Virginia. He figured we'd need a heavier gun than the long rifle for the West. They've designated this one the eighteen-o-three. Do you think it'll stop buffalo?"

"I say she'll stop anything you shoot at," Stephen said.

Clark looked doubtful. "Maybe not everything. There's a kind of bear out here the fur traders and trappers talk about. Supposed to be the meanest, toughest critter on earth and the hardest to kill. Ordinary bullets either bounce off of him, or he absorbs them in his body . . ."

"The grizzly, you're talking about."

"Grizzly, silvertip, call him what you like, he's supposed to be a mean devil."

There was a knock on the front tent pole, and a soldier respectfully cleared his throat. "Cap'n, you said to tell you when we're ready."

Clark sighed. "Yes." He stood up, strapped a pistol around his blue-uniformed body and put on a heavy coat. Since December, when they had made camp here at the confluence of the

Mississippi and the Woods rivers, eighteen miles north of the village of St. Louis, both captains and all army enlisted men had worn uniforms. The officers invoked strong discipline, with garrisonlike daily drills, sentry challenges, and countersigns. There were now thirty army enlisted men in the Corps of Discovery, plus the two captains. Stephen and eight others were civilians. "You don't have to come out if you don't want to," Clark said. "I know how you feel about this sort of thing."

"No, I'll come."

They walked out into the cheerless afternoon. Behind the headquarters tent, the soldiers who had been drilling now stood in stiff, solemn ranks. Before them, kneeling in handcuffs and stripped to the waist in the cold, was a shivering young soldier.

Captain Clark positioned himself in front of the kneeling man and spoke gravely. "Private Manuel Fogg, you have been tried and found guilty of stealing whiskey belonging to the Corps of Discovery, getting drunk on duty, and being absent without leave. You were sentenced under the articles of military procedure to one hundred lashes on the bare back, fifty at a time. Each flogging is to be administered on each of two successive days. Such sentence is now to begin in the presence of this company. Do you have anything to say?"

The youth, who was nineteen, swallowed hard. "No, sir."

"Very well, then." Clark stepped back and nodded to a sergeant grasping a flail-type whip. "Proceed."

Stephen noted that the whip was quite supple, indicating that it probably had been warmed. It also did not have the beaded lead pellets on the thong ends, such as navy whips had, which would tear a man's back to shreds. The sergeant shook out the ends, raised the whip, and brought it whistling down. *Whack!*

Stephen winced, remembering the little bookdealer Zachary Palmer and his bitter aversion to such treatment of men. Even some of the Indians who had visited the winter camp of the Corps of Discovery were abashed. He remembered an Oto chief telling Captain Lewis through an interpreter, "We do not even whip our children. It is a barbaric custom." Still, both captains insisted on rigid discipline and military order, and whipping was part of the army life. Stephen's protests, having been duly registered, were ignored. But he did notice that the whip was sparingly used, and then not with full force. When this lashing was done, therefore, Private Fogg was able to put on his uniform coat and walk back to his quarters unaided.

"I don't think we'll have any more trouble with Private Fogg," Captain Clark muttered, and he returned to his tent.

It had been a bitter winter in the river camp. Now, in early March, the wind and sleet still howled down occasionally, and patches of snow clung to the hard ground. Personnel had undergone frequent changes as soldiers came and went, some of them as messengers, and the captains hired or replaced civilians for specialized duty.

An hour after the soldier's whipping, Captain Lewis returned by pirogue from downriver, rowed by six oarsmen. The captain was in full dress uniform, sword and all, for yet another visit to the Spanish commander of the St. Louis garrison, Don Carlos Duhault Delassus, governor of Upper Louisiana. The governor was a difficult man, pompous and hostile to Americans. Until the Louisiana Territory was officially turned over to the United States in due and proper ceremony, he had refused to permit Captain Lewis and his company to journey on the Missouri River, or anywhere in the territory. "Captain Lewees" and his band were viewed as dangerous intruders, not to be trusted. But this March 9, 1804, marked the end of the lengthy standoff; for this time, Lewis had gone to St. Louis to take part in a formal ceremony acknowledging the changeover to American control.

"Halloo, Captain Lewis!" shouted a pleased William Clark, watching the approach of his co-commander's pirogue.

"Hallooo, yourself!" came the reply.

Lewis stepped ashore dry-shod and in fine spirits, accepting the company's congratulations. "Now it's official," he declared.

"And that," said Captain Clark, "calls for a drink."

The mood of the camp changed abruptly now. A new sense of purpose and excitement swept the Corps of Discovery. While the actual order to strike out up the Missouri did not come, the commanders busily began winnowing down the force to its final form. "We'll need forty men going into Indian country. Any less is too few, more is unmanageable." There were more changes in manpower and duties, interpreters hired, fur traders questioned as they arrived from up the Missouri.

Stephen remained in civilian status, giving the captains more flexibility in his use. In addition to having charge of the armaments—rifles, handguns, swivel guns for the keelboat, pocket pistols, smoothbore rifles for Indian trade, powder and ammunition—he would be the master boatwright when repairs were needed and do surveying and map making ashore. This, at least, was the plan in theory. In practice, theory would quickly give way to harsh necessity, for Stephen and every other member of the Corps of Discovery.

March passed into April, bringing at last a warming trend. Gray trees burst into bud, wildflowers and dogwood bloomed in the woods, the grasslands along the river turned to rich green. Spring rains brought the Mississippi nearly to floodcrest, but the waters soon receded. May brought warm, balmy days and pleasant nights. They began to break camp and load supplies into the keelboat and two pirogues.

At last the day arrived. Excitement surged through the ranks as the Corps of Discovery formed up for inspection on the morning of May 14. "Gentlemen," Captain Lewis announced, "today is the day. By noon I want every man ready to board his assigned vessel. This expedition is going up the Missouri!" His words were drowned in a cheer.

The keelboat now spread its single sail. For added power it had been fitted with twenty-two sweep oars. The two pirogues also were oar-powered by six rowers. A gentle breeze stirred the stern flag as they stood out from the ruins of the Woods River camp and moved across the Mississippi. Ahead, the mouth of the Missouri made its presence known by a brown sweep of muddy water that poured into the Mississippi but refused to mix. As they progressed under cloudy skies, the muddy current strengthened. Still, oars and sail prevailed for the balance of daylight, with the aid of a following breeze. At dusk they were only a short distance up the Missouri and made camp on the shore. The clouds let go finally with a light drizzle. It was still falling the next morning as they boarded the boats once more, to meet the onslaught of the Missouri head on.

And now the wild, wicked nature of this river began to exert itself. Stephen, stationed as bow watch on the keelboat, was awed by the power of those muddy waters as they swept down as if bent on turning the expedition back. On that day they encountered the first of the deadly floating snags—gnarled tree trunks, wallowing along just beneath the roiling surface—that threatened to smash their hull and overturn the escorting pirogues. By the third day they found a new phenomenon: giant mudbanks, undercut by the mighty current, abruptly giving way and plunging into the river to float downstream with the torrent in a turgid, thickening mass. "Jesus!" breathed Pierre Cruzatte, a Frenchman taken on the previous fall at Louisville. "One of them cave-ins would do us in for sure."

Captain Clark mustered the men on deck and announced a new difficulty. "We're not making enough headway with the oars, and there's not enough wind for the sail. This means it's back to poling, lads. And when that fails, we'll just have to send men ashore to haul the keelboat upriver. I expect every man to do his best." With that, he summoned the three sergeants, including John Floyd, for a meeting to plot details.

The river twisted and turned in a fury of boiling mud and silt. Its rush raised a roar of water in such volume that men had to shout to be heard. So varying was the caprice of this mad torrent that on good days they could sometimes make thirty miles; on bad days they were lucky to make six. On some of the tricky bends there was no choice but to move in close to a towering mudbank for poling. As they struggled at the task, men kept fearful watch at the brooding brown masses rising above them.

Every man took his turn at the poles now, Stephen included. Putting aside the graph charts on which he kept a running map sketch, with compass headings, he went ashore with a gang of soldiers and civilian boatmen. Yard by yard, slipping and sliding in mud or scrambling around trees, they physically hauled the keelboat upriver. John Floyd moved ahead, wary of the banks. At dangerous spots they moved back from the shore with even longer lengths of tow rope, and suffered even more. Even the process of finding a decent campsite had its risks; if they happened to pick an island at midstream it might just break apart, with great chunks swirling downstream like some brown iceberg broken loose.

But if the river was wild, it was also provident. The land along the Missouri was rich and teeming with game; the waters provided an infinite harvest of fish. At intervals of peaceful travel, Captain Clark and Stephen took two riding horses ashore—which they had brought along on the keelboat—for hunting expeditions. The 1803 rifle quickly proved its expectations. They shot a fine elk, a great deal of smaller game, and even an occasional buffalo. For Stephen it was a sojourn in a wild, untamed land of incredible beauty. His eyes roamed hungrily over rich bottomlands and wooded slopes, now in the full green leaf of early summer. Regular hunting parties were detailed to move ashore each day, and he relished the chance to accompany them.

His most priceless possession, after the hunting rifle that could save his life, was a bundle of letters. Most of them bore the smooth, flowing handwriting of Jamie Catherine Colby, although a few were from his mother, and three were written in the heavy, crabbed script—splotched over and badly spelled—of his father. The letters had followed him down the Ohio, sent on flatboats and keelboats of Stewart Boat Works customers who delivered them faithfully if they came upon the distinctive Corps of Discovery keelboat, or handed them to other travelers bound for St. Louis if they did not. Some of the letters actually came in the leather pouch of the courier from Washington, who'd picked them up at the house of George Rogers Clark in Louisville. The roundabout routing and months of complicated travel seemed to make delivery at all nothing short of miraculous. But the letters stopped, of course, when they had made their departure from the Woods River camp. There would be no more until their return, two or three years hence.

Catherine's letters were chatty and warm. From them, he learned of the tremendous new surge in business and the heavy pressures on his father since his departure. It gave him a pang of guilt to read: "I'm afraid your mother worries too much about him. But he insists on doing everything himself now that you are gone, and his temper seems to get shorter and shorter with age. Even Burl is shoved aside and permitted only the most menial of work. Poor Burl! And as for Maybelle, Isaiah Stewart practically refuses to acknowledge that she exists at all. I hate to see this happening, for all of their sakes, as I know that you did . . ." Catherine's candor made him almost wish anew that he had never left Pittsburgh, but remained to attend to his responsibilities. And yet, in another vein, she wrote: "We are so proud of what you are doing. The word of the expedition is out now, and everybody is talking about the Louisiana Purchase. To think that our Stephen is part of this magnificent adventure! It takes my breath away. And your father basks in the light of his eldest sons." All of the letters arrived smudged and worn from much handling, and some appeared to have been dunked in a river. But he read them and reread them, often at night by the light of a fish-oil lantern in a mud-caked camp. And his heart expanded, knowing that Catherine cared.

And so the days followed days; the weeks slid by in toil and muddy torrent, with the men growing tougher and more resistant to suffering and toil. A month passed, then two. By mid-July,

Stephen was a mass of hard muscle, browned by the sun and
bearded for extra protection from the elements. His thinning
buckskins were bleached from sunshine, his boots so often
muddied that they took on the color of the Missouri itself. His
gray eyes squinted out from beneath a floppy wide-brimmed hat
of buffalo leather. Of the three '03 rifles, one was now permanently
assigned to him, as a crack shot second only to Georges
Drouillard, the hunter-interpreter who was the son of a French-
Canadian father and a Shawnee mother. As Stephen went ashore
more and more, the captains themselves took over the map-
making chores.

The midsummer heat bore down upon the river and the rolling
countryside. They had borne steadily westward on a twisting
course, but finally veered to the northwest. From passing fur
traders, floating downriver on rafts laden with pelts bound for St.
Louis, they learned that the River Platte was just ahead, a
powerful stream vomiting silt and mud into the Missouri. "Beyond
the Platte, you're in Indian country," said the fur traders.
Rugged, profane men, they drank expedition whiskey and palavered
far into the night in a strange mix of tongues.

Stephen and Drouillard went ashore the following morning
with three of the soldiers detailed for hunting. They shot a deer
and many wildfowl within two hours and returned to the river
with their burdens. After turning over the game to a shore party,
they moved inland again a quarter of a mile, heading for a rocky
promontory.

The sudden roar came from a stand of pine just below the
rocks. Stephen checked his rifle load and the other men dropped
into crouches, waiting. Then from behind the trees there emerged a
monster on four feet, ears laid back on a massive head, great
lumbering body moving rapidly down the slope toward them.
The fur of the bear was like no color any of them had ever seen,
brown and tipped at the ends with silver. Even from a distance,
his size was immense. Another roar exposed giant white fangs in
a gaping mouth.

"Good Lord!"

Stephen stood his ground, tracked the chest of the beast over
the '03's gunsight and carefully squeezed off a shot at less than a
hundred yards. The bear did not drop but seemed to absorb the
heavy ball into his body. His speed increased. Two more rifles
spoke, finding their targets, and still the rush came on. As a
man, they whirled around and took to their heels. "Fire your

weapons," Stephen shouted. "Get another ball into him!" The two remaining guns, both Kentucky long rifles wielded by expert marksmen, fired with no apparent effect. Bellowing now, the bear rose on his back legs, towering a massive eight feet, his noise seeming to make the earth tremble. It was a wild dash then, every man tearing toward the river and shouting to warn the shore party still dismembering the early kill. Stephen would never know afterward how it was done, but the French Canadian Drouillard somehow managed to prime, reload, and ram home patch and ball in his '03 rifle at a dead run. At the river the men scattered like fleeing birds. Two of them plunged into the swift water and started swimming for their lives. The bear plunged after them. While Stephen and the others watched in stupefied fascination, not thinking to reload their weapons too, Drouillard took careful aim at thirty yards. This time the ball plowed into the great head. The bear stopped swimming, seemed to try to turn back to shore and sank in a spreading mass of scarlet bubbles.

"That, son," said Drouillard gravely, spitting tobacco juice into the mud, "was one mean grizzly."

It took eight men using a jerry-rigged block and tackle to haul the monster out of the Missouri and onto the deck of the keelboat. When they opened the body, they found five rifle balls lodged in the chest area, two of them in the lungs. The two great upper fangs and hide were given to Drouillard. The French Canadian handed one of the fangs to Stephen. "Put that on a thong around your neck as a reminder," he said.

"A reminder?"

"To reload your rifle next time."

Stephen sputtered and began to laugh. The laughter became so convulsive that he had to sit down, wiping his eyes and gasping for breath. The others stared, as if he had lost his wits. When the seizure subsided, Drouillard asked curiously, "Now what was that all about?"

"I remembered something that happened years ago to my older brother Nathan," Stephen replied with another giggle. "And I told him the same damned thing."

A week later they passed the mighty Platte as it swept into the Missouri, disgorging sediment. And then one day they saw Indians following their progress along the eastern shore, on foot. Captain Clark smoked his pipe and studied the newcomers, who neither beckoned nor called out. "Otos, more'n likely," the captain said. "Or Missouri." He turned away from the gunwale and went aft to where Meriwether Lewis was writing in his journal. "I guess it's time to break out the trinkets," Clark said, "and call a council."

They met the Otos on a high bluff overlooking the river, having lit a grass fire to signal the main body of the tribe to parley. These were the first wild Indians Stephen had ever seen. He felt a disappointment at their seemingly placid natures and craving for whiskey and barter. John Floyd stroked his chin, listening to Captain Clark's formal speech presenting the greetings of the Great White Father in Washington. "Just don't turn your back on 'em," the sergeant said. "An Indian'll steal you blind."

The council talk and whiskey drinking went on late into the night, and the following morning the captains learned that these Otos were merely the vanguard of an even larger official welcoming party. Captain Lewis was impatient to move on, but was restrained by Drouillard. The French Canadian stressed the importance of cementing friendship with tribes living this far downriver, on the chance that their help might be needed on the return journey. Lewis relented, but he lost none of his anxiety to make contact with the next tribe upriver, the Omaha.

Finally, irritated, the captain spoke to Stephen:

"Take four men, Mr. Stewart, and go on ahead as an advance party. Make a powwow with the Omaha, if you can. Take two canoes and presents with you. We'll follow along when we're finished here."

Stephen was delighted. With Captain Clark's consent, John Floyd came along bringing a congenial crew, including the fiddle-playing *engagé* Pierre Cruzatte. They loaded the canoes with extra provisions and weapons and pushed off. Compared to the slow progress of the keelboat, the canoes fairly flew, slicing lightly through the sluggish current in response to their paddling. Within two days they were in Omaha country, as delineated by the Oto chiefs, and making overnight camp on the east bank of the river. There was a clear creek here, its mouth partially blocked by an old broken beaver dam. Working the canoes past the dam, they drew them onto a grassy, shallow bank, posted a lookout, and went inland a few hundred yards to set fire to the prairie grass. Tongues of flame raced through the dry growth, sending smoke billows into the clear sky in the customary Indian signal for gathering and parley. Then they checked weapons and provisions and settled down to wait.

This was good land, with a varied topography and natural growth. Along the floodplain to the south, the trees were mainly scrub cottonwood and willow. Here, Stephen recognized ash and hackberry, walnut, mulberry, linden, and sycamore. The higher land away from the river was gently rolling, with lush plains of grass and wooded copses that looked, from a distance, like oak and blue ash. Here and there stood a mighty sycamore, its bark splotched in grayish browns and white beneath a broad green canopy. There had been a long period without rain, however, and the undergrowth was tinder dry and browning. Occasional splotches of bare earth lay cracked and fissured from the sun.

Stephen, Sergeant Floyd and one of the privates, Harrison, whiled away several hours seining the creek for fish. The catch was marvelously abundant, each pulling of the net yielding a fine wiggling catch of catfish, bass, salmon, and perch. By late afternoon they had caught more than a score of fish in various sizes and also collected a quantity of large mussels from the mudflats. John Floyd changed the lookouts and kindled a cookfire. Soon the savory aroma of baking fish wafted over the camp. They ate voraciously, pulling apart the flaky white meat with their fingers and stuffing it into their mouths. When every man had eaten his fill, there was still plenty left over. This they put aside for a later meal. John Floyd drew a small flask of whiskey from his pack, which quickly passed from hand to hand. Pipes were lit, and Cruzatte unpacked his fiddle.

They stretched out on their backs above the creek. Sunlight came at a steep slant now, bathing the plains in a glow of burnished gold. Stephen breathed in the mingled odors of grass, river water, and pipe smoke. Cupping his head in his hands, he gazed up into a sky streaked with blue, gold and vermillion, sweeping to infinity. Behind them, the smoke pillar towered at a steep slant away from the camp as the fire ate eastward from the river. By turning his head slightly, Stephen could see the lookout standing motionless on a rock, rifle cradled, staring across the rolling plain. Cruzatte's fiddle made a plaintive pattern of sound.

John Floyd sighed with contentment. "This is God's country. The great, silent, open land. Imagine, as far as you can see, nothing but land. And it's there for the taking. I always wanted to have me a small spread, some pigs and cows, a horse and some chickens. Get me a wife to share it with. I grew up in a village back east, Lancaster, Pennsylvania.''

"That's nice country, I hear. Rich country.''

"True. But most of it's taken now. Lancaster ain't like what you see here, wide open and free. And the beauty of it don't catch in a man's throat the way this does. Know what I mean?''

"I think I do.''

"So after this army hitch, I'm gettin' out and try to make a life of it. I've got a little saved up and I'm willing to work hard. But first . . .''

"Yes?''

"First, I want to see me a mountain,'' John Floyd said. "A real mountain, with ice and snow on top, all glistening in the sunlight.''

Stephen laughed. "I've dreamed of that, too, since I was a kid. The shining mountain, I called it.''

"That's right. That's what I mean. The shining mountain.'' John Floyd plucked a blade of grass and chewed on it thoughtfully. "And what about you, Stephen?''

"Me?''

"What do you intend to do, once we get back from this? *If* we get back . . .''

Stephen chuckled. "We'll get back all right, John. I've got a lot of confidence in the captains. They're good men, and they keep tight discipline. We'll get back, all right.''

"Sometimes I wonder.'' The sergeant knocked his pipe against the heel of his boot.

"I've got somebody waiting for me,'' Stephen mused. "Her name is Catherine. Her hair's the color of that gold in the sky up there. She's in my mind all the time. I can close my eyes and see her face.''

"You're lucky. I haven't got anybody waiting for me. I wish I did have.''

"You will, John. You'll find the right girl—''

"Here they come!''

Stephen sat up quickly. The lookout was pointing to the northeast. Cruzatte's music stopped, and he put his fiddle aside. John Floyd jumped up and grabbed one of the '03 rifles. Harrison came running from the creek, where he had been securing the canoes.

There were three of them, rangy, slightly bowlegged men wearing breechclothes, ragged moccasins, shirts fashioned from animal skins, and hawks' feathers in their braided hair. About them there was the look of hard times. One warrior's face was peppered with deep pockmarks. Two of the men might have been in their early thirties; the third was older, thinner, and wore a more distinctive headdress. This one rode a spavined pony while his companions walked. They stopped a short distance from the campfire in gathering twilight. Stephen raised his hand in greeting and beckoned them forward.

"Them's Omaha, all right," said Cruzatte. "I've seen 'em before and know a little of the lingo. But, by damn, they've been sorely used. I don't remember no Omaha looking that scraggly before."

The Indians came forward warily. Stephen made friendship signs and offered presents—a hand mirror, a beaded necklace of seashells, a red bandana. To the older man, who appeared to be a minor chief, he gave an old army jacket with brass buttons. A smile lit the Indian's face, displaying toothless gums. He nodded and grunted something. Cruzatte grunted in reply. "He say you are the tallest white man he ever seen, and thanks you for the gift." There were more grunts. Cruzatte smiled. "He asks for whiskey."

"No whiskey yet. Maybe later," Stephen said. "Tell him we would like to vist his village tomorrow. Ask him if they will escort us to the village."

It was agreed.

They gave their leftover fish to the Indians, who fell to the meal ravenously. Harrison brought a fresh catch up from the creek, which was quickly cooked and served all around. They finished eating in darkness, squatting on the earth around the campfire. The Indians eyed the weapons curiously, pointing and nodding. Stephen did not offer a closer inspection. Finally, with the guard duty arranged for the night, they gave the visitors buffalo blankets. As the men rolled up to sleep, Stephen lay for a long time looking up at the night sky ablaze with stars. Something John Floyd had said troubled his mind, but he could not recall immediately what it was. He drifted off to sleep thinking of Catherine. And then, half in dream, he remembered the sergeant's words. *"If* we get back."

They were up at dawn, sharing a breakfast of fried meat, gooseberries, huckleberries, and wild plums foraged from a nearby woods. They broke camp, dragged the canoes into a brushy thicket and built a cairn of stones. Atop the stones

Stephen secured a note for the main party. The sun was already an hour high when they set off behind the Indians across the fire-blackened grassland toward the northeast. For all their seedy appearance, the Indians stepped out at a rapid pace. Stephen, wearing his buckskins and encumbered with rifle and heavy pack, soon was feeling the strain. By the time they covered five miles to the Omaha camp, the white men were puffing heavily and drenched in sweat.

The Omaha village was a pitiable symbol of the bad times befalling what had been a proud and warlike tribe. Caught in the bend of a creek, shaded by several stands of sickly trees, it consisted of rude shelters built of logs and hides around a central ceremonial campfire area grown weedy from neglect. Stephen and his companions soon found, however, that for all their poverty the Omaha were a hospitable people and—once their initial shyness was overcome—even personable. Harrison and Gallin, a half-breed French soldier, went off to hunt with the rifles and killed a fine elk, a buffalo, and a good quantity of wildfowl. Omaha men rushed out to help retrieve the game, and the squaws began preparing a feast for the occasion. By the time Stephen broke out the whiskey jugs, the bonds of friendship were being forged.

Cruzatte proved to be a vital link. Not only was he a maker of fiddle music, he also could interpret enough of the Omaha language to be understood. Stephen and his companions sat cross-legged around the council fire, smoking pipes and talking with Blood Feather, who had been the Omaha medicine man and now was the chief of what remained of the tribe. A squat, wizened Indian with clear eyes and prominent cheekbones, Blood Feather amplified his words with sign language. Cruzatte translated: "He say four years past a great disease swept over the rivers and the plains. A pox, it sounds like. Yes. A pox. This great disease sickened the Omaha. It spared neither the baby in its swaddling furs nor the young maiden nor the warrior nor the chief. By the hundreds they grew fevered and broke out in great running sores that reeked of corruption and perished. Even the medicines of the medicine men did no good, and the Great Spirit was deaf to their pleas. They died. In all, perhaps two thousand died including the best of the tribe. Even the chief medicine man died, leaving only Blood Feather as both medicine man and chief. Now they are a handful, reduced to living like this. They are at the mercy of their neighbors, the Sioux, the Otos and the

Missouri, who insult them and prey upon their women and steal what horses they have left."

They roasted the meat in great quarters, drank whiskey, and danced half the night away. Then they rolled in the furs and slept, with one man on guard. Stephen awoke in the first light of morning to find even the guard snoozing at his post. Suddenly wary, he came to his feet and looked around anxiously. Their guns were all in their places. The sacks of presents and cask of whiskey seemed undisturbed. Nothing appeared to be missing. Angrily, Stephen aroused the sleeping guard, a youth named Fairweather. The fellow was surly and indifferent, knuckling sleep from his eyes. "I'll have to report you to the commanders for this," Stephen said. Fairweather shrugged. "Suit yourself." His breath gave off the stale odor of whiskey from the night before. The whiff of it brought Stephen up short; abruptly he realized that it was his own fault, for he had been too lenient with the drink.

Nearby, a form stirred in a buffalo robe. Stephen looked down into the hard eyes of Blood Feather. Stephen smiled. Blood Feather stood up, still wrapped in the robe. Rousing Cruzatte to interpret, Stephen said, "I am grateful to Blood Feather for valuing our possessions and seeing that no harm came to them." The Indian frowned slightly and seemed puzzled. He said, "What do you think would happen to them?" Stephen shrugged. Blood Feather walked away into the bush.

Even the little creek became a food source. If the Missouri River, wild and unruly, was a provident storehouse, so was its tributaries, no matter how small. The creek yielded up small but succulent fish to the white man's nets. So abundant was the catch that even the Indians, who had no nets, were impressed. Carrying his '03 rifle, Stephen also went on a solitary hunt. It took him a while to realize that he was being followed. Turning swiftly, rifle ready, he saw an Indian boy about eleven years old, crouching beside a bush. When Stephen beckoned, the boy ran away. But when he resumed walking, the follower followed again.

It became almost like a game between them. Stephen would walk a short distance, aware that the boy was about thirty yards behind. Then he would stop, hoping the boy would catch up. But the boy stopped too. Finally he gave up stopping and went on without looking back. In time, he could hear the occasional break of a twig, indicating the distance between them had closed a bit. He shot two wild turkeys, but left them unretrieved. At last he came to a chuckling stream and sat down to drink water and rest. The boy came up short of breath, laboring under the weight of the turkeys. Stephen laughed and took one of the birds, tucking it into his belt, and handed the boy a chunk of pemmican to eat. After that, the youngster walked by his side back to the Omaha camp.

"His name Running Wolf," Cruzatte said. "He is the nephew of Blood Feather, the medicine man chief. You've made an important friend."

Wherever Stephen went after that, Running Wolf was not far away, watching with round-eyed interest. When Stephen dismantled portions of the '03 rifle for cleaning, the boy crept up beside him and watched. Stephen taught him how to handle the seine for fishing and how to load and fire one of the fusee smoothbore rifles. He gave the boy a bone-handled knife that was the envy of the camp. After two days they were able to communicate in limited sign language. When Stephen sat down to write of the day's events in his pocket diary, Running Wolf sat in rapt silence, watching the words scribbling down on paper. Stephen was able to tell him that this was a sign language, too, only in written form with symbols representing thoughts.

And still there was no rain. The grasslands parched and browned for want of water. Even the trees were tinder dry. Occasional thunderheads rose on the horizon, flickering lightning, but they did not release their rain. The sultry heat pressed down. Even the log huts of the Omaha had dried out. Stephen saw that the Indian women were careful of their cookfires, clearing away sticks and clumps of grass.

It was not cookfire sparks, however, but a freakish lightning bolt that started the disastrous fire in the Omaha camp.

Stephen and his companions had settled down for the night. As usual, he removed only his boots for sleeping and was otherwise fully dressed in buckskins. They were on their blankets, out of doors. The Omaha men also preferred sleeping in the open air, but the squaws and children slept in the huts.

All evening, heat lightning had played over the distant prairies, making a flickering fireworks display that diverted Stephen's mind from his sweaty discomfort. He had dozed off to sleep when a loud report, like a cannon shot, exploded in sparse trees surrounding two of the huts. There was an acrid smell of smoke and electricity. Flames shot up in the high grass behind the huts, and a gust of wind swept them quickly into the flimsy structures. Even the lookout was caught unawares, on the far side of the camp. Jarred from sleep, Stephen was confused by the sudden pandemonium. Already the huts were wrapped in flames and screams came from the fire. Indians and white men rushed to help. Several women and children came staggering out of the inferno.

By instinct, Stephen did not dash instantly to the fire. Pulling on his boots and gathering up his blanket, he ran to the creek instead. He doused the blanket and his own clothing in the stream and then sprinted the thirty yards to the flames.

An ancient woman was screaming and pointing to one of the huts. Cruzatte shouted, "It's the boy! He's in there!" Stephen wrapped his head and upper body in the wet blanket and plunged into the flames. Breaking through, he groped wildly in smoke-filled blindness. His hands found a body and grabbed. He tried to take a breath, choked, and without trying to find the doorway again simply crashed his body through a fiery side wall. He hit the ground rolling in a shower of flame and sparks, came to his feet again, lurched into the welcoming darkness. Around him, hands snatched the flaming blanket from his body. Stephen collapsed in a fit of coughing, and the smoldering body of the boy rolled free. Indian women came running with full buckets from the creek to slosh water over both of them. They swarmed over the smoking form of Running Wolf, keening and wailing by the light of the flames. Stephen could do nothing but cough, and it seemed that his lungs would come out. Not for a quarter of an hour was he able to stand again with the help of Sergeant Floyd, who led him to the creek. "That was the damndest thing I ever saw, boy," Floyd kept muttering. "You could have been killed for sure. Damndest thing I ever saw . . ."

Two squaws and an infant were dead. One of the braves was burned about the face and hands. Running Wolf was terribly burned. Great pieces of cooked skin peeled from his back and legs. Burns of varying severity ranged over much of his body. The squaws laid him out on a soft bed of hide, wailing the Omaha death chant. The boy stared up at the paling night sky, jaws clenched agains the pain. He made no sound. Stephen went to him and looked into his face, but there was no flicker of recognition. At last Blood Feather came. He wore the ceremonial buffalo headdress and the sacred black panther skin of the medicine man. With a grunt, he ordered the women away,

sprinkled powder around the body of his nephew, and shook a
snake rattle over him. An ancient squaw hovered near the
medicine man. Blood Feather took a large pouch from around his
neck, opened it and shook out a mass of grayish dried herbs.
These he handed to the squaw, who took them and went away.
Then the medicine man knelt beside the body of his nephew,
looked to the gray wash of dawn and began a wailing, guttural
chant to the accompaniment of a tom-tom.

"The boy'll be dead before night, poor devil," muttered
Sergeant Floyd. "The sooner the better. No human can survive
burns like that. I seen men die with burns half that bad."

"Don't be too sure," said Cruzatte. "These redskins have got
their ways."

Stephen turned away, sickened and troubled of mind. Why
couldn't he have moved faster? Why had he gone to the creek
and wet down, when every second was vital? He cursed himself
for a fool and a laggard. And in his consciousness there burned
the round eyes of his young friend, listening and watching the
wondrous things of the white man's magic. Well, there was
nothing white man's magic could do for him now, nothing
anybody could do.

The keelboat arrived the following morning and was met by a
small party of Omaha who led the captains and half a dozen
soldiers to the camp. To the surprise of Stephen and his men,
Running Wolf had survived all the previous day and the night.
And still he lay on the soft animal skin. His burns now were
covered in a wet compost of the herbs, which raised a foul odor.
And still Blood Feather chanted his doleful chant, shook the
sacred rattles and swayed to the beat of the tom-tom. The old
squaw kept replacing the composts with ones that had been
freshly wetted; and each time she did this, her fingers plucked
away more loose shreds of skin from the boy's body. Stephen
winced, watching, knowing that the pain must be intense. He
wanted to shout out to them to stop this madness and leave the
boy to die in peace! But he kept his silence.

The captains were greeted by a subchief named Minniwha.
Stephen described the disaster, and Sergeant Floyd recounted the
heroic rescue of the Indian boy. Captain Lewis had had some
medical training in Philadelphia prior to starting the journey. His
offer to do what he could for Running Wolf was politely
declined. Minniwha insisted on going ahead with the welcoming
ceremony, saying that it was Blood Feather's wish. Captain

Clark then distributed the usual gifts and made his speech, interpreted by the Frenchman Pierre Dorian. "We have journeyed many marches up this great river to the land of the Omaha, our friends. We come with personal gifts and greetings from your new White Father in Washington City, President Jefferson. He instructs me to bind our peoples in perpetual friendship and to assure the Omaha that he will look after their interests, honoring their tribe, their lands and hunting grounds..." The Omaha braves and elders sat on their blankets, nodding with stoic courtesy at the words which none of them could really comprehend. Afterward, the captains handed out more trinkets, beads and cloth goods and opened a small cask of whiskey. That night they feasted again, but the celebration was forced, for in the background sounded the ceaseless wail of Blood Feather as he ministered to a nephew who was obviously dying.

They made ready for departure the following morning. To Stephen, it seemed impossible that so much had happened in just five days with the Omaha. He wished that he could say farewell to Running Wolf, but the eyes of the boy were glazed and unresponsive. Stephen went to Winniwha and handed him a smoothbore fusee rifle and sack of powder, ball, and flint. "This is for the boy," he said. "And if he cannot use it, then it shall pass to Blood Feather." The rifle was decorated with a distinctive serpentine design of hammered brass, prized by Indians. The Indian accepted the weapon with an impassive nod, along with a hunting knife which Stephen presented for his own use. Captain Clark shouted for the men to move out, and Stephen had to trot to catch up. They marched back to the river, trailed by playful Indian boys and several barking dogs.

The Missouri eased now, beyond the Platte. The going continued to be against the current, but there were fewer bank cave-ins, sandbars and submerged tree snags to bedevil them. Many of the men were ill, complaining of colds, sunstroke, and boils. Captain Lewis was kept busy treating the sick. A herd of buffalo was spotted to the northeast and a hunting party sent out to restock their supply of fresh meat. Stephen accompanied the hunters, loading his '03 rifle with a hundred-grain charge of powder. They also took along the two horses. The buffalo proved to be skittish and veered away from the main body of men advancing on foot. Stephen and John Floyd managed to circle the herd on horseback, turn them toward the hunting party and—with constant circling and whooping—set them into milling confusion. Slowing to a trot, Stephen moved in close to a huge bull, placed the muzzle of his rifle against its head, and pulled the trigger. The gun boomed, recoiling heavily. The great beast fell to its knees and rolled over in a heap. They made three kills, quartered and skinned the animals, and brought the meat back to the river tied to the horses.

John Floyd was not well. Pale and weak, the sergeant complained of a sharp pain in his lower abdomen. Captain Lewis said it sounded to him like bilious colic. He bled the sergeant and dosed him with niter, followed by a stiff jolt of whiskey laced with sugar. It seemed to help. That evening they roasted the meat onshore and, to lift the spirits of the men, Cruzatte tuned his fiddle and struck up a merry reel.

"I'm not going to lay here and suffer," John Floyd shouted. "I'm a'goin' to shake a leg!" The sergeant got to his feet and started dancing. Several others joined him in a joyous, spinning dance that set hands to clapping. Stephen laid aside the journal in which he had been writing. He was glad for the distraction, because he had been describing the events in the Omaha camp. Taking a long pull from the whiskey jug, he clapped hands in time to the music. It was good to see John Floyd feeling better again; the sergeant's illness, on top of everything else, had added to his gloomy mood.

John Floyd spun out of the dance, suddenly short of breath. He came over to Stephen and sat down heavily. "Whew! That took the wind out of my sails." The sergeant's face had gone white again, and he clutched at his stomach. "It must be all them fish we ate among the Omahas." He took a long drink from the whiskey jug and lay down, breathing heavily. He remained there after the merriment had subsided. As the fire died down, the sergeant became feverish and chilled. Stephen brought a buffalo robe and spread it over him. Floyd thanked him.

"You'll feel better in the morning," Stephen said.

In the morning, John Floyd's condition had worsened. His pulse was weak, and he could keep no food in his stomach or bowels. They did not travel that day but remained in the camp, the alarming turn of events casting a pall over the company. Late in the day, the young sergeant asked for Captain Clark.

The red-haired captain knelt down. "What is it, son?"

"I'm going away," Sergeant Floyd whispered. "I want you to write me a letter."

The captain nodded. "Do you want to do it now?"

"Later, maybe. I'm too weak just now."

"All right. Whenever you say."

Stephen, Harrison, and Cruzatte took turns sitting beside the patient. They made a weak fish broth, hoping to give him some strength. They shot a fine mallard and made a stew. The sergeant refused it all and steadily weakened. By the middle of the afternoon, there was a rattle in his throat. He opened his eyes and, with feverish intensity, said to Stephen: "Tell them to put me on that bluff yonder."

And then he died.

They buried John Floyd on the bluff overlooking the Missouri and a secondary stream that angled in from the east. Captain Lewis spoke the words over the grave. "Lord, we commit to your everlasting care the soul of our deceased brother, John Floyd, whom you chose to take from our midst so young in life. We honor him and love him." The late afternoon sun struck fire to the river and bathed the peaceful countryside in its glow.

Stephen had never seen a more beautiful sunset.

The following morning they pushed upriver again, toward Sioux country. Their objective now was to reach the village of the Mandan, on the upper river, before the first snowfall.

Ahead lay the great northwest and the shining mountains.

V

The problem was there, chronic and deep, and anyone could see that it originated with Isaiah. Perhaps it was his age or the onset of some new and pervasive dark humor. But the man she knew and loved, had loved all these years, was changed. He drove himself and others; he was abusive and belligerent; he suffered periods of dark despair, he drank. They slept now in separate bedrooms.

"Mother, I hate him. I absolutely hate him, and I can't help myself." Maybelle was talking, her face streaked with tears.

They had had another row, father and daughter. It had left her flushed and angry. "Sometimes I just want to leave this place."

Martha winced. "Please. You're speaking about your father." How many times had she said that to this child, over how many years? She tried to keep her voice subdued, lest someone should hear them. It was a foolish habit; everybody knew anyhow. But Catherine was nearby, somewhere, and old Charlie puttered in the kitchen, and the windows of the house were open. But Maybelle would not follow her lead, would not speak quietly and be mollified. "If I even look at a young man, he accuses me of moral turpitude. Mother, I'm an *adult*. He thinks I'm unclean. But I am also his daughter, his flesh and blood. And then there's Burl. He treats Burl as if he's less than dirt..."

"Stop it, I say. *Stop it!*"

Martha Stewart's voice ricocheted through the house. She had not intended to speak so loudly and in that tone, had never spoken in that tone. It was the voice of a fishwife. Both of them suddenly stood quite still, staring at one another. Martha was sickened inside.

"I—I'm sorry. I didn't mean..."

Maybelle turned and walked out of the house, slamming the door behind her.

It was wrong, all wrong. Once they had had peace and love in this house. Martha returned to her sewing room, where the argument with Maybelle had begun. Standing there, in this very personal place with its chintz curtains and rose-covered wallpaper brought all the way from Philadelphia, with the sewing things and the needlepoint so intimately hers, she knew again the nagging despair. It was almost an alien presence, intruding on the order of their lives, and she could give it no name. The thoughts tumbled through her mind, about Isaiah, about the children, about her. Had she gone wrong? Should she have been stronger with him, less submissive? How could she make life better for Isaiah? And what—in God's name, what—was happening to the man who was her husband?

Martha stepped to the window and looked out into the busy compound, at the freight wagons hub-to-hub, the piles of lumber, cargo, and supplies, the constant clutch of customers waiting to do business, the boatyard. My heavens, did they have to have all this in order to be happy? Was it necessary to control the world before Isaiah would be satisfied? He was driving himself too hard. He never caught up, never even had a Sunday for relaxing any more.

She pushed the curtain aside and watched as Maybelle untied the young dappled gray mare, leaped astride the animal bareback and galloped through the wide double gate toward the town. Her red hair flew in the wind, her back was straight and she was beautiful. Martha thought: Isaiah Stewart, are you blind?

Maybelle knew that her mother was watching, but it did not matter. Nothing mattered now. There was no need to think about it or to look back. She let the mare gallop. Chickens, goats, and dogs scurried out of the way as the horse thundered up Water Street. Finally, Maybelle slowed her to turn up toward the square. As crowds thickened, she reined in and let the mare walk, blowing and streaked with sweat. The gallop had distracted Maybelle somewhat and stabilized her mind.

It was such a deep and chronic thing with Father, almost unreal. Since her childhood, he seemed to resent having a daughter instead of a fourth son. Isaiah Stewart also insisted that she act and think and be subdued like a female. Once he had spanked her, at the age of twelve, just for going riding up the river with a boy. Isaiah had been drinking whiskey, and to this day she could see the fury in his eyes and hear his voice. "Damned little slut!" Well, it had gone far enough now; a life like this could no longer be endured. She put her hand to her cheek, felt the slight mottled swelling there, and made her decision.

Maybelle came to the Irontown Inn, a squat, three-storied stone building a block from the courthouse. Tethering the mare to a hitching post, she walked through a lobby filled with men—loungers and traveling drummers and riverboat hands—aware of the admiring stares. Deliberately, she exaggerated the sway of her behind. She climbed the stairs to the second floor and knocked at the door of room 23. The man who answered was dark and handsome, with snapping eyes and flaring nostrils. He was in shirtsleeves and trousers. Behind him, she could see the rumpled bed and half-empty whiskey bottles on a dresser. His name was Ahmad Ahzeeb, and he was an Arab drummer in yard goods.

"So you have come back, my flower," he said.

"I've decided, Ahmad," she said. "I'll go with you downriver next week."

She stepped past him into the room, strangely excited by his mingled odors of sweat, whiskey, hair dressing and cigars. Ahzeeb smiled and closed the door.

Catherine had watched Maybelle go and felt intuitively that this time she might not return. The quarrel between father and daughter that morning had been worse than any that had gone before, their shouting heard all over the compound. Isaiah had called her a trollop and a whore for being seen with an Arab salesman at the Irontown Inn the night before. "That hell hole is no place for my daughter!" Isaiah's face was flushed and bloated beneath his shock of snow-white hair. And then he had slapped her across the face.

The man had become obsessive this past year. Catherine remembered what Stephen once told her about the Stewarts, quoting his complex father: "A Stewart has a lust. The blood is a concoction of wild Scot and Englishman, spiked with other fiery brew and mixed at fever heat. There's also good Stewarts and bad, and even God doesn't understand the bad ones." Now, with both of the favorite sons gone, the bitter truth of this was emerging in the father. It was as if in his headlong rush to make life perfect, and his children perfect, he'd lost touch with reality. Those offspring failing to meet Isaiah's standards of worth, moreover, were cruelly shunted aside.

"Catherine, the mail." Burl came in, carrying his delivery pouch. The office screen door banged shut behind him. As usual, the least favored of the brothers was untidy and needed a shave. He had come from town with the buckboard wagon, and there was liquor on his breath. "I brought the newspaper. And"—he gave a conspiratorial wink—"there's a letter . . . "

"A letter?" Catherine flushed and stood up. "What kind of a letter? You mean a letter for me, personally?"

Burl grinned. "You're Miss Jamie Catherine Colby, ain't you? Of course, now, it could be for some other Jamie Catherine Colby—"

"Stephen. Stephen wrote me a letter!" She ran around the desk, reaching. Burl laughed and backed away, holding the letter aloft. "Burl Stewart," she cried, "you give me that letter!" He relented, and Catherine ripped open the soiled and travel-worn envelope. It contained but a few lines on a single sheet of paper, headed "St. Louis" and written in apparent haste:

"Catherine. We are back from a journey beyond my poor

ability to describe. Expedition recovering for a few days here in St. Louis. Am well, but skinny as a tent pole and twice as tough. Got to give this to a man pushing off on the river. Home soon. Love to all. Steph.''

Three years. He was now gone nearly three years!

She rushed from the office into the house. "Miz Martha! Miz Martha! It's from Stephen!''

Martha Stewart came from her sewing room. Catherine saw that she had been weeping. She took the letter with trembling hands and read it. "Thank God,'' Martha said. "Oh, thank the Lord!''

The news from Stephen bouyed everybody's spirits. Even Isaiah Stewart joined them at the supper table for the first time in a fortnight. He read the letter over and over, tracing the words with his fingers. "Well, now,'' he muttered, "if that don't beat all. He's coming back. The boy's safe and coming home.''

"That's right, Isaiah,'' Martha said gently.

"The boy's coming home.''

Catherine reached across the table and squeezed Isaiah's hand. "I'm glad you're happy,'' she said.

Maybelle did not come home that night.

Long after midnight, Catherine lay in the bed of her downstairs room listening to footfalls from Isaiah's bedroom overhead. She knew that Martha must be awake too, and she ached for their suffering.

Why, she thought, must we make our own lives such torments?

But the man whose pacing kept her awake thought only of himself and his outrage. Isaiah Stewart glared into the shadows of a room lit by moonbeams and peopled with ghosts. He remembered his father, the gruff, hardhanded man who had beaten him in a drunken rage. Isaiah had been a lad of seven, ready to go to the mines with his brother Bartholemew, who was but a couple of years older. The old man had staggered home to their smoke-blackened hovel and laid about him with those hands, smashing anything within reach and bellowing like a bull. "Take that, ye squirts. And that! Living milksops ye are, and not worth a farthing out of me.'' Now, in the shadows, he saw the glittering eyes, heard the drunken voice, felt the blows afresh. Strange, how such things could come back to haunt a man.

Well, Bartholemew was doing all right, he supposed, with a fishing fleet and a son of his own at Cape Cod. Occasionally there was a letter from his brother, crudely written and taking

months to arrive at Pittsburgh. Why he bothered, Isaiah did not
know, for he never wrote in return. From the letters, however, he
knew that Bartholemew's wife had died, and the boy was
half-grown and working his father's fishing boats along the
Grand Banks. So be it. A son should be about his father's
business.

Pace, pace, pace. The thoughts sifted through his mind like
shadows. A goodly son, they whispered. A goodly son, smart and
strong. He, Isaiah, had sired two. They would make their marks,
God's blood. And the third? A runt, soft and addled in the head;
always was. Not a Stewart of the good blood, but a Stewart of
the bad. Burl should have been drowned as a pup in a tote sack.
Too bad they did not condone such practices. And the girl was
worse. A slut. A bad one, rotten to the core. And now she's
gone, and good riddance to bad rubbish. Ah, the pain she'd
caused her father; pain, pain, pain. And what did she care, for
all that? Not a snap. Not a fig.

The notion seemed to echo in a whiper, among the shadows of
this room. A mocking whisper. "Not a snap. Not a fig. Not a
snap. Not a fig . . ."

And the rage engulfed him afresh, engulfed his mind and his
soul with its black consuming bile, engulfed him and would not
let him breath. The rage poured from his mind down into his
chest, filling it—filling it so full, well nigh to bursting.

He paced until the dawn turned the window to silver. And then
he dressed in his suit, with a cravat and high hat and shiny
shoes, and went down to the porch to see the first workmen into
the compound.

He loved her. It was as simple and inescapable as that. Burl
loved her and longed to be with her and wished fervently that she
could love him back. He tried to imagine consciously when this
feeling had begun, but could not. It was something that had
grown in his heart and mind like a flower, a flower having both
sweet scent and prickly thorns, that entranced and beguiled and
also caused pain. At night he lay on his cot in the small room
behind the house and thought: Catherine, Catherine, can't you
see? At other times he watched her furtively from afar. Little
things about her stabbed him with delicious pain. The tall,
lithesome sway of her walk. The shine of her hair in sunlight,
like spun gold. The merry flash of blue eyes when she laughed.

The fullness of her mouth. The creamy white smoothness of her skin. Once, when he brought mail to the office, Catherine leaned over to look into a drawer and exposed the marvelous milky swell of her breasts. Guiltily he glanced, looked away, glanced again. Sensing the delicious lechery of his act, he also felt base, a despoiler of something holy.

And he tried not to think of Stephen.

Burl had no wish to hate this laughing, handsome brother, not as he hated Nathan. Hate? No, perhaps resentment was the word. Yes. He resented Nathan. One did not hate one's brother, for to do so was to bear the mark of Cain. He resented Nathan for his superiority, for the esteem with which their father held him ("Ah, Nathan. The finest sort of son a father could have," Isaiah declared at random moments, unaware that his words caused a hurt like hot coals. "And Stephen. What a handsome lad!"). Well, Nathan had gone. And then Stephen had gone. Burl delighted at their departures, certain at last that he would receive a sign of warming, of acceptance. It did not come. He longed for that, just as he longed for a sign from Catherine. But Catherine did not change either. Her mind and heart continued to be on Stephen, even in his absence. Burl knew, because he carried her letters to start on their journey downriver.

What could he do? At one time, he thought to tell her, to bare his heart and soul; and he made pretty speeches in his reverie. "Catherine, I've been meaning to tell you. Catherine, I love you." No, no. He could do better than that. "Catherine, I can't hide any longer what's in my heart..." But the chance never came, nor could he find the courage. He even dreamed of creeping into her room at night, to stand over her bed looking down at that blessed, blessed face. One night he actually went to her door and stood with his hand on the knob, heart pounding. Heart! Heart! Be still! Suddenly terrified and breaking into a sweat, he hurried away, knocking over a small table in his flight.

Isolated, dejected, he drank instead. More and more he drank, for the whiskey dulled the ache in his stomach and gave his fancies freer flight. He took the generous weekly allowance from his father, walked to the Irontown Inn, and elbowed through the crowded saloon to a small table. There, amid the noise and revelry, he drank until his mind was numb.

The summer night closed over Pittsburgh; not a soft and moonstruck night, but one of cloying heat and a sky filled with flickering thunderheads. No air stirred. People sat in their yards in the darkness, fanning themselves and gossiping. Children chased lightning bugs. Lovers writhed and panted in the bushes. The taverns did a booming trade in half-and-half. Wastrels, sweating and drinking, filled the fetid air with smoke and oaths. At the Irontown, a mob clustered around a fiddler—rivermen and gamblers and mill hands—singing bawdy songs against a background of shouting and raucous laughter. Burl Stewart kept to himself, swallowing his fourth half-and-half of the evening. The concoction, dark ale chasing a dollop of gin, kindled its familiar glow in his stomach, followed by a creeping numbness. His face numbed, his hands numbed, his vision played tricks. It was as if he was looking at life through a hole from inside a barrel. He found himself laughing at nonsensical things.

He fancied that he saw his sister. Maybelle swam into view in the company of a black-haired handsome man. Maybelle smiled down upon him, saying, "Well, there's my brother Burl, in his cups." Laughter enveloped him. A man said, "Burl, how are ye, old man?" It was not the black-haired handsome man, but someone else speaking. The black-haired handsome man scowled and was silent. The woman who looked like Maybelle knelt down and kissed him on the cheek, saying, "Burl. My poor, poor Burl." And then she rose up again. Someone else said, again, "Burl, how are ye, old man?" He looked up, trying to focus. He laughed. He said, "Fine. I'm fine. Ol' Burl is just fine." He repeated the phrase, and the laughter bubbled inside him. The black-haired handsome man scowled. The woman who looked like Maybelle seemed concerned, almost to tears. He felt his head nodding forward, nodding, nodding, nodding. He heard the woman say, "Come on, Ahzeeb. It's time to go. Let's leave here." And then it was dark, and he slept.

They carried him back to the compound that night and dumped him in the yard. Half an hour later, it started to rain. He awoke at daybreak with his father standing over him. He scrambled to his feet in the dirt. Isaiah Stewart cursed and kicked him in the behind, sending him lurching toward the house. "Drunken fool," the old man said. "Besotted, filthy idiot, get out of my sight!" Burl staggered to his room, tumbled facedown onto the cot, and slept.

That was the day Stephen came home.

* * *

They arrived by canoe, two lean, sun-bronzed, and bearded men in faded buckskins. Stroking the last few yards, they turned in from midstream and rested the paddles on their knees while the canoe slid through the water, losing way. With another deft stroke, the man in the stern came about and brought the craft expertly broadside to the wharf. Ashore, some of the workmen looked up from their labors. There was nothing unique about canoes on the Monongahela, but this one had the look of a Shawnee war craft, and the men stepping out of it were clearly long traveled and hard worn. It was the ancient master carpenter, John Crafton, who spoke. "By God if that tall feller don't look like... I declare. Stephen. It's Stephen Stewart!" Tools tumbled from workmen's hands, and boards fell with a clatter. Men clambered down from half-completed keels and decks, rooftops and scaffolds. They raised a ragged cheer and swarmed around the sunblasted young man, pounding his back and pumping his hand.

From the house, Isaiah heard the commotion and stormed out onto the porch. "What the hell's happening down there? Charlie, see what's going on in the boatyard. Oh, never mind, I'll go myself." He strode muttering toward the mob, looking for John Crafton or one of the foremen. "It's gotten so a man can't depend on a day's work around here..." Then he saw the buckskinned newcomer, standing tall above the rest, and checked his stride. "God damn, it's my boy!" Isaiah broke into a gimpy, shuffling trot, bulled through the crowd, and locked Stephen in a bear hug. "If you ain't a sight. By heaven, if you ain't somethin' to see!"

Stephen and his companion, the Frenchman Cruzatte, moved up the slope toward the main house carrying their rifles and gear. They were halfway there before Martha and Catherine appeared on the porch. Catherine gave a startled cry and came running, petticoats flashing. Stephen thrust his rifle to Cruzatte and opened his arms. Catherine buried her face in his neck as he swept her up. "You're home," she shouted. "Stephen, you're home!" The house workers and stablehands came out to join the throng. So tumultuous was the welcome that it was a quarter of an hour before they finally got into the house.

Stephen kissed his mother while she dabbed at her eyes and rattled on about how thin he was and how she wouldn't have known him in that beard, and—my land—hadn't he gotten taller! She told old Charlie to put the kitchen help to work killing chickens and gathering garden vegetables for supper, and told Isaiah to bring wine from the cellar. Martha Stewart laughed and hugged her son and then fled to her sewing room under a fresh onslaught of tears. At last, Stephen and Cruzatte climbed the stairs to their rooms, each man experiencing the closed-in feeling of being indoors again after so long a time. Stephen caught a whiff of himself and grimaced. "Damn, Cruzatte, if I don't smell like a grizzly." The Frenchman's white teeth flashed through the heavy black beard. "You look like one, too."

Old Charlie heated washtubs of water for their use in the bathhouse off the back porch. Stephen soaped his long, tough body and soaked luxuriantly, smoking a cigar. Finally, the black servant poured rinsewater over him. Stephen sputtered and coughed. "Damned if I didn't plumb forget there were pleasures like this." He stepped out and dried himself on a huge soft towel. Old Charlie trimmed the ragged beard and brought sweet-smelling toilet water. The servant had picked out some of Stephen's best clothing from three years past, but when he attempted to dress, they all burst into laughter. The pants were too big in the middle and too skimpy in the legs. The shirts no longer had enough arm and shoulder room. Cruzatte, being shorter, was even more ludicrous in Stephen's old clothes. Finally, they decided to put on fresh buckskins, taken from their packs and pressed with a warm iron. By the time the two explorers presented themselves at Martha Stewart's table, the result was fairly respectable.

Isaiah Stewart was suddenly a man redeemed. Smiling and energetic, he gave his workers the rest of the day off—which brought another cheer from the boatyard—and unleashed a flurry of instructions to the domestic help. "This calls for a celebration, by God!" And again, for the first time since Nathan's going-away party eight years before, the lamps blazed throughout Stewart House.

It was not until after supper that he could be with Catherine. They met on the porch and walked together, hand in hand, through the soft evening. The moon rose early, high and full. Crickets sang in the sycamores along Water Street. Frogs raised a chorus from the riverbanks. There was the sound of a nightingale.

Their strides matched. He had forgotten that she was so tall and willowy. Her eye level came to his shoulder, and the eyes were frank, expressive, and intelligent. Between them there coursed a magic that was fresh and new and startling.

"I can't tell you how often I've dreamed about this," he said, "—walking with you and holding your hand."

"And I. Oh, Stephen, I thought you were never coming home. And if you didn't, I couldn't imagine what life would be like. Isn't that silly? I'm a grown woman now, and yet I feel like a child."

"I read your letters over and over. They've been to places no white man ever saw before. I toted them up the Missouri as far as the keelboat would go and carried them when we changed to canoes in the headwaters. When we portaged, and the men were growing weak for want of food, I carried them still. I think I would have thrown away my rifle before I parted with those letters. There was one or two in my pocket all the time, when we confronted the Sioux and wintered in the Mandan village, when we came to the big mountains and went down the Columbia to the Pacific. Even"—he chuckled, but without mirth—"being chased by grizzly bears."

Her hand was strong in his, stronger than he'd imagined it would be. But then he remembered her strange childhood. These hands could drive a team, shoot a rifle, and handle a bullwhip like a teamster. He squeezed the hand, and the hand squeezed back.

And he talked. How long had it been since he had talked like this? Probably never. In the company of men, the talk was different, not on a personal level. Men spoke of superficial things, if they spoke at all; and in the company of men, Stephen usually kept his silences. How different it was now, with this beautiful young woman whose presence seemed so—so close, so intensely identifiable. He talked freely now. He talked of the Indians he had seen—Arikara, Shoshoni, Minnetarees and Flatheads, the Otos and Missouri and, yes, the Omaha. How strange that some Indians, such as those they'd encountered on the Columbia River, were surly and dirty, thievish and insolent; and others, like the Mandan, were disciplined people and excellent hosts. What contrast between the Teton Sioux, who were aggressive bullies and scoundrels for all their strength, and the Omaha, a weak and tragic people, nonetheless dignified.

"I have a friend in the Omaha tribe. His name used to be Running Wolf. He is a miracle." He told her of the fire in the

camp, the terrible ordeal of Running Wolf and the strange
healing ritual performed by the medicine man. "When we left
there nobody expected the boy to live. But live he did. On the
way back downriver a year later, we stopped to see the Omaha.
Blood Feather was still chief and medicine man. And Running
Wolf himself came out to greet me. Only his name is no longer
Running Wolf, but Crippled Wolf. He is lamed and scarred, but
he lives." Stephen paused, deep in thought. Then: "We are
blood brothers." He glanced at Catherine. "That means a great
deal to me. Maybe I've been away from civilization too long,
though. After all, he is a redskin, and I'm a white man. You
know what my father would say. He despises Indians."

"Skin color does not matter, Stephen. And when it comes to
blood, yours is as red as his."

"Thank you," he said.

There were some things he did not talk about. He did not talk
about the cruel winter trek overland to the Upper Columbia,
when they were reduced to a band of starving scarecrows. He did
not speak of the death of John Floyd. He did not mention the
experience of subsisting on fresh dog meat, or of the near-
blindness of his friend Cruzatte, who had mistaken Captain
Meriwether Lewis for a deer and shot him in the behind. It
would be better for them all to know Cruzatte as the fine fiddler
he was, rather than as the man who'd almost killed a national
hero.

Finally, he was silent. They walked on for nearly an hour,
sharing the magic of it, the completeness of it. At last they
returned to the compound. Martha Stewart had left a candle lit
for them in the front window, along with a plate of cookies. They
ate the cookies in the kitchen and then parted for the night.
Catherine returned to her room filled with the elation of it all.
She fell asleep happier than she had ever thought possible.

"What do you mean, Maybelle's left home? When? Where is
she going? And with whom?"

The anger clouded his face. Catherine had never seen him so
angry. Stephen glared at his father with such intensity that Isaiah
Stewart backed away a step, at loss for words. Martha plucked at
her son's sleeve. "Stephen, you mustn't . . ." But he turned
away, beckoning for Catherine to accompany him. She had to

trot to catch up as he strode angrily to the barn. They saddled horses, mounted, and rode away at a gallop.

It was midafternoon. The saloon of the Irontown Inn was almost empty. Stephen handed the bartender a gold piece, got the information he wanted, and—with Catherine still close behind—took the stairs two at a time. His knuckles banged at the door of the Arab's room. From inside came the creak of bedsprings, footsteps, and a raspy male voice. "Who is it?"

"Let me speak to Maybelle Stewart. I'm her brother."

He heard a woman's voice, low and urgent. The man said, "There ain't no Maybelle here. You've got the wrong room, mister."

Stephen stood back. "Open the door or I'll kick it in," he said.

More movement inside. Then: "I said there's no Maybelle here. Now go away and leave us alone."

Stephen raised his booted foot and drove it forward, lock high. The door burst open with a splintering crash and he moved into the room. Maybelle sat up in the bed, wide-eyed, holding a sheet across her body. Ahzeeb stood in the middle of the room, pointing a brace of pistols at Stephen's stomach.

"I told you to go away," the Arab said.

Catherine walked in and calmly stepped in front of Stephen. "If you intend to use those, you'll have to shoot me first."

Ahzeeb's eyes widened. The pistols lowered and hung at his sides. His mouth worked, but no sound came. Stephen went to his sister and glared down at her.

"Get dressed," he said. "You're coming with us."

Maybelle's eyes flashed, and her face hardened in defiance. "Since when do you tell me what to do, brother?"

"I'm telling you now."

"Oh, no you're not. You don't just kick your way in here and start giving orders. Mister Stephen might rule the roost with some folks, but not with Maybelle."

"How long have you been living like this?"

"That's no business of yours." Her eyes shifted to Catherine. "Tell him, Catherine. He does not have any right."

Catherine sighed and nodded. "I'm afraid she's right, Stephen. I hate to take sides in this, but . . ."

A crowd had gathered in the hallway and stood ogling the scene. Stephen walked over and slammed the door in their faces.

Ahzeeb still gripped the pistols, white-faced with fury. Catherine watched the man carefully. "If you've got any ideas," she said quietly, "forget them."

Stephen's anger abated. He moved to the bed and sat down heavily beside his sister. "Tell me what's going on, Maybelle."

"Ahzeeb and I are leaving tomorrow. We're going downriver. There is nothing you can do or say, because I've made up my mind." She clutched her knees beneath the bedsheet and rocked. "I guess you're not aware of how things have been at home. Of course, you're not. It's hard to keep track of little things like that when you're off in the woods for three years. Well, I'm not going to burden you with a lot of details now. But I will tell you this much, Stephen Stewart. I don't care if our father lives or dies." She glanced at him to measure the effect of her words, saw the surprise in his handsome face and offered a grim smile. "I thought that might get your attention. Isaiah Stewart thinks more of his hound dog than he does of his daughter. That's how it is, and Catherine can bear me out. She will, too, if you ask her..."

"Come home, Maybelle," Stephen said. He spoke softly now, and without rancor. "Whatever's wrong, let's fix it."

She shook her head, the hair tumbling loosely over her bare shoulders. Her eyes brimmed with tears. "No, I can't go home, Stephen. Not now, not ever. I've made up my mind."

Stephen turned to Ahzeeb. "Get out of here."

Maybelle flared. *"No!"*

"Just for a moment," Stephen said lamely. "I want a private word with my sister."

"I said no! He stays. Stay, Ahmad."

The Arab stayed.

"All right, then," Stephen said. "You'll need money, because I'm sure you don't have any."

"I'll get by."

From the pocket of his buckskins he drew out a small sack of gold pieces and tossed it with a clink onto the bed. "There. It isn't much, but it's all I've got. My earnings from the expedition. Take it."

She stared at the wall, saying nothing. To Catherine, Maybelle had never seemed more vulnerable and alone. She reached out to touch her hair, but Maybelle shrank back.

"We're leaving tomorrow morning, Ahmad and me," Maybelle said.

Stephen bent over and kissed his sister on the cheek. She did not respond. Then he and Catherine walked out of the room.

The crowd no longer hovered at the doorway. A lone man stood there now, and he was angry. "Mister," he growled to Stephen, "you owe me a door."

"Send me a bill at Stewart's Boat Works."

The man's face drained of its anger. Two piglike eyes screwed up in partial recognition. "Ain't you one of the Stewart boys?"

"Yes."

An oily smile crossed the face. Hands rubbed in happy obsequiousness. "Yes, sir. No trouble at all, Mr. Stewart. It's just a little thing anyhow, hah, hah. You be Stephen, then? The explorer. Well, by golly, right here in my place. Happy to oblige, sir. Yes, indeed. Yes, indeedy." He bowed, glanced at Catherine, offered a fawning smile. "Your servant, ma'am."

As they walked out of the Irontown Inn, the late afternoon sunlight struck them like a cleansing fire.

The next morning, Maybelle and Ahmad Ahzeeb left Pittsburgh on a keelboat, headed downriver. She had pinned Stephen's sack of gold, four hundred dollars worth, into her bodice.

For the first time in her life, Maybelle was afraid.

They moved downriver in stages, according to the whims of Ahmad Ahzeeb and the availability of transport. First there was the keelboat *Cincinnati*, running out of Pittsburgh piled high with goods. Plows, harness, kegs of whiskey, boxes of rifles and ammunition, spinning wheels, yard goods, needle and thread—whatever fetched a profit in the village and clearing settlements downstream found a place on her decks and in her cabin. Tethered on board were a sheep, two goats, two horses, and a milk cow; chickens clucked from crates. The *Cincinnati* carried passengers as well, but only as an afterthought. What few there were found sparse accommodations indeed, suffering to share their lot with the profane, hard-drinking rivermen who alternately poled, rowed, and cursed the vessel on its uncertain course.

Maybelle Stewart stayed close to Ahmad. The trader, while no match physically for even the slightest of the river hands, gave protection of sorts simply by being male. It was assumed, moreover, that they were man and wife. Even so, when Ahmad was not beside her, the bolder men made advances with winks, pinches, and ribald whispers. "Here, now, how's about you and meetin' tonight for a little toss behind yon boxes and bales, eh?''

She flushed, ignoring them as best she could. For added security, Maybelle made the acquaintance of the keelboat's captain, a bewhiskered, Bible-toting ancient named Zeb Tutty. "Ah, Captain Tutty, it is so good to find a Christian man in this world of sin." She fluttered her eyes and tossed her flaming hair. "My dear father, God rest his sainted soul, always read the Bible to us after supper." She looked toward heaven. Captain Tutty, flustered, kept his eyes from straying to the ample bosom straining under her high-necked bodice. "Indeed, my child, he must have been a good man. And what is your favorite Biblical passage?" The battered old hands thumbed his weathered Good Book. Maybelle dropped her eyes and blushed. "I always felt it was Father's place to select the passage, being but mere female and having no head for such important things. If you'd be so kind . . ." After that, she spent several hours each day in the old captain's company, listening as he read God's word in a voice of heavy piety. The nuisances stopped.

They got off the *Cincinnati* at the town of Gallipolis. Maybelle helped Ahzeeb carry his sample valises ashore and followed the drummer dutifully as he went from door to door peddling yard goods. Many of the townsfolk spoke French, and Maybelle was surprised to hear the Arab rattle off their tongue with practiced ease. Housewives reddened under the admiring scrutiny of his moist brown eyes, and the orders came thick and fast. They put up at the only inn in town. But in the evenings Ahmad would leave her to find a game of cards or to tryst with a willing maid down by the river. Maybelle chafed in idlenss for three days, until he grew tired of the town and was ready to move on. The pattern repeated itself consistently as Ahmad Ahzeeb peddled yard goods by day and pleasured by night from Marietta to Cincinnati and Louisville. Maybelle protested his absences to no avail. Her protests became a nagging, running quarrel. And in time she rebuffed his physical advances.

At last they passed from the Ohio into the muddy Mississippi, arrived in yet another river town and put up at a lodging house. Ahmad disappeared for two days while she seethed with helpless rage. On the second night, however, she was awakened by noises outside. The door burst open, and Ahzeeb stood swaying in the lamplight, wild-eyed and disheveled, gasping for breath. "Get up! We're leaving!"

"What is it? What's wrong?"

The noises grew louder and nearer. Maybelle ran to the window. Advancing uphill from the town was a crowd bearing torches. Voices punctuated the night with angry shouts. "He's in the house. We've got him now. Tar and feather the Arab! Despoiler of women. Cheater. We'll do for him . . ."

Ahmad grabbed up his valises and bolted for the door. Maybelle threw a coat over her nightdress. Suddenly remembering, she snatched open a dresser drawer, found Stephen's sack of gold coins, and thrust it into her coat pocket. She ran after the Arab, who was already pounding across the yard. They sprinted in darkness down the river road away from town. Behind them, the mob approached the house in a fury. There were more shouts and sounds of breaking glass. Fear put wings to Maybelle's heels, and she managed to keep pace with Ahmad as he labored under the weight of his goods. Finally, gasping for breath, they slowed the pace.

"Ahmad, what did you do to stir up that hornet's nest?"

"It doesn't matter. Those rubes would have killed us both, or ridden us out on a rail tarred and feathered."

They trudged on, keeping to the road. Shadows loomed up, cast by a sliver of moon. Maybelle's coat was snagged repeatedly by hidden branches, reaching like hands from the darkness. She stubbed her toe and once tripped over a stone and fell sprawling. Ahmad did not stop, and she ran to catch up. They passed a few cabins set back in the woods, rousing choruses of barking dogs. At one place a hound came bounding after them, but Ahmad chased the brute away with a rock. Finally, the moon went down, the road disintegrated into a bare forest track, and they sat down to await the dawn. A gnawing cold drifted up from the river, enveloping her as she huddled on the ground. Finally, pressing her body against the Arab, she fell into a fitful sleep. She awoke in a gray wash of morning, cloaked in dense fog.

Cramped and musclesore, they got up and started walking again. Maybelle was hungry, but the fog was too heavy even to search for berries. They walked for another two hours before the watery sunlight filtered down through a dripping forest.

"We'll try to catch a fish, Ahmad," she said.

Maybelle ripped a heavy thread from the hem of her gown and found a straight pin in her nightgown. The Arab turned up rocks until he found a fat grubworm. With this he baited the pin, and they went down to the river and dropped it, bent and afixed to the thread, into the water. They used a pebble as a sinker. In a short time they managed to catch a small bass. Ahmad rummaged in his pockets and found a clasp knife but no matches. "We don't have matches, so we can't start a fire," he said. "We'll have to eat it raw." He skinned the bass and sliced the meat into thin strips. Maybelle had never tasted raw fish before. She chewed and swallowed quickly, making a face at the unpleasant taste. "It's better than nothing," she said.

They waited for the fog to clear, hoping to sight a passing barge or keelboat. The Mississippi was quite wide here, however, and the only craft they sighted was passing downstream on the other side. The boat did not heed their calls and waves. Finally, they climbed back up to the forest track and resumed their walk, still heading upriver away from the village.

"If we keep on this way, we'll get back to the Ohio," Ahmad said. But the prospect did not cheer him. "I don't know where we'll go from there."

Maybelle did not ask him again the cause of so much furor in the town. Perhaps it was better not to know. A card cheat and womanizer with a taste for liquor and unsavory friends could find trouble easily enough. She resolved to part company with the Arab as soon as possible.

By evening her feet were numb, and the flimsy shoes she wore began to come apart at the seams. She washed her feet in the river and bound them with strips of torn nightgown. Then she put on the shoes and wrapped more strips around them. She cursed Ahmad for a hasty flight, and for the first time realized that she herself probably had no need to run. "I was a damn fool for coming with you," she grumbled. "That made me a party to your guilt."

Ahzeeb chuckled, his white teeth flashing in the gathering dusk. "We live and learn, little flower."

They slept on the trail again that night, shared a meager breakfast of wild apples and gooseberries the next morning, and then found a wide beach of dried mud on which to wait for a boat. It did not matter which way the boat was headed, as long as it floated.

They were rescued by a crew poling a flatboat upriver on the shallow side. Half-a-dozen men, two young women, and a small child were aboard. They were astonished to see the dark Arab and the red-haired woman in rags waving from the mud beach. The flatboat grounded, and the men quickly helped them aboard.

"Where might ye be bound, folks?"

"Anywhere you're going is fine with us," said Ahzeeb. "Right now, we're nowhere at all."

"That's a fact. We're all going to St. Louis, the Lord willing."

"That's quite a distance," Maybelle said. "And upriver, at that."

"We'll be beyond the Ohio in two days time. Then the current gets easier."

The spokesman was a huge man with a wild red beard and hair down to his shoulders. Maybelle felt that she had seen him before but could not remember where. Pittsburgh, more than likely. So many of them came through Pittsburgh. In her present circumstances, however, she had no wish to let her own identity be known, and so she asked no questions. The others called the red-bearded man Mr. Faber, and spoke with respect. Even the name seemed to strike a chord of memory somewhere.

The women replaced Maybelle's ragged garb with a cotton dress, petticoats, and worn shoes that did not precisely fit but were serviceable enough. She was grateful.

"Well, then, off we go, lads."

Their progress was slow, the labor heavy. To move upriver, the flatboaters were bushwhacking it, yard by yard, hauling by sheer muscle power at low-hanging trees and bushes and poling through shallow spots. Two men worked a great sweep at the stern which also provided some power. Occasionally, they came to stretches of river where several men had to go ashore and pull the flatboat by a rope.

"There's the Ohio, dead ahed!"

The great river down which Maybelle and Ahzeeb had come seemed even broader and more powerful now, looking at it from the opposite direction. Five hundred miles up that river lay home and safety. Maybelle knew that her mother would be worrying, and Catherine and Stephen too. Perhaps even Burl cared, if he was sober. But then the thought of her father came to mind, and her homesickness was swept away by anger and wounded pride.

"St. Louis must be an exciting place," she said.

"Oh, child, it really ain't much," one of the women said. Her name was Marylou and she was the wife of Mr. Faber's son, Arthur. "St. Louis is a rough river town, filled with fur trappers and Indians and renegade French. You've got to be careful there." Her eyes passed from Maybelle to Ahzeeb in a casual way. River folk, Maybelle had learned, were not the kind to pry and accepted life pretty much as it was presented. This was frontier, after all, and many of the civilized niceties from back east became secondary to survival. "We ain't planning to stay there. Mr. Faber wants to bring a load of furs downriver, to New Orleans. Two of these young men, including my husband, are his sons. That"—she indicated another tall man at the stern sweep—"is Terence, and the other woman is his wife." She pursed her lips thoughtfully. "They was settling downriver and got attacked by renegade Shawneee. Lost everything they owned, except their scalps."

Wild rivers and renegade Indians, toil and flatboats; was there nothing gentle in this world anymore? Did it all have to be this way, living on the fringe of disaster? Suddenly Maybelle was hungry and tired—they'd shared the meager provisions of Mr. Faber and his people, augmented by fish and some berries from ashore—and uncertain about tomorrow. St. Louis. A rough river town, Marylou said. The tone of her voice did not offer much reassurance.

That night, when they tied the flatboat to a tree and all settled down to sleep, Maybelle lay awake for a long time looking up at the blaze of stars and listening to the gentle lap of the Mississippi against the wooden hull. And for no apparent reason at all, she began to cry.

They were nine days moving upriver—nine days of poling and rowing and hauling. Other vessels passed them under sail and oar, blowing their curiously noted horns in friendly greeting. Ahzeeb neither offered to help with the toil nor was asked; the Arab kept to himself as much as possible, except to take meals. It was as if he did not wish to become acquainted with people who might ask questions.

At last the town of St. Louis came into view, spread over a rise that gave it a broad riverfront. The place was an odd mix of buildings and tents, false fronts and dusty streets. Dominating all, its life and purpose, was the river. And as they tied up at the shore, Maybelle was surprised at the variety of river craft clustered there: pirogues and keelboats, scows and barges, some fitted with sails or oars or sweeps. There were boats with tall heavy masts, fitted for towing by gangs of men ashore. And scattered among them were all manner of canoes, some of beech bark and many of hollowed tree trunks, burned and hewn. As they prepared to take their leave of Mr. Faber and his group,

Maybelle whispered to Ahzeeb. But the Arab shrugged and pulled out his pockets. "I have no money. Not a single gold piece." Turning away from him in disgust, Maybelle drew from her underclothes Stephen's sack of coins. She gave Marylou five dollars. The woman was startled. "It's not necessary. You'll need this."

"You saved us," Maybelle said. "It's little enough."

She shook Mr. Faber's hand then, and followed Ahzeeb into the busy human hive that was St. Louis.

The streets filled with drunken idlers and roisterers. Rough laughter burst from the saloons. Maybelle stepped around a moaning body in the street. They turned a corner and heard the clashing of a piano, badly out of tune. "A piano," Ahzeeb said. "How the hell did they get a piano this far upriver?" They found a room over a feed store and managed to get water for a tub bath and food for their empty bellies. Ahzeeb went out for a drink and returned at midnight, to fall muttering into bed. He was still sleeping when Maybelle arose the next morning. She went for a walk in the town. At that early hour only a few merchants and working folk were out. In a weedy yard beside a wooden shack, a young woman boiled clothes in a metal tub and hung them up to dry. The laundry included a baby's things. Maybelle envied the young woman. After about an hour, she returned to the room above the feed store.

Ahmad Ahzeeb was gone. His valises were gone. And so was Stephen's money sack.

Angered and upset, she thought about going after him. But then the idea of roaming alone through the streets and into saloons changed her mind. She waited instead, through the remainder of the day and into the evening. The room let out onto a small second-floor porch. Maybelle moved out there, to sit in a straight-backed chair and watch the activity along the dusty street below. Sunset brought a golden glow to the town and the river and filled her with a powerful sense of being alone. Still she waited, but she knew instinctively that this time he would not return.

Maybelle did not go to bed that night, but sat on the porch listening to the noises of the bawdy river town, the raucous shouts and banjo music, the quarrels and fights and laughter. Occasionally, she nodded off but awoke again imagining that she had heard a sound, a step on the stair. But it was nothing. At last the sun came up on another day. She had not eaten and had no money. At midafternoon she left the room and went down to the street. After an hour of aimless walking, ignoring the propositions of drifters and street louts, she came to a huge wooden building displaying a sign proclaiming that it was the Gown and Slipper. Stuck to the window was a hand-printed note, "Female Help Wanted."

It was part saloon, part dance hall. Maybelle pushed past the double doors into an atmosphere of stale whiskey and cigar smoke. Afternoon sunlight filtered through a stained glass window onto the bar. There were a few red velvet hangings and brass spittoons. Some men sat at wooden tables, drinking. Signs along the walls said, "No Fighting," "No Profanity," and "No Indians Allowed."

A bartender polished glasses. Maybelle asked for the proprietor. He called over his shoulder, "Dove. Somebody here to see you."

A buxom, middle-aged brunette came out through a doorway of beaded curtains. The face was fleshy and heavily rouged, the eyes set in folds of painted skin. She wore a red gown that matched the wall hangings and her ample bosom was a white expanse swelling from a plunging neckline. The woman weighed at least three hundred pounds.

"Yes?"

"I saw your notice outside. I need a job."

The fleshy face was noncommittal. "I seen you come into town off the flatboat. You was with the Arab, Ahzeeb."

"Do you know Ahzeeb?"

"Honey, everybody on the river knows Ahzeeb."

"Do you know where I can find him."

"He left this morning, heading downriver."

Maybelle felt giddy, as if she had been struck in the stomach. She sat down heavily in a chair.

"Left you flat, did he?" the woman said.

"Something like that."

"That's Ahzeeb, all right. A real snake." The massive bosom heaved, the fleshy face softened. "I'm Dove Lovelady. I run this place. What can you do?"

"I can entertain, I think."

"Entertain?" The painted eyebrows lifted. "How do you mean, entertain?"

"I used to play the piano and sing in church back home."

The bartender snickered. A glare from the proprietor silenced him. The eyes shifted back to Maybelle, looking her up and down. Maybelle felt a flush of embarrassment as the appraisal lingered on her breasts and thighs. Dove Lovelady murmured, "You've got a fine figure and a pretty face, honey. We'll find work for you to do. You'll start this evening as a hostess. I pay meals and tips."

"Meals and tips?"

"Take it or leave it."

Maybelle thought for a moment. Dove Lovelady yawned, displaying a mouthful of bad teeth. Maybelle tried to think of alternatives, but there seemed to be none.

"I'll take it," she whispered.

The Gown and Slipper gave pleasure, pleasure for an hour or pleasure for the night. Dove Lovelady watched over a bevy of twelve hostesses whose profession was to cool the fires of male customers, some of whom had just come back from two years in the wilds. It was a world of whiskers and buckskin, loud voices and strong drink. A battered piano, muscled upriver on a flatboat the previous year, clashed in the corner. It was the same piano Maybelle and Ahzeeb had heard when they arrived, and in fact the only piano in St. Louis. If the instrument was hopelessly out of tune, its sounding board warped and hammers bent, no one seemed to mind. In a world without pianos, or little else in the way of music, anything was wondrous.

Dove Lovelady found a silken gown of emerald green for Maybelle, set off with sequins. After an hour of arduous tucking and pinning, Maybelle was so tightly encased that she could barely breathe. The white mounds of her breasts now bulged from cleavage that plunged almost to her naval, and the probing warm eyes of every man in the Gown and Slipper caused her a confusion of inner responses, part revulsion and part pleasure. The costume was completed by a glittering necklace of fake diamonds. Her bright red hair was upswept and caught in a black ribbon. So striking was the effect that Maybelle's first walk down the stairs and through the crowd to the piano caused conversation to lapse. The regular piano player, a weasel-faced man with bad complexion, quickly relinquished the ancient bench. She sat down quickly, aware of a sudden stampede of males to gather around her.

"Play us a tune, honey."

"Yeah. Play somethin' peppy, from back east."

"Give us a number. Mmm?"

Maybelle smiled and struck up a medley of the only tunes she had ever played. The babble around her subsided but was soon replaced by a chorus of groans.

"Hey, ain't that a hymn? We don't need no church music around here, sister."

"Boo!"

"What the hell is that? Some kind of music. Haw, haw!"

"Quiet there. Be quiet and let the little lady play."

"Hey, sister, get off the piano and bring back weasel-face."

"I said quiet!"

"Hymns. We don't want no fucking hymns . . ."

"*I said shut up!*"

In sudden fright, Maybelle stopped playing. A burly, bewhiskered man in buckskins pushed through the crowd. His matted long hair was plastered down with bear grease, and he sported an eagle's feather in a leather thong, worn as a headband. His hands were the size of hams, and the handle of a huge hunting knife jutted from the top of his boot. One of the huge hands patted Maybelle's bare shoulder, and the man turned to the crowd.

"Next man that says a word about this little lady's piano playing answers to me." His jaw jutted and a massive brow knotted angrily. "And if you're wondering who I be, the name is Mountain John Slye, and I can whup a grizzly bear. And I done it, too."

Maybelle wrinkled her nose. The huge paw still lay heavily upon her shoulder, and the buckskinned giant gave off penetrating odors of stale sweat and bear grease. When he bent over her to speak, his breath reeked of whiskey. "All right, little honey, you just go right ahead and play whatever comes to your mind." Her protector drew up a chair beside her, sat down, and ordered a bottle of whiskey.

Her fingers beat at the battered keys in a kind of desperation. Maybelle played every hymn she knew and then started over again with a different tempo. The tempo didn't really matter and neither did the tune, so atrocious was the sound. As the hulk drank, his great body leaned closer and closer to hers, and his leg began to press amiably against her thigh. Her attempts to push him away failed, and by the fourth playing of the hymns she was saying, "Don't do that, please. No. Don't do that, it isn't nice . . . Look, I just play music here, I'm not—"

"You're not what, little honey?" The hands pawed at her back and thigh, and the giant murmured something into her ear. Desperately, she looked around for help, but the crowd had given up and gone back to the tables, the bartender and two massive men hired as bouncers ignored her. Dove Lovelady was nowhere to be seen. Her thoughts tumbled now, and she paid no attention to the piano keys. It was all just a clash and clatter of meaningless sound. Midway through the fifth playing, she stopped and got up to move away.

The great hand circled her waist with an iron grip. The whiskey voice said, "Honey, you and old John Slye, we're goin' upstairs." The massive body pressed against her, a towering presence.

Fear jolted Maybelle, and she tried to wrench free. She screamed for help. Faces turned to watch, but no help came. Suddenly she was being lifted off her feet, and a great shaggy muzzle pressed against her face with a sloppy kiss. "Honey, John Slye's gonna show you how a mountain man does it!" The crowd faces broke into laughter as Slye tossed her over his shoulder, kicking and beating with her fists. He lumbered across the room stroking her bottom with one hand and carrying the whiskey bottle with the other.

"Oh, no! Please, let me down. Let me down!"

The giant bore Maybelle up the stairs, rounded a corner, and kicked open a door. From a rumpled bed, a naked man and woman looked up, startled. Ignoring them, the mountain man kicked the door shut behind him and dropped her onto the bed. The other couple rolled out and fled.

Maybelle screamed and bit, but the huge hand closed over her mouth and pinned her head to the pillow. Volleys of laughter rolled from the giant as he put down the whiskey bottle, grasped the neckline of her gown and ripped it off like so much tissue paper. Then the undergarments went, and the shaggy head bent to cover her breasts and stomach with wet kisses. With one hand, he unbuckled his belt and took off his trousers. In terror, she glimpsed the massive, throbbing member as he moved astride her and forced her thighs apart. The hand loosened from her mouth. She screamed again and bit through the flesh, bringing a spurt of blood. But the giant merely laughed, spread her wider and moved the rigid thing against her, so that she could feel its scalding heat.

"Now, my little hymn-singin' honey . . ."

The blow came from behind him. It struck the base of his skull, snapping the head upward. The eyes widened and rolled up in their sockets. A blob of spittle flew from his mouth, and he fell forward, his weight smashing the wind from Maybelle's body. With the strength of terror, she drove her elbow into the side of his head and pushed it away. Then she squirmed out from beneath him and rolled off the bed, clutching her nakedness and staring wild-eyed.

"That ought to give him a nice little nap." The speaker was a muscular woman with short blonde hair, wielding a heavy club. She wore a gown that bared her shoulders. Her old-young face was square and masculine, her mouth a red slash. One side of the face was thinly scarred, as if from an old knife wound. "We ain't been formally introduced," she said. "My name's Violet."

"Violet?"

Putting aside the club, Violet inspected the massive body on the bed. "Talk about a stallion, look at the size of that meat." She looked closely at the eyes. They were open and unblinking. The mountain man was not breathing. "Hmm," Violet said. "I guess I tapped him too hard. They'll have to take him to the river."

"Do you mean he's—he's dead?"

"Looks like it."

"Now listen here, Violet," an imperious voice said from the doorway, "I didn't mean for you to bash him clear to eternity." Dove Lovelady walked into the room, looked down at the giant, sniffed. "But that's what you went and did."

"Sorry, Dove."

"Go get Buckles and George. Tell 'em to clean up this mess." For the first time, Dove acknowledged the presence of Maybelle, crouching nude beside the bed. "And you, put some clothes on and get back downstairs. We've got customers to attend to."

"I don't . . ."

"Did you hear me?"

"Don't you see what happened? He tried to rape me."

Dove's face softened slightly. "I know. That's why I sent Violet after you. I don't like my girls getting manhandled; I won't stand for it. But you've got to expect some of that in a place like this." She opened a closet, found a robe, and gently helped Maybelle to her feet. "Here, put this on." The painted eyes lingered lovingly over Maybelle's body and took on a glow. "No wonder he went crazy. Can't say as I blame him."

Maybelle shivered. Again she was uncomfortable under Dove's intense scrutiny. "I'm sorry," she said.

"Listen to me, honey, this ain't no polite social you're into now. The Gown and Slipper is a whorehouse and a gin mill, plain and simple. You can work here or you can leave. But let me tell you, a woman alone is next to useless in this country, and you might as well face that fact. Besides, you ain't all that virtuous, or you wouldn't have come downriver with the likes of that greaser Ahzeeb. So make up your mind."

Maybelle tied the belt of the robe and pushed hair back from her eyes. She felt calmer now. "Well, I thought there might be something I could do that wouldn't involve...you know."

Dove Lovelady smiled. "Actually, it ain't all that bad a life. There's good money to be made, better than you can make doing anything else. Most of the men who come here are gentlemen. Some of them don't even want to go to bed with you, believe it or not. They just want somebody to talk to and hold, somebody who's soft and warm and female. That's why this is the world's oldest profession, honey. There wouldn't be no whorehouses without willing women to work in them. Ever think of that? So they must get something out of it in return. Freedom. Good money. A sense of being needed. I can tell you, I've made a lot of friends in this business. Back east, years ago, I had some real important customers. And let me tell you, if you want to get the lowdown on what's going on in this world, find out who's who and what's what, just work in a whorehouse for a while."

"I never thought about it before," Maybelle said.

"Well, think about it now. And I'll tell you what I can do, just for the hell of it. I'll keep you on here as a hostess, pick the men that come to you—gentlemen, you understand—and you do what you please with 'em. If you don't want to go to bed, then don't go. Tell 'em you're sick or tell 'em the truth. But don't tease. Understand me? Don't pretend to promise something you won't deliver. Is it a deal?"

The bouncers, Buckles and George, arrived, followed by Violet. Dove merely nodded at the silent giant on the bed, and the two grabbed his feet and pulled. The body struck the floor with a sickening thud. As Maybelle watched, they dragged it out through a side door, bundled it into a blanket, and carried it down the back stairs. Violet quickly changed the bedding and straightened the room.

"What will they do with him?" Maybelle asked.

"Him?" Violet said. "Oh, he'll be fish bait, floatin' down the Mississippi. The river asks no questions and tells no lies."

To Maybelle's surprise, the town of St. Louis asked no questions either. On the frontier, people came and went as they pleased, and life was reckoned in wilderness values. The constabulary saw its duty to protect the law-abiding citizen. Those outside the law tended to settle things among themselves. Strangers who entered the twilight world of the Gown and Slipper, or any one of half-a-dozen other such places purveying pleasure, whiskey, and cards, did so at their peril. Only the most blatantly open cases of homicide, involving a breach of the public peace, got official attention; and the attention usually came in the form of quick trial and quick justice at the hanging tree. A massive body dumped with a splash at midnight from a rowboat into the Mississippi elicited no interest at all. As the body sank in *rigor mortis*, the current carried it gently southward like so much flotsam, turning over and over, hair and beard wildly awash, and eyes bulging in the depths.

She would try life, then, in the Gown and Slipper. For a while, at least. Dove Lovelady, true to her word, steered gentle, good-looking men to Maybelle, saying: "If you just want nice company, there's your girl; if you want more, it's up to her."

Maybelle took them to one of the upstairs parlors and they talked and drank. She developed a knack for listening, and found that oftentimes this is what a man really wanted. Some, surprisingly, reminded her of her brothers, Nathan and Stephen. One evening she found herself speaking of Stephen to a lean, handsome young fur trapper who had just come downriver with a fine load of pelts. "I've got a brother who's the most beautiful man you've ever seen. He makes women weak, just walking past them." As she spoke, looking into the friendly brown eyes of the stranger, Maybelle remembered old times and other loves and a familiar excitement stole over her, warming her mind and body. Strangely, she thought of the night of the party in Pittsburgh, long ago, and the brown-eyed stranger whom she had taken to the wagon, and Nathan's unexpected arrival . . .

"You're a handsome man, too," she whispered. "You make me feel weak. Did any woman ever tell you that?" She leaned close to him, breathing the masculine aromas of toilet water and cigar smoke. Their lips met, softening and widening. The hunger expanded. It had been so long, so long. Her breath quickened. Lightly, lightly her tongue flicked her want to his. Gently his hand closed over her breast, and the thrill poured through her like molten fire.

He stayed the night, loving her hugely and tenderly, and she lost track of their climaxes. When she awoke with the first sunlight, he was gone, but he had left her a hundred dollars and a note. "Thank you, angel."

Never does the human spirit master its own destiny. Life is fashioned from thwarted hopes and ambitions half fulfilled. One makes compromises. One accepts. One exists. So it was with Maybelle. At first, she found herself thinking: Oh, my God, I'm a whore. A prostitute in a St. Louis bordello. Where was the Stewart pride and the Stewart values? But then, she thought again. Who gives a damn? And as time went on, the thoughts came to her less and less frequently, buried in the welter of daily trivialities and domestic cares. She came to know the other women and girls, Fawn, Bella, Lisbeth, Folly, Violet, Ginger, and others. Some were frivolous and gay, some introspective and deep. Among them, Maybelle sensed a common gentleness of spirit born of shared hardship. They considered themselves entertainers, whatever the world might say. Some of the older women took pride in their art and had regular customers, who would go to no others. Occasionally, a girl left the Gown and Slipper, having fallen in love. There was even a wedding in the house, performed by a preacher who'd come to the house first to save the souls of sinners and later as a customer. "A preacher ain't no different from any other man," Dove Lovelady said philosophically. "He's cursed with a cock." For the wedding, they decorated the Gown and Slipper with white streamers of paper. Somebody baked a cake. Maybelle played her hymns on the piano.

And then tragedy struck. And the idyll shattered like glass.

One of Maybelle's favorites was Folly, a tall mousy blonde with quick, infectious laughter and tantalizing blue eyes. Folly was only seventeen, taken in as an orphan after her parents were killed when a keelboat sank on the river. The older women looked after Folly like foster mothers, and Dove Lovelady was careful to pick nice, clean young men for her. The girl dreamed of having a husband someday and a little family of her own. She confided to Maybelle that she really did not enjoy giving her body to strange men for money. "It just don't seem right to me, Maybelle. I feel like Ma and Pa wouldn't approve at all."

"You've got to survive, Folly."

"Yes, that's true. And Miz Lovelady, she's awfully good to me. I would never want her to think I wasn't grateful. It's just that I wasn't brought up this way, Maybelle. I was brought up, well, a Christian."

Folly was also a favorite of the men, especially the younger ones. More than once a rowdy customer making a play for Folly found himself looking into the business end of a pocket pistol and was asked, not too politely, to leave.

Nobody ever knew how the half-breed French trapper got to Folly and managed to take her upstairs without being noticed. Dirk Fleur was as ugly as a coyote and had the disposition, after a few drinks, of a diamondback rattler. He always carried two knives, one in the belt and one in the top of his boot.

Maybelle was entertaining a customer in the parlor when Dove Lovelady barged in shouting, "Where's Folly? I can't find that girl anywhere." Maybelle abandoned her customer and joined Dove in a search of the second floor, accompanied by Buckles and George. They banged on doors and pushed into rooms, heedless of the protests, but Folly was not to be found. Finally, in the bar, a customer said he had seen the girl in the company of Dirk Fleur. "I think they went out the side door, Dove." The search swept outside as customers joined in, bearing torches and shouting.

They found Folly's body behind a shack near the Gown and Slipper. Her throat was cut, and she had been raped. The tracks of a man led away in soft ground, toward the river. At the wharf, Dirk Fleur's canoe was gone. No one had seen him leave in the darkness, and it was impossible to know if he had gone upriver or down.

"They'll never catch the brute," muttered one of the men. "Hell, he's halfway up the Missouri by now."

They buried Folly on a hillside in the autumn cold. The preacher read the Twenty-third Psalm from a battered Bible. "Yea though I walk through the valley of the shadow of death, I shall fear no evil..." Dove Lovelady wept. The Gown and Slipper was closed for three days of mourning.

Soon after that, one of the other young women, Ginger, contracted the French Disease.

The death of Folly affected Maybelle deeply. Now, Ginger's illness filled her with a nameless dread. The French Disease, everyone knew, was incurable, and in time it could drive one insane or cause the body to break out in horrible sores. Anxiety hung over the house like a pall. No one knew which customer carried the disease and who would be infected next. It was time, Maybelle felt, to be leaving. She had saved more than five hundred dollars in less than eight months. That would serve her needs nicely. She announced her decision to Dove Lovelady. The painted eyes filled with tears.

"Where will you go, Maybelle?"

"To New Orleans, more than likely. I always wanted to see the place."

Dove nodded. "A good town, New Orleans. There's plenty of money and all sorts of people. You will do well there."

Maybelle kissed the heavily rouged cheek and went to gather her things. In addition to her savings she now had a decent wardrobe of gowns, fake jewelry, good shoes, and even a winter coat of mink fur provided by an admiring trapper. Even more important, she would walk out of the Gown and Slipper confident and self-assured—qualities she sorely lacked when she had arrived.

Violet gave her a bone-crunching hug. The others embraced and kissed her by turns at the bar. Even Buckles and George, the bouncers, were moved. Maybelle looked around for the last time, put on her coat, picked up her small bearskin suitcase, and walked out into the freezing December day.

At the wharf, the keelboat on which she had bought passage was waiting. The vessel was piled high with pelts for shipment to New Orleans. Keelboaters respectfully helped her to board and made a place for her in the cabin, with a door that latched for privacy. What a far cry, she thought, from her trip upriver with Ahzeeb! The keelboat captain raised a horn to his lips and gave a mighty two-tone blast. There was a pounding of feet and clamor of voices. Poles dug into the shallow water, and muscles strained. Slowly the keelboat moved into midstream, where the current caught hold, and the polers relaxed.

At the stern sweep, a fat man with a luxuriant growth of black beard raised his voice in a melodic chanty song:

"Well it's down to New Orleans we go.
Yo ho, yo ho! Down and down the muddy flow,
Yo ho, yo ho, yo!"

Maybelle sensed that life had a fresh new beginning.

VI

The summer was fierce. Heat broiled the city. In the shops and factories, workers defied the rules by peeling off their shirts. Even on Wall Street, men went without coats and loosened their neckties. Children who were neither in school nor at work splashed in the warm waters of the Hudson and East rivers. In waterfront taverns, the fortunate drank away their afternoons with American-made stout and ale. In stately homes overlooking the Hudson, the wives of merchants, lawyers, and owners of landed wealth took afternoon naps, fanned by black servants. Behind the docks, longshoremen and teamsters brawled over trifles. Everywhere tempers were short. The police reported a record number of homicides. People slept at open windows or on porches, hoping for a breath of air.

Horses stood in their traces, sweating.

The strange craft rode low in the water between two massive fifteen-foot paddle wheels, a tall smokestack jutting skyward amidships. Smoke curled from the funnel, accompanied by random sparks, spewing like fireflies. Emblazoned on her prow, the paint still fresh, was the name *Clermont*. That also was the name of Robert Livingston's country estate, and Robert Fulton thought it a fitting tribute to his patron. Dock loungers had another name for it. A burly fellow perched atop a pile of lumber called down, for the pleasure of a loutish crowd. "Haw, haw, haw, 'Fulton's Folly.' Hey you there, big fella. You gonna ride on 'Fulton's Folly?'" Nathan Stewart ignored him.

Another heckler, inspired by a fresh gush of black pinewood

smoke, joined the merriment. "Looks like a floatin' sawmill, and she's done caught fire. Haw, haw, haw."

Excitement had been mounting all morning as final preparations were completed for *Clermont's* maiden voyage. Shortly before noon, Robert Fulton's guests began to arrive, elegantly dressed men and women drawn from his wide circle of friends in New York. Nathan had begun the day dressed for the occasion, but mechanical trouble had sent him belowdecks. Now, wrench in hand, he emerged drenched in sweat and smeared with grease. He had filled out physically in the three years since Paris and was toughened and heavily muscled from hard labor on the *Clermont* in Charles Brown's New York shipyard. Fulton had insisted to the builder that Nathan have personal charge of every detail of the works, with complete authority for design changes if necessary. The task had been more than even Nathan had bargained for. Now, in the sweltering heat, his mind was consumed by a flurry of last-minute details.

"Ladies and gentlemen," Fulton said. "Permit me to introduce my associate, Nathan Stewart." Nathan checked his stride, nodded, and smiled. Several of the women murmured and moved toward him. Nathan looked to Fulton for help, but saw only his amused grin. The inventor, as was his custom now, was attired in a natty, lightweight suit and fresh linen, every button buttoned. How, Nathan thought, can one man manage to look so damned fresh in heat like this?

"Oh, Mr. Stewart, do tell us all about the *Clermont*. You must be excited absolutely out of your minnnnd!" A doe-eyed blonde put her hand lightly on the bicep of his right arm. "Goodness!"

And so he found himself surrounded by guests and describing the vessel. It was a loving task, for by now Nathan felt a strong kinship with this boat that soon would become, under the guidance of her creators, a living thing. "She stretches one hundred and thirty feet, ladies and gentlemen, from up there"—he pointed to the ornate gold-painted nymph at the bow—"to the end of the flagpole at the stern. She's got a seven-foot draft and is eighteen feet across. That boiler behind the steam engine is twenty feet long, set in asbestos brickwork for fire safety. You can just see the boiler belowdecks there . . ."

"How fast will she travel on the way to Albany, Mr. Stewart?"

"Well, ma'am, we figure close to five miles an hour, upstream. A little more than that coming back down. Round trip ought to take us five days."

"How thrilling!"

"Yes'm."

Nathan glanced at Fulton, who had moved aft and was talking to an elderly man accompanied by a strikingly handsome woman. He estimated her age to be about thirty. She wore a tasteful gown of blue silk print that set off a remarkable, full figure. Her hair was so blond that it gleamed almost white in the sunlight. She wore no hat. Fulton caught Nathan's eye and beckoned for him to join them. He bowed his way free of the crowd.

"Nathan, permit me to introduce Claude Durange and his wife Lucy. Mr. Durange is one of our most important backers."

The old man was visibly pleased. Nathan found his handshake surprisingly firm. "Not *the* Claude Durange?" he said. "This is a privilege. And Mrs. Durange . . ." Her eyes had seemed blue from a distance, but now he saw that that was an illusion. They were gray; gray and steady.

"Mr. Stewart," she said.

Afterward, Nathan would find himself unable to recall the details of their conversation there on the deck of *Clermont*. It was mainly idle pleasantry. He would remember the striking contrast between Durange the man and Durange the legend: tycoon of business and banking, a power in the state legislature, friend of President Jefferson, Robert Livingston, and New York's mayor, DeWitt Clinton. In person, Durange was soft-spoken, almost shy, and quite cordial. But it was Lucy Durange, the celebrated beauty of New York society, who dominated his memory of that meeting. The steady gray eyes looked deeply into his own, as if searching for something.

The Duranges did not remain long on board but went ashore to observe the launching from their carriage. Most of the other guests did stay aboard, to be taken off later by rowboat. Nathan went below again to help the fireman feed cords of pinewood to the firebox and keep an eye on the steam pressure gauge. The heat was stifling, and he mopped sweat from his face and eyes. The guests warily eyed thickening billows of smoke that gushed from the stack. "My goodness, Robert," breathed a young matron, lifting a parasol against flying sparks, "I do hope it doesn't explode!"

"Fear not, my dear."

At last Fulton gave the command. "Cast off lines! Helmsman, steer into the channel."

The great paddle wheels lumbered into action, churning white water as they slowly revolved. From the engine there came a great gushing and chugging. Machinery clanked and steam hissed. The crowd ashore applauded. Abruptly, the paddle wheels slowed and stopped. Fulton shouted reassurance and hurried below, made an adjustment and returned to the deck. The paddle wheels were turning again, slowly pushing *Clermont* forward. The crowd raised a ragged cheer. Fulton responded by vigorously ringing the great ship's bell.

The *Clermont* moved into midstream and progressed steadily against the Hudson River current. Onlookers hurried along onshore, waving joyously. People came running from their houses and fields, shouting. Church bells pealed in the distance.

Nathan came on deck and leaned at the railing beside Fulton and his guests. A thrill went through him as he watched the shoreline sliding past them and felt the light breeze stirred by their forward progress.

"We're doing it, Robert! We're actually under way!"

"It's history in the making, Nathan. Only the beginning, my young friend. We've just turned a page, and things will never be quite the same again."

They stopped to let off those guests who desired to go ashore. Then the *Clermont* resumed her forward motion, consuming cords of firewood from the great pile heaped on deck.

Twenty miles north of New York, a plowman stared in disbelief at the smoking, snorting monster laboring upstream. Dropping the reins of his mule, he sprinted toward the barn, shouting: "The devil's comin' upriver in a sawmill!"

The afternoon rushed by, and evening settled over the lovely river and its lush, rolling hills. They dined by lamplight with white linen and silver, while the hills and valleys gathered purple twilight. The night came on ablaze with stars, and the sparks made a brilliant plume from the smokestack. A late half-moon rose, casting enough light for them to keep to the middle of the river, and the *Clermont* chugged on through the night. Fulton and Nathan took turns at the bow watch. And finally the dawn came, spreading a light mist over the river and the virgin wilderness along both shores. Nathan drank in the beauty of it all as sunrise tipped the hilltops with its rosy glow. And he sensed that he was, at this moment, in this time and place, in the presence of the Almighty.

They made the one-hundred-forty-mile journey to Albany in thirty-two hours. As the *Clermont* steamed into shore in the late afternoon, the whole town came running. Three days later they were back in New York, to be greeted by a huge crowd, cheering and exploding fireworks. Mayor DeWitt Clinton himself read a proclamation extolling "the magnificent achievement of Robert Fulton and his friends." Afterward, in his hotel rooms, Nathan wrote a long letter to Pittsburgh, telling his father about all that had happened. "*Clermont* is going to start regular service the first part of September, carrying passengers and freight. The fare to Albany will be seven dollars a head. Mr. Fulton thinks he can declare a profit for the company by the end of the year. His principal shareholders include Robert Livingston and Mayor Clinton. He wants me to go to work building up the freight business. And he says it won't be long until we'll be building a steamboat for the Ohio and Mississippi, probably right there in Pittsburgh. I'm sure he'll want the Stewart Boatworks to make a bid on the project." As he finished the letter, Nathan realized that he had not been home in more than six years. There had been no time, and the thought gave him a sense of abject loneliness.

He drew out another sheet of paper, dipped his quill into the inkwell, and wrote another letter. The words poured out easily and seemed to give him comfort. The letter consumed two pages. Then he signed it, sprinkled it with drying powder, tucked it into an envelope and affixed his waxen seal. He addressed it: "Mademoiselle Yvette Marchand, 31 Rue de la Concorde, Paris, France." He went down to dinner with the letter in his pocket for posting. It had been an impulse, no more. A foolish one, more than likely, for surely she would not deign to reply.

And yet Nathan had a feeling that somewhere, sometime, he would see her again.

"Wishful thinker," he said aloud.

Where had the months gone? Time fled in a ceaseless rush of activity. Everything demanded Nathan's attention; and still, it seemed, the enterprise of Fulton, Livingston and Clinton wanted more. Barely had the *Clermont* settled into its regularly scheduled Hudson runs than more steam-powered paddle wheelers were on the way. And then there were the constant meetings with shippers and merchant groups, generating more freight business. What had been a novelty in late summer was a demand by fall.

The winter freeze had given him a breather, but spring was upon them already, and demand had become a hue and cry.

"Our summer work's cut out for us, Nathan. We're going to be building a lot of steam-powered paddle boats. Ordinarily, I would put you in charge of that, but I think your talents will be of even better use elsewhere."

"Elsewhere, Robert?"

Robert Fulton took a pinch of snuff, sniffed, sneezed, and dabbed at his nostril with a ruffled cuff. "First we want to go to Washington City with DeWitt Clinton to see President Jefferson about the Erie Canal. And then, a little later on, I'll be wanting you to go to Pittsburgh—"

"To Pittsburgh!"

"—to help build a new steamship. Mainly it's Nicholas Roosevelt's plan, and I have my doubts about the design; but he is a partner, and I want him to have the best technical advice available. That means you."

"Thank you."

"Oh, don't thank me, dear boy. I'm a pragmatist. You happen to be quite brilliant in several ways that we find both useful and profitable."

They had shared dinner in Nathan's rooms overlooking the Hudson. Then as his housekeeper cleared the table, they moved to the balcony for cigars and brandy. Fulton was married and a family man now. He also had grown portly again and added a small paunch, which he adorned in a waistcoat with a gold watch chain. The creator of the Hudson River's burgeoning steamboat enterprise was looking prosperous indeed.

Nathan asked, "Do you think there's a likelihood of President Jefferson rejecting us on the Erie Canal?"

Fulton smiled into his brandy snifter. "You never know about politics, Nathan. We're asking for federal money on a canal project that will cost millions. But by asking federal participation, DeWitt has more than the money in mind. He thinks the added government leverage would help to overcome resistance right here in New York, with the state legislature and his enemies elsewhere. Those damn fools are too blind to see the ends of their noses."

"Even with regular steamboat runs on the Hudson?"

"Even so. Regional jealousies and personal grudges don't always yield to reason. A lot of people don't like DeWitt

Clinton, period. His forebears were British aristocracy, after all. Others can't get comfortable with the idea that our company stands to profit hugely from the canal. But that's plain, gut free enterprise of the kind that will make this country. And then there are the people who resist any kind of change."

Nathan shook his head. Human nature baffled him.

"To Washington City it is, then," he said.

The journey was an agony. Robert Livingston had provided them with his personal heavy carriage. The ponderous vehicle was equipped with extra heavy leaf springs, in contrast to the leather straps of a common stagecoach. Still they lurched and swayed miserably behind a six-horse team. The road from New York to Washington City ranged, for the most part, from bad to abominable. Portions were paved with logs, corduroy style, which rattled one's very bones. Great stretches had no paving at all, and the winter past had left many gullies and washouts and potholes, often slowing them to a walk. To make matters worse, the spring weather turned foul, with an unseasonable sleet storm and cold, blustery days.

Even DeWitt Clinton lost his usual, Olympian composure. The mayor of New York clutched at his tall hat and cursed. "My God, Fulton. This is terrible! I'm coming back by ship, if I come back at all. At least one can take a turn on the deck without being cooped up in this horrible lurching cubicle day after rotten day." Fulton, suffering greatly from motion sickness, merely stared straight ahead, his face the color of chalk.

Before leaving New York, they had been amply warned not to expect much of the new nation's capital. Most critics could not imagine what madness had seized Congress anyhow, to build the city in those foggy bottoms along the Potomac. "God-awful place, really," a journalist had sniffed. "The humidity, you know, is extreme." The warnings, dire as they were, did not nearly do justice to the reality.

Streets were quagmires of mud and filth. Few buildings were completed. Everywhere, from that curious domed Capitol to the White House, scaffolding bristled. Life in Washington was a never-ending hammering and clatter, with swarms of workmen, beasts of burden and foul-mouthed mule skinners, usually drunk. Much of the city consisted of dreary shacks of raw lumber, leaning in the wind. Few women were to be seen, and those who did appear on the streets were usually prostitutes or labor camp followers.

They managed to find lodgings in a half-constructed hotel, but the food was ill prepared, the rooms drafty, and the service terrible. The manager warned them not to go out on the streets after sundown unless it was absolutely necessary. "The city, gentlemen, is positively alive with ruffians and thieves."

"And this, dear friends," DeWitt Clinton said gravely, "is the new cradle of the republic. Would you believe that I'm actually thinking seriously about running for president?"

Thomas Jefferson received them the following morning, apologizing profusely for the state of the capital city and the shambles of his own office as well. Even the President was in temporary quarters while they worked on the White House. He confessed to "a vexation of spirit" over it all. He was tempted, he told them, to move bag and baggage to his beloved Monticello, the mountaintop retreat overlooking Charlottesville, Virginia; but even there, one could not escape hammering and brick dust. "Monticello is only partially done, I regret to say, and I can't spend enough time there to do all the things I've got in mind."

As Nathan knew, these were but petty difficulties. Jefferson was harassed as well by recalcitrant New England shipbuilders and fishermen, in near revolt over the continuing embargo on foreign trade. To get back at the British for impressing American seamen on the high seas, it seemed that the administration was punishing Americans even more. And then there were those who vigorously criticized the Louisiana Purchase; they saw it as a monumental folly, expanding for Jefferson's ego a struggling young nation beyond the limits of good sense or, for that matter, his ability to govern.

All this added to Nathan's sense of awe to be in the presence of the President. He found himself surprised, however, by the great man's diminutive stature. One presumed, somehow, that the author of the Declaration of Independence would be tall and lanky, to match his giant words. Jefferson was, on the contrary, rather short. His hair, in the absence of a wig, was of a common reddish hue.

They took chairs and discussed the usual preliminaries—the hardships of their journey, the weather, the muddy streets of Washington. Abruptly, Jefferson turned to Nathan and said, "I understand you are the brother of Stephen Stewart?"

Nathan was startled. "Yes, sir. I do have a brother named Stephen. He is in Pittsburgh."

Jefferson smiled. "Your brother enjoys the esteem of my

former secretary, Captain Meriwether Lewis. He was a member of the expedition to the West, with Captain Clark, was he not?"

"It's true." Nathan's pleasure was expressed in a broad smile. "We are all proud of Stephen. Even though I haven't seen my brother for several years, I feel very close to him."

"Good. Good." Jefferson seemed to want to pursue the subject in more detail, especially as it related to the expedition and the many samples sent back by Lewis and Clark. DeWitt Clinton, however, was visibly restless. The President turned the conversation to the purpose of their visit. "Well, DeWitt, I can see that you've got other things on your mind."

"Mr. President, we came to talk with you about the Erie Canal."

"Ah, yes." Jefferson put his fingers together and studied them closely. "The canal."

"As I wrote in my letter, I consider the Erie the most momentous project ever undertaken in America. Cheap, efficient transportation, Mr. President, is the key to opening up our great nation for settlement and trade. Mr. Fulton here has launched his steamboat, the *Clermont*, on regular runs up the Hudson to Albany and back. We plan to build at least twenty more paddle steamers in the next decade for general service."

"I'm familar with Mr. Fulton's work. As a gadgeteer of sorts myself, I stand in awe of his achievements."

"We propose to continue our New York to Albany service. But we also want to dig our canal from Albany overland to Buffalo, on Lake Erie. This will open a direct route to the western territory. The entire northern tier of the Ohio Territory is waiting to be settled. In a few years, enterprising engineers could also cut canals southward through Ohio to the Ohio River. Think about that, Mr. President. By direct water route, we could settle the Michigan country and the lands north of there along the Canadian border. Water transportation is the only way."

Jefferson listened politely as Clinton made his points with the aid of a wall map of the United States. The New Yorker described some of the successes already created from canals in England and France. He reminded Jefferson that Robert Fulton had been engaged in some of those projects. The possibility of the Erie Canal had been in men's minds for three quarters of a century. "This is our opportunity, Mr. President, to achieve a real success!"

When Clinton had finished, the President rocked back in his

chair and gathered his thoughts. "DeWitt, I have the greatest respect for you and your associates," he said. "Certainly my friend Robert Livingston did an incredible service for this country by negotiating the Louisiana Purchase. All of you are to be congratulated for opening up the Hudson with the steamboat. I don't doubt that steam power on the rivers will bring about a revolution in trade, commerce, and travel in a very short time. Lord knows we need it, for the British already are casting hungry eyes upon our western territories as far south as New Orleans. Geographically, we've been strapped. There has long existed an enormous gulf between Americans along the eastern seaboard and those beyond the Alleghenies and the Appalachians. Those mountains rise like a wall. For added measure the major rivers in the heart of the country flow in one direction: south. Two-way commerce is extremely difficult; from a practical standpoint, well-nigh impossible."

He paused, letting his words sink in. "But the Erie Canal?" The President shook his head. "I've made my position clear in the past, and nothing you have told me changes my mind. This administration is committed foremost to the building of a national road westward from the Cumberland and into Ohio Territory. That road, gentlemen, borrows from the ancient Romans. It will be wide and paved with crushed stone for all-weather travel on foot, by wagon or horseback. And that happens to be the mode of travel for ninety percent of our people. The road will have bridges and culverts crossing creeks and streams. Work on it has already begun at Cumberland, Maryland. And by the time it's completed, that road is going to open up the Ohio Territory in a way that will make canals seem obsolete by comparison. The work has already started, and when it's done you'll be able to travel on foot all the way to Illinois Territory. Mark my words."

"Mr. President, the National Road is going to be a great boon to Baltimore and the state of Maryland. But it does nothing to increase trade for New York, New Jersey, and even northern Pennsylvania." Clinton spoke vehemently now, and his voice had a cutting edge. Nathan had never seen the distinguished New Yorker so close to losing his temper. "And I remind you, Mr. President, that we New Yorkers provide your administration with a great deal of political support..."

"DeWitt, what you say is true. All true. But let me point out that talking about building the Erie Canal is one thing, actually *doing* it is something else again. Why, you can't even get your own state legislature to go along. You are proposing to dig and build aqueducts and locks through hill country for a distance of three hundred and sixty-three miles! You will require more than eighty locks. The highest point along your route is nearly seven hundred feet above sea level." The President wagged his head. "I've said it before, and I say it again. A splendid project, gentlemen, and it might even be executed a century from now. But to think of it at this day is little short of madness."

They left the President's office in dark humor. DeWitt Clinton rode in silence back to the unfinished hotel. Over a tasteless luncheon, he brooded. Finally, he struck the table a heavy blow with his fist. "By God, we're going to build that canal. I don't care what Tom Jefferson says or what my enemies say. We're going to get an appropriation bill through the legislature and build it!" He sighed heavily and slumped in his chair.

Robert Fulton stroked his sideburns, plainly dubious. "Yes, well . . . In the meantime, Nathan, I think we should be getting back to the steamship business. Time and tides wait for no man, you know."

Spring came late to the Alleghenies. An unseasonable freeze in late March nipped the early buds and browned the grasses along the rivers. But when the change did come, it brought a concentrated rush of fresh life more dazzling than anyone could remember. Dogwood flourished in forests bursting with new leaf. Jonquils and bluebells danced in the meadows. The grasses were a deep, rich green. And the rivers, for a change unflooded by the spring rains, meandered through burgeoning hills with splendid calm, shining blue-green in the distance.

The panorama overwhelmed Nathan. As his big bay stallion topped the final hill, and the smoky valley of the three rivers spread out below, the weariness of travel evaporated from his body. He thought: Home. Dismounting and removing his rifle, travel cloak, and heavy saddlebags, he let the bay forage and stood for half an hour savoring the splendor of it all. The town had grown immensely in the decade since he had looked back for the last time from this very crest. Old Fort Pitt was still there, a crumbling dark ruin of dark battlements and brooding memories. Everywhere else, new smokestacks, factories, and buildings had risen in his absence. The town spread well back from the rivers and up the slopes. There were new structures across the rivers as well, and the shores of the Monongahela were alive with boatbuilding activity. One saw warehouses and loading docks and every imaginable sign of commercial boom. From here, too, he could see the Stewart Boatworks and compound. It was difficult to recognize the place, so vastly had it expanded. And the house—the once frame Stewart House—was now a handsome structure of quarried stone with a high cupola and widow's walk overlooking the river.

They would be waiting, he knew. He had written six weeks earlier of his intentions and sent his trunks ahead from New York. From the exchanges of letters with the family, however, he sensed that the changes would be far greater than surface prosperity. Stephen was in command now; and from the tone of the letters, the younger brother had become a man of his own mind. To Nathan's dismay, already there was conflict about the building of the steamboat *New Orleans*. Stephen had refused to submit a bid for the work, saying he would explain things to Nathan in person. And so Nicholas Roosevelt's craft was now being constructed in a competing boatyard. Nathan had silently cursed his brother for a headstrong young fool, but managed to curb his anger until they could discuss it face to face. And then there was the matter of Maybelle's disappearance. His sister had been gone for three years. Except for two brief letters, one from St. Louis and the other from New Orleans, they seemed to have no real idea of where she was or what she was doing. Even this apparently would have to wait, however; for in the latest letter from his mother, Nathan had learned that his homecoming would be celebrated with the wedding of Stephen and Catherine Colby, his parent's ward. "Catherine is such a beautiful person, both inside and out. I know you are going to love her as we do."

His mood a welter of conflicts, Nathan whistled up the bay, mounted, and descended the road into Pittsburgh.

They came swarming out of the compound drawn by the shouts of old Charlie. Someone started ringing the fire bell. "Nathan! Nathan's back!" But it was Martha Stewart who reached him first. Her once-lovely hair had gone to gray, and age had lined and seamed her face. The transformation so startled him that he almost wept, gathering up his mother in a joyous embrace. A similar shock came with the appearance of his father, but for all his aging, Isaiah Stewart had lost none of his iron handclasp and authoritative vigor. "By God, Nathan, what a handsome big devil ye are!" Nathan's parents and several of the old employees

ushered him up a wide, curving brick walkway lined with flower
beds toward the great stone house, dominated by a broad front
verandah and massive double doors.

"How do ye like this?" Isaiah rumbled.

"Magnificent."

"It's your brother's labor of love," said Martha. "He wanted
a proper homeplace for us and his bride-to-be."

As she spoke, the double doors opened, and Stephen emerged,
smiling. Nathan broke his stride, so impressed was he by the
appearance of his brother. Gone the boyish build and look of
juvenile whimsy. Stephen Stewart was muscular, tall, and extraordinarily handsome. He had their father's thrusting jawline
and the chiseled, even features they both shared with their
mother. His bearing bespoke strength and self-assurance. Stephen
strode across the verandah and gripped his brother's hand.
"Welcome home, Nathan. Welcome to Stewart House." Moments later, Nathan came into the presence of Catherine Colby.
Tall, blond, obviously intelligent, she seemed to be everything in
a woman that Stephen was in a man. The hand she gave him had
a surprisingly strong grip, and her bearing radiated a confidence
almost of command. "Thank God you're home, Nathan. What a
marvelous day in our lives. We're so happy to see you."

But it wasn't all marvelous, and it wasn't all happy. The first
strains became apparent that very evening as they sat down with
a few friends from town for Nathan's homecoming dinner. He
was delighted by the arrival of Zachary Palmer, the tutor and
bookdealer. Jenny Carver also came, stout and still unmarried
though approaching thirty. She had an intense loyalty to the
Stewart family. Brother Burl did not appear, but Stephen passed
this over lightly. "Burl went to town this morning and probably is not aware of your arrival."

Isaiah Stewart took a mouthful of rare beef and growled,
"Drunk, you mean."

"I didn't say that."

"No, but I said it."

It was Nathan's mention of Maybelle that set things on edge.
When he asked Stephen about their sister, Isaiah noisily smacked
down his water goblet. A hush came over the table.

"That name is not to be mentioned in this house," Isaiah said.

Nathan flushed. "What do you mean, not to be mentioned?
This is her family too, her home . . ."

"Not while I draw breath it isn't."

Martha paled. "Your father . . ."

"Mother, don't get upset," Stephen said quietly.

"Thank you, Stephen. I'm all right. Your father, Nathan, has disowned your sister. Struck her out of his will. She ran off with a—a merchant three years ago."

"I know that. But where is Maybelle now? Is she well? Does she have any money? Is she safe?"

"I said we will not discuss it!"

"Father, I damn well intend to discuss it."

"Nathan," Stephen said. "Later."

Isaiah pushed back his chair. "Not later, not any time. Your sister is disowned, do you understand me? Disowned. As far as I'm concerned, as far as this family is concerned, she does not exist." He glowered around the table. The guests stirred uncomfortably. Zachary Palmer fiddled with his fork. Jenny Carver coughed. Stephen wore a curiously detached expression, but Catherine's eyes were filled with concern. Martha Stewart seemed flustered and confused.

"What's wrong with this family?" Nathan said. "Have you all lost your senses? Don't you care what happens to your own flesh and blood? Or what might have happened to her already?"

Isaiah threw down his napkin and left the table, his face mottled with fury. So abrupt was his departure that he overturned a water glass. In his wake, they sat frozen and unspeaking, listening to the water drip.

Martha was the first to recover. "Poor man. Poor, poor man. He has suffered so much over this. I feel sorry for Isaiah."

"What about Maybelle?" Nathan persisted. "Does anybody feel sorry for her?"

Stephen spoke quietly: "We all do, Nathan. I've sent inquiries downriver trying to locate her without success. We know that for a while she worked in a place in St. Louis called the Gown and Slipper. Then she left St. Louis, supposedly for New Orleans. But if there is anybody named Maybelle Stewart working in New Orleans, in a public place, we haven't been able to locate her."

Dinner resumed without enthusiasm. Even wine did not put any sparkle into the table talk. Finally, Nathan looked to Catherine and asked when the wedding would take place.

"In ten days," she said, quickly brightening and looking at Stephen with a warm smile. "That is, if your brother will still have me."

"Still have you?" Stephen squeezed her hand. "Must a man have air to breathe?"

As they looked into each other's eyes, Nathan felt an envy disturbing in its intensity. The presence of so much love gave him an acute sense of empty bachelorhood.

Business waited until after dinner. The men gathered on the verandah for brandy and pipes filled with mild Virginia tobacco. Even Zachary Palmer, who normally abstained from alcohol, accepted a glass. Nathan came quickly to the subject of the steamship *New Orleans* and Stephen's refusal to bid for the work. "This would have given the family an inside line on building steamships for the Mississippi," he said curtly. "The *New Orleans* is merely the beginning. Fulton and Livingston will be constructing steam-powered vessels in a big way. We're making a fortune with the Hudson River steamship monopoly, Stephen. Now they plan to do the same thing along the Ohio and Mississippi: gain a monopoly from states and territorial jurisdictions adjoining the rivers and build the vessels to serve it."

Stephen smoked his pipe, saying nothing. Nathan did not conceal his displeasure over the *New Orleans* contract going to another boatyard. But he believed that he could salvage future business for Stewart Boatworks, provided that Nicholas Roosevelt, the boatbuilder who was in association with Fulton and Livingston, was not overly offended.

Stephen knocked out his pipe in a shower of sparks. "I don't want their contracts," he said.

Nathan blinked. "What on earth are you saying, you don't *want* their contracts? My God, man, this is a fortune I'm talking about. Any boatbuilder would give his eye teeth to get a chance like this one."

"But most of all, I don't want their monopoly on the rivers," Stephen continued. "The western rivers are free for any man to navigate, with any kind of vessel. As far as I'm concerned, they'll stay that way. New York state can do what it pleases with its rivers; but this isn't New York."

"Don't you see, though, we'll be part of that monopoly too! I can virtually assure you, Stephen . . ."

"Besides, I've seen Roosevelt's craft. He was a farmer and a tinkerer with steam engines, not a boatbuilder. That boat, the *New Orleans*, has got a five-foot draft, Nathan. She might be fine for the Hudson River, but a vessel drawing that much water is going to have a hard time of it on the Ohio and upper

Mississippi, especially at low-water season. Oh, she'll make it all right on the spring and fall floods; but we've got to have boats that can navigate between Pittsburgh and New Orleans and up to St. Louis and beyond, all year around. Tell him, Zachary."

Zachary Palmer was now the publisher of the *River Almanac*, an annual compendium of facts and figures about the Ohio and Mississippi, highly respected by travelers and rivermen. He confirmed what Stephen had said, reciting from an encyclopedic memory mean water tables along certain stretches of the Ohio and describing the shifting nature of sandbars and currents along the Mississippi. "With all due respect to you, Nathan, I must concur with what Stephen is saying."

"And Father? What does he say?"

"Father has left these decisions to me. We've so expanded our operations, with both the boat works and the freight business really booming, that he's just too busy to think much about contracting for Roosevelt's steamboat. Besides"—Stephen looked down from the verandah to the sprawling Stewart works along the Monongahela, where men now toiled by lamplight to catch up on orders for new river craft—"I'm damned if I know where we'd find room."

Nathan bit his lip angrily. "Well, I ought to have some say-so in the matter. Am I not a member of the family too?"

"Yes, Nathan, you certainly are a member of the family. And any time you feel ready to come back and work with us, you're more than welcome."

The remark had a blunt edge. Stephen well knew that Nathan's success with the Fulton-Livingston enterprises was too profitable to abandon and return permanently to the family business in Pittsburgh. Besides, the prospect of both the western river monopoly and the Erie Canal fired Nathan with a zeal that no amount of brotherly opposition was likely to dampen.

Nathan left them in a foul mood and went to his rooms. The quarters consisted of an apartment on the third floor of Stewart House, with a richly paneled interior and fine carpeting. A servant turned down his bed and brought whiskey and water for a nightcap. As Nathan drank in silence, he thought he heard someone pacing from his father's room next door. When he finally blew out the lamp and went to bed an hour later, he was sure of it. He drifted off to sleep to the sound of soft, measured steps.

The formal wedding of Stephen Stewart and Catherine Colby

ten days later was the biggest social event ever to take place in
Pittsburgh. The Rev. Jonathan Duncan, an Anglican bishop from
Philadelphia, arrived personally to perform the ceremony at
Stewart House in the company of a full choir and hundreds of
guests. They included wealthy ironmongers, boatbuilders, and
merchants whose friendship could serve the church well in times
of need.

Despite the business differences. Nicholas Roosevelt also came
with his wife Lydia, whose father Benjamin had planned
Washington, D. C. They were accompanied by a strikingly
beautiful woman with hair so blond it was almost white. Nathan's
pleasure surged. Lucy Durange! His intense stare across the
crowded vestibule drew her attention. The gray eyes widened,
and the lovely face lifted in a smile. Nathan worked his way
through the crush of people to her side. "Madame Durange. I'm
delighted!" He took her hand, and the long tapering fingers
squeezed his lightly in response. They were caught up in small
talk with the Roosevelts. When the subject turned to Nathan's
visit to Washington two years before, he managed to avoid
speaking critically of the new city. It was Lydia who laughingly
spoke what was on Nathan's mind. "Frankly, I think it's a terrible
place, all mud and flies in summer and terribly cold in winter.
Nicholas, darling, if we never go back to Father's city, that will
be just fine with me."

Catherine Colby was radiant. Her blonde hair shimmered beneath the white veil. Her lithesome body was encased in white
and trailed a long train as she moved down a red-carpeted aisle
on the arm of Zachary Palmer. Stephen, in full formal wear,
towered over his friends and the bishop. Even Burl, seeming
short and nondescript in comparison to his brothers, managed to
remain sober long enough to serve as an usher. Jenny Carver
wept through the entire service, her nose growing redder with
each tear, and she was still mopping her eyes with a hankie when
it was over.

"Jenny, what's the matter?" Nathan asked, teasingly.

"I just w-wish," she sobbed afresh, "that something like that
would happen to me!"

Lucy Durange watched the bridal couple with open admiration. "Mr. Stewart, I've never seen two more beautiful people in
my life," she whispered. "And I'm positively jealous of your
new sister-in-law."

The wedding was followed by a reception and dancing in the

garden. Stephen and Catherine changed into traveling clothes then emerged to cut a huge five-tiered wedding cake that Martha Stewart herself had designed. Isaiah, already tipsy from celebrating, rose for a toast. "It warms an old man's heart, dear friends." He teetered a bit, and sloshed a dollop of wine. "I've never decided whether marriages were indeed made in heaven. Some of them, I suspect, came from the other place. No matter." He belched softly. "I think God meant for these two special, special people to be together always." He drank off the glass. The crowd drank off their glasses. Catherine kissed him on the cheek. Martha wept. And a fiddler struck up a merry reel.

Nathan and Lucy Durange shared a table with the Nicholas Roosevelts, Zachary Palmer, and a few other friends. The combination of it all—the wine, the gaily dressed crowd, the afternoon sunlight filtering down through tall sycamore trees and the heady nearness of Lucy Durange—served to warm his blood. Stephen and Catherine joined them briefly, but were constantly besieged by well wishers. Nathan saw the flush of happiness and wine in his brother's face. He leaned toward Catherine and said: "I've never seen my little brother so happy. I hope your love endures forever."

Catherine seemed startled. "Why Nathan, you're positively poetic."

"A lovely sentiment and I share it," Lucy said.

Catherine watched Stephen accepting congratulations. Her face glowed with an inner light. "Stephen is all I've ever wanted. If I could not have married him, I doubt if I'd marry at all."

An hour later a sparkling green carriage trimmed in gilt and drawn by four white horses came rattling into the compound. The vehicle was loaned by an ironmonger with a fondness for romance. As the liveried driver leaped down, snatched open the door, and unfolded the step, Stephen and Catherine rushed through a storm of flying grain and cheers. Then, with a whistle and a whipcrack, hooves clashed, and the wagon lurched in a wide turn through the double gates and away, paper streamers flying. Martha Stewart stood waving at the gates, a damp handkerchief crushed in one hand. Nathan thought that his mother suddenly seemed very alone and vulnerable.

And now the fiddles flew, the dancing increased its tempo, and the wine changed to hard liquor as the party roared through the afternoon and into the evening. Nathan delighted in the company of Lucy Durange, who drew admirers and stimulated conversation like an electric presence. He marveled at the social grace of the woman as she deftly turned aside an invitation to dance from a handsome young merchant and yet accepted the offer of an ancient ironmonger crippled with gout. She neither mentioned nor seemed to notice that Nathen made no offer to dance; but when finally, from acute embarrassment, he confessed his inability, she gave a sigh of relief. "I'm so glad. I was beginning to think I was dull company." And promptly, her laughter and a touch of her hand settled his momentary confusion. After that she did not accept any dancing invitations at all. As darkness stole over the garden, and servants put out lighted lamps at the tables, they shared dinner with Nicholas and Lydia Roosevelt.

"They'll enjoy honeymooning in Philadelphia," Lydia was saying. "Catherine will be able to do a lot of shopping there. It certainly sounds more civilized than our wedding trip last year, don't you agree Nicholas?"

Roosevelt laughed. He was forty-three years old, had a pleasant disposition, and doted on his young wife. "Lydia's bridal journey," he said, "was downriver on a houseboat. Fulton and Livingston sent me out to survey the water route to New Orleans, and so we combined business with pleasure."

"I'd call that roughing it," Lucy Durange said.

"Not really. We had a pilot, three deckhands, and a cook. Lydia did a lot of sewing and reading while I worked..."

"Nicholas was so busy mapping channels and currents and surveying fueling places that sometimes I thought I was honeymooning alone," Lydia said.

Roosevelt chuckled. "It'll be better next time."

"Next time?" said Lucy.

Nathan laughed. "When the *New Orleans* is built, Lydia and Nicholas intend to take her on a maiden voyage the full distance downriver."

"Then that explains why you surveyed fuel stops."

"Wood stops, really."

"But won't it be dangerous, a man and woman alone?"

"We won't be alone exactly," Roosevelt said. "We'll have our crew on board." He turned to Nathan and his expression became serious. "I gather that your brother still doesn't wish to participate?"

"No. He's stubborn as a mule."

"And the monopoly?"

"He's not going to help us there, either. Stephen seems dead set against river monopolies in the West. I suspect that his experience with the Lewis and Clark expedition shaped his thinking."

Lucy Durange smiled. "Do you mean to tell me that the mighty Stewart family of Pittsburgh has disagreements?"

Nathan nodded ruefully. "More than you could possibly imagine."

The Roosevelts remained at Stewart House all evening. They were among the last guests to leave, accompanied by Lucy Durange, who was their houseguest in Pittsburgh. Nathan surmised that the lingering visit had to do with Lucy, and he was grateful. Martha Stewart sat up with him until long after midnight, talking family talk. At one point she gazed at her son with concern.

"Mr. Durange did not accompany his wife to Pittsburgh?"

"He had matters to attend to. Besides, his health is not of the best for travel. Lucy—that is, Mrs. Durange—is a close friend of the Roosevelts. They invited her to visit them here for a couple of months this summer."

"Beautiful woman. And at least thirty-five years old, wouldn't you say?"

"Perhaps," Nathan said.

"Her husband is a much older man, I'm told. Quite wealthy, too."

"Yes." Nathan was uncomfortable with the subject of the conversation. "He is a great deal older, but an extremely important man in New York, both in business and politics."

Martha Stewart pursed her lips. "Nathan," she began, "I know it's none of my business, but—"

"You're absolutely right, Mother. It's none of your business."

Stung by the rebuke, she left him and went to bed.

In the days that followed, Nathan was drawn as if by some magnetic force to the company of Lucy Durange. They rode horseback side-by-side for long distances up the Monongahela to take picnic lunches in forest meadows by the river. They went rowboating and caught perch, bass, and catfish at Nathan's boyhood fishing holes under towering cliffs and off grassy points. Borrowing a pair of Stephen's rifles, they hunted for small game and wildfowl. Lucy proved to be an excellent shot and bagged two fine wild turkeys, which they took to the Roosevelt house. But the Roosevelts had gone upriver to spend the night with friends, and even the servants had left for the night.

"Well, then, we'll just do our own cooking," Lucy said. Expertly, she cleaned and plucked one of the turkeys, stuffed it with chestnuts and dark grain meal dressing, and roasted it with carrots and white potatoes. The table was set on the terrace with crystal, silver, and gleaming white cloth. They dined by candle-light with a fine view of the Allegheny River. A full moon rose, turning the night to dappled shade and the river to silver. Warmed by wine and brandy, Nathan lit a pipe, and they strolled down the broad lawn to the water's edge. They stood there wordlessly, holding hands and listening to the night sounds.

She reached up into her hair and unclasped two pins. The hair tumbled down in silvery waves as she shook it out. She half turned, her arms still raised, and Nathan gathered her to him. His mouth sought hers.

"Oh, Nathan. Oh, Nathan."

Her mouth was full-lipped, warm and sweet from wine. Her breath quickened, and she seemed to melt against him. His arms encircled her and the power of his embrace drove the breath from her. She moaned. Nathan's mind came aflame. The night covered them with its warmths and its scents. There was a fragrance of crushed violets and daffodils.

"Lucy. My God, Lucy..."

So suddenly it happened. So suddenly. One moment they were standing, locked together, and the next they were melting down into the rich grass. The firm breast, clothed, thrust against his cradling hand, and then the breast was free; free and smooth and firm-nippled against his face and his mouth. She panted and made soft sounds in her throat; her breath and body gave off the musk of her heat. His hand fought more cloth, freeing her thighs and freeing himself until he jutted out, immense and aching. Her fingers found him, and she gasped. And then his hands explored her, explored the opening flesh, the fine wedge of silken blond hair, the warm wet opening places. She trembled beneath him.

He entered her slowly, slowly, slowly, and the heat of her enclosed him. "Nathan, you're so...so..."

Slowly he moved with her as she moved, felt the constriction of her tautness, demanded, thrust. She whimpered. And then the shaft went home. Her body arched; her eyes grew lynxlike in the moonlight. And then savagely, like mating animals, they writhed and pumped, breathing mixed, sweat rising. He locked her hips in his two hands and pumped into the spread of her thighs.

"Nathan! Nathan! Oh, my God...Oh, my *G-G-Goddddd!*"

He exploded deep inside her; and deep went the flood of his manhood, each spurt coming from some volcanic depth, while she cried out into his ear, and her body made answering spasms.

They lay together in their disarray, drained. Her hair was a tumble of silver on the grass. Somewhere, an owl hooted. And the river flowed past them timeless and eternal, washing its sand grains and rock grains, its leaves and humus and flotsam, down to the Ohio, down to the Mississippi, down to the sea.

Afterward, long afterward, they spoke in whispers and watched the moon ride across the night. The wonder of it filled him with an aching sense of beauty beyond reality, beyond life. His mind and senses had gone into a different dimension, and the hunger of it kept repeating itself until the night at last became a wash of gray and curling mists, and the grass gleamed with dewdrops, and she stood up at last—pale like a blossom drained of its last vestige of color—and said that it was time for him to go.

And so they moved into a magic summer. Nathan had nothing to compare it with, nothing against which to measure such an experience, and he took this to be the infinite and everlasting love. By day he worked in a boatyard, overseeing construction of the *New Orleans:* keel to hull, warped boards and pitch caulking, sawdust and glue and sweat. The machinery arrived by wagon and was installed, the great boilers belowdecks, the engine next to them and linked to the paddle wheels by steel arms and pistons and great connecting rods. That was by day. By night, again and again and yet again, it was Lucy. Always Lucy. Dear, loving, sweetly scented, passionate Lucy. They loved on the grass and beneath the trees and by the river; they loved on couches and in quiet rooms, at stolen moments.

She spoke of her husband. "He is a good man and treats me like a queen."

"You are a queen."

"Claude adores me. He is a gentle man. Yes, he is twice as old as I am; but Nathan, look at all that he gives me. He is a worldly man, Claude, with a questing spirit."

He learned to accept the idea of sharing her with Claude. He thought that he loved her, wanted desperately to love her. In the mornings he shaved before the mirror and looked into his own eyes and told his reflection: "I love her. I love her more than life." The thought of her was with him constantly. And yet, within two months, his ardor began to cool. He knew it; she sensed it.

"You're changing," she said. "You don't feel as you did before. The flame dies, yes?"

He denied it, spoke his reassurance. They quarreled. He stormed from her presence and was gone for two days.

She left Pittsburgh during one of those quarrels, to return to New York. A note told him good-bye.

Nathan was bereft.

Martha Stewart watched him with pain in her eyes. "You're not well. What's ailing you, son?"

"I'm all right, Mother."

"Maybe you should see the doctor. Have him bleed you with the leeches. You look pale. You are losing weight. You work too hard on that steamboat."

"It's nothing. I'm fine."

"The woman, then. You're eating your heart out over that woman."

"I'm a grown man. Leave me alone."

She watched him ride out of the compound astride the big bay stallion. She thought: We're never fully grown. Our bodies grow and age, bend and wrinkle; but inside, there is always the child.

Nathan returned to New York in August, riding a stagecoach in the sweltering heat. Part of the journey, from Wheeling, Virginia, to Cumberland, Maryland, took him over portions of the new National Road. Gangs of laborers toiled at the western extension with picks and shovels, sledgehammers and great horse-drawn roller machines. He was astounded by the breadth and smoothness of the finished pike. Already travel was picking up in both directions. He remembered Thomas Jefferson's prophecy, and he had to admit that in some ways the President was right. The National Road indeed was beginning to open the West. But then, beyond Cumberland, the stagecoach was back on the old roads, lurching and bucking. They were three weeks reaching New York, and every muscle in Nathan's body rebelled from its punishment.

The reunion with Lucy was tumultuous, their passions seemingly inexhaustible. She also began to introduce him socially, and Nathan accompanied Lucy and Claude Durange to parties and dinners everywhere. The old man remembered him from the *Clermont* and seemed delighted to have him along. "Somebody to talk to besides the fops. Parties are such a bore." But if the parties were a bore, they also served to enhance the fortunes of an ambitious young man. As summer passed into autumn,

Nathan met the wealthy and influential of New York. As a hostess in her own right, Lucy specialized in small, bright dinners for select people where conversation went beyond the banal. Nathan moved into the rarified circle of the DeWitt Clintons, the Livingstons, the Adamses, the Claytons and the Rosenfoerts. The latter was a Dutch banking family. There was talk of trade agreements and talk of the British impressing of American seamen in international waters. "Bloody outrages on the high seas," grumbled old Robert Rosenfoert, whose investments included shipping. There was talk of war.

Nathan liked Claude Durange and respected the old man's skill at bargaining and political subterfuge. Durange shared DeWitt Clinton's belief in the Erie Canal and vowed to invest in it if the New York legislature ever approved the project. "Damned bunch of nincompoops," fumed Clinton. Durange smiled and patted the mayor's arm. "Now, DeWitt. Every man has his self-interest. Your job is to identify and reward it."

The trysts with Lucy became more furtive and brief. He found ways to visit her in daytime, when Durange was not at home. But he felt like a sneak thief, and the threat of discovery nagged at him, making their lovemaking perfunctory and often incomplete. "I don't care," Lucy whispered urgently. "Let them find us. I don't care. I want you. I'll leave him and marry you." But this also troubled Nathan. To himself, he thought: Do I throw away my career, my ambitions, for a love affair with a married woman? He hated thinking this way, for it was clearly selfish and vain. She sensed his preoccupation, accused him again of growing cold, accused him of infidelity. "Who else are you seeing, Nathan? You're seeing another woman. Tell me the truth!" She wept. Once, during a stolen evening in his own rooms, she flew into a towering rage and struck him. And then, a sudden overwhelming passing, they fell to frantic lovemaking that left them exhausted.

Cargo business thrived on the Fulton-Livingston monopoly. The steamships were bringing about a rapid expansion of settlement up the Hudson. Towns and villages now flourished where only farms stood before. And as the line prospered, so did Nathan. He was growing rich. And the tall, handsome Pennsylvania bachelor with his Oxford polish and powerful friends was now regarded as the most eligible man in New York. Rumors that the beautiful Lucy Durange was madly in love with him did not lessen his appeal. He was sought after by hostesses having unmarried females in the family. Party invitations poured in at such a rate he could not possibly accept them all. But when an embossed card arrived inviting him to a weekend of pre-Christmas celebration at the Rosenfoert country estate, he responded with enthusiasm.

Fresh snowfall transformed the rolling hills along the Hudson into a wonderland. Nathan traveled by hired sleigh, bundled against the cold. The Rosenfoert estate spread back from the river along a winding road, the main house rising in columned splendor. He arrived at dusk. Liveried footmen helped guests from carriages and sleighs and took their things into the house. Icicles drooped from roof overhangs. Lights blazed.

Nathan was ushered inside by old Rosenfoert himself, who gave him a dry handshake. "Delighted you could come, Nathan. I think you're going to enjoy this." A servant took his damp cloak, and a butler brought hot buttered rum on a tray. "Nothing like buttered rum," Rosenfoert cackled, "to drive out the cold from a man's innards." He sipped gratefully, lips puckered against the heat of the brew. Rosenfoert hurried away to greet more guests, and Nathan moved about the house. A gigantic Christmas tree, still barren of decoration, dominated the living room beside a great stone fireplace in which a log fire burned cheerily. Elsewhere about the house, decorations abounded. There were sprigs of holly and spruce, bright beads and baubles, and colorful candles at the windows. The interior of the mansion was all polished floors and European-style furnishings, with stuffed settees in gold fabric, gleaming woods, and soaring white walls displaying rich paintings and sculpted moldings. In the dining room a long formal table was set for two-dozen guests, and from the kitchen area came a heady blending of cooking odors.

A servant approached him. "Your room is ready, sir." Nathan climbed broad, winding stairs. His quarters for the weekend consisted of a large bedroom with a fireplace. He bathed, shaved, and dressed in evening clothes. At nine o'clock, he went back downstairs.

The house was now filled with guests. A piano tinkled from the music room, where people were singing carols. Many recognized Nathan and called his name. He worked his way toward the great Christmas tree.

A familiar voice called, "Ah, Nathan. There you are!" Robert Livingston, tall and elegantly clothed, detached himself from a group and came over to shake hands. "I've been looking for you. There's someone I think you'll enjoy seeing." Nathan followed him across the room. Then Livingston was saying, "Yvette? Look who we have here."

She was still petite and perfectly formed. The soft oval face looked up to him. The eyes had a glint of whimsy. "Mr. Stewart. How nice to see you again." She wore a gown of shimmering brown, and her hair was done in a bouffant, caught with a clutch of seed pearls.

He stood at first, openmouthed. Then, recovering, he took her proffered hand and lightly brushed it with his lips. "Yvette. Uh, Mademoiselle Marchand." Without thinking he lapsed into French. "What an honor. What a lovely surprise." He glanced at the left hand for a ring, saw none. "It is still 'mademoiselle,' is it not?"

She laughed. "Yes." The large brown eyes searched his face. "You look marvelous, so fit and handsome. And certainly as tall as ever. It's a good thing you didn't join the emperor's imperial guard, for you'd be on your way to Russia by now."

He was having difficulty thinking of what to say. Confound it! How many times had he dreamed of a meeting such as this and spoken to her with such easy charm and conviviality. Now came the reality, however—the amazing, stunning reality—and his tongue was tied again. Damn. What a dolt he was!

"Monsieur. You're having difficulty?"

Nathan smiled, his embarrassment showing. "I'm overwhelmed. I can't think of a single clever thing to say, except that I'm very, very glad to see you. And that isn't clever at all, is it?" Her eyes smiled again. Were they mocking him? He tried to correct himself. "That is, I'm . . ."

She took his arm, murmured to her friends, and walked away with him. He could feel the swell of her breast lightly against his arm. They passed Rosenfoert, who smiled broadly. "Ah, I see that you two found each other." But Nathan had not found his tongue. He nodded, smiled, moved on, conscious only of her nearness, her arm in his arm, the soft scent of her perfume, and the murmur of her voice.

Later, he tried to recall every moment, every detail of that magical weekend, but could not. It all blended into an ecstatic blur of impressions. They skied on the steep slopes behind the mansion, and he was so clumsy that he fell repeatedly in clouds of flying snow. They went ice skating on the pond, her gaiety bubbling, and he fell again, this time taking her with him. At dinner, her eyes sparkled at him across the rim of a wineglass, and their fingertips met as they touched glasses in a toast. Then, decorating Robert Rosenfoert's great Christmas tree, he held tightly to her trim waist as she stood on the ladder, placing strings of tinsel and colored sugar cookies baked in the form of stars and dangling from thread. The two nights and two days rushed past them, and suddenly it was Sunday evening, and they were all saying good-bye and climbing back into sleighs and carriages for the journey back to the city, a fresh snowfall lightly swirling down.

A week went by before he saw her again, for Yvette was staying at the Livingstons' country place. Then, wonder of wonders, a note came informing him that the family was moving to their townhouse. After that he saw her almost daily; indeed, he could not keep away. They walked through the city in the cold, laughing and shopping and tossing snowballs. When a warm spell came, thawing the ice along the edges of the East River, he took her down to see the original *Clermont*, fired up her boilers and—cracking the ice—took her chugging out onto the river, smoke boiling from the stack.

And then came the evening in February. New York lay under a fresh blanket of snow. They rode in a horse-drawn sleigh through the silent streets, down to the river. She had brought hot tea in a warming jar, and they sat huddled under lap robes looking at the swirling black river and sipping tea from china cups. The steam rose in their faces.

For days, the question had haunted his mind, and he was tormented by the thought of her refusal. He had phrased it all, time after time; but for all the made-up speech, it came out not at all as he had planned.

"I've got something . . . something I want to say to you, to ask you."

"Oh?"

"Yes. It has been on my mind."

"You don't like the tea?"

"Oh, I love the tea. It's wonderful tea."

"It's me you don't like, then. You're bored. You want to go back."

"No." He glowered at her. "That's not it."

She giggled. "You're angry. I always know when you're

angry, because your brow darkens, and that lock of hair falls down. You remind me of a little boy when that hair falls—"

"I love you."

"—down, like a spoiled little boy who . . . What?"

"I love you," he said. "I want you to marry me. That is, I hope you love me and will marry me. I mean . . . Well, you know what I mean."

There. It was said. Now he was miserable. For she sat there in a sudden silence, just looking at the river. Now I've ruined it, he thought. Now she will go away, and I'll never see her again, and if that happens . . .

"It took you long enough to say so," she said. "Almost six weeks. That's a terribly long time to keep a young woman dangling."

"Then you will? You will marry me?"

"Well . . ."

"Please say you will, Yvette. It means everything to me, my life. I can't think of a future without you. You don't have to love me. You don't even have to say anything at all right now."

"Of course I love you."

He gaped at her. Then he looked at the river, trying to calm his racing thoughts. "You do?"

"I've loved you since we first met, in France."

"At Napoleon's ball?"

"Oh, before the ball. I fell in love with you when you and Mr. Fulton were sloshing around in that silly submarine, and every time we met you seemed unable to say a word. You'd just stand there, so self-important, like a big blowfish."

"You loved me then?"

"I loved you then."

"And you loved me after I stepped on your gown at the ball?"

She sighed. "Yes, after you stepped on my gown."

"I wrote to you two years ago, but you never replied."

"Well, a girl doesn't just fall into a man's arms because he writes her a letter. Besides, the letter was cold and all business. I kept waiting for you to write again, but you never did. So finally I decided to come to America and visit the Livingstons."

"You came over here deliberately, to see me?"

"To find out if you wanted to marry me."

He laughed. He laughed and flung his arms around her and drew her close. Then she laughed, too, and they kissed, spilling the tea on the lap robes. He was giddy with pleasure, and when finally it was time to take her home, the horse and sleigh seemed to fly over those frozen streets. But when they arrived at the Livingston townhouse, she looked at him gravely.

"But before I can say yes to marrying you, you must speak to Mr. Livingston. After all, he is my guardian."

"Mr. Livingston?"

"It's the proper thing to do."

"Very well."

He met Robert Livingston the following Sunday, after church. They retired to the library. The businessman was in a somber mood, and it took him forever to get around to the subject at hand. Livingston wanted to know Nathan's plans for the future, and if he intended to remain with the Fulton-Livingston enterprise, and if he was willing to accept additional assignments involving travel. Then, with a cold detachment, he said: "And what are your intentions toward my ward? Will you forsake all others for her? Will you be loyal and steadfast? You know, Stewart, I have heard troublesome rumors about your, er, private life. There's no need to discuss them, but I want you to know that I value my ward's good name as I would value my own. She is not to be trifled with."

"I'll be steadfast, Mr. Livingston. You have my word on that."

Livingston sighed. "Very well. She's a headstrong girl and has made up her mind anyway. Nothing I could do or say would make a whole lot of difference. You have my permission." Livingston extended a long, manicured hand and Nathan shook it. "My congratulations, Stewart. You could not have made a wiser choice."

Notice of the engagement appeared in the New York society columns. Two nights later Lucy Durange confronted Nathan as he worked late at his riverfront office. The beautiful face was livid with rage. "Bastard!" she said. "Snake! How dare you do this to me."

"Lucy, I . . ."

"Marrying that little baggage from Paris. The very idea. Well, let me tell you something, Nathan Stewart. Go ahead and have your pleasure. But I promise you that you'll pay. Oh, yes, you'll pay. I shall see to it."

The fury flashed from her eyes. Nathan had never seen such

hatred. Her bosom heaved, and her fists clenched, white-knuckled. "I'll destroy you. Yes! I'll absolutely destroy you!" She moved toward him as if to attack. Nathan stepped backward, toward his desk. But then her lower lip began to tremble. The sobs came from deep within her and erupted in great, gulping sounds, twisting her features into a grotesque mask. She put her hands to his chest and slowly sank to the floor, clutching him around the legs and burying her face against his knees. "Oh, Nathan, it's all wrong! Oh my God, darling, it's all wrong!"

He stood there stroking her hair as she sobbed out her agony. Finally she grew quiet, got to her feet, straightened her clothing, and dabbed at her eyes.

"I'm sorry," Nathan said.

She nodded, took out a hand mirror and fixed her face. "Somehow, I'll survive it," she said. And then she walked out into the cold night. He listened to her carriage rattle away.

Nathan Stewart and Yvette Marchand were married in a small church on Wall Street in late May of 1811. Only close friends and business associates were invited. Afterward, the couple left by steamer for a honeymoon trip up the Hudson, to Albany.

The times were ominous. The nation was on the verge of war.

VII

A ragged line of clouds scudded out of the northwest loosing rain and sleet. Ward Stewart braced at the wheel of the schooner *Shark*, squinting into the gray murk ahead. The mate, Kuykendahl, shouted down from his masthead perch, "There she is again, Mr. Stewart, off to starboard. A British man-o'-war, no doubt about it. Thirty guns, I'd say, maybe more. Still bearing down and all sails set." Stewart let his eye drift in that direction and caught the fleeting shadow of his nemesis. Damn! Kuykendahl had the instincts of a fox and was never wrong on lookout. A

British man-o'-war, and all he had in the cabin was an ancient blunderbuss.

"Are the bastards after us?"

"Yes sir, unless I miss my guess."

For a week now they had codfished the Grand Banks, blessed with decent weather: six vessels of his father's fleet out of Provincetown. Like a fool he'd sent the others farther north yesterday, to work as far as the Labrador coast and Chaleur Bay. The *Shark* was half full of cod, riding the heavy swells. She was a long-sparred topsail schooner, very fast for a fishing boat; but not fast enough, he reasoned, to outrun flying cannonballs. It was a choice, then, of taking the chance on eluding the Englishman or heaving to and trusting to fate. He surveyed the crew, now huddled in storm gear awaiting a decision. Cod fishermen they were, not Jack-tars; brothers and cousins and fathers and sons. They were the employees of his father Bartholemew Stewart, ranging in age from twelve to forty-five, veterans not of war but of the Grand Banks, the Nantucket Shoals and the dreaded Georges Banks. They could take fog and wind and sudden blow, and they lived the strange free lives of fishermen beholden to no authority but their own and their families' needs.

"We'll hold course and speed, then," Ward Stewart said. "Let the devil come on."

It was an hour before His Majesty's Ship *Vigorous* came within hailing distance. The megaphoned command struck Ward Stewart like a blow. "You are ordered to heave to and prepare for boarding."

"Cheeky bastards," Kuykendahl hissed. "These are American waters."

Ward sensed the resentment among his men. He wished devoutly to tell the blighters to bugger off, but he held his tongue. No need to let stubborn pride jeopardize lives. "All right, Kuykendahl," he said. "Strike sail and heave to."

They were boarded by a British lieutenant in full uniform accompanied by a squad of Royal Marines. The lieutenant wrinkled his nose fastidiously at the powerful mingled stenches from years of hauling cod.

"I don't suppose that I need inform you," Ward said icily, "that this is a violation of maritime law. You are acting in American waters, against an American vessel."

"Indeed." The lieutenant motioned armed men fore and aft. "I have reason to believe that you are harboring a British

Explore <u>Silver Canyon</u>, your first handsome, hardcover Collector's Edition, for 14 days FREE!

As a reader of Louis L'Amour's tough and gritty tales of the Old West, you'll be thrilled by <u>The Louis L'Amour Collection</u>—a series of hardcover editions of Louis L'Amour's exciting Western adventures.

Savor the feel of rich leathers. Like a good saddle, these volumes are made to last—to be read, reread and passed along to family and friends for years to come. Bound in rugged sierra-brown simulated leather with gold lettering, <u>The Louis L'Amour Collection</u> will be a handsome addition to your library.

<u>Silver Canyon</u> opens the series: It's the memorable tale of Matt Brennan, gunfighter, and his lone battle against duelling ranchers in one of the bloodiest range wars the West had ever seen. After <u>Silver Canyon</u> you'll set out on a new adventure every month, as succeeding volumes in the Collection are conveniently mailed to your home.

Receive the full-color Louis L'Amour Western Calendar FREE —just for looking at <u>Silver Canyon</u>. Like every volume in <u>The Louis L'Amour Collection</u>, <u>Silver Canyon</u> is yours to examine without risk or obligation. If you're not satisfied, return it within 14 days and owe nothing. The calendar is yours to keep.

Send no money now. Simply complete the coupon opposite to enter your subscription to <u>The Louis L'Amour Collection</u> and receive your free calendar.

Dear Reader,

One question I've been asked again and again over the years is when a first-rate hardcover edition of my books would become available.

    I'm pleased to say that the time has come, thanks to the folks at Bantam Books. They've put together a collection of which I am very proud. The books are handsome, permanent, and what I like best of all, affordable. Plus you enjoy the privilege of a 14-day free examination for each volume in the series, without any obligation whatsoever.

    I hope you'll take this opportunity to examine the books in the Collection, starting with _Silver Canyon_, and see their fine quality for yourself. I think you'll be as pleased as I am!

Sincerely,

Louis L'Amour

Send no money now – but mail today!

☐ **YES!** Please send me _Silver Canyon_ for a 14-day free examination, along with my free Louis L'Amour Calendar, and enter my subscription to <u>The Louis L'Amour Collection</u>. If I decide to keep _Silver Canyon_, I will pay $7.95 plus shipping and handling and receive one additional volume per month on a fully returnable, 14-day free-examination basis. There is no minimum number of books to buy, and I may cancel my subscription at any time. The Calendar is mine whether or not I keep _Silver Canyon_. 05322

☐ I prefer the deluxe edition, bound in genuine leather with gilt-edged pages, at $24.95 each plus shipping and handling. 05330

Name _(please print)_

Address

City State Zip

In Canada, mail to: Bantam Books Canada, Inc.
60 St. Clair Avenue East, Suite 601, Toronto, Ontario M4T 1N5

D 1 2 3 4

BUSINESS REPLY MAIL

FIRST CLASS   PERMIT NO. 2154   HICKSVILLE, NY

Postage will be paid by addressee:

The
Louis L'Amour
Collection

Bantam Books
P.O. Box 956
Hicksville, New York 11801

deserter, and my orders are to find the man and take him into custody."

"Deserter? There's not an Englishman on board this vessel. These are Provincetown men, and some from Chatham, Duxbury, and Plymouth, born and bred."

"And who are you, pray tell?"

"Ward Stewart. I'm captain of this vessel. My father, Bartholemew Stewart, is owner."

The lieutenant smiled thinly and turned away. Over his shoulder, Ward looked up into the towering presence of the man-o'-war. Several officers clustered on the poop deck, surveying him with spyglasses. Armed sailors stood at the railings. All guns had been run out and stood ready to smash the *Shark* to pieces with a single broadside.

The cod fishermen were ordered to stand in a single line. The lieutenant and a petty officer inspected each man, peering intently into the impassive faces. Abruptly, a tall young fisherman—one of the Cheatham brothers, from Plymouth—was jerked bodily from the line and wrestled toward the ladder.

"Mr. Stewart!" shrieked the captive.

Ward shouted his protest, but he might as well have bellowed at the wind. Two burly marines clapped the man in iron manacles and hauled him down the ladder to the launch. The lieutenant ordered the others to withdraw as well. He said to Ward: "Harboring deserters is a very serious offense." Then he followed his men into the launch, and its rowers quickly pulled away.

Ward Stewart leaned at the rail and watched them go in white-lipped fury.

"But why can't we do anything. My God, are we so helpless? Must we grovel at the feet of England? Hell, I thought we won the Revolution! Was I wrong?"

He paced the broad-beamed floor of his father's house giving vent to the fury that tormented him. Brows knit, black eyes flashing, Ward Stewart was a human storm, subconsciously punctuating his thunderous tirade by beating a fist against his open hand. Bartholemew Stewart watched and listened, knowing he could do little more than sympathize.

"It is the way things are," he said. "Ye handled it well enough, I think. What else could ye do, Ward?"

"Nothing, I suppose. But that's not the point, Father. Where do I take my complaint now? To the government? The government don't give a damn, and certainly not for us codfishers. We don't even have a navy worthy of the name, because Mr. Jefferson didn't hold for navies. And frankly, I don't think his successor, Mr. Madison, is much better. And then there's the Cape Codders themselves. They sat around for so long cursing the embargo and drinking tavern grog that they don't know whose side they're on anymore. How do ye like that, eh? They're still so mad at the men in Washington they haven't got room to be angry at the British."

"Son, son, I hate to hear ye go on like this," Bartholemew said. He spoke what was in his heart. Ward was a son filled with tempers, like the sea, subject to sudden squalls and furies. He took after his mother that way, God rest her soul. Rosa had given this boy her hot Italian blood and fine features. Mixed with the rugged nature of Stewarts, it was a spectacular combination. He himself was growing old now and staying ashore to recoup the business, while the boy went after the cod as all Cape Cod sons were expected to do. But he knew, deep inside, that Ward was restless; a father's instinct told him there was more to this than stung pride from being boarded by a British ship and having a seaman impressed.

"The embargo almost destroyed us," Bartholemew said. "People had a right to be angry. We could not trade abroad at all, and the ships rotted at the wharves. Look what happened to fishing; half our fleet sits idle to this day. Even with the embargo lifted, they can't resume all that business overnight. So the British . . ."

"The British are doing the same damn thing they've done for years, harassing American vessels and impressing our seamen," Ward said. "I've talked to some of these idlers in an effort to get their backs up, to stand up and fight for themselves! They won't do it, Father."

"And how should they fight?"

Ward crossed the floor in three great strides and knelt at his father's side. Suddenly the anger in his face was replaced by excitement. "Listen, Father, I've got a plan. We can outfit one of our own big schooners for battle; refit her with heavier, bigger sails, and mount enough guns to make her worthy of anybody's respect. I have a notion that this situation is not going to last much longer. It can't last. We'll have to go to war with England. And when we do, the government is going to need fighting ships. With no navy to speak of, Washington is going to turn to privateers. We'll go out and take prize vessels—English merchantmen—on our own, go into admiralty court, and claim a share of the money. And even if that doesn't happen, at least we'll have something to raid the British with, and get back some of our own vessels when they're impounded for fishing Canadian waters. Do ye understand what I'm saying, Father?''

"You're talking about piracy," Bartholemew said. "No, I'll not be a party to it." There was a stubborn set to his jaw. The old gray brows knitted, and the chin jutted in Stewart resolve. "We'll not be committing crimes on the high seas!"

Ward jumped to his feet. In exasperation, he blew out an explosion of air. Then he stormed from the house, shouting: "Well, what the hell do ye think the British are doing?" The door banged behind him, and he strode rapidly through the streets of Provincetown, past the great smelly racks of drying codfish, past the great shallow vats of his father's saltworks and the windmills for pumping in seawater and down to the harbor where the fleet rested in a tangle of masts, spars, and netting. To his back, the massive, encroaching sand dunes marched away on bleak, windblown courses. Over his head, seagulls wheeled and quarreled in the chill, gray air of morning.

Cape Codders were a stubborn lot, he thought. They would not change, but followed their own courses. Some of 'em still made salt by boiling water in the great iron kettles, knowing full well they were destroying forests to feed the fires. In the bad times, it was salt, not fish, that kept them alive: forty-thousand bushels of salt a year now, and four times as much of the Glauber's salt—those bitter dregs of the salt-making process—used by tanneries. And thirty-thousand quintals of cod per year and five thousand barrels of herring, to keep Cape Cod alive. He shook his head. It was not enough. Not nearly enough. And besides, he did not wish to fish all his life.

Truth was—and he never told his father this—Ward Stewart hated codfishing, hated it in his soul. From the age of twelve he'd gone out on his father's boats, early spring to the first of October, after the cod. It was a monotonous business, taking the fish with handlines from their dark submerged lairs off the Grand Banks or Labrador; pulling cod from morning to night, until his shoulders and arms ached and his hands were hard as leather. No, the merry mackerel was more to his liking, more to his spirit. A surface fish, the mackerel, a creature of shimmers and ripples

playing the sunny surface in schools. When the mackerel ran for
weeks in Cape Cod Bay, a schooner barely need journey beyond
sight of home port. You broadcast minced menhaden over the
water to attract them, and then could handline at the rail without
even bait; the leaden jog would do, scraped to silvery shine and
serving as both bait and sinker. A man pulled and slatted as fast
as he could move, filling the barrels with silver fish. Ah, but the
mackerel was a will-o'-the-wisp, here today and gone tomorrow.
Cod fishermen could not subsist on anything so undependable as
that, and no man had yet figured out the strange migrations of
the mackerel, so as to predict where he'd be next.

That, too, appealed to Ward. The mackerel was not locked on
these inhospitable shores but swam where he pleased, dancing
and splashing to his heart's delight. Would that a human creature
could live as free!

Well, other Stewarts had found ways to chart their own
courses. His father had spoken of a brother, Isaiah, who came to
New England but had no love for a cod fisherman's life and left,
eventually to make his own successful business in Pittsburgh. A
rich man now, Isaiah. Ward knew of two of the sons, Nathan and
Stephen; the one had gone to England to school, the other
explored with Lewis and Clark. He felt a sharp pang of envy and
wondered where these cousins were today? Lucky bastards.

He dug an oyster shell from the sand with the toe of his boot,
picked it up and flung it, skipping, out toward a rotting skiff. In
time, he knew, his father would relent. And if not, there were
others who could be persuaded to invest in a privateer, for a
share of the booty if not for patriotism. To change the mind of a
Capecodder, he mused, you had to reason with his stomach.

At midday the sun was a watery disk in a gray overcast,
shedding no warmth at all. The sea came off the starboard quarter
in steep, heavy swells, causing the *Shark* to pitch and roll as she
drove on the wind. All morning it had gusted to gale force out of
the northeast, ripping plumes off the wave crests and dousing the
decks in spray. Captain Ward Stewart eyed the set of the
mainsail, pondering whether to make changes. But she appeared
to hold nicely, and the new heavy-duty mast was solid enough.
So he simply ordered Kuykendahl to reef the foretops and then
went aft to check their quarry through the glass.

She was a fine, fat prize, by the look of her; a British East

Indiaman trying to run the blockade. It was dangerous business along this stormy coast, the more perilous for its hidden rocks and shoals. Even Stewart had a leadsman at soundings now, and he'd sailed these waters all his life.

"By the mark five," tolled the leadsman, "and a half!"

Good. That was very good. He felt reasonable comfort with five fathoms under his bottom on a making tide. It would change soon enough. No such luck for the stranger. The merchantman struggled under partial rigging, her mizzen seemingly torn away and foresail flapping in shreds. The damned fool had waited too late to take in sail and now plunged perilously close to that dark smear of rocky headland, exploding in surf off his port bow. He was gambling to make the headland, obviously, but he would have fared better with a balanced-reef mainsail and reefed jib. Ah, the risks a man will take for gold! A heavy sea took the boat and davits, leaving him at the mercy of his fates.

"Christ, we'll lose her for sure," grumbled a bosun at Ward's elbow.

"Maybe not, maybe not," he said. "Besides, Mr. Trask, your pockets are already lined with gold. What's one more?"

The gamble had paid richly. For more than two years, under Letters of Marque, the *Shark* had prowled the coast as a privateer. She was a different vessel now, completely rebuilt for the duty at hand, rigged as a small frigate and as heavily gunned as she'd bear. Already they had seized five prize vessels of the British merchant fleet and, as specified under the new American Embargo Act, registered them in court for sale and division of spoils. Ward himself took both the captain's share and that of part owner, the balance of the owner's portion going to his father. His bank account in Boston got steadily richer, to finance the high life ashore that now was his pleasure.

On board, he had manned his vessel with Cape Codders, induced for their own gain and working like devils despite the air of easy discipline. Even in wartime, he knew these men would not bend to the savage commands that drove a typical navy ship. But there were no better fighters anywhere, as they'd proven well enough when led in pitched battle to board a potential prize under fire. The hands that once mastered lines and nets could adapt to cutlass and musket with surprising ease.

"By the mark four!"

"We're gaining on her."

"Look, she's raising more sail!"

"By damn, that takes balls."

The squalls increased their fury, and the spray now mixed with stinging rain. A league off their starboard quarter, a roiling black cloud suddenly vomited a nasty gray coil that dipped down on a writhing course.

"Waterspout, Captain!"

"I see it."

"God's blood, would you look at that!"

The merchantman heeled heavily now, flying before the wind with all sails set. Ward had to admire the raw nerve of her captain to take such risk, although admittedly he had hardly less choice. The following sea threatened to dash over her at any moment. Beyond, the surf of the headland now burst in white fury as high as her mizzen. The light grew weaker as the afternoon wore on and cloud masses thickened. If she did cross the headland and make it around, they might still lose her in early darkness. Stewart adjusted his glass and brooded. He knew his advantage: home waters and the tremendous maneuverability of a Grand Banks vessel and crew. The only thing he lacked was patience.

Suddenly, the break came. The merchantman rounded the point, her bottom dancing just above the rocks that would smash her. A low tide would have spelled disaster. In the lee of the headland, the sea became less tortuous, the waves changing to heavy swells.

"By the mark three!"

Ward brought the *Shark* around slightly, felt her take the fresh onslaught of wind and sea, and drove in toward his quarry.

"Mr. Kuykendahl, put a shot across her bow."

"Aye, Captain."

His maneuver was closing off the merchantman's swing into open water. The forward gun spoke, a flat report in the teeth of the wind. He saw the ball arc away. That settled the matter. Forced to cross *Shark's* guns or tack into certain destruction aground, the merchantman swung off before the wind. Ward, exhilarated now, saw her canvas go slack and men swarm aloft to take in the mainsheet.

"We've got her, by heaven!" he shouted. "Smartly aloft now, lads. Ready at the main braces!"

Twenty minutes later, as darkness began to close over the late afternoon, *Shark* drew to within easy hailing distance. Ward Stewart picked up his megaphone and spoke.

"Prepare for boarding. I hereby commandeer your vessel as a prize of war under the Embargo Act of the government of the United States..."

As usual, he had difficulty masking his elation.

The uniform was new, of his own design for evening wear, and had cost him a small fortune. No matter; it pleased him to look well, and if that required the finest tailor in New York, then so be it. The results were evident in the responses of the women. Expensively coiffed and gowned, showing the daring décolleté borrowed from European fashion, they clustered like soft bright birds to the parties and soirees. One could hardly suspect that a war was still going on after more than two years, with Washington City sacked and burned and the entire coast under blockade. If anything, the war tended to invigorate those segments of society which gave Ward Stewart his pleasures; war and uniforms added to the zest of the gaming tables and boudoir. The mystique of danger had a luster all its own.

"Ah, Captain Stewart. How delightful." She was a lovely creature, aglow with champagne, coming to him out of the elegant crowd. "I'm pleased that you came to my party after all. And how rakishly handsome you are in that uniform." She took his arm. "You must meet my guests."

Ward Stewart felt the hand squeeze his arm. It was a shared intimacy that delighted him. The memory of her on the previous afternoon crossed his mind, writhing naked beneath him on silken sheets. It always amazed him that society's beauties preferred dull and respectable husbands and yet could be so insatiable in their demands for carnal pleasure. And he was more than willing, of course, to oblige. Now, smiling as if exchanging a pleasantry, he murmured to her ear, "You are a marvelous fuck."

She flushed, eyes glowing, as they moved into a lively group of party guests. "May I introduce Captain Stewart? Captain, this is the Baron Reinholtz. Um, Mr. and Mrs. Van Dyke. Miss Clinton. Captain Stewart..." Faces swam past him. He navigated through smiles and handshakes.

There were other whispers, out of his hearing. "Privateer. Made a fortune, I hear, taking British prizes." "Devilishly handsome. My word." "A stallion, they say. He's slept with every woman in Boston and half in New York." "How interesting." "Cora, you can't be serious."

More wine flowed. The talk was a murmur around him, rising and falling like a gentle sea. He sipped champagne, feeling the numbing glow in his face. A small string ensemble was playing, off somewhere behind the potted palms. He thought of Provincetown, the bleak sand dunes and quarreling gulls, the cold and stench of the codfish boats. Never, he thought. Never again.

"So pensive, Captain Stewart. What on earth could you be pondering with such gravity?"

Huge brown eyes. Lovely breasts. Heady scent. He'd met her earlier. Marla something. Marla, Marla... "Um, the war, madame." He sighed. "So many shipmates, gone down in the deep." It had the right touch of sonority, he thought. Yes. The brown eyes filled with patriotic concern. He gave her a craggy smile. "It's of no consequence. Tell me, do you live here in New York?" Within ten minutes, it was mutually agreed that they would meet again in a more, er, private setting. For lunch next Thursday. Thursdays were such busy days for her husband on the Exchange.

"You are a devil." It was his hostess again, placing her gloved hand softly on his arm. "But then, we must share the wealth, mustn't we? Now, I have a surprise for you. There is somebody very special I want you to meet. They've just arrived." She offered a conspiratorial wink.

A tall, handsome man in evening clothes stood in the middle of a welcoming crowd. Beside him was a stunning young woman whose presence seemed to radiate warmth. Ward noticed, somewhat ruefully, that she wore a wedding ring. The couple spoke easily in both English and French. His hostess drew him along by the hand, opening a path through the knot of people. Then she was saying, "Nathan, so good of you to come. May I present another Stewart. Nathan Stewart, Captain Ward Stewart—"

"Nathan! Not Isaiah Stewart's son!"

"Ward? Are you Bartholemew's boy?"

"Well, I'll be damned!"

Eagerly, like long-lost friends, they exchanged small talk. Bystanders would never have known that these two were strangers. Each, then, was distracted by others. The unexpected bond of kinship came as a surprise to Ward. He also reveled in a fine surge of pride in his cousin. Nathan was much in demand, an engaging conversationalist and listener. His air of self-suffiency was intriguing. Ward wondered if this was the product of a superb education or some natural gift. The old envy came back.

Watching Nathan move about with such ease and grace reminded Ward suddenly of his own deficiencies. He thought: You're a cod fisherman still. But it did not last. If men were not instinctively drawn to him, women certainly were, and several of them exercised their subtle demands for his attention as the evening wore on.

It was almost midnight when Nathan came over and invited Ward to join them for a late supper. "Just a few friends, Captain. Yvette and I are dying to get to know you better."

They rode in Nathan's enclosed carriage, small but superbly crafted. It had a driver and a pair of spirited matched grays. As Ward settled back amid the odors of fine leather and polished woods, his cousin deftly plied him with questions. What was he doing in New York? How had his father's business weathered the embargo? What was the state of Bartholemew's health? Nathan seemed to want to know anything and everything. The man had broad knowledge of ships and maritime matters. Ward deftly avoided discussing his own relationship with his father. The strain had been apparent on his last visit to Provincetown, where a British man-o'-war was based full time now, and British seamen filled the streets and taverns, flirting with the local girls. Captain Stewart came and went disguised as a civilian, and his father implored him to give up privateering. "This war is not of our concern, lad. I was wrong to help ye build *Shark* into a fighting vessel." Ward had left on a sour note, hating it.

"The war has brought good times and bad," Nathan was saying, as if divining Ward's thoughts. "But then wars always do. My father's freight business is healthy; the coastal blockade forced merchants to use inland shipping. And you, Ward, have a ship now and a fine stake."

"That's true," he said.

They arrived at a stately brownstone house overlooking the Hudson. Lamplight glowed in downstairs rooms and the driveway. Other carriages drew up behind Nathan's and half-a-dozen guests filled the foyer. Servants gathered wraps. Soon afterward, they were taking a candlelight supper of roasted chicken and light vegetables. The wine was excellent, white with a delicate bouquet. Ward had met the other people only casually earlier in the evening. They were six couples, the men obviously business associates of Nathan's. As conversation flowed he saw that Yvette, unlike other wives, took full part in whatever was being discussed. Yvette's beauty was captivating.

"Captain Stewart, your vessel is the *Shark*, out of Boston?" It was an older man speaking, portly and red-haired with a full mustache. The question caught Ward off guard.

"Yes. The *Shark* is a . . ."

"I know what she is. A privateer." The red-haired man took a sip of wine. "And a damned good one, too. I suspect that you've made a bundle for yourself, young man. Do all Stewarts have this Midas touch?" He looked at Yvette and smiled. "And this gift for attracting magnificent women?"

Yvette nodded. Her hair, in this light, was a rich auburn color done in soft waves. Her smile made the great brown eyes sparkle. "It is their marvelous ability," she murmured, "for dancing."

Nathan choked on his wine, grabbed up his napkin and turned away, coughing. It took several minutes for him to recover. Yvette thumped him soundly on the back. At last, he gasped, "You could have waited until I finished swallowing . . ."

"Poor dear," she said.

Ward and the others were left with their puzzlement.

"This war will be finished soon," the red-haired man said. "Bonaparte is done for, and the British are sick and tired of fighting. When it does end, there's going to be a boom in this country the likes of which we've never even imagined. Isn't that right, Nathan?"

"Absolutely," Nathan said. "The West is opening. When the National Road reaches the Ohio River at Wheeling, it's going to provide an easy route over the Appalachians. Steamships are going to be conquering every river that's wide enough, and you'll think Mississippi runs both ways. The firm holding the right monopolies will earn bonanzas. The potential is tremendous, absolutely tremendous."

"I hear your brother, Stephen, is giving you some competition down there," another man said.

Nathan frowned. It was, Ward could see, a sore point with him. Yvette patted his hand. He said, "A difference of opinion on some things, that's all."

"And do you really think the Erie Canal . . ."

"I do indeed." Nathan's eyes flashed. "That canal is going to be built, no question about it. She'll cut through from Albany clear to Lake Erie. And that will open up the whole northwestern territory. You'll see settlers and commerce pouring through the port of New York. That will be our answer to the National Road."

"Tut, tut, Nathan. A little sectional jealousy there?"

Ward's excitement mounted. He had never heard such talk. These were men who did things, who translated thought into action. A road spanning mountains. Canals. Steamships. What next? By the time they came to the brandy and cigars, in the middle of the night, he was bursting with enthusiasm.

"Tell me, Captain Stewart," said the red-haired man, "what do ye know about steamships?"

His bright bubble deflated. "Steamships? Well, I've seen Fulton's crafts in New York harbor. But to tell you the truth . . ."

"No matter. You're a seafaring man, and that's what's important. A man that can sail and navigate, as you do, has mastered the hard part. Machines are simple enough, steam pressure, driving pistons, things like that."

Nathan was listening intently. "Why do you ask?"

The red-haired man drew on his cigar and flicked ash into a brass cuspidor. "As you know, Nathan, I'm interested in steamship investment. I think we can build a steamship that can cross the Atlantic on her own power . . ."

A responsive murmur went around the table.

"I'm serious about it. If a ship can go one hundred and forty miles to Albany and back, or fifteen hundred miles down the Mississippi, then she can cross the Atlantic. It's just a question of how much wood you can put on board."

"Well, it's more than that, Howard," another man said. "You've got to have a sturdy vessel, one that will weather the storms at sea and give you plenty of storage for both fuel and cargo. And what do you do in case of breakdown? It's one thing to break down on the Hudson, fifty yards from shore; it's something else to break down in the middle of the Atlantic with a gale blowing . . ."

"We'll build the ships that will do it," the red-haired man said.

The other man wagged his head and chuckled. "Maybe fifty years from now. But I don't see it happening anytime soon. No, Howard, I think the brandy's gone to your head."

The red-haired man smiled and looked thoughtfully at Ward. "Nevertheless, you think about it, Captain. There's going to be a real need for men like yourself who can run these vessels for their owners, men who're flexible and not afraid of change."

Ward Stewart savored his fine cigar. "I'll keep that in mind," he said. "Yes, indeed, I'll certainly keep it in mind."

When the last guest departed and Yvette had gone off to bed,
Ward and Nathan sat talking until dawn. He declined Nathan's
invitation to remain as their houseguest and took the carriage to
return to his own lodgings.

The narrow streets of New York stirred to life. A bright
sunlight broke through to burn the fog off the river. As the
carriage rattled along, Ward settled back with his tumbling
thoughts.

He felt that a door had been opened for him.

VIII

The rivers were the navigable routes and steam the secret of
their mastery. Damn! He'd been a fool to let Nathan and the
Fulton crowd steal such a march on him. A man can be forgiven
for pride and forgiven for blindness, but to be both proud and
blind at once was unconscionable. The irony was that he had
been too busy criticising Nicholas Roosevelt's deep draft *New
Orleans* to think about creative alternatives. But Stephen was a
boat man, not a steam engine man; and in order to design a
vessel to conquer the rivers, one would require that both talents
be combined.

From Catherine came the usual reassurances. "You'll work it
out, Stephen. I know you will." In order to free his mind and his
time, she quietly assumed more of the burden of managing the
Stewart enterprises. Catherine now involved herself not only in
the bookkeeping but also in dealing with customers and operations
of the boatyard itself. Workmen quickly became accustomed to
the presence of the tall, willowy blond scrutinizing results,
learning, making suggestions.

For Stephen, everything seemed to be happening at once, and
the demands multiplied. The War of 1812 dragged on, and now
was the War of 1814. Battles raged on the Great Lakes and in
upper New York and at Detroit. The British raided and burned

Washington. Maritime commerce was stymied along the coast under total blockade. And the war seemed shapeless, sporadic and without plan. General Andrew Jackson secured the Mississippi Territory, only to be diverted with a force of Tennessee and Kentucky sharpshooters to New Orleans amid rumors of a British assault there. Military goods poured through the Stewart compound, bound for the western regions and downriver. Rumor circulated that peace was being negotiated at Ghent, in Belgium. Rumor, rumor, rumor.

The Fulton group, undaunted by war, was expanding its operations. As the original steamship *New Orleans*, deep draft and all, chugged into regular service on the southern end of the Mississippi, more steamships with fiery names—*Aetna* and *Vesuvius*—were in the stocks at Pittsburgh. Launched with dash and ceremony, they went chuffing away downriver, paddle wheels flashing, as if to flaunt their presence before Stephen Stewart. Even more disturbing to him were the persistent reports that Fulton-Livingston agents were working among state and territorial politicians downriver, trying to lock up a monopoly for these steamships. Rivermen wrote to Stephen for help, knowing of his prestige as a former member of the Lewis and Clark expedition and hoping, of course, that he would have influence with his brother Nathan.

One day there arrived at the Stewart compound a delegation of rivermen headed by the colorful maverick of the Mississippi, Captain Henry Miller Shreve. The group had traveled far, having been drawn from Ohio, Kentucky, Tennessee, and Illinois. In the library of Stewart House, they lit pipes, drank bourbon, and talked.

"I heard downriver that the *New Orleans* sank off Baton Rouge. She grounded after taking on wood and the boiler room flooded."

"Just over two years in service; that is, since Nicholas Roosevelt took her down on the maiden voyage."

"Bad luck boat, if you ask me. Right from the beginning."

"Do ye think so?"

"Damn right. That was a hell of a trip Roosevelt made, taking the fall flood with a pregnant wife and all."

"The boat couldn't have made it through the falls without the flood. They say she almost capsized."

"Fine place for a baby to be born, at a stopover there in Louisville. Must have been plumb scared right into life."

"All that, and then the fire aboard ship and the earthquake they experienced at Cairo, Illinois. The damned river started running backwards, and Roosevelt couldn't find the channel for weeks."

"If General Jackson don't turn back the British at New Orleans, that boat would have had new owners anyhow."

"He'll turn 'em back. Jackson's got sharpshooters with him. Look what they done to the Creek Indians."

Henry Shreve interrupted the small talk. "We come here to discuss the monopoly, not Andy Jackson. I want to know, Stephen, if you can get your brother to back off. The Fulton crowd has got men in every capital and lawyer's office from here to New Orleans. There's going to be trouble for sure."

Stephen shook his head. "Henry, my brother is pigheaded when it comes to business. But he's also got a lot of other irons in the fire these days. They're having a real fight in New York state over the plan for the Erie Canal—"

"That's why DeWitt Clinton ran for president two years ago, to force that canal through. Ain't that so?"

"The Erie's not the only reason Clinton got beat."

"You fellas hush up and let Mr. Stewart talk."

"As I was saying, they're fighting to try to get a canal bill through the New York legislature. And then there's the Hudson steamship business. Robert Fulton is in failing health, and everything has fallen onto my brother's shoulders. On top of all that, they're expanding on our western rivers and trying to get the monopoly for steamship traffic on the Ohio and Mississippi."

Angry mutterings rippled around the room.

"They'll get their monopoly in Louisiana," Henry Shreve said. "Robert Livingston has got a brother there, Edward. He's a lawyer and political power in the state. They'll win for certain there."

"And that means nobody else can legally put in at New Orleans with steamboats?"

"That's about the size of it. Besides, who's got steamships other than Fulton?"

Henry Shreve pulled a brass cuspidor to the side of his chair, leaned over, and spat. "I've got some ideas about that. I think it's time somebody else started building steamboats."

Stephen's interest quickened. Shreve and a partner already had built a crude flatboat mounted with an engine. Named the *Comet*, it had journeyed from Brownsville, fifty miles up the Monongahela from Pittsburgh, all the way to New Orleans this past spring. Henry Shreve was widely viewed as eccentric, but Stephen knew the man was no fool. "What have you got in mind, Henry?" he said.

"The way I see it," Shreve said, "Fulton's boatbuilders have got a problem. They just can't get away from designing vessels that take the steam engine belowdecks. That means a deeper draft, because it takes space for the boilers and the piston assembly, all that. It's a big mistake, but like a lot of smart fellas they got set in their ways and can't change. The master, Fulton, builds his boats with deep draft, and that's the way everybody does it. This is all very fine for deep rivers and harbors, but it won't do for the Ohio, the Mississippi, and the Missouri. We've got us some rivers that don't follow the rules like rivers do back east or over in Europe."

Someone snickered. "Old Henry, he's smarter than Robert Fulton." Laughter filled the room.

Captain Shreve put up his hands. "Go on and laugh, if you've a mind to. But I say if you're going to navigate in shallow waters, then build shallow boats. Look at our flatboats. They ain't nothing but glorified rafts with superstructure on top, but we've done a whole lot of traveling with 'em on these rivers and carried mountains of cargo. Even our keelboats seldom draw much over three feet."

"That ain't no steamboat, Henry. Haw, haw. That's a sweat boat."

"Hush up and let the captain talk."

Shreve scratched his head. "Who says you've got to put a steam engine belowdecks to power a river craft? Why can't you put it abovedecks? Put the boiler, the piston assembly, the smokestacks, the gears and side-wheel housing, the whole darn thing right on deck. Build superstructure housing around and above that as high as you like, same as you do with a flatboat."

There was no snickering now. Suddenly the men were listening in respectful silence. Henry Shreve glanced around with a certain air of triumph. "So that's what I've got in mind," he said.

"What about the engine, Henry?" Stephen said. "Fulton has got the Watt and Boulton engine locked in tight, every patent covered."

Shreve smiled. "That's true." He looked around the room. "Where's Daniel French? Ah, there he is." He motioned to a nondescript man in work clothing who had not spoken since the meeting began. "Dan here has a patented marine engine with an

oscillating cylinder. It's radically different from the Watt and
Boulton type, but just as efficient. Show 'em, Dan.''

French stood up nervously with a roll of mechanical drawings.
The drawings consisted not only of a steam engine design but
also of a flat-bottomed boat. Henry Shreve looked on admiringly.
"By God, there's a boat that'll float on the morning dew."

When French had completed his technical explanation, which
few men in the room could understand, someone asked: "What
happened to the *Comet*?"

"We sold it to a fella in Louisiana," Shreve replied. "He
wanted to use the engine to power his cotton gin."

The plan now was for a much larger vessel, of about forty-five
tons. Like the *Comet*, they intended to build it at Brownsville.
"We need capital, though," Henry Shreve said. "And"—he
looked at Stephen—"we need to bring in a first-class boatbuilder."

Within an hour, Henry Shreve had promises of all the investment capital he needed. Stephen agreed to help build the new
vessel and also to lead the fight against the downriver monopoly.
The mood of the rivermen took an abrupt change.

As the meeting broke up for dinner, and Catherine arrived to
meet their guests, Stephen asked Captain Shreve: "What do you
intend to name the new steamboat, Henry?"

"I figured I'd name her *Enterprise*."

Stephen nodded and followed him out of the room. A smile
masked his own deep misgivings. Now he faced direct conflict
with Nathan, knowing that their relationship would never be the
same again.

She knew love now, knew it deeply and completely in her
heart. And in the knowing there was life. Catherine could feel
the wonder of it, feel herself the luckiest of women, blessed by
God to live with this man and thrill to his glance and his touch.
In the night, the blessed night that was theirs together, she stirred
and opened her eyes, seeing his shadow next to her in the bed.
"Stephen." It was a whisper, no more, but he slept lightly, and
she knew that his eyes fluttered open quick as a heartbeat.
Catherine stretched, luxuriantly naked, and rolled over next to
him, breathing his scent. She touched his face with her fingers
and traced the smoothness of those features, from the broad
forehead and long, silken eyelashes down the long, rock-hard
cheeks and the firm, wide mouth that smiled and dimpled deeply

at the corners. She touched the chin that was like touching warm marble. "Did anyone ever tell you," she whispered, "how beautiful you are?"

"Beautiful?" He chuckled softly that deep, rich chuckle she knew so well. "A man is not supposed to be beautiful. A woman is beautiful. A man is . . . a man."

"You're beautiful, Stephen, more beautiful than I am. And we'll make beautiful babies, too. Would you like that?

"Yes, I'd like that. Babies that look like Catherine and have their mother's intelligence and wit. Strong babies that will thrive."

"Well, then?"

He laughed out loud and drew her tightly to him with one powerful arm, squeezing her in a way that was so arousing. He kissed her face and the arch of her throat and warmly, smoothly, suckled her quick-swelling nipples. Electricity surged through her being, bring a molten weakness to her belly and thighs, taking her breath away. "Darling, Stephen. I love you so. I've always loved you, and I always shall. How could one woman be so lucky? Oh, darling, do that. Yes. Do that . . ."

She opened herself to receive him.

Then the morning came, the morning that she had dreaded. This was the morning that he would leave her, to go downriver on the *Enterprise* with Captain Shreve. Except for the brief trips upriver to oversee the construction at Brownsville, they had never been separated more than a single night of marriage. Strange that she would feel such need of him now, such a hunger to treasure their every moment together. It was almost—almost a foreboding that Catherine felt but could not define; a sense that something brooded just beyond the horizon of their lives, waiting to strike at Stephen. She had a terrible urgency to fill the cup now and savor it and drink it all down. Now. Right now. And he was leaving, this time downriver.

Catherine did not tell him of her thoughts.

They breakfasted with Captain Shreve. He was a burly man who filled a room with odors of machine oil and chewing tobacco. They had become fast friends, for he had developed enormous respect for Stephen's ability and his way with men. "We'll make good time downriver, I'll wager. This is a much improved engine Dan French has built for the *Enterprise*, twice as good as *Comet*. We'll make Louisville inside four days."

Four days! To Stephen it seemed hardly possible. They had

labored for weeks taking Meriwether Lewis' keelboat down that stretch and suffered torments of the damned. When he reminded Captain Shreve of that, the steamboater smiled. "Times change, Stephen. You're in the new age now, the age of steam. By God those rivers are going to be filled with fast packets before you know it. You'll see 'em racing up and down loaded with cargo and fancy women and gamblers and velvet plush; regular floating palaces they'll be, mark my words. And we'll build them!"

Catherine went out with them to the wharf. There, a great, breathing presence now stood, a monster almost alive, spewing smoke and live steam into the morning air. The *Enterprise* was forty-five tons, with paddle wheels on each side and a stack amidships. Her cabins rose on a single level fore and aft, with a pilothouse jutting above. Captain Shreve had placed it so for an all-around view of the river, with a bell-signaling device and a great spoked wheel.

Since dawn, when the stokers had begun firing her boiler, a crowd had been gathering along Water Street under the sycamore trees. Now it appeared that most of Pittsburgh was on hand to watch. Old Charlie, now bent and gray, saw to the last of the provisions put on board. Isaiah Stewart stalked up and down, quarreling at the laborers as they finished stacking a large pile of firewood on deck. Stephen watched his father badgering the men and said to Catherine, "The older he gets the more crotchety he gets." He was smiling, and the affection he felt for the old man shone in his eyes. "Remember, don't let him get the upper hand."

She laughed. "Don't worry."

And finally it was time. With a quick hug and a kiss for her, he turned and strode down the slope behind Henry Shreve. They boarded and climbed to the pilothouse. Black smoke curled from the stack, and the boiler gave off a rhythmic gush of steam. Captain Shreve barked commands to the deck. Lines slipped from moorings. Steam hissed and sighed. Stephen jerked the bell cord, and the brass bell atop the pilothouse sent its clanging warning across the morning. The steam whistle gave a keening, double-throated blast. With a shudder and a chuff, the piston arms began to move and paddle wheels bit up white froth. Then they were moving, grandly and relentlessly, away from the dock and into open stream, heading for the Forks, heading for the Ohio. Birds wheeled and dived for morsels churned up in the wake.

Catherine stood watching until the *Enterprise* was out of sight. Martha Stewart came and put an arm around her. "Don't worry, child. He will be all right."

They moved smoothly downriver with intermittent fall rains. The new engine did not have the power Henry Shreve wanted, but it did well enough. Stephen was not satisfied with the basic hull design, either; a bigger version of this craft would draw too much water for his liking. And so they pondered and discussed as *Enterprise* thumped along past hillsides just beginning to turn autumn colors. As cargo they carried a load of military supplies for General Jackson's troops at New Orleans. But along the way they stopped to make contacts with more rivermen and local politicians, among whom Stephen enlisted support against the Fulton monopoly. "The waters belong to everybody. They're as free as the air we breathe! Fulton and Livingston cannot control what you breathe, can they? Or the food you put into your mouths. Give them the monopoly they seek, gentlemen, and you will be handing over a precious freedom. The next thing, they'll control every piece of goods, every commodity that comes downriver. They will build into the price of everything you use—your guns, your plows, the clothes on your backs—profit for Fulton, Livingston and, yes, for Nathan Stewart!"

Stephen talked to church socials and independent groups. He spoke quietly to merchants and lawyers and noisily to crowds gathered on riverbanks. The more he spoke, the more he overcame his early shyness. And finally even Henry Shreve was impressed. "Boy, you keep on this way, and you'll be going into politics for sure."

Finally, they arrived at New Orleans and passed by two new Fulton-Livingston steamers—deep-drafted vessels—plying between the port city and Natchez. At the dock they were met by a colonel of General Jackson's staff. "Gentlemen," he shouted, "we are glad to see you!" When the supplies, including fresh arms and ammunition, had been transferred to wagons, they accompanied the colonel to the general's headquarters outside the city. Jackson hugged Captain Shreve and pounded him on the back, saying, "Henry, you old son of a bitch!" The general was lean and toughened from his arduous campaign against the Creek Indians in the Mississippi country. He was now directing his men in the strengthening of fortifications and breastworks along a dry canal bed between the Mississippi River and a swamp. Manning the redoubts were leathery, buckskinned men of the Tennessee militia who had fought the Creeks, later taken Pensacola, Florida, and then forced-marched to southern Louisiana, all in a few short months.

"Unless I miss my guess, we're going to have us a hell of a fight right here," Jackson said. "The British have got seventy-five hundred men sailing from the West Indies, wanting to take this city. But thanks to the supplies you brought down in that floatin' tea kettle of yours, Henry, we'll whup the pants off of 'em." Old Hickory, as his troops called him, spat tobacco juice into the dust. "And that's a fact."

They left Jackson's positions and went into New Orleans. The city was crowded, troops and military wagons everywhere, but hardly seemed braced for siege. Henry Shreve chuckled. "This here town's been under too many flags to give a damn who occupies it next." They roamed the narrow, teeming streets with their mixture of Spanish and French atmosphere, of double doors and wrought-iron balconies and shaded patios in secluded nooks. The babble was many-tongued, and even baffled the French-speaking Stephen Stewart. "That's Creole you're listening to," Shreve told him. "It's a little bit of everything."

Maybelle was on Stephen's mind. Would it be possible to find her in a place like this? They roamed among fleshpots and cafes. Henry Shreve asked no questions, but kept looking at him suspiciously. At one point the captain allowed that this was no pastime for a married man. Stephen smiled. Occasionally he asked for a red-haired woman named Maybelle who might be working as a hostess or entertainer. But no one seemed to know anything. New Orleans kept its secrets well. One of the more interesting places even offered strolling violinists and expensive decor. The Nocturne, it was called. The customers were elegantly dressed men, attended by some of the loveliest women Stephen had ever seen. The featured performer, according to a billboard, was a singer named Rose Lark. But they did not stay for the show. "Let's move along, Henry. I don't think Maybelle would be here."

Even the public mood over the pending monopoly was different in New Orleans. People either did not care or they strongly endorsed the plan and resented outsiders. After several shouted debates, Stephen saw that he was getting nowhere. Anxious to return home to Catherine, he suggested that Captain Shreve fire up his boiler. "Let's get back to Pittsburgh."

This was the test they had come for. Now, the steam engine would have to struggle for every yard of progress against a river that flowed eternal and never tired. The *Enterprise* swung into the stream making loud, laboring sounds. As they progressed, the firebox consumed firewood at twice the rate of the downstream voyage, and the speed of the steamboat was cut by a third. Shreve, listening to the hammering piston, had his doubts. But they resolved to run her until she broke down. "Nobody's ever made it upriver clear to Pittsburgh before, Stephen. And frankly, I don't know if we're going to do it either."

They traveled by day, ever watchful for snags and floating tree trunks that could disembowel the boat. By night they tied up at the bank. With high water in their favor, they avoided the current where possible by running through flooded fields and cutoffs.

And at last, clanking and groaning after two thousand miles of it, the *Enterprise* made the last turn of the Ohio with Pittsburgh dead ahead. They put into the wharf at Stewart's Boatworks on a sunny December afternoon, and a deckhand leaped ashore with his mooring rope. "We did it!" Henry Shreve exulted. "River, you've met your match!"

Stephen did not reply. He was watching the house. And he saw her come running out and down the slope, blonde hair streaming in the sunlight.

In the months that followed, as a hard winter closed over the boat works and the riverbanks thickened with ice, Stephen and Henry Shreve began sketching and planning for a massive new vessel. The more they worked at it, the more excited the captain became.

"By God, Stephen, she'll be four hundred tons of riverboat this time, but with a draft that'll float on a mud puddle. We'll give her your flat-bottomed hull, double decks all around and, for real power, a high-pressure engine that'll run her against a damned flood. She'll take a boiler for big steam—put the engine right here on the main deck—and a pair of smokestacks big as chimneys."

Stephen shared his rising enthusiasm. Four hundred tons of riverboat!

At dinner with Catherine that evening, they discussed the momentous news of General Jackson's victory at New Orleans.

But with it, travelers also had brought word that the state of Louisiana had granted the steamship monopoly to the Fulton-Livingston group, barring any other steamship company from entering the port of New Orleans.

Henry Shreve grumbled into his soup. "We'll just go down anyhow, with the new steamboat. This is 1815, not the damned Dark Ages. She'll be ready to make the journey next year."

Stephen asked: "And what do you plan to name this new boat, Henry?"

"We'll name her for the old commander-in-chief himself. We'll name her *Washington*."

Catherine shivered, for no apparent reason, as if an icy finger had touched her heart.

IX

The weather grew colder, a cold December with gray days to match Nathan's mood. Robert Fulton was dying. For months his health had deteriorated, giving the once-lively face a drawn and somber cast. Finally there was no hope left. But then, irony of ironies, it was Robert Livingston who died first! The blow was unexpected and devastating. Yvette hurried to the Livingston estate, to be with the family. Nathan took rooms near the Fulton home and visited every day. "Did he suffer?" the inventor whispered. Nathan shook his head. "No, he didn't suffer."

And Fulton grew deeper into his illness. The flesh melted from him, his features sharpened, his skin became the consistency of parchment. Gone, the vital man; only the flesh was left. Nathan sat by the bed while Fulton's family moved about the house, hushed in the reverence of the dying. But finally there came a day when he seemed to brighten, and the eyes had a luster of life again. He asked about the business, and Nathan answered his questions as if they really mattered. Yes, he told Fulton, they had twenty steamships now plying the Hudson and New York harbor and the Mississippi. The mouth formed a twisted smile. "We never . . . sold the submarine, did we?" There was a dry chuckle. No, Nathan told him, they never sold the submarine.

He did not report the latest reversals of the monopoly or tell Fulton that his own brother, Stephen, had defeated them with a campaign that ignited the fierce resistance of nine states, with only Louisiana coming through. It was a measure, after all, of personal defeat. Fulton did not ask about that, either, but remained preoccupied with the Hudson River business and the coming showdown in the legislature over the Erie Canal. "Nathan," he whispered, "I want you to look after our interests on the Hudson."

"I will, Robert."

Robert Fulton died that night.

In their grief, Nathan and Yvette now supported each other. He was impressed by her strength. But then in more than four years of marriage, she had emerged as a trusting, uncomplicated person, possessed of social graces and practical common sense.

"Now," she said, "there's even more reason to help DeWitt Clinton push across the canal."

The canal. Its fortunes had been on-again, off-again. The legislature had finally come through with a five million dollar appropriation and had named a commission with DeWitt Clinton as chairman. But then for more than two years the war had brought inland improvements to a standstill. The enemies of the Erie, headed by the firebrand Martin Van Buren, saw their opportunity to have an authorization bill cancelled. "In these days of national peril," Van Buren argued to the legislature, "we do not need Clinton's Ditch!"

Clinton's Ditch. Clinton's Folly. Well, the political opposition did not represent public sentiment, of this Nathan was convinced. At dinner with the New York mayor, he urged a renewal of the canal battle. Clinton moved with alacrity, calling a meeting of New York business and political leaders shortly before Christmas. "Gentlemen, we are on the threshold of 1816. The war has been over for nearly a year. It is time to build ourselves a canal." Claude Durange and Robert Rosenfoert were the first to leap to their feet, shouting, "Hear, hear!"

Words spoken in private rooms could not make it happen, however. Nathan recalled ironically his brother's successful trip down the Ohio and Mississippi, as described to him by associates. He had stirred up grassroots opinion against the Fulton-

Livingston monopoly. Now, Nathan proposed to DeWitt Clinton a campaign to muster support for the Erie Canal in villages up the Hudson and inland along the route the canal would take. The prospect put a glint in Clinton's eye. "Capital idea, Stewart. I'll agree to it on one condition: that you personally take the lead. In that way, they can't say it's all DeWitt Clinton's idea, now can they?"

With the spring thaws, Nathan and Yvette took a steamship up the Hudson to Albany. From there they struck inland on horseback, following a string of villages along the canal's intended route. From Schenectady to Amsterdam and Canajoharie they went, from Little Falls to Herkimer and Utica. Nathan addressed massed rallies, spoke in barns and churches and from platforms out of doors, lit by torchlight. "The Erie Canal, my friends, will bring a new era to the Mohawk Valley and our beloved New York State. More than that, it represents the biggest single project in our nation's history to open western settlement and navigation!" His words fell on fertile minds, bringing cheers and pledges of support. "Write to your legislators. Tell 'em what you want, what you demand!"

To Rome, he went. To Oneida and Syracuse, speaking what was in his heart, shouting at them, and pleading with them. As his campaign spread, crowds grew larger and hecklers appeared, obviously sent by enemies of the Erie. "Boondoggle!" they shouted. "You want the taxpayers to make you an even richer man, Stewart? Hasn't Fulton steamboats made you wealthy enough already?" He lashed back angrily and challenged one husky heckler to a fistfight. It was Yvette who plucked at his arm, drawing him back. "Don't do it, darling. That's what they want. Don't lose your temper. The people are with you."

And so it progressed, from Syracuse through the Montezuma Marshes, to Lyons, Rochester, Lockport, and, finally, Buffalo, a town of less than five hundred souls on the shores of Lake Erie.

Then they made the hard trek back, back to Albany and downriver to New York. Nathan was welcomed home by something that amounted to a state dinner. DeWitt Clinton was beaming. "I don't know what you told those people up there, Stewart, but the legislature is being deluged with mail. This state has never experienced such an outpouring of public sentiment for any kind of project. The timing is perfect, because the legislature goes into session next week. From now on the fight is up to us politicians, me and Rosenfoert and Claude Durange."

"Claude Durange?" Nathan said.

"He is the floor leader for the bill."

And now the whispers began. They came to Nathan in indirect ways. First he became conscious of the inquiring glances and lapses in conversation when he approached a group of acquaintances; then the outright stares, especially from women. A line appeared in a New York scandal sheet newspaper controlled by the powerful Irish political club, Tammany Hall: "What distinguished elder of the legislature has joined the Erie Canal forces to help his wife's lover?" Nathan threw down the paper with a curse. Yvette asked mildly, "What's wrong, dear?" "Dirty work," he muttered. It was dirty work. There were attacks, too, on DeWitt Clinton's motives in the canal debate, suggestions that the New York mayor's friends stood to profit hugely at public expense.

"And who's to profit more than Nathan Stewart, with his steamship empire?"

From nowhere, it seemed, there also emerged a flesh-and-blood foe. The man spoke at a rally, out loud: "If you ask me, Nathan Stewart is a tool of the rich, and part of the conspiracy himself. All they care about is sucking at the tax tit, and to hell with the common man!" He was a thickset Irishman sporting a cloth cap and a heavy sweater. His hands were knotted and strong. He surrounded himself with toughs from the expanding immigrant environs of New York City. His name was Michael Ahearn, and he was a functionary for Tammany Hall. Wherever Nathan spoke the man followed; and now, as the campaign moved into a new dimension of intense behind-the-scenes work, Ahearn seemed to be everywhere, needling, goading, prodding. Nathan was affronted, and exchanged the man glare for glare.

"I wouldn't mess with Ahearn, Mr. Stewart," an aide said quietly. "He's a bad'un, for sure."

If Ahearn delighted in making life more difficult for Nathan Stewart, he also had a knack for pleasing the crowds with feats of strength. The man could break a log over his knee or smash a brick with a blow of one fist. So blatant did the challenge become, that it was all Nathan could do to avoid direct confrontation. The urge was strongest on the afternoon of a pro-canal public rally at the Battery, when Ahearn sauntered to his side trailed by two of his bullies. "Tell me, Mr. Stewart," he muttered, "is Lucy Durange as fine a piece as they say?" Nathan whirled, face darkening. The man laughed and ambled away.

DeWitt took it all with surprising aplomb, unmoved by Nathan's undisguised fury. "Tut, tut, Stewart. When you've been in politics as long as I have you take things in stride. It's nothing personal, old man."

Nothing personal!

But now came an even harder part of the campaign for Nathan: inactivity. His work done, he moved to the sidelines while other men, well experienced at the task, manipulated votes in private and debated the canal issue with the brokers of power, man to man. Old Claude Durange, white-thatched and stooped, became a sudden dynamo of energy. Bursting into Clinton's legislative office, the floor leader announced the winning over of legislators from several key downstate districts. "That so, Durange?" Clinton mused. "And what did you promise 'em?" Durange cackled gleefully. "Hell, I promised we'd build canals for them, too."

From his sidelines position, Nathan was awed by the subtle shadings and barter that went on in such a campaign. While the public at large saw the issue simply to build or not to build—and assumed a long-term state debt in the process—these were not the essentials discussed in political privacy. Durange smoothly mustered the support of contractors, jobbers and suppliers of everything from nails to mules; he pressured merchants whose trade would expand enormously from a direct water link between the Hudson and Lake Erie and called in political debts, real and imaginary, wherever they could be justified. Like a master puppeteer, the Old Fox, as he was nicknamed in legislative corridors, pulled every string. And while the puppeteer manipulated, Clinton stage-managed the public drama. At a joint session of the legislature's two houses, the mayor stood up and announced a major coup. "Gentlemen, the Holland Land Company, owners of half-a-million acres in the canal area, has offered us free right-of-way half-a-mile wide through its holdings. I need not remind you of the enormous expression of confidence this represents in the future of the Erie Canal." At Nathan's side in the gallery, Robert Rosenfoert chuckled. "He needn't remind them, either, that Holland Land's holdings will triple in value when the canal goes through." Across the chamber from Clinton, the faces of Martin Van Buren and the Tammany Hall group seemed to collapse.

When at last the issue came for full debate on the floor, spectator galleries were packed and the corridors outside teemed with lobbyists. As the session opened, Nathan happened to glance across tiers of seats and saw, in a reserved box, Lucy Durange! She was surrounded by friends. The golden-white hair gleamed in a stunning play of light against the rich gallery setting. Smiling, she accepted the greetings of well-wishers who came all the way up from the legislative floor to kiss her hand. Someone behind Nathan whispered, "Ravishing woman." Another voice said, "Shhh." He sensed the finger pointing to his back. Abruptly, Lucy looked across the gallery and saw him. Her eyes widened slightly, and she quickly looked away. Nathan felt a sudden pleasurable tautness in his stomach. Beside him, Yvette said nothing.

If the gallery expected more verbal brawling in this decisive session, they were disappointed. The tough trade-offs and manipulating, Nathan knew, had been completed behind the scenes. Now the pivotal personality was Van Buren, leading the opposition.

Claude Durange, his voice unusually strong for one so physically frail, made a rousing speech declaring this a "day of destiny" for New York state. Several others followed him. And then a hush fell over the chamber as Martin Van Buren came to his feet. The voice of the canal's most voluble critic filled the chamber in measured cadence. "My fellow legislators. All of us here have searched our consciences to do what was right. It is time, I believe, to place public interest above party loyalties. I have wrestled with this with an intensity unprecedented in my public career. In consequence, I hereby cast my vote in *favor* of the Erie Canal!"

The floor and the gallery were shocked. For an instant even the breathing seemed to stop. And then the hush was broken by a spontaneous burst of applause and cheers. With the human mass, Nathan found himself surging to his feet, applauding. "Darling, you've won!" Yvette cried. "You've won!" She flung her arms about his neck. Others swarmed around him in the gallery, thumping his back and pumping his hand. Nathan stammered, "But—But I didn't . . ." The pandemonium went on for a full five minutes before the president of the joint session could gavel things back to order. From his place as a legislative member, DeWitt Clinton rose to declare his heartfelt thanks to Martin Van Buren and issue a plea to bind the wounds. Clinton added: "My friends, many people have worked hard and exercised their gifts, both political and personal, to help bring about this day. But I would be gravely amiss if I failed to acknowledge here the tremendous efforts of one man who focused public attention on the Erie Canal. Without his personal involvement, I assure you that it would not have happened. He is in the gallery today. Gentlemen and ladies, I give you"—Clinton turned and looked up, extending his hand—"a great citizen, the general manager of Hudson River Steamships, Mr. Nathan Stewart!" And now every eye turned to Nathan, and fresh waves of applause rolled through the packed chamber. He stood and nodded, heart pounding. It was too much, too much. But he was too overwhelmed to speak.

That evening Nathan and Yvette joined DeWitt Clinton and other key supporters of the canal for a celebration dinner. Lucy Durange accompanied her husband. She acknowledged Nathan as one would a friendly acquaintance. When dinner and toasting were done, DeWitt Clinton drew Nathan aside. "Stewart, I have a request to make of you. I know it's asking a great deal, but it is important that we move forward vigorously with the canal and obtain the services of the best men available. The other four members of the canal commission concur. We would like for you to serve as our general superintendent."

Yvette's eyes sparkled as the mayor spoke. "Nathan!" she said.

"You might wish to give it some thought, Stewart. Your private business certainly is to be considered."

Nathan smiled. "I don't have to think about it. I accept."

"Wonderful," Clinton said.

"And thank you for recommending me."

"To be honest, Stewart, the idea was not originally mine, although I agree with it wholeheartedly. The suggestion came from Claude and Lucy Durange."

"Claude and Lucy . . . ?"

"They felt, unquestionably, that you were the best man for the job."

Nathan glanced into the parlor, where the other guests were gathered in conversation. Lucy Durange was watching him. As their eyes met, the lovely faced seemed to smolder, framed in shining hair and a loosely caught dark veil. This time she did not look away.

Life abruptly took a fresh tack. With a hired manager seeing to the steamship business and Edward Livingston in charge of

the monopoly at New Orleans, Nathan plunged into preparations. "I envy you, boy," declared old Robert Rosenfoert.
"You're about to build the longest, most challenging canal
ever attempted by man. And without a bit of hydraulic expertise!"

Overnight, a chief engineer was selected along with a group of
smart, energetic young men who—as Rosenfoert had shrewdly
observed—possessed more enthusiasm than skills. But if most of
them knew little more than how to peer through a theodolite,
they made up for it in stubborn resolve and willingness to work.
Nathan trudged with survey crews through rugged terrain, hillsides and marshes, taking sightings and measurements. From
Buffalo to the eastern terminus at Albany, the canal would extend
exactly three hundred and sixty-three miles. As plans took shape,
it became obvious that they would have to build eighty-three
locks to handle two-way traffic, twenty-seven of them in a
distance of fifteen miles between Albany and Schenectady,
skirting around Cohoes Falls.

Problems developed thick and fast.

"Nathan, we've got to have a reservoir of cheap labor. Listen,
it's going to take three thousand men to dig this damned thing.
Three thousand!" DeWitt Clinton sat in the cluttered office for
hiring and purchasing in New York. "Then there are horses and
mules to buy, wagons and tools. My God."

"I've been going over the budget, DeWitt. Are you sure the
canal commission can't pry loose more than one million dollars
in a single legislative appropriation? They're strangling us.
We've got to have start-up money."

Clinton sighed. "That's it. That's the limit."

"I'm telling you, it leaves precious little for wages. And on
top of that, we've got to feed and house the men."

"We'll build shacks, Stewart. Hell, let the contractor worry
about it."

"If men are on starvation pay and living in hovels, with rotten
food and no medical care, we're responsible, not the contractor."

"First, we've got to find the labor."

There was a knock at the office door. Nathan opened the door
and frowned. Michael Ahearn stood there, cap tilted over one
eye, a smile playing at his mouth. "Mr. Mayor? Mr. Stewart? I
hear ye need men to dig that canal."

Nathan bristled. "What would you know about that, Mr.
Ahearn?"

"Word gets around. Me associates and I has got a proposition."

"I'd rather deal with the devil than Tammany."

"Now, now. I'm here on a peaceable mission. Let us say that the Tammany Irish Club is prepared to provide all the men ye need at a price ye can afford to pay. Now what do you think of that?"

Clinton said, "Careful, Stewart."

Nathan frowned. There were no options. The legislature had left him none. He would have to hear Ahearn out. "You're doing the talking, Ahearn."

"Well, it so happens we've got some terrible troubles in the old country. Terrible. There's Irishmen dying to come to this new land, so's they can earn the money to feed their wives and little ones in Erin. 'Tis sad."

"Yes, I'm aware of the problems in Ireland."

"They need jobs, Stewart. And they'll work hard, we can guarantee you. There ain't no brawnier, tougher, more roughscufflin' man alive than an Irishman with a hungry family." Ahearn sucked at his teeth. "We'll dig your canal for you, at the goin' wage."

Nathan took the dilemma home and pondered. Yvette had misgivings. "That's slave work, Nathan. Ahearn and his people will bring them over like cattle, to reap the gain and the profits. They'll use those poor people! The Tammany contractors will—"

"I know, I know. I don't like it either. But what else can we do? We've got contracts already let."

"You can try to get more money out of the legislature."

Nathan went to the canal commissioners, pleading for a bigger chunk of the five million dollar appropriation for the total canal. "One million dollars is not enough to get us started properly and not enough to pay a decent wage, gentlemen!" But the purse strings for the Erie were clutched not by its friends, but by the same power clique that had opposed it. Sadly, Nathan went to see Michael Ahearn. The face of the enemy was wreathed in a smile.

"You win, Ahearn. Bring your Irish at the going rate."

"We set the wages, and no questions asked?"

"As long as they're within the budget."

Ahearn stuck out his hand for a shake. "Agreed."

Nathan ignored the hand. "And let me warn you, Ahearn . . ."

He caught the man's eyes and held them, feeling a small muscle twitch in his face.

The Irishman's smile faded. He glanced nervously to one of his hangers-on for reassurance. "What's that, Stewart?"

"Don't cross me," Nathan growled. "And don't get in my way."

On a sweltering Fourth of July, 1817, at the village of Rome, New York, a small crowd sweated through speeches. A ragtag band played something that passed for a march. A judge who had been designated as prime contractor for the first stretch of canal, a seventy-mile segment of easy digging known as the Long Level, sank a shovel with his foot and threw the first gob of earth. There was a spattering of applause.

Yvette squeezed Nathan's arm. "Darling, now it begins!"

"Yes," he said. "Now it begins."

Why would she be fearful of a boat? It was nothing, after all, but a steam-driven vessel. They were indeed in the age of steam, and for boatbuilders such as Stephen Stewart, steam was the way of the future. But in Catherine's mind it was not merely steam-driven boats that troubled so deeply, it was *this* steam-driven boat. Henry Shreve's creation. The *Washington*. If a vessel ever seemed less menacing and more the butt of humor, however, it was this one.

"Haw, haw, haw," a docklounger chortled. "Old Henry's got himself a beaut there, ain't he?"

Isaiah Stewart had to agree. "Henry, she's the ugliest damn boat I ever seen." He grinned and spat tobacco juice. "She's so ugly, she's downright beautiful."

Beautiful? Catherine smiled ruefully and held Stephen's arm as they crossed the gangplank to the deck. It was like boarding a floating building. Indeed, if you took the *Washington* out of the water and set it on its nose, the building would rise fourteen stories high. She was, after all, one hundred and forty-eight feet long and weighed four hundred tons. Nothing of that size had ever floated on the Ohio or the Mississippi. Onto her main decks, Henry Shreve had bolted four steam boilers. ("Stephen, we're goin' to build us a boat that'll *move!*") For maximum power, the great twin side-wheels were set back toward the stern. Above her jutted twin smokestacks with ornamental crowns. But the most unique feature of the *Washington* was her sheer bulk. She was double-decked on a massive framework of timbers bolted together on trusses eight feet above the decks, with passenger cabins and state-rooms. The whole was topped by a lofty pilothouse with windows that opened all round. To drive the mass, the canny Shreve had devised twin steam engines, one for each wheel, with a new type cutoff valve that would reduce fuel consumption by a third. Bulky she was. Powerful she was. Ungainly she was. But beautiful?

"Yes," Stephen Stewart said, "she is beautiful."

Catherine shrugged. Oh, well.

They had built the *Washington* at Wheeling, Virginia, downriver from Pittsburgh. Already Stephen was making plans for steamboats of his own, utilizing innovations that he and Captain Shreve had devised together. "But the first thing we've got to do," he said, "is break the monopoly at New Orleans."

Henry Shreve grinned. "All right, my boy. Let's go do it!"

Catherine and Isaiah rode the *Washington* with them back to Pittsburgh. The great vessel, blasting her steam whistles, made the ninety-odd miles in ten hours. From the taverns and fleshpots in town, they signed on a crew of burly bargemen and keelboaters, men who not only knew the river but could fight their way out of trouble, if need be. "Sometimes," Captain Shreve observed wisely, "ye need to have a few good brawlers around." Two mornings later, Stephen again kissed Catherine at the Stewart wharf.

She hugged him fiercely. "We're always saying good-bye."

"I know. But it won't be long this time."

The *Washington* blasted downriver, steam whistles tootling, spray flying, crowds cheering from every town and hamlet. In just twenty days ("Unbelievable, Henry. Utterly unbelievable!") Stephen stood on the prow as the great vessel made her final turn into the riverfront at New Orleans. But he was grim-faced now. Awaiting him was the usual large crowd of onlookers, but led this time by a group of somber officials and uniformed police constables.

"Who is in charge here?" asked a chief constable.

Stephen stepped onto the dock. "I am. Stephen Stewart."

"Mr. Stewart, you are hereby charged with violating the laws of the sovereign state of Louisiana and the city of New Orleans by bringing a steamboat into our waters, contrary to special regulations . . ."

The crowd behind the officials began muttering. Stephen glanced warily at Henry Shreve and the dock brawlers they had brought along as crew. Then to his surprise someone yelled: "Let 'em through, Constable. You can't block off free rivers." Other voices of the citizenry joined in. "That's right, Constable." "It ain't constitutional, blockin' off trade." "Let them fellas be."

The chief constable, tight-lipped, said to Stephen, "Mr. Stewart, I don't like this any more than you do, but I've got my duty. I'd advise your men there not to interfere. Your own brother, after all, had a part in this monopoly. I am placing you under arrest and impounding this vessel."

"Impounding!" Henry Shreve snarled from the deck. "How dare they!"

From behind the chief constable, a tall man in civilian clothes stepped forward. "Really, Mr. Stewart, I wouldn't expect you to deliberately violate the laws of trade."

"And who might you be?" said Henry Shreve.

"Marsh Blackman, attorney for Mr. Edward Livingston." A courtly bow. "At your service."

Stephen smiled. "My compliments, Mr. Blackman. At least you don't send underlings to do your dirty work."

"We have a legitimate monopoly, Mr. Stewart. And you are legitimately under arrest, and this vessel is impounded."

It was Stephen's turn to bow. "If that's the case, let me remind you that we have access to the courts too. We intend to file suit for full damages. Not only will I demand recompense for all losses incurred by being denied the use of this vessel, I myself will sue you personally if I'm put in jail."

Blackman flushed. "Take him, Constable," he snapped, and turned away.

Stephen was escorted to jail with more courtesy than he had imagined possible. Instead of being locked into a cell, he was given the freedom of the constable's office.

"And what do you do now, Mr. Stewart?" a deputy asked.

"I'll just wait and see what develops."

Developments were not long in coming. At the docks an uneasy standoff began between the constables and Henry Shreve's river toughs, neither side caring to do battle with the other. Shreve himself left the *Washington*, found a lawyer on Canal Street, and began drawing up a lawsuit. In the city, meanwhile, the mood turned sour as citizens gathered for angry speeches against the monopoly. At nightfall, a harassed chief constable came back to his office. "Mr. Stewart, you're free to go. Someone has posted your bail."

"Posted my bail? Who?"

"A lady. She asked not to be identified." The officer shrugged. "That's all I can tell you."

Puzzled, Stephen left the constable's office and returned to the steamboat. Henry Shreve was there with his attorney, having dinner on board. "Well, well," said the captain cheerily, "I thought you'd be dining on jailhouse hardtack and salt pork this evening."

Stephen described his release. Neither Shreve nor the lawyer could account for it. "One of your many female admirers, no doubt," Shreve mused.

It was almost midnight when Marsh Blackman arrived. The lawyer was in a conciliatory mood. "Mr. Stewart, I understand that you are indeed filing suit for damages. I, uh, rather hoped this could be settled amicably."

Stephen and Shreve looked at him with surprise. The Canal Street lawyer started to speak, but he was waved into silence.

"I am willing to release you, Mr. Stewart, and your vessel provided you withdraw from New Orleans and hereafter honor our company's monopoly rights."

"Honor the monopoly? You must be mad."

"Those, um, are the terms." Hurriedly, he gathered his papers and beaver hat. "I will take my leave now so that you can think it over. Consider your breach of the monopoly overlooked . . . this time."

He left them sitting speechless.

Lawyer Blackman walked off the gangplank of the *Washington* to a waiting enclosed carriage and quickly got in beside a beautiful, red-haired woman.

"You let them go?"

"Yes, damn it, Rose. I let them go."

"Good. Now you can take me to dinner. I'm starving."

Blackman tapped for the driver to move off.

The following day, attorney Edward Livingston, representing the Fulton-Livingston interests in New Orleans, wrote a letter to Nathan Stewart in New York. He believed that the monopoly was not constitutionally defensible, especially in view of their failure to secure commitments from the nine other riverfront states. There was strong risk of losing heavy damage claims in the event of such failure. Public sentiment in New Orleans, moreover, was strongly against the measure and being further stirred up by unsavory elements in the city, including a leading brothel madame. "I strongly recommend that we no longer attempt to invoke the monopoly in Louisiana waters. A prudently quiet withdrawal seems appropriate . . ."

It was not her pleasure to rise before ten. Maurice insisted that early rising was not civilized. With her acquired tastes for luxury and ease, she happily agreed. But then how could one not agree with Maurice Rambeaux? He was an exquisite man, and he quite openly adored her.

"Miss Rose, will you wear the yellow gown today?"

"Which yellow gown is that, Mossy?"

"The one with the parasol to match."

"Yes, that will be nice."

The delicate little mantel clock, the one with the crystal face and the carved ivory case, struck ten-thirty. The tiny chime had a silver sound. She sat at her makeup table and attended her toilet. The shutters were open to the morning. Doves cooed from the tree-shaded high terrace. There were distant sounds of street life and a fisherwoman crying her merchandise. "Sweet fish! Fresh fish! Sweet fish! Fresh fish!"

With deft strokes she applied eye makeup with a brush. A dab of rouge finished the highlights of her cheekbones. Using her pinky finger, she placed a dark beauty spot just under the left eye. This made her giggle. The beauty spot could be worn sometimes on the right and sometimes on the left. The transformation was subtle to her appearance; not enough to be noticeable, and yet intriguing to men. "What is it Rose?" they would ask. "Upon my word you look ravishingly different today, but for the life of me I can't . . ." She put on a light lipstick. She removed the night netting and brushed out her hair, so that it would catch fire in the sunlight. There! Silly, foolish creatures, men.

She put down the hairbrush and thought about Stephen. *Mon Dieu,* he had developed into a handsome man. Surely Nathan must be the same. Her brothers were blessed by the Fates to bring aches to the hearts of women. Rose Lark sighed.

There was a soft knock at the door. She was still in her chemise. "Who is it?"

"Maurice."

"Ah!" She slipped into a robe and let him in. He wore his dark silk dressing gown over silk morning pajamas. She had given him the gown for Christmas. His small-boned face lifted with pleasure.

"I hope I'm not too early."

"Not at all, Maurice. I've ordered breakfast on the terrace."

As she finished dressing, Mossy brought the breakfast. The servant's massive black bulk all but filled the latticed double door as she passed through, bearing the tray. Mossy had been a slave before Maybelle bought her and set her free. Now she worked for a salary and had her own living quarters behind the Nocturne. ("Mossy, nobody should be a slave. People ain't got a right to own other people. Always remember that. Even if your body is shackled, your mind is free." "Yas'm, Miss Rose. But everybody ain't as smart as you.")

Maybelle wore the yellow gown now, with its tight uplifting bodice edged in silken ruffles. The gown fell in soft pleats, adorned with printed pink tea roses and pale green stitching. Her white silken shoes with tiny high heels peeped out from beneath the bottom ruffle. The petticoats were just full enough to flash slightly when she walked. Her waist was naturally small. She joined Maurice at the breakfast table.

"You've had quite an adventure for yourself this week." Maurice spooned into a poached egg. "That took real organization, the public demonstration and all. And the very idea, persuading Judge Mattlebaum that the monopoly is unconstitutional. Poor Marsh Blackman, he didn't have a chance." He shook his head in admiration. "Rose, you're a wonder."

She reached across the table and squeezed his hand. "I've had a good teacher."

"Did your brother suspect?"

"I'm sure he has no idea that I am in New Orleans. Otherwise, he would have found me by now. He's not going to be looking for Rose Lark, Queen of the Delta."

"True."

Rose Lark, Queen of the Delta. The name had been hers for so many years that any other, even Maybelle Stewart, seemed strange. At times, in reflection, she would chide Maurice for his choice of names. The quick arrival and departure of Stephen had put her into a nostalgic mood.

"Maurice, whatever did you think of me when I stumbled into your saloon out of the rain?"

He chuckled, spreading butter on a piece of toast. "I suppose I should say that you reminded me of a drowned rat with red hair. But to tell the truth, I thought you were the most enchanting creature ever to stumble into my saloon out of the rain."

"You said I had a rotten voice and looked like a schoolmistress."

"That's because you had a rotten voice and looked like a schoolmistress. But remember, you weren't up against much competition."

"Competition? You didn't have any girls at all. Just that dinky saloon, the Rive Gauche. And you told me to put on white tights with a huge paper rose on my thigh and a ruffled blue body suit and sing in a French accent. I didn't speak a word of French!"

"Who cared?"

Her laughter pealed in a way that delighted him. Maybelle could see the love in his face and feel it in his moods. He had that same expression when he played a nocturne on the piano: a strong, inward look full of life and passion. There was so much mystery about him, about his past, that even after sharing five years of his life and having his child—the baby, Brack—there was so much that she did not know. She settled back with a cup of the fierce black coffee so beloved of New Orleans. "Maurice, what was it like before?"

He dabbed at his mouth with a napkin. "In Paris, you mean? Dull, really. As I've told you before, hardly worth talking about."

"But I'd like to know. You're so—so well educated. You know music, art, literature. My word, you've taught me things I would not have learned in finishing school."

She did not mention the element of mystery. He kept loaded pistols about and was watchful of customers who came and went, as if expecting someone. Maurice was a gentlemen, Maybelle told herself. But he was also a rogue.

"Ah, yes." He offered a wry smile. "And today we run the finest whorehouse in New Orleans."

The light flickered from her face. He saw, and was immediately sorry. "I didn't mean to be cruel," he said. "The Nocturne is really something special. We're giving the public what it wants. You've made this business what it is. My God, we'll both be rich someday. There is nothing we should want for."

"It's still a whorehouse, Maurice." She sighed, feeling the guilt. "You've had confidence in me, given me freedom to build the business. I added a whorehouse to your bar and changed the name of the place. We put in continental food and a wine list. Already a lot of dandies and duelists come here. In time, we'll get the gourmets, too. But it's still a whorehouse." She looked down at the pretty yellow gown with the tea rose print that matched a parasol. "And I'm still a whore."

He looked away quickly. "Please, Rose."

"Maybelle," she said tartly. "My name is Maybelle Stewart. I'm a whore. I am also a mother. I am unwed."

"I told you, we cannot—"

"Yes." It was her turn to be contrite. "I know. Your wife in France, your religion. You are a good Catholic, and that's fine. I have no religion except life, so I can't quarrel with yours. The fact that she is in France, somewhere, and we are in New Orleans doesn't matter either."

Why did it happen like this? Why did they quarrel, when so much of life was spread for them as on a gigantic table? Why did they spoil the idyll? It happened infrequently, but with any frequency was too much.

"I—I'm sorry," she said.

Maurice shrugged. "We are human. We have our pleasures and our pains."

"And our frustrations."

"That, too."

He pushed away from the table and changed the subject. "So what do you plan to do today?"

The idyll came back. She brightened. "I'm taking Brack for a ride in the carriage. And then I'll do some shopping on Canal Street. And I must have an hour for the piano."

Maurice was his old self again. A smile played over his handsome face. "Ah, the piano. If you keep on, the pupil is going to outperform the teacher."

She laughed. "That will be the day."

An hour later Rose Lark swept into Bourbon Street in her open carriage. It was colored a pale rose and drawn by a matched pair of black mares. Her face glowed beneath a mass of flaming red hair and a yellow parasol to match her gown. Beside her, in a suit of blue velvet, rode the two-year-old Brack. Male heads turned to stare at the passing carriage. And when it stopped, there was a rush of volunteers to let down the folding steps, on the chance of glimpsing a flashing ankle.

"Ah," murmured a French expatriate, "*la rose est une belle fleur!*"

An old crone hissed: "Strumpet."

She ignored them both.

X

Stifling. God, he was stifling. It was the void, the swirling, fetid, heated void choking and enveloping him, cutting off the light and the air. The void spun, drawing him down. Then abruptly it brightened and changed. He was floating, drifting upward into the brighter air. But this was more frightening still, for the faces expanded about him and broke into hideous laughter, mocking, jeering, laughing. His eardrums were bursting. He clapped his hands to his ears, the fear eating at his insides. He screamed. He screamed again. And again...

Ward Stewart woke up screaming.

His eyes opened in the murky darkness. He fought to regain control. The fear was receding now like a great wave. His heart pounded. He was drenched in sweat. A hand moved over his chest, lightly. The hand was cool and dry. A whisper came to him intimately, out of the night. "Sweetheart, you were dreaming. You had a bad dream. Are you all right?" Only she spoke Southern, languidly, slurring the words Savannah-style. Ah yuh all right?

"Yes." It was a croak. He cleared his throat. "Yes, I'm all right."

Moonlight filtered through the slatted shutters, casting the room in diffused light. The light was a silver shimmer on the mosquito netting surrounding the bed. He rolled over, and the netting trembled. He kicked off the covers and still sweated. The woman beside him said, "Shall I get you a cool drink?"

"That would be nice," he said.

She slipped naked from the bed. She was a moonlit body moving away from the netting. A door opened and closed. He stared at the gossamer web of the mosquito bar. It reminded him of a shroud for the dead. He groaned and flung his arm over his eyes and lay there. After a while she came back. His hand reached out and took the glass, and he drank. It was bourbon and water. The bourbon warmed his throat, going down. The warmth flooded the area behind his eyes. His fear melted away.

She caressed his chest, saying nothing. Her mouth, wet and warm, kissed his earlobe and worked over the side of his face and neck and shoulder. She murmured something. The hand moved down from his chest to his stomach and down, down, to fondle him. He swelled. The mouth followed the hand down, and his swelling hardened and rose up. The mouth found his hardness and gently began to suck.

Oh, he thought. Oh. Oh. Oh. What, he thought, was her name? Dumb, oh, stupid, oh, thing to . . . Oh. Her name was . . . God. Her name was . . . Oh. Her name . . . Oh, Jesus. Oh, take it, honey. Take it, uh, oh, uh . . . Her name . . . Name . . . *Name* . . . NAME . . . "I'm . . . I'm, ohJesusChristI'mgoingtorightnow . . . NOW!"

The spasms shook him.

And then he remembered.

Her name was Reba.

He slept again.

Four hours later he left Reba and walked out of her house into the languid, tree-shaded heat of Savannah. Passing horses and buggies raised a fine dust from the streets, and children played in dappled shade beneath massive trees. He took off his coat and hooked it over his shoulder and sweated. Not a breath of air stirred, and the mosquitoes hummed off the marshes, greedy for human blood.

"Mawnin', Captain Stewart. How you this mawnin'?"

"Pretty day, ma'am," he said. "Yes, indeed."

They could take Savannah and shove it into the sea, for all he cared. The new wealth was breeding and inbreeding on tides of shipping and cotton and slavery. There was a stench of human sweat and duplicity. After two months of life in Savannah, Ward Stewart longed for the amenities of Boston and New York. He was drained from too much whiskey and too much sex. He was culturally sapped and emotionally dried. The only thing hotter than the weather in July was the women. Jesus. They went after a single, handsome man like animals in rut.

But what troubled him most was the absence of concern for human suffering. The first view of slavery shocked him. There were slaves in the north, yes, but on a more humane level. The buying and selling of slaves was not flaunted; the public was spared its cruel realities. Here, he had been introduced to the misery of the slave market, where men stood in chains on the block in heat, dust, and stench. The white crowd ogled. White men bargained for their bodies, in auction.

He went out and stayed drunk for a week.

Later, when he mentioned his disgust at a dinner party, the hostess had drawn him aside. "Goodness, Captain, it's not polite for you to talk like that. We know you're from the Nawth and all, but I really wouldn't like for you to spoil my lovely dinnah party. I'm sure you mean no harm. Why, these nigras ain't nothin' but animals. Really, Captain, it's not like they had any *feelings* or intelligence at all."

After that he kept his opinions to himself and took his pleasures where he found them. To hell with slavery. Women were what mattered.

"Why, Captain Stewart, how *nice* to see you. I declare, I've been thinking about you for days. Did you get my note? You must come to my little dinner party next week. I mean, you simply *must* come, or I shall be terribly disappointed." She was a gasping, wide-eyed vision in white with matching parasol and too much powder on her face. "Now, you wouldn't want me to be disappointed, would you?"

He thought: Ah, Miss Clive, of course I'd be delighted to come to yore little ole dinner party. Unfortunately, I have a date to screw yore pretty little ole cousin, Miss Priscilla Herndon, that evening. Miss Priscilla's got one of the hottest bodies in Savannah.

"I'd love to come, Miss Clive," he said. "You are really good to ask me. Unfortunately, I have a most important engagement that evening. Business, you know. Nothing else, I assure you, would keep me away. Even wild horses..."

"Oh, my, such a pity. That strange-looking vessel of yours, I suppose. Well, business is business, as they say, and far be it from me. Do you really plan to sail across the ocean in that *steamship?* Upon my word. But if you happen to change your mind—about dinner, I mean—then you know where to find me."

"Yes, ma'am." He tipped his hat. "Charmed."

He continued his walk. From several passing carriages, well-dressed men glowered down. Ward could feel the malice and knew its cause. They were the husbands of women he had bedded. Damn fool, he thought; if I don't get out of this port soon, I'm liable to get my ass shot off.

There is an instant and mutual respect between certain men of a breed. Its roots can neither be plumbed nor understood. Friendship, like enmity, is a matter of temper, values, and the blood. So it was between Ward Stewart and Captain Lucas Petersen of the steam-powered sailing vessel *Atlantica*. In part, the bond was their common affection for the strange, ungainly ship that now tugged at her anchor line in Savannah harbor. The *Atlantica* was quite unlike anything that had put to sea before: three hundred and twenty tons of wood and iron, with three masts and two paddle wheels that could be folded and lifted on deck for rough weather. For months they had seen to her fittings, and entertained wealthy visitors from the North who had come down to inspect their investment. Novelty of design and power set tongues to wagging but did not inspire confidence. Investors on more than one occasion went away muttering and red-faced, vowing to get their money back.

Capt. Petersen was a dour Norwegian in his early sixties with the look and rolling gait of a lifetime spent at sea. It mattered not at all to him that Capt. Stewart, who would sail as his first mate, cut a merry swath ashore. The man knew ships and was enthusiastic, and that was enough. And so they made their peace and kept it.

Ward found the captain in his cabin, poring over a blueprint of the last engine fittings. If it was hot on deck, it was broiling below. Capt. Petersen seemed not to notice. He even kept his gold-braided uniform jacket buttoned.

"Well, then, Captain. That's about it, I see," Ward said gaily. He sat on the bunk and mopped sweat from his eyes. "Don't see how you can stand this heat."

"Ah, Captain Stewart." Petersen offered a craggy smile and motioned to the cupboard. "You'll find a tot of something in there, to slake ye thirst."

Ward poured them two glasses of West Indies rum. They

touched glasses and downed them at a gulp. The fire raced down his throat. "The morning tide, then?"

"Aye," Petersen said, "the morning tide."

"And the hands?"

"Coming aboard tonight."

Ward then repeated the talk that by now had become ritual.

"How many passengers will we be carrying, Captain?"

"Not a soul, I'm afraid. Still can't sell a single ticket. Can't even give one away."

"Well, then, we'll just make it up on cargo. How much cargo?"

"Not a pound."

Ward poured another glass of rum and tossed it back. He swallowed, grimaced, belched. "Pity."

"Indeed it is. And I'll thank you"—Capt. Petersen held forth his empty glass—"to pour."

So there would be no dinner party after all, and no rendezvous with Miss Priscilla either. He was grateful. It would be good to feel a moving ship beneath his feet again and a bit of wind in the face.

The *Atlantica* left Savannah on the morning tide with a flurry of shouted commands, creaking tackle, and men scurrying aloft. Stashed on deck and below was an enormous quantity of pine-wood logs to feed the fires of her great steam boiler. For the first time in history, a vessel left an American port bearing, in addition to her sailing crew, men whose jobs would be to stoke fires and tend to engines. For all the skepticism ashore, there was a fine show of farewells. Cannon boomed, ladies fluttered their handkerchiefs—a good many in distress over the departure of the handsome Capt. Stewart—and a Navy frigate provided escort. Finally, offshore, the work gang belowdecks fired up the boilers, the *Atlantica* belched plumes of heavy black smoke, all sails were taken in, and she chugged resolutely ahead, her holds laden with sand ballast.

In years to come, Ward Stewart would remember the historic voyage as being dull but happy. Capt. Petersen was good company. Unfortunately, there was only enough wood to provide seventy hours of steam; but during those seventy hours, the crew had idle time on hand and spent it sprucing up the ship. The weather did not turn foul. No one quarreled. Even the engineers were happy, having an engine that worked quite well indeed as long as there was fuel to burn. Finally, keeping a single stack of wood in reserve, they hoisted sail. On the twenty-seventh day, they made landfall off the coast of Ireland. Capt. Petersen ordered steam up once more for a triumphant entry to port. A large crowd awaited them, including several dozen men in uniform arrayed alongside the town's water-pumping equipment. Capt. Petersen emerged on deck in his best uniform and began to make a speech. He was interrupted as men began toiling at the pumps. A heavy stream of seawater gushed forth, soaking him through.

The captain sputtered and cursed. *"What,"* he roared, *"is the meaning of this?"*

Finally the water was turned off and a red-faced official explained. "Sir, we thought your ship was on fire!"

Officers and crew of the *Atlantica* were wined in Ireland, dined in Scotland, and mobbed on the docks in England. Elated, they made the return trip to America under sail—the boiler was balky and Capt. Petersen did not wish to risk an explosion— expecting a heroes' welcome. There was none. At the offices of Howard Untermeyer, the red-haired financier who had put together the investment group for the *Atlantica*, a preoccupied assistant to the president told them there would be no further need for their services.

"But—But damn it, man, we made it!" Ward protested. "Where is Howard? Why doesn't he come out to meet us?"

Mr. Untermeyer was out of the city. There were no plans to follow up the voyage of the *Atlantica* with another. The venture had been entirely too expensive, with neither passengers nor cargo to show an income. "Let us say, gentlemen, that the project was premature."

"Premature?" said Capt. Petersen. "But what about oceanic steamships? Aren't we going to build and sail them?"

The assistant to the president picked up a sheaf of papers and turned on his heel. "I'm sure I don't know. If so, somebody else will have to do so. Now, if you don't mind, I'm terribly busy." He left them standing in the anteroom.

It finally took Nathan to explain. Untermeyer had taken a heavy loss on the *Atlantica*. Merchants were in no mood to take risks on transatlantic steamships. Nathan saw the dejection in his cousin's face and sympathized. Would he care to throw in his lot with riverboats? Ward shook his head. "Thank you, Nathan, but no. I'm a seafaring man. I wouldn't know the first thing about a riverboat. Besides, I'm not lacking for funds. It's just a damned disappointment, that's all. The *Atlantica* . . . Well, she's a great ship."

And so he went back to Provincetown. Bartholemew greeted him warmly, as if nothing had happened. They dined together and were careful in their speech, two stubborn men unwilling to broach the subject on their minds. The spoons clinked in bowls of fish chowder. The dining room was as it had always been, austere and devoid of decoration. The house had been thus since Ward's mother died, in his childhood. Bartholemew cared for nothing beyond utility. It was enough to serve one's basic needs. "Your room is as it was," he said gruffly. After supper and a pipe, Ward went up the narrow stairs to bed.

Why had he come here, to lick his wounds and be a child again? The war was over and done, the *Shark* converted again to the fishing fleet, and he was a grown man already showing lines in his face. What was he looking for? Certainly not codfishing. That was plain. What did he seek from his father, understanding?

The confrontation came three days later. Bartholemew was growing old and his health failing. More and more of the office business was handled by Throckmorton, the clerk whom Ward had known from childhood. The fleet consisted of eight vessels, fishing the Georges Banks now. They were treacherous waters, where swift current could sweep a boat right off the shallows unless securely anchored. Men still held the Georges in superstitious awe. But fish were there for the taking, and the journey from Provincetown was nothing compared to the distance to the Grand Banks. Fishing prospered. The saltworks prospered. His father had added new salt vats and windmills. He had orders to build dories and small schooners.

"It's all here for you, Ward. I want you to take it over from me. There's a fine business in cod. Listen, we're going to have a boom. Everybody says so. A fortune's to be made, several times over . . ."

The set of Ward's face stopped him. He became perplexed and bit his lip, as if to bite off a word.

"No, Father," Ward said.

"But a Cape Cod son always steps into his father's shoes. It's our way, lad. You're a fine strong man now, and have had time to sow your wild oats. Now's the time to settle down, get you a good wife, start a family and a business. That's the way of life, son. There's no happiness any other way."

He thought: Why can't I be like other men? For what his father said was true, had always been true. And yet his restlessness gave him no peace. It was still too soon for codfishing boats and saltworks, too soon.

"I'm just not ready, Father. Perhaps in another year or two. I want to find my own way."

He left the following morning in darkness. The cold stars glittered overhead, and the first snowfall of autumn crunched underfoot. He felt his father's eyes looking down from the window at his back, but he did not turn. He caught the stagecoach that labored down the road toward the mainland, its horses struggling for footing in the sand. He watched the sea and the soaring gulls. He wept, but not for his father. He wept for himself.

There are women of beauty, women of personality, and women of intelligence. Rarely did Ward Stewart encounter a woman who was all three. Lilly Crandon, featured actress in the new hit play of Boston, *Lady of the Niger,* was such a rarity. He went to the play with friends. The next night he went alone. And the next, and the next. Her magnetism across the footlights drew him like a cold soul to the fire. Ward resolved to meet her, and if the opportunity did not create itself, he would create one.

He had arrived in Boston on a drinking binge. The bitter parting from his father ate at his memory. Guilt gave him no rest. And so he drank. In the early stages of the bottle, numbness took over, and the face of old Bartholemew faded. Only later, when the bottom had been reached and he lay on his bed in a stupor, did the face come back. Then he suffered in abject wretchedness. From the fog of his delirium, Bartholemew spoke to him, his old face etched with pain. "A Cape Cod son always steps into his father's shoes . . ."

The wayward son. Why was he cursed to be the wayward son? And the *only* son, at that! There was a line from Shakespeare that haunted him. "How sharper than a serpent's tooth it is to have a thankless child." And he was that child. But he was not a child; he was a man, full-grown and possessed of his own faculties and sense, a man of substance and friendships. He could walk a quarterdeck and command a vessel. He groaned, pushed up from the bed, saw the bloated image in a mirror. He shouted at the reflection: "Just let me be my self!" He threw a vase, and the reflection exploded into a shower of bright shards and diamonds.

He resolved to drink less, go out more, busy himself. It was then that he went to the theater and saw Lilly Crandon. It was then that he vowed to make love to her.

"Lilly Crandon? Why, Ward, I think you've been smitten." His friend Conrad Appleby, the young jeweler, chuckled. "Ward Stewart, terror of the boudoir, smitten. Upon my word!" Fashion plate, Appleby. Wealthy family, fussy about his clothes, a dandy. Ward found him useful, if superficial. The man had connections. "And an actress at that! Really, Ward, you do astonish me at times."

Ward played on his considerable vanity. "Try to get me an introduction, Appleby. If anybody in Boston can do it, you can. Just for the hell of it, eh? Where's your gaming spirit?"

He waited in his rooms, not daring to go out for fear of missing Appleby's visit. He sat at the window and watched a cold rain sluice down upon the dreary streets of Boston. Finally, on the fifth day, Appleby came bounding up the stairs, whistling.

"We're in luck, Stewart. I've got us invitations to a cast party. The play's assistant producer is now a dear friend of mine. Lovely fellow, excellent family. It's tomorrow night, and Lilly Crandon will be there."

"I knew you could do it! Let's have a drink."

"Hold on a minute." Appleby plucked at Ward's sleeve. "There's something else you probably ought to know. Your precious Lilly has got a full-time gentleman friend. She's the mistress of Barnard Hefling."

"Who's Barnard Hefling?"

"Heavens, you are out of touch. Barnard Hefling, dear boy, is merely the richest fur dealer in Boston. He is also a power of Massachusetts politics and a brother-in-law of the governor. Rather an avid sportsman too, I hear."

"Sportsman?"

"Fishing. He's really keen on fishing."

Ward smiled, drew a cigar from his pocket and bit off the end. He leaned into Appleby's lighted match and drew the flame. "Is that a fact?"

The cast party for the *Lady of the Niger* took place in one of those new mansions rising along the Charles River, in the backwash of Boston wealth. Lilly Crandon and her escort arrived suitably late. He was a corpulent man, given to too much port and heavy perspiration. Lilly was whisked away into a clutch of adoring friends, leaving Hefling to his own devices. No one here seemed remotely interested in politics and less in business affairs, dash it all. Ward bided his time, letting the man suffer to listen to actors talk about themselves. Finally, then, he stepped to Hefling's side and said, mildly, "Ah, Barnard Hefling, isn't it? I hear you're really keen on fishing."

Thirty minutes later, Lilly Crandon joined them, and Hefling murmured, "My dear, permit me to introduce Captain Ward Stewart. We've been having an absolutely capital chat . . ."

Her eyes met Ward's and he sensed her sudden kindling of interest. "Really, Barnard? How charming."

Did she really love him, or was it some cruel and monumental pretense? And could it happen at last that he would have such feelings as this, and they would endure? At odd and hellish times, doubts assailed him. Nonetheless, Ward Stewart recognized that he had never had such completeness before. A woman had been a challenge, a pursuit, a diversion, nothing more. Beyond the conquest lay emptiness and, inevitably, the bitter scenes. He had never understood their angers; in his own heart, the climactic act of lovemaking was complete of and for itself. Afterward, one walked away. And yet, how deeply he had envied those having more permanent relationships; how he had envied his cousin Nathan, for Yvette.

Now, at last, he was whole. Lilly. God, he loved Lilly! When he was with her, in those urgent trystings, he could not have his fill of Lilly's delights. And when they were apart, he agonized.

"I love you," he whispered. "I adore you."

She laughed that small, breathless laugh with its oddly hinted detachment, almost of scorn. "How much do you love me?"

"I would do anything for you. I would go to the ends of the earth for you."

Lilly pouted. The China-blue eyes enlarged. The lower lip curled. It was her Little Girl look. "Now you're going away from Lilly. You don't love Lilly any more."

And so she was heaven, and she was hell. Her days and nights were turned around. Nights, after the curtain and the bows, were for play and lovemaking; days were for sleeping. He always awaited her at the stage door, flowers in hand. But sometimes, for no explained reason, she eluded him and disappeared. He would not find her again, either in her normal haunts with lively friends or at her residence hotel. His torment at such times knew no bounds; he could neither sleep nor sit still, but paced away the terrible hours tortured by visions of his Lilly in the arms of another man. It lay in the pit of his stomach, the suspicion, like a hot iron. Even whiskey gave him no relief. He writhed on his torture rack, and only her presence again with that flirty, taunting smile provided release. And always, she had an explanation which he accepted greedily, too grateful to question.

They spoke, in the delightful intimacy of her bed, of how they had come together, the magic splendor of their first nights together and the humorous irony of how he had won her. Barnard Hefling had been stupidly, ridiculously easy. The politician had introduced them himself, after Ward captured his interest at the party. Ward laughed, remembering the scene. He puffed out his cheeks and puffed out his stomach, sitting up in bed like a pompous fool, and said gravely, "My dear, permit me to introduce Captain Ward Stewart, late of the privateer *Shark*. Captain Stewart is now going to set a course for your sweet little ass." Lilly laughed and laughed at his imitation of Hefling, laughed until she could hardly catch her breath, shouting, "Stop it! Stop it, you're killing me. You look—you look like a toad!" And then, abruptly, her laughter would stop, and she would grow pensive. In one such mood, she spoke fleetingly of Hefling with a look of mingled sadness.

"He adored me, you know. He was quite good to me. He is . . . That is, I understand he is quite hurt over this."

Ward shrugged. "Hefling is a big boy."

"Yes," she said. But the China-blue eyes were hooded in thought.

There were occasional mentions of Hefling from other quarters as well. Boston was a small town, delighting in its gossip. And what better morsel than the spectacle of the rich, powerful financier out of his mind over an actress, forced to share her favors with a handsome sea captain. And "share" was the word. "My dear," whispered the knowing lips, "you don't think that Lilly Crandon would throw away a man like Barnard Hefling, do you? She's much too smart a baggage for that."

Ward received hints, but he ignored them. Dirty minds. They would do anything to discredit Lilly. He swallowed his pain. When Conrad Appleby suggested as much, Ward flew into a towering rage, and the jeweler beat a hasty retreat stammering apologies. Ward mentioned it to Lilly later, and she burst into tears, "Oh, darling, why do they hate me so?" He comforted her that night, until the sunlight bathed her window with its rosy glow.

"I love you, Lilly. I'd go out of my mind without you. I think I'd kill any man who tried to take you from me. I've even started carrying a pocket pistol."

"Oh, Ward. Oh, darling, what a perfectly fearsome thing to say."

Well, she was his for now. She lay here beside him, with her sweet odors and her warmth. He looked at the ceiling in the half-dark and reveled. Then he kissed her bare shoulder and the side of her blessed little neck. "Angel," he whispered. His arm encircled her naked body beneath the covers. "You have my heart," he said, "my soul . . ." He tried to caress her, but she deftly enclosed herself so that his hand moved clumsily in the wrong places. Damn, why was he clumsy with Lilly? It was as if she divined his moves and thoughts in advance, making him seem foolish.

"I love you too," she said.

He wanted her again. He tried to draw her close, so that she would feel his need. But she was lying on her stomach now, doing something to her hair.

"Let me."

"Not now, darling." She yawned and stretched, catlike. "I've got an awfully busy day tomorrow. Casting call at eleven for the new play, hairdresser at noon and then luncheon with Carlyle. He wants me to help him select the costumes. I think that's darling of Carlyle, don't you?"

No, Ward did not think it was darling of Carlyle. Always there was a Carlyle or a Teddy or a Blakemore inviting her to this or that, consulting Lilly and generally skulking about. He rolled away from her, sulking. "Carlyle can bloody well stuff it," he said.

"Now don't be like that. Really, your moods can be so tiresome. I think you don't trust me at all sometimes. I wonder, 'Whatever must he think of me?' I'm a simple working girl, Ward. I've tried to tell you that. This is my career." She had turned to him again and the China-blue eyes regarded him gravely. "Do you not want Lilly any more? Are you getting tired of Lilly?"

He threw back his head and sighed in utter exasperation. *"Tired* of Lilly! Would you listen to that? My girl, I happen to be very much in love with you. I really am. But for some reason, I can't share your life. We've been together for six weeks now, and still you push me into a corner like some lapdog. I'm supposed to sit and wait till you're ready for me again. And then we sneak around—"

"You're being silly."

"Tired of Lilly? Not hardly. You're always saying, 'I love you too.' But you don't act like a woman in love."

"I can't please you at all." The eyes were hurt now, soft and vulnerable and hurt. It wasn't Little Girl Lilly any more, but Innocent Lilly. "You don't want Lilly." She sniffed. The blue eyes misted. "You don't love Lilly." Softly, then, she drew close to him. The pouty mouth grew full and near. She stroked his chest. The touching inflamed him. She knew. The China-blue eyes took on a smoky glow. The hand slipped down his chest and across his stomach. "Do you like Lilly, just a little bit?" she whispered, and kissed him openmouthed, tongue darting. "Big beautiful man. How much do you love Lilly?"

Afterward, the night settled down over him again, and he slept. But it was fitful. A storm gathered over the city, with thunder and flickering lightning. He stirred. The rain finally loosed and pattered softly at the windows. Shortly before dawn he came half-awake again, to a sound. What was it? A footstep on the hallway stairs? He thought of the pocket pistol in his trousers, within easy reach. The thunder muttered again, softly. His senses quieted. The thunder, nothing more. He drifted again toward sleep.

The door burst open with a splintering crash.

"Harlot! Whore! Cheat!"

Ward's eyes snapped open. Another flicker of lightning burned the image into his mind. Barnard Hefling stood framed in the shattered doorway, arms upraised, cloak spilling over one shoulder. His eyes bulged, and his mouth was an angry wound, opening and closing.

"By heaven, you'll pay!"

The shadow came lurching toward the bed.

Lilly was struggling with the covers, screaming. Ward broke free of them, naked, rolled to the floor, grabbed for his trousers on the bedpost, plunged a hand into his pocket.

"No, Barnard! No. Please!" Lilly screamed.

Ward's fingers closed over the pistol. The smooth, cold, deadly shape was in his hand, coming up. Wildly he looked up to find the lurching, stumbling man. He did not aim.

Blam! Blam!

The shots seemed extraordinarily loud. They struck home deeply, he knew. They struck point-blank, at an upward angle, deep into the chest. Barnard Hefling grunted, gurgling in his throat. Another lightning flash caught him clutching at a spreading stain on his white shirtfront, looking down in surprise with bulging eyes. The eyes swiveled toward Ward in an instant of disbelief. And then he fell, half-sprawled across the bed.

Lilly's screams raked across the darkness.

He got to his feet, still grasping the pistol. The barrel was warm in his hand, and there was an odor of burnt gunpowder. He turned to Lilly, saying, "I—I—I—" But she scuttled off the bed and away, shrinking into a corner.

"Murderer," she said. "Murderer!"

"I thought . . . he was going to . . ."

He knelt swiftly, frantically, groping over the body for the weapon he was positive would be there, had to be there. He found a bulge in the pocket. A wallet. He groped more. Nothing. No weapon. No weapon at all. He looked at Lilly again, beseechingly. "Please . . . I didn't mean . . ."

"Murderer! *Murderer! MURDERER!*"

There were voices on the stairs, feet pounding.

He fled then. He flung the pistol aside and fled, down the stairs, past startled people with startled faces in the gloom. He darted into the street in the cold wash of dawn and ran as hard as he could run.

He was stark naked.

XI

The word was power. Power to drive pistons and paddle wheels. Power to tame rivers and shrink distances, giving man seven-league boots. For tens of thousands of years, men had moved on water by wind or muscle or simple current. And now, abruptly, devastatingly, he could use steam. Small wonder that it so captured the enthusiasms of Robert Fulton and Nathan Stewart and Henry Shreve. And now the passion for steam power consumed Stephen. Within months, Stewart Boatworks underwent a transformation. No less than three steamboats went on the racks for construction at one time. Old craftsmen who had painstakingly built keelboats and flatboats, barges and scows, now hauled at winches and pulley blocks to hoist huge trusses into position; they worked at drilling and cutting and bolting massive structures that did not resemble boats at all.

Henry Shreve was his ardent supporter. It mattered not at all to the captain that Stewart steamboats would be competition for himself. "Hell, Stephen, there's more business on these rivers than either of us can handle in a lifetime. We can't build steamboats fast enough."

With his first vessels, Stephen refined even more the engine and superstructure designs. But beyond this, he announced his intention to build a fleet of luxury steamboats. "It's all very well to carry livestock and plows downriver. But people want to travel, too. They want to travel in style. We'll give 'em elegance and entertainment, plus a hell of a lot more room for cargo. Downriver, cotton is king. All right, then, we'll carry baled cotton. And we'll push up the Missouri, too, as far as steam will take us, to bring those pelts and hides back down to St. Louis and back east on the Ohio."

The work went on practically around the clock. His zeal was

infectious. Catherine was swept up in the spirit of it. Their first vessel, the *City of Louisville*, came off the ways in five months, followed closely by the larger and more powerful *Pittsburgh* and *River Princess*. Secretly, he persuaded Daniel French to design a smaller steam engine and mount it on a superbly crafted thirty-foot flatboat, with two state-rooms, lockers, and a large after-deck. It was painted a gleaming white and named the *Jamie*. He gave it to Catherine on their wedding anniversary.

Within two years Stewart steamboats were making record runs to New Orleans and St. Louis. Hiring the best captains he could find, veterans of keelboats and flatboats, he urged them to push into new rivers, the Kanawha, the Tennessee, the Missouri. But it was hard going. "The Missouri? Stephen, that wild river ain't worth navigating." He insisted. They tried. And they came back awed by the force of the Missouri and its lurking perils, which could rip the bottom out of a boat in the wink of an eye.

"I know the Missouri," Stephen said. He did not push the captains further.

Then the tragedies began.

A rival steamship, the *Pride of the Ohio* making its maiden run out of a Cincinnati boatyard, burst into flames and burned to the waterline. So rapidly was the wooden superstructure engulfed that a dozen people lost their lives. A month later, Stephen's own *River Princess* blew up off Gallipolis with more than one hundred aboard. Twenty-four were killed. Pieces of bodies rained down on the riverfront and the town. Stephen rushed to the scene of the disaster in the *Jamie* and helped to fish mangled corpses from the water. He returned to Pittsburgh, shut himself into his office, and drank himself into a stupor.

"Darling, it was not your fault," Catherine said. "There are going to be more and more steamboat accidents. Captain Shreve says it's to be expected, and there's nothing anybody can do as long as we have high-pressure boilers and wooden vessels."

But the memory haunted him, the memory of disaster and the injured writhing and screaming on the dock and of life going out of human beings as easily as a breath of air. Stephen could not sleep. He brooded.

"He's been working too hard, Catherine," Henry Shreve said. "I need to get him away from the routine, take him downriver on the *Washington*."

Something plucked at her mind. She was suddenly uncomfortable without knowing why. The feeling had been there before, and it always involved the *Washington*. She was being silly. "Maybe you're right, Henry. Maybe he needs to get away."

With a mighty whistle blast, the big steamboat pushed off from Stewart Boat Works and went booming into the Forks and down the Ohio. It was mid-May, the weather fine. Stephen's spirits lifted in the hearty company of Captain Shreve and old riverboat friends. They made a record run to the Mississippi and then upriver to St. Louis. The town had grown tremendously since he had last seen it a dozen years before. "Hell, this is eighteen-nineteen," Henry Shreve said. "St. Louis is booming. So's every other town along this river." The steamboat was fueling the boom. They had passed boatworks in practically every town of size from Wheeling on down. Moored beside the *Washington* at St. Louis were three other steamers, in all of which Captain Henry Shreve owned at least part interest.

"Henry, you've got more partners than any man alive."

Shreve snickered. "They do all the work; I get all the glory."

On the first of June they left St. Louis for the run back to Pittsburgh. After several stops along the way, picking up cargo and passengers, the *Washington* cleared the falls at Louisville. "I'm going to open her up now, Stephen. You ain't never seen this old boat when she's really running. I tell you, the *Washington* under a full head of steam goes like a scalded dog!" The captain signaled his engineer to pour it on. With a gush of woodsmoke and a snort of pressure, the big steamboat breasted the current, pounding upriver with a power that raised whitecaps and flying spray. Stephen exulted, standing on the upper deck with the wind in his face. This was excitement! This was life! And he was part of it. Off to port, coming downstream, he saw another vessel. It was his own steamer *Pittsburgh*. The two craft exchanged horn salutes. Glancing over his shoulder, he noticed that sparks were pouring from the *Washington's* stacks, and the smoked billowed more heavily than he had ever seen it before. Stephen moved to the pilothouse and called in to Captain Shreve. "Henry, shouldn't we back her down a couple of notches? Those boilers are getting mighty hot."

"Naw, Stephen. Hell, she'll handle this much and half again more. Marietta's a few miles ahead. I'm going to run her full steam all the way in."

"Well, I just thought I'd—"

The explosion erupted in the starboard boilers.

With a deafening blast, the *Washington's* starboard side came apart. Stephen saw the pilothouse bearing Captain Shreve disappear. Something smashed him in the left side. He was snatched aloft as if by a giant hand. Then his body was hurtling skyward through a cloud of steam, tumbling and twisting across a gigantic arc. He plummeted down and struck the water with the force of a cannonball. Then there was neither night nor day but a wild gray eternity of thrashing, floundering, gasping terror. His eyes bulged, and his arms flailed in the depths; instinctively he held his breath, fighting upward in a shower of bubbles. The light grew brighter and brighter, and he broke surface in a red void, with a searing burst of pain.

Pain!

PAIN!

Something nudged the side of his head. He reached up, grabbed on, opened one eye. Only one eye would open. Pain engulfed the other. Pain engulfed his entire left side. In a dreamlike state, he focused the one eye onto a red thing that stuck out of the water. It was the stump of his left arm. The hand was gone. He gripped with his right hand onto a floating wooden frame. His consciousness washed away into a gray void.

They found him miraculously afloat, clutching the debris. Gently, gently they lifted him out and into a rowboat. "Oh, Jesus Christ," a voice said. "Oh, holy mother of God."

"His face. Careful with his face. His hand. His foot. Oh, my heaven."

"Careful."

"Easy now. Uh. Lift. Uh. Gently. Uh."

"Hold him. He's thrashing. There, there, Mr. Stewart. Don't struggle. Lie still, Mr. Stewart."

"Get him on board the *Pittsburgh*. Then we'll go after the others."

They had seen the explosion from a mile away. The *Washington* had blown apart, and her hulk gone adrift in a cloud of fire and steam. She drifted toward deep water on the Kentucky shore, burning fiercely. And there she sank.

A dozen crewmen and passengers were dead, a score—including Stephen—injured. Captain Shreve and his engineer were blown free into the river. Neither was hurt. The *Pittsburgh* gathered them up and then, with its cargo of horror, steamed upriver to Marietta. A doctor took one look at Stephen and shook his head. "Poor devil. Take him into my office."

He sawed off Stephen's shattered left leg just below the knee. He cleaned and dressed the stump of the left wrist as best he could. So severe were the burns on the left side of the body and face that he dared not even touch them. When it was done, he stepped back and sighed. "He's in God's hands now."

"The eye? How's the left eye?"

"There is no left eye."

The journey back to Pittsburgh seemed to take forever. Screams pierced the afternoon and the night and the dawn. Every man was shaken. When finally they put in at Stewart's, Captain Shreve, his clothing charred and water-soaked, walked up the slope to tell Catherine. From the deck, as they brought off the makeshift litter, the men heard her cry:

"No! Oh, nnnnooooo!"

And then she came down the slope, her face twisted oddly, her eyes great pools of shock, looking at him sideways like a curious wounded bird. She was trembling and pale, the blonde hair in disarray. Her glance focused on his single open eye, but it was glazed and unrecognizing. A jolt of the litter and the body twisted. The mouth opened to scream, baring for the first time the mutilated flesh. The scream slammed through the compound and up to the house. It brought Isaiah Stewart, running on his gimpy legs, and Martha, openmouthed and choking for breath, and old Charlie and the workmen and . . . and . . .

"Take him up. Take him upstairs. Our room." It was Catherine who had recovered first. The lovely face abruptly turned cold and the mouth resolute. The voice was steadied and filled with command. "That's where we will tend him. Upstairs."

And so they bore the burden into the house.

A workman whispered to his mate: "They brought her home half a man."

The noise of the boatyard ceased. The afternoon wore on. Men stood in hushed groups, hands idled, watching Stewart House. The screams came from the second floor room, front. They sounded like a wounded animal. They rolled in volleys over the Stewart compound. The day became evening. The evening became night. The screams subsided, volleyed again, subsided. The night became dawn. Some of the men still waited, seated in silent clusters in the dirt, smoking. Isaiah Stewart came out onto the porch at his usual hour. For the first time in twenty years, the old man did not wear his business suit. He was unshaven. His face was a rumpled mask. "Go home," he said quietly. "There will be no work today, or tomorrow either. Go home."

Some of them stayed through the second day.

They had drawn the shades in the upstairs room. In the semidarkness of noon, the figure lay unmoving on the bed. Catherine sat in silence, watching. Already a scent of superation lay on the air. There was a sound from the figure on the bed, a gurgle in the throat. Catherine moved closer, bending over. The mouth was working, half-burned and grossly swollen.

"Darling?" she said.

"B-B-Bl . . ." the mouth said.

"Yes?"

"Bluh-Bluh-Blood . . ."

"Blood? No, you are not bleeding. There is no blood."

"F-F-Feath . . ."

She concentrated intently. By sheer force of will the mouth was trying to speak. The effort brought the one eye open and bulging. Muscle cords strained in the neck. The sound was a gurgling whistle of air.

"B-Blood F-F-Feather . . . B-Blood Feather . . . Gehh Bl . . . G-Get Blood Feather. Get Blood Feather!"

"Yes!" Catherine shouted. She stood bolt upright. "Get Blood Feather. Yes, darling. I will. I'll get him. I'll bring him back here to you. I'll bring Blood Feather!"

She summoned Martha. "Take care of him. I'm going for help."

"For help! Land sakes, Catherine, what kind of help? A doctor? We've got a doctor."

"Not that doctor. A special kind of doctor."

She was down the stairs and out the front door, then, shouting orders.

They fired up *Jamie's* boilers and stacked her decks with cords of firewood. Catherine, hurriedly changed into trousers and boots, took two horses aboard to tether on the afterdeck. Men loaded up blankets, bedrolls, harness, and provisions. Old Charlie brought down Stephen's '03 rifle and powder and ball, along with John Colby's old bullwhip.

Henry Shreve was astonished. "Catherine, where the hell do you think you're going?"

"To find the Omaha Indian village."

"And where is that?"

"Up the Missouri," she snapped angrily. "And I'm in a hurry."

"Woman, you're crazy. You can't take this here boat up the Missouri. What do you know about running a boat in wild water? You need a captain. So you'll just jolly well wait till I get my gear."

"Your gear?"

"Damn it, I'm going with you!"

The *Jamie* was already under steam when they boarded. Isaiah Stewart came storming. "Where's that fool woman going? Catherine, come back here. Have you lost your mind?"

"Just take care of Stephen!" She nodded to Henry Shreve at the controls. The *Jamie* blew steam and chuffed ahead, her single stern wheel kicking water.

"Come back, I say!" Isaiah Stewart bellowed.

"Keep him alive, do you hear me?" she shouted over the widening expanse of water. "That's all that matters now. You keep Stephen alive!"

The *Jamie* put her stern to Isaiah and gathered speed. Catherine closed her eyes for an instant of concentration. "Please, God," she said.

News travels with astonishing swiftness on the frontier. Minds eager for every scrap of intelligence, fact or fancy, are quick to grasp and quicker to carry. The superstitious would think that even the breeze carried its tales and portents. As June faded into July and heat bore down on the rivers, talk rippled across wilderness campfires about the tall blonde woman on the little steamboat. She could shoot and ride like a man and handled a blacksnake whip with deadly accuracy. She was on a quest, they said, for Indian magic to save a husband who was half a man. Even the Indians heard.

"That woman, they say she's here in St. Louis."

"What woman?"

"The one that's goin' up the Missouri to find an Omaha medicine man. She's looking for a guide."

"What about the old captain that's with her?"

"He's a boatman. He don't know the wilderness."

"Whoever gets the job better not have any notions in his head."

"How's that?"

"A fella tried to cozy up to her on the street last night, and she like to cut him to pieces with that bullwhip of her'n."

"Upon my word."

Another man said, "What about you, Mr. Faber? You know that country like the back of your hand."

The big red-bearded fur trader scratched his jaw thoughtfully. "Anybody know her name?"

"Name of Stewart, they say. Catherine Stewart."

Geoffrey Markowitz Faber came forward with a start. "Where from?"

"From Pittsburgh, they say."

"Well, I'll be damned!"

The big man was on his feet, lumbering out the door.

"Hey, where you goin'?"

"Upriver. Up the Missouri. On a steamboat!"

Faber found her with the old captain on the little steamboat, tied up at the wharf. She was saying impatiently, "Henry, I don't care. Time is precious. If we don't find a guide by tomorrow morning, I'm going without one. We'll take the steamer as far as we can . . ."

"Miz Stewart?" Faber called from the wharf. "I hear you're lookin' for a guide?"

Catherine eyed him warily. "That's right, mister."

"They say you're from Pittsburgh. One of the Pittsburgh Stewarts . . ."

"I'm married to a Pittsburgh Stewart."

"And who might your husband be?"

The tall woman reached for a peg and drew down a looped bullwhip. It was an ugly weapon, of tightly braided snakeskin. The old welts on Geoffrey Faber's back seemed to smart again as she tapped the handle lightly against the top of her boot. He stood his ground.

"My husband is Stephen Stewart," the woman said.

Faber smiled. "You've got yourself a guide, Miz Stewart. Your husband and his brother Nathan did me a favor once that I never forgot and always swore to repay."

Catherine relaxed, but only slightly. "What kind of favor was that?"

"I was on the public whipping post at Pittsburgh, and they started a riot to get me loose. Twenty years ago."

For the first time, she smiled. "I've heard the story. You'd be Geoffrey Faber, then."

"Geoffrey Markowitz Faber, at your service, ma'am."

Catherine hung the whip back on its peg. "Come aboard, Mr. Faber."

On the run to St. Louis, Henry Shreve prudently had kept the *Jamie* at three-quarter speed. He surmised that a woman would not be aware of such a technicality. But two days out of St. Louis, as they breasted the power of the wild Missouri, Catherine Stewart took command. "We'll open her up now, Captain Shreve. I want every bit of steam you can give."

"But Catherine, I'm afraid the boiler won't . . ."

"Don't you worry about that boiler, Captain. Dan French built it special for Stephen and this boat. She's got high-pressure reserve and a blowoff valve in case of trouble. So rev her up, if you please."

Shreve added pressure. "Whatever you say, ma'am."

She was right, of course. At three-quarter speed they never would overcome the current on this river. Henry Shreve had never experienced anything like the Missouri. Every wild story about this untamed river now seemed true, and then some. Whole tree trunks came sweeping down toward them, to be dodged in the nick of time. Great segments of mudbanks gave way in mighty slides. Mud caked up the paddle wheel so thickly that Geoffrey Faber, when he wasn't standing lookout for snags at the bow, was busy clearing the mechanism with a poking rod. At Faber's suggestion they had acquired at St. Louis an extra riding mount—a mule—and a heavy canoe.

Just downriver from the mouth of the Platte, the *Jamie* struck a hidden sandbar and shuddered to a halt, stuck fast. Even after unloading the vessel they could not work her free. "From here on," Captain Shreve said unhappily, "we travel less comfortably."

They moored the steamboat securely to a stand of cottonwood onshore, to hold when high water floated her free. Shreve and Catherine then pushed off in the canoe while Faber moved along the riverbank with the mounts.

It took them another ten days to find the Omaha village. The tribe had moved several times over the years, and now occupied teepees and lodges on a bluff overlooking the river itself. Catherine rode in at the lead, to a welcome of scampering children and barking dogs. Omaha braves were astonished at the color of her hair and her height. By means of sign language, Faber managed to communicate with a tribal elder. Catherine distributed gifts among the squaws and children, but was followed everywhere by a crowd of young men, speaking volubly in the Omaha tongue to an uncomprehending Captain Shreve. Faber came to her looking grim.

"Bad news, Mrs. Stewart. Blood Feather died three years ago. There is a new chief, a younger man. He is away on a buffalo hunt and could be gone for two months."

Faber's words fell like a blow. Sickened, Catherine sat down on a stone and buried her face in her hands. The men stood by helplessly. At last she looked up at them.

"What do we do now? It never occurred to me that Blood Feather might not be here. I couldn't even let myself think such a thing. Surely somebody, somewhere . . ."

The crowd of Indians watched gravely, keeping a respectful distance. Even Catherine's entourage of braves had fallen silent.

"Do they have a medicine man?" Catherine asked.

"The chief is the medicine man."

She sighed, clasping her hands. "Oh."

During the hour they had been in the camp, Faber several times had mentioned the name Stewart to the tribal elder. Now, a tall, somber Indian with a heavy limp pushed through the crowd. Cradled on his arm was a handsome smoothbore fusee rifle, its stock decorated with a serpentine design. He stood over Catherine and said, "Stewart?"

The man seemed half-witted, his speech thick and slurry. Catherine looked up at him apprehensively.

"He's heard the name around the camp," Faber said. "The elder said it was remembered. He looks harmless enough."

"Stewart," the Indian said. He thrust the rifle toward Catherine. She drew back. "Stewart. Stewart." Then: "Shtephen!"

"What's he saying? What's he talking about? Stephen. He said Stephen."

"Sure. The tribe remembers Stephen."

"Stephen Stewart," the man said. One of his hands was gnarled and drawn. With that hand, he pointed to himself. "Me, Stewart . . ." The rest of the sentence was a garble of Omaha tongue.

"He thinks he's a Stewart, too."

Catherine stared at the gnarled hand. Something triggered in her memory. "What—what's his name? Can you find out his name?"

Faber spoke to the man in sign language. It was a difficult process, but finally a kind of understanding came through. "His name is Crippled something. Crippled Dog. Crippled Fox. Something like that. I can't make it out . . ."

"Crippled Wolf!" She jumped to her feet. "Crippled Wolf!" Her obvious tone of recognition pleased the Indian. He smiled broadly and chattered something. The other Indians nodded and grunted with pleasure.

Faber beckoned to the tribal elder. They conferred for a long time. Then: "Crippled Wolf is his name, all right. And it seems that this Indian and Stephen are blood brothers. He says he owes Stephen his life."

"He was Blood Feather's nephew, the nephew of the medicine man!"

"That's right," Faber said, looking at her curiously. "How did you know?"

"Ask him if he knows how Blood Feather treated his burns, and if he could do the same thing for Stephen?"

Again, it was a lengthy and complex business in sign language. There was great difficulty in communicating concepts, and to get across the idea that Stephen Stewart had been terribly burned in a steamboat explosion. Finally, however, it was done. Faber was suddenly beaming. "Of course, he knows how Blood Feather did it. And his wife, Moon Flower, knows even more, for she helped to nurse Crippled Wolf back to health with her mother . . ."

"Will they come with us? Will they come to Pittsburgh, to help Stephen?"

This time, the tall Indian seemed to comprehend her words. Crippled Wolf made sign language to Faber which the fur trader quickly understood.

"Crippled Wolf says he would give his life to help his brother Stewart. And yes, he will go to Pittsburgh, too."

They left the Omaha village the following morning. Moon Flower, a young squaw with square, stolid features, rode silently in the canoe with Catherine and Captain Shreve; Crippled Wolf traveled astride the mule on shore, following Geoffrey Faber. The tall Indian's hair was matted down with bear grease, and he clutched his smoothbore rifle. Rolled in a small packet of skins in a mulepack was a wad of grayish, foul-smelling herbs.

* * *

He would not have it. By heaven, he would not stand for it. Bad enough to have red Indians anywhere on the property, in violation of his orders for twenty-five years. But to bring them into Stewart House! To let them in to try to work their godless magic on a man's own son... Never.

"Get them wild savages out of my house. They'll not touch my son, do you hear me. They will not!"

Isaiah's face reddened with fury. His breath reeked of whiskey again. His bellowing voice could be heard clear down at the boatyard. In the agony of certain loss, fate was too cruel, life too bleak. Men whispered that the whole lot of them had lost their minds over this, including Catherine. And indeed, Isaiah thought so too.

"Martha, we've had the best doctors money could buy. They've come clear from Philadelphia, and all they did was stand over that boy and shake their heads and try to bleed him again. Bleed him! Hell, he ain't got no blood left. And so there he lies, rotting away with a stench that fills this whole house. Phew! We've tried everything. Even prayer does no good. The boy weakens each passing day. And now this..."

"Isaiah, please. Try to calm yourself. It can't do any harm now." Martha, herself pale and agonized over Stephen, tried to pat her husband's cheek, but he knocked her hand away.

"... And while we're doing our level best, his wife—his own wife—goes off on some wild chase west for nearly two months and comes back with two ragged Indians who can't speak a word of English and stink of bear grease. For what? To try their damned mumbo jumbo on my boy. I don't give a hoot if that redskin is Stephen's blood brother, to me he looks like something that's been dragged out of a swamp!"

But Catherine would not be denied. Pushing past the sputtering Isaiah, she had taken Crippled Wolf and Moon Flower up to Stephen's bedside. The Indian, his face impassive, stood in the darkened room looking down at the semiconscious half-man.

The fury of Isaiah's wrath rose in volume downstairs. Catherine went to Stephen's bureau, drew two pistols from a drawer, and loaded them with powder and ball. She then walked out of the room and closed the door behind her.

Isaiah stood at the foot of the stairs. Two of the boatyard's burliest workmen were beside him. He glared up at Catherine, eyes filled with hurt and hatred. "Now you listen to me, young woman. I've had enough. We're coming up them stairs, and we're going to throw them heathen savages out and let my son die in peace."

As he moved forward, Catherine raised the pistols. "Mr. Stewart, I'll shoot out the knee of any man who takes another step, and that includes you."

Martha gasped. "Catherine!"

Isaiah Stewart froze. Uncertainty flickered in his eyes. His breathing grew labored. "You wouldn't."

"I would, and I will. The man in there might be your son, but he's *my* whole life. I'll do anything for a chance to save him."

Isaiah Stewart seemed to lose air, like a balloon. The workmen retreated and walked out of the house. Five minutes later Isaiah went out too, slumped in resignation.

In the bedroom, Indian hands deftly removed the putrid dressings from tortured flesh. The animal skin pouch was unrolled, and the grayish herb was formed into damp poultices. Gradually, piece by piece, they covered the worst of the yellowish, running wounds. Moon Flower opened the window shades, flooding the room with light. Crippled Wolf sat down cross-legged on the floor, staring into a square of sunlight. He remained motionless as the hours passed. Finally, in gathering twilight, the Indian began a low, keening chant as his fingers lightly stroked a tom-tom.

The sound permeated the compound. It could be heard along Water Street and into town. People stood at their windows, whispering. The sound seemed to penetrate the very pores of one's skin.

"Brrrr," said a watchman in the boatyard. "That sends a shiver up me back."

It went on all that night, and the next day, and the next night, and the next day, and . . .

The eye was open, watching him. The eye contained intelligence. Crippled Wolf sensed this gradually at first, as a blind man might sense a beam of light. He kept his eyes closed, in deep concentration. Nearby, Moon Flower moved as lightly as a shadow, and he knew that her hands were changing the poultices again. With each change, her fingers pulled at bits of dead tissue around the burns, peeling them away.

It had been four days and nights.

But the fever was down. The putrid odor was less strong. And Stephen's one eye was open, watching, aware.

In the Omaha tongue, the Indian said to Moon Flower: "The gods are smiling."

Six weeks later, Catherine came downstairs to speak to Martha, Isaiah, and Burl. Her face was set and resolute. She asked them and the servants to gather at the foot of the stairs. Puzzled, they complied. When all was ready, she called up the stairs: "All right, Crippled Wolf."

The bedroom door opened slowly. The Indian woman emerged, her face impassive as ever. Someone was holding onto her braided hair with one hand, holding on in a dead weight. She displayed no sign of pain. And then the tall Indian appeared, but stooping and backing out very slowly. And then . . .

"Stephen!"

He was more apparition than man, clutching the woman's hair in a death grip, his left knee cradled in Crippled Wolf's cupped hands. Thus he moved upright, leaning heavily against the door for added support.

One side of his face was pale as death and drawn from the agony of effort. The left side of the face was partially melted, the eye socket blank. Even his father gasped.

He stopped moving, panting for breath. The shattered mouth moved. A voice, as from the grave, spoke in a raspy whisper: "I am a Stewart. I am going . . . to live . . . again."

The river is life, pouring downstream in slackwater and in flood, carrying with it the flotsam of nature and of humanity and of commerce. Times sweeps with the river; for the waters are timeless and only human life finite and small. And yet man challenged the waters; and with his smoke-belching crafts thrashing the Great Muddy with their paddle wheels, surging and snorting like monsters, man triumphed. Steamboats were beginning to transform the mighty Mississippi, the Ohio, the Missouri, the Arkansas, the Tennessee into avenues of commerce. Down the valleys and the gorges, their multinoted shrieks pierced the nights and the curling mists of false dawns; great smokestacks gushed plumes of sparks, like star trails, in the darkness. And often, too often, the river erupted in explosion and fire. The blast rained debris and bodies. The river washed blood . . .

And life went on.

"Hold me, Stephen. Hold me, darling."

"I am so ugly."

"You are my husband. My flesh is your flesh. You are a man."

"I'm afraid..."

"You can. I know you can, darling. Here, let me touch you. There. It is all right, darling. There, you are whole there, whole and beautiful. My, how big you're getting."

"Catherine."

"My darling, my love, my beautiful Stephen. That's it. Oh, yes, that's it. You are my beautiful, my adored...Yes, and...Oh, yes...I want..."

"Yes, Catherine."

"Now, Stephen. I want you *now!*"

The river is a vast community of people, and yet possessed of its own unique close communication. And so on every wharf and loading dock and landing they knew of Catherine Stewart, the stunningly beautiful woman who was building the Stewart Line of luxury steamboats. And they knew her husband, a familiar sight with his peg leg, his face half-masked in flesh-tinted silk and a claw for a hand. Always, he was accompanied by the tall lame Indian and the young squaw.

There were those on the river who whispered darkly that Catherine Stewart was a blonde witch, with a husband she had brought back...from the dead.

XII

The fugitive's lot galled him. A man could not live like a rat, scurrying among the shadows of his own country. He had to come out into the sunlight, stand up, and walk. But the hue and cry was strong. One did not murder a Boston politician of the substance of Barnard Hefling and expect the matter to blow away. In Baltimore, he saw the wanted leaflet. In Washington, he thought someone followed him. He fled south to Charleston, growing a beard and casting off his seaman's identity as best he could. But the characteristic rolling gait of a seafaring man would not disguise behind a beard, and the challenging eyes of Ward Stewart were still there, causing men to give way and women to draw nearer.

He drank in a waterfront saloon. He thought of Lilly Crandon with an ache in his heart. Damn, he had been a fool; a fool to fall in love with her, a fool to commit a deed so rashly, from jealousy more than fear. In the long months that followed his escape from Boston, Ward Stewart relived the seconds when the pistol went off in his hand and the body of Barnard Hefling tumbled across Lilly's bed. Repeatedly he heard her scream: "Murderer!"

One had to live. He had no money. He went to the dock and shipped out on a schooner, but found the life of a deckhand brutal and unsatisfying. He thought of Savannah. There were friends in Savannah. He discarded the idea. They would recognize him there; someone might have heard, or read a New York newspaper. He quit thinking about Savannah, spent the last of his money, borrowed, grubbed, worked odd jobs on the docks.

The slave market was there with its block and its brutalities. Poor devils, they were worse off than he. Ward stood in the crowd and watched as the auctioneer sold off a young woman for breeding. She stood, as docile-seeming as a young deer. "What am I bid for this fine, nubile nigra girl? She is about fifteen years of age, gentlemen, and the finest breeding stock. Mandingo stock, gentlemen, with fire and spirit"—the auctioneer rolled his eyes and snickered, indicating her light skin—"and a little Anglo-Saxon thrown in. I need not remind you that ever' pickaninny she breeds is worth two hundred dollars. In her productive lifetime, my friends, this girl can produce twelve, fifteen pickaninnies!" A fat, baldish planter drenched in sweat bought the girl for five hundred dollars and led her away. As the afternoon wore on, the auctioneer sold studs and field hands and more women and children, bringing them up from a pen behind the block. The pen was a place of stench and sweltering heat, with rolling white eyes peering out from the darkness. A recalcitrant male could draw the lash, the thumbscrew, and the gag. But sales were slow. Finally, the auctioneer gave up and went behind the pen to have a drink of whiskey, mopping sweat from his sunburned brow.

"What do you do with the rejects?" Ward asked.

"What do you mean, rejects?"

"The ones nobody buys."

"Oh, them. We sell them off in gangs to the traders. They go on down to Alabama, Florida, Mississippi, maybe Louisiana and work the plantations. Cotton, sugar cane, tobacco. Most of 'em go overland to Natchez and then downriver on a steamboat..."

Ward had seen the black gangs. They shuffled cross-country in double lines, strung out like animals on a coffle chain, manacled wrist-to-wrist. Once, in the misty dawn of a woodland clearing, he had come across three hundred in a gang. They traveled over long distances that way. They shuffled along in scorching heat and raw cold on rutted roads. They sang a kind of moaning dirge. They bore babies and died on the march. Nothing stopped them. Nothing.

Yes, some wretches were worse off than a man on the run.

He hung around the docks, drinking cheap whiskey when he could earn or beg a few dollars. The weight dripped from his tall body. He thought of his father and Cape Cod. If he had listened to Bartholemew...

"Ward! Ward Stewart!"

Alarm jolted him. He whirled, ready to run. The man advanced through the smoky crowd, wide-eyed with recognition. The face was round, pink, fleshy. He struggled to remember the face and the rolling walk. He stood warily by the bar, trapped. The newcomer extended his hand and smiled, talking of home. Then Ward remembered; this was a cod fisherman from Provincetown who'd left to go to sea.

They drank ale from tankards. The newcomer bought.

"I've been back to Cape Cod, you know." The fleshy face turned solemn. "Bad news for ye, Ward. I reckon you haven't heard. Old Bartholemew, he's dead."

Shock swept over him like a dark wave. "Oh, my," Ward said. "I did not know. When? How?"

"A seizure, they say, three months past. It was..." The man hesitated, dipped his mouth quickly to the ale glass, drank, mopped foam from his lips. "It was the shock of what you done, they say. He heard you'd shot the fellow in Boston and was on the run. Old Bart, he clutched at his chest, like, and just fell over. That was it."

Old Bart dead. Ward thought guiltily of their quarrels and his hardheadedness. A hardheaded Stewart; there was no more stubborn creature. He had done the deed, as surely as if he'd plunged a dagger into his father's heart.

Ward Stewart leaned over the bar and vomited.

And after that he was the total outcast.

The months went by and he drifted. From Charleston he took ship and worked his way up and down the coast, from Boston to Baltimore, Norfolk, Wilmington, south to St. Augustine and the Caribbean, down to Jamaica. It was no life. It was no future. He was broke again in Kingston; broke and prevailing on the generosity of a hard-eyed Englishman for fierce Jamaican rum, horsebacked down neat. The Englishman had money and seemed on the lookout for sea captains at loose ends, men with a past that was better forgotten.

"There's money to be made, Captain," the Englishman said. "A man might even recoup his fortune, play his cards right." He poured rum into Ward's glass. His skin was oily, his face very pale. "It ain't exactly without risk, I don't mind sayin'. But then, that's what my company pays for, the risk. Get what I mean?"

The next morning, at sunup, they stood at a deserted point looking out on the dirty hulk of a brigantine anchored apart from other ships, as though infected. Even from a quarter-mile distance the vessel seemed to emit an evil. "There she is, Captain. No beauty, to be sure, but at the moment vacant of command. She'll take on a cargo of rum and shove off for West Africa inside a week." The Englishman fixed him with a glittering eye. "That is, if you're interested."

And so Ward Stewart took command of the slave ship *Congo Traveler.*

The human mind, it is said, can inure itself to anything. Given time and repeated exposure, even the most civilized among us will regress to some primeval state, numb to conscience and suffering.

The crew of the *Congo Traveler,* taken from fleshpots and prisons of the Caribbean, were the dregs of the sea. From the moment they hoisted anchor at Kingston and beat northeastward toward the Windward Passage, Ward kept a brace of pistols in his belt. The mate was a surly Spaniard not long out of a Santiago jail, and even he hated them. "They'll slit our throats, the scum, quick as a wink."

Even a fair wind over open deck did not dispel the stink of the ship. It was a dire mix of old sweat and blood and human excrement that permeated the timbers themselves. Below, an extra deck had been built into the hull, allowing only five feet of headroom and with chains and manacles—hundreds of them—bolted into the floor. Around the sides of this deck ranged an additional shelflike structure, six feet wide and eighteen inches deep, with more chains and shackles. Down there, the air was almost too thick to breathe. When he ordered the crew to swab down the entire area with a quicklime solution, they refused. He did not press the matter.

After twelve weeks' sailing they dropped anchor off a fortress village in West Africa. As the rum cargo was unloaded, it was counted by a fussy official speaking in Portuguese. Leaving the mate on board the ship, Ward was taken ashore. On the way, the official abruptly switched from Portuguese to English. "This is your first voyage, Captain?"

Ward nodded, grim-faced.

"There are, uh, certain formalities to attend to." The man's hooded eyes searched his face speculatively. "It is not uncommon, by the way, for the captain of a vessel such as yours to make a small side investment of his own. We are traders, you understand; it doesn't matter to us with whom we trade. I am called Hassaam."

As they stepped ashore from the dinghy, Ward heard a deep, moaning sound from the hills behind the fortress. Squinting into the blazing sunlight, he saw a dark line snaking down from a crest. The moaning was a rhythmic dirge from the throats of more than three hundred men. As they drew nearer he saw that they were chained two by two, left leg to right leg. They were driven by whip-wielding black slave merchants, the Slattees.

"Those are Ebos, mainly," Hassaam said, "mixed with some Hausa and Yorubas. Excellent stock, taken in recent raids." He made a sucking sound in his teeth. "I don't know where we will put them. Negro House is overflowing already." He beckoned for Ward to follow, and they descended broad circular steps down to a sunblasted earthen courtyard. The surface was beaten smooth and hard by multitudes of calloused bare feet. High above them armed sentries paced stone battlements. From a dungeonlike area off the courtyard there arose a stench that made him want to gag.

At Hassaam's command, guards unlocked an iron barred door and brought out a line of shambling black men and women. Each was naked and carried a wad of ragged clothing under one arm. Two white men appeared and systematically began to examine each slave, peering into eyes, ears and mouths, squeezing here, probing there, inspecting hands and feet and genitals. "It is our desire to provide you with healthy stock," Hassaam said. "What happens to them later, aboard your ship, then becomes your responsibility."

When inspections were done, Hassaam presented his calculations on a sheet of paper. "Your brigantine, Captain, is fitted out for ninety slaves. We are trading at a rate of one hundred gallons of rum for each Negro." He made a notation on paper. "The amount of rum taken off your vessel more than covers the shipment. Therefore"—he gave Ward an oily smile—"you may choose to take on a dozen more in trade for the extra rum. Needless to say, these additional Negroes will not be reflected on the ship's manifest . . ."

Among the excess slaves, not taken in his shipment, he had seen a shapely young woman with high firm breasts and rounded thighs. He pointed to her now. "I will take her," he said, "and the others as you suggest."

Hassaam nodded, yelled to a guard in African dialect. The woman was pushed forward into line. Her eyes blazed. Hassaam said, "She is an Ebo woman. Proud."

When the *Congo Traveler* prepared to weigh anchor again, the lower decks were packed with human beings lain out like codfish on a rack. Each naked, shackled adult male occupied a space six feet long by sixteen inches wide; each woman's space was five and one-half feet long. The slave hold, just five feet high, denied even the crew space to stand erect. More slaves were crowded into the shelf areas, with eighteen inches of clearing. They had shuffled aboard in a weary stream, heads down, like cattle being herded into a pen. When the last body was secured, Hassaam advised Ward to batten down the hatches.

"But those people will suffocate in this heat," he said. "We've got at least ten weeks of sailing ahead."

The trader's eyes were thin slits. "I presume, then, that your employers did not tell you about the patrols."

"The patrols?"

"There are armed antislaver patrols by United States vessels in these waters. They are quite widely scattered and slow, of course, and up to now have not seized a single ship. But there is always a first time. Under your new American law against slaving, the penalty for violation is death."

Ward swallowed hard. "I was not told that."

"Yes, Captain. If you are caught by an American patrol, you will be hanged."

The voyage back to Jamaica seemed to take forever. The *Congo Traveler* was old and slow under any circumstances. But they also passed through several squalls at sea, which made life belowdecks intolerable, and then they entered into a region of eerie calm where for days not a breath of air stirred and the sun beat down with merciless intensity. The stench of vomit, excrement, and urine rose through the hatches so powerfully that Ward was driven from his cabin.

Sharks began trailing the ship.

Dysentery broke out in the slave hold, along with other nameless fevers and humours. For no apparent reason a seemingly strong black would break into sweats and chills and die in his chains. The crowding set a madness loose. Men strangled their neighbors to gain a few more inches of breathing space. A woman drove a spike into the brain of a sleeper next to her.

Each day crewmen struggled onto the deck with fresh burdens and dumped them overboard, setting off a furious crimson boiling in the sea.

Ward paced the deck, suffering a terrible loneliness and despair. He looked to the heavens and thought: If I could save them, I would. I'm caught in something I did not create. God in your infinite mercy, I'm not to blame! He descended to the cabin, stench and all, and began to drink. He drank until his mind was a fog. And then he sent for the Ebo woman.

The ragged shift she wore was shapeless and torn, exposing her breasts. She was black as night, but with finely molded features and a body that might have been cut from obsidian. He ordered the shackles taken from her wrists. And then they were alone, and she stood in silent defiance.

"Take that garment off," he said thickly.

She tilted her head, uncomprehending.

Ward walked to her, seized the top of the shift, and ripped it away. The thing fell into a formless heap at her feet. He rummaged in a sea chest and found a wide bolt of red cloth.

Slashing off a sheet of it with his knife, he threw it at her. "Put this around you." He gave her leftover food from his table, which she ate voraciously.

For long hours into the night, then, she sat motionless on the floor in her red wrapper while he drank and talked to phantoms in a drunken mumble.

"You think I'm going to rape you, don't you? You think all men . . . all men are beasts. Well we're not beasts. Not all of us, anyway. I am a Stewart, of the Provincetown Stewarts." He chuckled giddily. "What d'ye think'a that? Yes, and my father is Bartholemew . . . *was* Bartholemew, and my mother died when I was but a child, and I have cousins who are . . . who are very important men. One of 'em, Nathan, is rich and handsome; and another of 'em, Stephen, builds big steamboats on the river, and their father Isaiah is probably one of the mosh . . . most important men in Pittsburgh, Pennsylvania. What d'ye think'a that?" His head wobbled as he turned to stare at her again, bringing her into focus—a blob of jet black and blood scarlet with two great white eyes shining in the lamplight. "And all around us, around you and me, there's nothing but cruelty and degradation on a colossal scale; nothing but filth and death and man's inhumanity to man. We are supposed to be civilized, right? I come from a country where it says, it says, 'We hold these truths to be self-evident, that all men are created equal and are posh . . . posh . . . poshessed of certain inalienable rights . . .' Hah, hah, hah. Get that? And all men are created equal . . .'" He sputtered and began to laugh. He looked down at her, huddled on the cabin floor and looking at him with those great defiant white eyes. He sputtered and said, "And the man who wrote that has got slaves!" And his laughter rolled out of the cabin and over the ship as it labored westward on a rising breeze; his laughter touched the ears of the helmsman at the wheel and the Spanish mate, honing his knife against his boot, and it filtered down through the grillwork into the hold, where the silent multitude heard it as demonic and were afraid; and it floated up and out and behind, across the broad reflection of a full, standing moon, and the silhouettes of dorsal fins as they slashed soundlessly through the silvery wake.

Deep in the night the Ebo woman removed the red wrapper, crept naked to his bunk, and slipped in beside him.

*   *   *

Profit was quick and substantial. On voyage after voyage the captain of the *Congo Traveler* bought slaves in West Africa for 100 gallons of rum apiece, worth fifty dollars, and sold them on the slave docks of Jamaica for one hundred and twenty dollars apiece in gold. A single run netted the vessel six thousand dollars, of which the captain's share was one thousand. To this was added the income from slaves he managed to bring in as contraband, bribing the headcounter on the Jamaica docks to overlook his tally. For an even greater profit he could deal directly in slaves, buying in Kingston, Jamaica, and running them to smuggler coves along the coasts of Georgia, South Carolina, and Virginia. In time he quit the *Congo Traveler* to work on his own, and the gold poured into his accounts in West Indies banks.

Ward Stewart took scant pleasure in his new wealth. He drove a splendid carriage with matched bays, wore elegant suits and linen, dressed his Ebo woman like a black queen, and drenched her in diamonds. But he drank overly much, his step slowed, his features grew coarse. He did not sleep well. His sleep was disrupted by dreams of groaning voices and heavy stench and the sounds of lash, falling bodies, clanking chains. He fed slaves to a voracious system of human greed, its appetite insatiable; and the more he fed the monster the more it demanded. Finally the massive maw yawned to devour him as well . . .

"No! M-My God, no!"

He awoke drenched in sweat, bolt upright in the bed. From out of the darkness soft, perfumed hands curled around his neck and stroked his back; a husky voice soothed him. "You all right. You safe. Is bad dream." Mary-Mary, the Ebo woman, drew him to her.

In the spring of 1823 she gave him a son, a light-skinned mulatto baby. Ward was jubilant. As the infant grew, the handsome Stewart features began to shape the chubby face. The eyes were oddly colored, more grayish than brown, giving them a dramatic intensity. The baby stole his heart with its infectious laughter.

"A seafaring man, by the look of him." Ward scooped the toddler into his brawny arms. "And by God, why not a seafaring man, eh? We'll give him a name proper for command. Francis Drake!" He lifted the boy, gave him a toss to the ceiling and was rewarded with a laughing gurgle. "Francis Drake Stewart, I salute you!"

But a man could not live forever secure from his past. There came to Jamaica an austere American in a tall leather hat and black clothing, asking about a captain named Ward Stewart. Damn! He should have changed it long ago, but did not.

Well, it was time to be moving along anyway. He was homesick to see Cape Cod again, if only briefly. Homesickness ate at his vitals like a living thing and gave him no peace. The arrival of the detective was only added reason to call it quits. For the last time he lay through the night with the Ebo woman. From the persistence of his lovemaking, she knew that he would go. But this, too, was to be accepted. After all, hadn't this strange, haunted white man made her a queen?

He left her most of the gold, in her name at the Bank of Jamaica. With the boy in his arms he took ship from Kingston on the morning tide and watched the land melt away. On a fair wind, they beat northward into American waters and then along the mainland coast, making various ports. Carrying the boy and a suitcase, he left the ship at Boston and hired a sloop for Cape Cod. The last few miles of the journey was by stagecoach, rocking along the desolate sand dune road to Provincetown.

Home! The town seemed so much smaller than he had remembered, even though it had grown in population. Wind-scoured houses still put their backs to the great encroaching dunes. There was the pervasive odor of drying cod from racks and the timeless sounds of squalling gulls. Home. He came back to it not as a prodigal, however, but as a stranger; and the house in which he'd been born and reared was silent now, empty of its master and absent of welcome. He pushed open the unlocked door and walked in, feeling the desolateness of it, breathing the accumulated dust and age and old wood. A square of sunlight stole across the broad planking his father had put down as flooring, and up along the narrow turning stairway the whitewash flaked from lapboard walls. He thought he had not been seen arriving, forgetting that houses have eyes in Provincetown, that even the stout little boats dancing in the harbor could whisper secrets in their bobbing, chuckling way. A knock came at the door. Warily he looked out, but saw no one. Opening the door, he found a covered dish of steaming chowder on the stoop and chunks of bread in a plate. Down the street, the dark skirts of a woman went flapping away in the wind, turned a corner, and vanished from sight.

He could not stay. He could not stay. But he slept for a few hours in his narrow bed upstairs. In the late afternoon he awoke, splashed his face in cold water, tended to the boy. Francis Drake was a quiet tot, amusing himself with scraps of wood for toys. The boy's skin was a golden tan and his hair a tight cap of woolly brown curls. Ward cleaned him and dressed him, picked up the suitcase, and left the house. A few people were out, strolling along the narrow streets. Some of them he recognized, but no eye turned his way, and no one spoke. He took no offense. It was their way of protection, he knew; the eye that saw not betrayed not.

He carried the boy two blocks down the street to a small white frame building by the dock, surrounded with fish racks. A sign swung in the seabreeze: "Stewart's Cod & Salt. Bartholemew Stewart, Prop." He went in at a side door and found the old bookkeeper, Throckmorton, perched on a high stool at his desk, laboring over endless columns of figures in cramped ledger sheets. Throckmorton peered at him across square spectacles.

"Been expecting you, Mr. Stewart."

"Throckmorton."

The old man got off the stool, breathing harder for the effort, went to a small wood stove in the corner and poured tea. Without commenting on the presence of the boy, he handed Ward a steaming cup and spoke in generalities. The weather. Business. Bartholemew's insistence on correct accounts. A man of long silences, talk came uncomfortably to him. Ward learned, however, that things were still in the good hands of faithful employees, and the fleet now came home with codfish loaded to the scuppers. Times were good. Prosperity was being enjoyed at last in Provincetown.

Old Bart's bookkeeper brought out the ledgers. His impeccable honesty extended to the last decimal point. " 'Tis not a fortune, Ward Stewart, but a very good living ye have here. And of course it is all yours to do with as ye see fit. I am but a caretaker and make no decisions." The square spectacles bobbled as he spoke. Ward saw that one glass was cracked and the old man's linen frayed. He was obviously not a spendthrift, either.

"Throckmorton, I do not intend to take a penny for myself."

The bookkeeper drew up, blinking. He had never considered such a possibility. "But, Mr. Stewart, your father . . ."

"My father dreamed of his son coming home and taking over. Well, that was a dream and no more. I cannot stay in Provincetown in any event. Beyond that, I think that the business rightfully belongs to those who have tended it and cared for it since my father's death, and who by their labors and honesty continue to do so."

The bookkeeper remained motionless, his face set.

"There is, of course, a birthright, and I do intend to exercise at least a portion of it. But not for me"—he bent down and picked up the boy—"for my son."

Throckmorton's quick glance took in the shade of the child's skin, the hair and eyes. He cleared his throat. "Well, of course, whatever you say . . ."

"This mulatto child is my son and heir. His name is Francis Drake Stewart. I ask that he be taken in by the company, brought up as a man of the sea, and taught to command a ship. He is to be properly educated. At the age of twenty-one, I wish for him to be captain of his own vessel, a vessel provided by the company. That is all. Beyond that, he is to make his own way in the world, sink or swim. Everything else, including any demands that I might legitimately have on my father's estate, I turn over to you and to the men who have operated this business in Bartholemew Stewart's behalf."

When Ward had finished speaking, Throckmorton was silent, adjusting his mind to the new terms. It was a logical mind, accustomed to order and substance. Ward could visualize each bit of intelligence being tucked into its place, duly indexed and notated and classified. The boy made a playful sound and tried to poke a chubby finger into his father's mouth.

"As you wish," Throckmorton said.

"Good. Draw it up on paper, and I will sign."

The next morning, Ward Stewart took the stagecoach out of Provincetown.

No one saw him off.

He traveled alone.

XIII

Burl was weak and had always been weak. The runt of the litter, they called him. "Old Burl's the runt of Isaiah's litter." A do-nothing, a no-account. It is bad enough to be weak in a clan of great strengths, but infinitely worse to know it from childhood; to feel one's incapacity down to the marrow of the bones.

Even when he was a child, Burl could overhear them, overhear his father's scorn. "The boy is weak, Martha. No spine. No head. Can't hold his attention to anything. A dreamer. Worse, a trifling dreamer." And his mother: "Now, Isaiah. Hush, the boy might hear you." Well, he had heard and he had felt. The words, the glances, the slights burned into his memory. He was a loner. He played alone and lived alone; even among the family he lived alone. It was his brothers who took the attention. Handsome, they were. Tall, they were. And Nathan, the apple of his father's eye, going off to Oxford and doing great things and becoming rich. Even now, with Isaiah grown old and feeble of mind, with Nathan long gone and Stephen a strange ravaged monster . . . even now the pecking order of the family did not change. One existed forever in his place. "Nathan, now there's a success for ye!" Isaiah cackled into his bourbon. "Building the Erie Canal. Think of that! Rich? Oh, if I'd had that boy's money, what I could have done."

Manhood had not burst upon Burl, it had crept over him. Never tall and muscular like his brothers, he grew up stocky and moonfaced, with a slouch. His voice was weak. He'd had no knack for learning as a child—no head for sums or writing or consuming knowledge—and even less as a man. He tried his hand once, secretly, at a little business. He opened a small shop in town, repairing wagons. He could take the overflow from Stewart's without anybody paying much attention. But the business did not prosper. Customers were not drawn to him. A small sum he had borrowed from Zachary Palmer's cousin, a banker, went into default, and Zachary made good the debt from his own pocket. Burl closed the shop and went back to the Stewart compound, to do odd jobs and run errands and work beside Catherine.

His passion for Catherine had flamed as a shocking thing, stirring him deeply, making him afraid. He had spied on her and dreamed of her at night. In his dreams he carried Catherine away on a horse, her blond hair tumbling, to a hideaway in the forest where he, Burl, was lord of all he surveyed. But the dream crumbled in daylight. In time, Catherine and Stephen were married, and the fires of Burl's ardor were banked. But they remained alive beneath the surface, ready to flame again if stirred. Guilt troubled him. When Stephen was so terribly injured and lay in his agony, Burl caught himself hoping that his brother would die. If Stephen died then he, Burl, could attract Catherine, take her for himself. Even if Stephen lived, Catherine surely could not love a man so—so grotesque. This fantasy also crumbled. Stephen survived and grew strong again, walking on that peg leg, masking the horror of his face with a thin, flesh-toned cloth, going at life with a vigor even stronger than before. In almost losing life, Stephen gained an immeasurable zest for it, a zest that was transmitted to Catherine—who adored him even more—and encompassed that wild Indian and the squaw and Martha and Isaiah and the men of the compound and the people of the town. Strange, that a man's appearance did not matter; that a man could be so ugly as to be beautiful. Even Burl sensed it, from his distance. And his envy was the more consuming still.

Whiskey made life tolerable. Whiskey blunted the keen edges of reality and cast his light in a rosy glow, gave him courage and illusory congeniality. He took his whiskey in the several saloons of Pittsburgh, a familiar figure sitting alone at a small table, moonfaced and slump-shouldered and quiet. He never became quarrelsome, aggressive, or mean. "There's Burl. Nice old sot. Never give you no trouble." The constables knew him. Sometimes when he passed out at the table, they picked him up and took him to an unlocked cell, where he awoke the next day lying in his vomit.

Martha wished . . . Oh, how Martha wished. "Burl, Burl, when are you going to settle down, find some nice woman to marry, do steady work? You could handle light bookkeeping here in the office, dear. There's Jenny Carver. She never married. Nice girl, nice Christian girl from a good family. Do you like Jenny, Burl? Why don't you call on Jenny sometime?"

Yes, he said. Yes, he would call on Jenny, he said. But he never seemed to get around to it.

Finally, the notion came to Burl that he might take a little trip downriver. Not far; to Wheeling, maybe, or Marietta. Go someplace. Do something. "That's nice, son. A change will be good for you." And so he boarded the steamboat *Pittsburgh* and went to Wheeling, where he got off and wandered about the town feeling more alone than he'd ever felt in his life. He bought a jug of whiskey and sat on the riverbank drinking half of it until he fell over snoring, a line of spittle trickling from his mouth.

He awoke in the night. Someone was going through his pockets. Shadowy figures were around him. He blinked his eyes but could not come to grips with consciousness yet, so he passed out again aware that someone had grasped him under the arms and was dragging him along. When he awoke again, a campfire was burning, and someone was standing over him, speaking with great urgency. "Sinner," the voice said. It was a strong voice with a cutting sound, like a lash. "You are a sinner, my son. Admit it. Sinner! Sinner! Sinner! Oh, you should praise God for this night . . ." He opened his eyes. The speaker was reed thin and tall, tall as a steeple it seemed; the speaker wore black clothing and a tall, tall hat and had a face like a cadaver, the mouth a black hole that kept opening and closing, opening and closing. "Woe betide thee, wretch, drunken sinning whoreson! Thy sickness is the sickness of perdition; thy bile the bile of eternal damnation! God have mercy on your soul!"

Burl stirred. He roused himself on one elbow. He was sick. He wanted to heave. But the voice, the voice was a kind of palliative to his torment. It said what he had thought for so long, deep in his mind. Wretch. Sinner. Spawn of the devil. He needed it. He needed the voice. Oh, God. He blinked and focused on the face again, the cadaver face that now came down closer to him with blazing eyes that burned into his own. "Brother, I command thee. Beseech the glory of the almighty and benevolent God before it is too late, before He casts thy soul into everlasting hellfire! Brother, come to thy knees and repent of thy sins! *Repent, I say.* For whosoever believeth in me shall not perish but have everlasting life."

The stirring was inside him, deep inside him. The agony filled his breast so that he thought he would burst. The agony came up into the hollow of his mouth, demanding to be let free; rising like the very demon of his being would rise, to be expunged and excoriated. The voice flayed at him, hurling down its authority.

The tears sprang to Burl's eyes and he wept.

Then he vomited.

Then he slept.

When he awoke again, it was full daylight. There was an odor of frying fatback from a campfire. Blue smoke rose in the woods. He heard voices. The black-clad apparition and several other people, male and female, moved about. Burl struggled to his feet, suddenly ashamed of his filth and stink. He went down to the river and bathed. Then he came back to the campfire.

"Welcome, sinner," said the tall apparition. "My name is Brother Durango, and I am the Redeemer of the West. Have some beans and fatback."

And so Burl joined the Redeemer's blessed band. Under the verbal lash, he wallowed in penance for his sins, gloried in the shame, fell to his knees saying the name of the Lord. The salvation of Brother Stewart came at last one night in a clearing packed with worshipers. Brother Durango scourged the Devil and lay on his bony hands and tears of joy streamed down the sinner's countenance. "Hear ye, oh my children, that this sinner is saved! Hear ye, oh wilderness, oh birds of the air and fish of the stream, hear ye, oh mighty rivers, that Brother Burl . . ."

"Amen!" cried the multitude.

"That Brother Burl is born again! Hear ye . . ."

"Amen, oh Lord!"

"That we cast out the Devil from his soul, cast out the wickedness of liquor and sins of the flesh . . ."

"Amen! Amen!"

"Cast out the mortal carnal sins that afflict him, spawned of lust and child of the seed of Beelzebub!"

In the soul of Brother Burl there was all at once a rising, bursting passion, a cleansing fire, a light of the ages. In flickering torchlight, the cadaver face of the master danced over him, and the bony fingers laid on, and the multitude swayed and shouted blessings, and he felt the depth of his being rising up, swelling, a gorging spirit, a cleansing fluid of redemption, purifying and sanctifying ("Oh Lord, God, Jesus!") and thrusting to be . . . freed!

"Glory be!" he screamed.

They moved from town to town. Brother Durango exhorted sinners to find salvation and give of their tithes to his glorious ministry. He laid on his healing hands, scourging them of Satan's sicknesses that caused headaches and fevers and female disorders and night sweats. He preached God's Word from wagon beds, saloon counters, and barns, always drawing the curious, the doubters, the hangers-on, and the believing. They moved overland, the group varying in size and always consisting of several young women attending the master. They followed the forest track in the heat of the summer; the master rode a mule, and his saddlebags were stuffed with small Bibles. At the camp meetings, Burl watched the faces glistening in the heat behind hand-fluttered fans. Some of the eyes glazed, as if from fever, and some drooped in boredom.

In a Mississippi village they came upon a hanging. A slave buck, eyes bulging white with fear, stood in the noose on a makeshift platform of boards. He was said to have tried to molest a white woman. Brother Durango asked to preach God's Word upon the miscreant. The heavy, grating voice intoned richly, asking God to look down, yes, even upon this worthless sinner who would deflower the most precious thing known to man, a woman's virtue. A mob of slit-eyed and red-necked men listened gravely to the Word. The man in the noose shut his eyes tightly, whimpering. At last Brother Durango snapped closed the Good Book and turned away, saying: "Hang him, boys."

The scream was shut off. The body leaped skyward. The heels kicked. The toes twitched . . . and twitched . . . and finally were still.

That night Brother Durango took into his small tent one of the sisters of the flock, a plain young woman who had recently joined them seeking the cleansing spirit of the Lord. There was a murmuring and giggling, a quickening movement, a thrashing and moaning. Burl lay on the ground outside looking up at the stars and listening. Sweat drooled over his face. His manhood was stiff and throbbing. From the tent there came a shuddering, ecstatic cry. Burl grabbed himself and pumped fiercely. The stars exploded in a spasm of joy.

It was a hard calling, religion. Brother Durango demanded of them self-denial and avoidance of the horrors of the flesh. There was no sin like original sin. They must all pray and fast and ask the Lord's forgiveness. Burl was filled with remorse. Oh, weak and sinful spirit! The flesh was too mortal. Burl had lusted. He had failed Brother Durango, failed himself, failed the Lord.

They came to the town of Natchez. Dens of inequity flourished in squalid shacks and houses along the Mississippi under the high bluff. Nights erupted in drunken laughter and fistfights and breaking glass. It was a place of gamblers, whores, and triflers of the lowest sort. Burl sneaked away from Brother Durango's camp and went under the bluff, got drunk in a saloon and woke up in the bed of a prostitute, weeping for forgiveness. That day he drank some more to douse the fires of conscience in blissful, numbing alcohol.

"My, my, what have we got here, Molly?"

"Damned if I know, Harper. He keeps asking me to forgive him. He mutters about carnal sin and God and Brother Durango, whoever that is."

"He don't look none too sober to me."

"He ain't drawn a sober breath."

"We'll just take him along with us, then. The fellow might provide some sport. How about it, lads?"

There was a murmur of agreement among the men.

"Don't hurt him, Harper. He ain't done nobody no harm."

"Why, Molly, we wouldn't hurt him. A high-minded religious fellow? We wouldn't hurt him for the world, would we lads? Now, then, let's get an arm under him. That's it. Lift him to his feet. Upsy-daysy! There, lad. Off we go, then..."

They traveled overland toward the northwest along the wooded trail called the Natchez Trace. There were five of them in the band, hard-bitten, profane men fond of whiskey and cards. Burl was accepted as a butt of humor. He was nicknamed "Preacher," and his job was to fetch and carry, cook and tend. "Hey, Preacher, bring along that firewood." And, "I swear, Preacher, if I had to choose between your cooking and my starvin' to death, I don't know which is worse."

Few travelers were encountered along the way, and those they did pass were numerous and well armed. The man named Harper, leader of the group, wearied of moving on foot with only a pack mule to carry supplies and resolved to find horses. At last a man and his two grown sons came south along the trail with half-a-dozen horses. Harper and his men pounced from the woods, guns drawn. They stripped the men of their clothing, weapons, and food and drove them naked into the woods. Then they mounted the horses and moved northward again. Burl was shocked at the bold robbery but did not protest. Harper and his chief lieutenant, a surly half-breed Shawnee named Slagg, took the best clothing and boots for themselves and had the pick of the horses. That night they drank whiskey around the campfire, laughing raucously at the remembered discomfiture of their victims. "There they went, Slagg, a'runnin' bare-assed into the woods. I never seen white men light out so fast in all my born days. I couldn't get a ball into 'em fer laughing so hard."

"What'd you think of that, Preacher? Man, we went to all that trouble to get you a horse, and you ain't said one word of thanks."

"Preacher's a man of God. He don't believe in stealing."

" 'Zat so? 'Zat so, Preacher? Are you a real true man of God, no shit? Recite us a little outta the good book, Preacher."

"Aw, Billy George, you don't want to hear nothing out of the good book. Let him be, Billy George."

"I do, too. I want to hear me some Bible recitin'." Billy George took another swig of whiskey and leered at Burl. "Come on now, Preacher."

Burl looked at Harper. The leader spat tobacco juice into the fire, raising a sizzling puff of smoke. "Go ahead, Preacher," he said.

"The L-Lord is my shepherd," Burl whispered, "I shall not..."

"Louder, Preacher. A Christian man like you has got to speak up *loud*."

"...I shall not want. He maketh me to lie down in green pastures. He leadeth me beside the still waters. He r-restoreth..."

"All right, all right, that's enough."

"...My soul..."

"That's *enough*, I said."

Burl gulped and fell silent. Weary of the sport, they forgot about him and began to play cards again. Burl tried to drink himself into a stupor, but failed. For the first time since falling in with these men, he felt that he had been close to disaster.

They swung off the Natchez Trace finally and veered due north. Burl lost track of the days and weeks of travel. His legs had gone through the pain of adjusting to horseback, but they finally allowed him to ride comfortably. At last they came to the Ohio River. Harper led them upstream for several miles. They dismounted, chopped down trees and lashed them into a raft. It took three trips to float all the horses across the river. Then they moved upstream again until they came to a sheer rock cliff. High up in the cliff face, Burl could see a broad shelf and a large cave, commanding a full view of the river. They climbed up along the side of the bluff to the ledge and made camp.

After several days of hunting, gambling, and drinking, boredom settled in. Men began to quarrel. A fist fight broke out between Slagg and one of the others. Harper broke it up, and they settled down again. "What we need's some excitement, Harper. Can't sit here forever doin' nothing."

The cave mouth was partially sheltered from view on the river by tall trees. Burl had seen steamboats chuffing by. There also was an occasional flatboat or keelboat floating downstream, carrying goods, livestock, and people. Harper nodded toward the river. "Slagg, you'n Billy George see if you can catch us a nice fat bird. That'll give you some diversion."

The men snickered. "That's a fact, Harper. If we catch a bird, why even Preacher there might want a little piece. What about it, Preacher. You like a little piece of bird?"

"Haw, haw, haw."

Burl grinned, uncomprehending.

Slagg and Billy George picked up their rifles and climbed down the bluff. At the base of the cliff, eighty feet below the cave, Billy George stood on a rock to wave at a passing flatboat. "Help! We need some help over here." But the boatmen either did not hear him or deliberately ignored the signal. As the day wore on two more small craft also went by without approaching the shore. Not until late afternoon did a flatboat respond to Billy George's frantic waving and shouting. A lone man at the steering sweep worked the craft toward them. From a small cabin amidships there emerged a woman and two children. The boatman removed his hat to shade his eyes against the setting sun's glare. He was totally bald. The flatboat bumped ashore just downstream from Billy George.

"What's the trouble, neighbor?" the boatman said.

"We got a man bad sick here, friend." Billy George moved toward the flatboat. Behind him, hidden in the brush, Slagg worked his way along the base of the cliff, rifle at the ready.

As the boatman stepped ashore to tie off the flatboat, Slagg came out of concealment.

Harper and the others swarmed down the bluff. They joined Slagg and Billy George in plundering the boat. The boatman and his wife, a handsome woman of about thirty, pleaded for their lives. The small children, a boy and a girl, cried hysterically.

Bound with short ropes and their goods taken off the craft, the captives were herded up the steep bluff to the cave. Burl tried to shrink back out of sight, his own terror nearly matching that of the family. But Harper ordered him out to build a fire and open a fresh keg of whiskey. "We're going to have us a little party here, folks, and you're the honored guests."

"Please," the man said. The bald head glistened in the firelight and the blue eyes grew even paler. "Please let my wife and children go. You can have everything we own, but give us our lives. We mean you no harm. Please. Let us go, and we won't say anything to a soul, not a word. Please." Harper snickered, picking his teeth with a hunting knife. Burl stepped across the man for firewood, and the pale eyes fixed on him. "Please, mister, you look like a decent sort. Help us..."

The next six hours were a nightmare.

Harper and the band drank whiskey and played cards until the night was fully dark. Firelight played over the ledge and flickered into the mouth of the cave. One of the children, the little girl, had cried until she was exhausted. When Slagg accidentally stumbled over her, she broke out in a fresh wail of terror.

Billy George jumped to his feet, picked up the little girl, carried her to the edge of the cliff and threw her over.

The woman screamed and struggled at her bonds.

Slagg, with a brutal laugh, gathered up the boy and tossed him to Billy George across the open fire. Billy George caught the white-faced child by one arm and then flung him over.

It had taken only seconds. Burl sat rooted to the ledge, the scene playing against his drunken mind with shattering impact. His mouth hung slack and his eyes bulged. Harper looked at him and laughed. "Don't go away, Preacher. We're going to show you some more. How 'bout that bird now, lads?"

One by one, the men raped the woman while the bald-headed man watched helplessly, the blue eyes blazing with an insane light.

Then she, too, was rolled over the cliff.

Burl drank himself to sleep. The others, weary from exertion, were soon snoring, too. Only the crackling fire was left; the fire and the rope-bound man, sitting pale and wide-eyed.

Sometime during the night he managed to squirm free of his bonds and slip away.

Two days later, a cold sober, agonized Burl Stewart went out to gather firewood and kept on walking. He walked all day and the night and the next day. He rested for a few hours, ate raw fish and a handful of berries, and walked again.

He walked all the way home to Pittsburgh.

It was a different Burl Stewart now; quiet, as always, but introspective and sober. Since his return from downriver, he no longer drank at all. And he refused to speak of the journey, even under friendly family questioning.

Martha was delighted at the change. "Praised be," she said. "Burl has come to his senses at last."

Even Isaiah was impressed. "I never thought I'd see the day." At Isaiah's suggestion, Stephen gave his brother a steady book-keeping job in the office. From the first, Burl was punctual, sober, tended meticulously to his work, and never missed a day.

He also went calling on Jenny Carver.

They were married in a small ceremony at Stewart House. She was a good woman, a plain woman; and if there was no excess of passion between them, there was domesticity, security, and routine. Burl built them a little house on Water Street.

Jenny became pregnant. Excitement filled Stewart House. She gave birth to a son, the first grandchild for Martha and Isaiah Stewart. They named the boy Thaddeus, after Martha's father. And a year later, Jenny had a little girl, Mercy.

For the Stewarts of Pittsburgh, life suddenly poured sweet and clear. "Oh, Isaiah," Martha Stewart beamed, "we're the luckiest people God ever gave breath."

"Do ye think Jenny will let us keep Thaddeus for a couple of weeks while she takes care of Mercy?"

"Of course she will."

They brought Thaddeus to Stewart House with firm instructions from Jenny not to spoil him and not to feed him too many sweets. Isaiah, of course, promptly did both. And when Isaiah wasn't bouncing the child on his knee, Stephen was. For Thaddeus, a bright and bubbling child, was doted on by his uncle, too.

Ordinarily, Burl worked late at the office on Thursdays. But on this particular Thursday he left early to buy Jenny a gift. As he walked along the crowded cobblestone street, he failed to notice a man who turned in the crowd to stare at him in startled recognition. The man was bald. Hatred flashed from a pair of pale-blue eyes. He followed Burl to the little house on Water Street.

Neighbors found the bodies the next day. Burl, Jenny, and the baby Mercy, all dead, knifed in their beds.

Pittsburgh was stunned.

Only the boy Thaddeus—sleeping in a crib at his grandfather's house a mile away—survived.

XIV

"Prepare to blast!"

He looked up from the level and squinted ahead across gangs of toiling men. Heat waves shimmered in the distance. The heat pressed down on the work like a cloak, cloying and suffocating and sopping a man's body in his own sweat. Down the broad cut, an angry earthen scar gouged through fields and woodlands and, now, angling toward the marshes, the bogtrotters reminded Nathan of an army of ants. With picks and shovels, sledgehammers, wheelbarrows, mule teams, wagons, and brute strength they advanced to a steady cacophony of pounding, grunting, cursing, clattering sound.

"Mr. Stewart, sor, we're ready now."

"All right. Get those men clear, down there by the rock slide." Nathan cupped his hands and shouted. "You men by the rock slide, clear for blasting!"

It was straight powder, poured into the drill hole, plugged, and fused. Flame touched fuse; the fire sparkle danced across the distance and . . . *Boooommm!* Rock and earth erupted high into the midday air and showered down in a clatter of dirt and stones.

"Good shot, Curry."

"Thank'ee, Mr. Stewart."

The blast left a crater of wisping smoke. Slowly the bogtrotters came out of the woods and converged to attack the rubble with picks and shovels. Nathan watched. The energy of the bogtrotters amazed him. The gangs never seemed to lose spirit, no matter how cruel the heat or long the day. Perhaps it was the dollop of whiskey each two hours per man that moved them along. But it was also, Nathan suspected, the stubborn Irish will.

By the hundreds they had come, flushed out of western Ireland by the potato famine, brought to the New World in the airless, lightless steerage of sailing vessels. Masses were recruited and had their passage paid by Tammany, the powerful Irish political club, in league with its contractors. Nathan despised the system, even though his own Hudson River steamers also collected to bring the bogtrotters north to Albany. The system meant that they arrived as indentured men, owing everything they earned to Tammany; it was an economic bondage that left Nathan with a taste of gall.

But work. How those men worked! By the third season of canal construction they had driven the ditch through the Long Level, sixty-nine and one-half miles from Herkimer to Syracuse, and gained major lead time on other contracted segments. Now they mounted a major assault on the Montezuma Marshes, one of the most formidable barriers. They earned eight dollars per month, slept in tumbledown shacks provided by contractors, and ate the cheapest, coarsest food. Some men had families who shared their lot. Nathan had seen small children playing in filth around the labor camps and wondered if they would survive to be grown.

"Trouble, Mr. Stewart." An Irish foreman, squat and square-built, tugged the bill of his cloth cap.

"Yes, Finnigan?"

"One o' the men, sor. Barnaby. He's down. It's the fever."

"I'm coming."

Damn! They were driving them too hard. It was Clinton and his infernal deadlines. Nathan swung into the saddle of his big dappled gelding, gave Finnigan a lift up behind, and went off at a trot. They were working west of Syracuse, with Clinton demanding regular progress reports and making glowing promises to his political constituents. Nathan brooded as he rode. These were impossible schedules, heedless of their three weeks' delay due to weather. The spring had brought heavy rains, flooding tributary streams and saturating the marshes for too long into summer. This was supposed to be the grand assault on the Montezuma, but already it was July, and they were far behind. Nathan cursed.

The gelding picked its way downslope through a stand of cattails, raising clouds of mosquitoes and stink of swamp gas. Phew! No wonder the men all reeked of it.

"There they are, sor."

Slime-coated workmen gathered around a prostrate man. They stood calf-deep in muck, but every worker was muddied to the waist and more. Muck mingled with body sweat, caked into hair and ears and crevices around the eyes. Tools were covered with it; mules dripped in foul-smelling slime; there was muck even in the swill that passed for contractors' food. Nathan dismounted and pushed through, a head taller than most of the men. They gave way respectfully.

"What is it, Barnaby?" He knelt. The worker was no more than nineteen. They had lain him on a log. His face was white, his eyes nested in dark hollows. Shivers wracked his body. "How do you feel, lad?"

"I'm a w-wee bit under the weather, s-sor. Sorry. Maybe if I j-just rest a bit."

"He fell, Mr. Stewart, sor. Fell right into the muck there and like to drowned before we got him up."

"That's the third one this week."

Mosquitoes buzzed over the marsh. Several mosquitoes stood on the pale young face. Nathan angrily waved them off. He stood up and lifted the boy in his arms. Somebody said, "All right, make way there." The crowd fell back. Slipping and sliding, he carried the boy to the gelding. Willing hands helped him lift him onto the horse. Then he rode back toward high ground, bracing the shivering boy with one hand.

"Back to work!" bawled the foremen. "You shovelmen, give me a line across. All right, let's move!"

Barnaby died that night in his barracks.

Things worsened as the days passed. Contractors raised the whiskey ration, but it did no good. In the marshes, men toiled waist deep, and more and more of them dropped out. Medical men, such as they were, shook their heads. "You've got a lot of ailments coming out of that swamp, Mr. Stewart. The miasma, typhoid, ague, malaria. These men are working in heat that would kill an ox."

Nathan and the chief engineer went to Syracuse, to confront DeWitt Clinton. The chairman of the canal commission faced reelection for governor of New York. "Damn it, Stewart, I've made a commitment on this canal and I intend to see it through."

"Governor Clinton, we've got hundreds of men sick. There's a pestilence raging in those bogs, and we're jeopardizing lives."

"I know that, Stewart. Don't think I'm not in sympathy. Those bogtrotters are the finest workmen I've ever seen. They're doing miracles. Miracles. But we've got commitments, time schedules to meet, contracts..."

Nathan banged his fist on the table. Around him, a murmur arose among contractors and engineers who had been listening in rapt attention. Nathan sensed the disapproval of Ben Wright, the salty chief engineer, and Nathan Roberts, the brilliant technician whose career was on the line trying to devise locks to cross the awesome eleven-hundred-foot Niagara escarpment, a barrier of solid rock to the west. Nathan ignored their frowns. "Governor, time schedules don't mean a damned thing to me if men have got to die for them."

Clinton compressed his lips and surveyed the group. "Gentlemen, you've heard Mr. Stewart. What is the consensus?"

A veteran engineer stood up and leaned forward, knuckles on the table. "What Nathan says has certainly been in back of everybody's mind. Let me remind you, Governor, that in politics as well as construction, a little humanity never hurts. We've had the public's support on the Erie Canal. That's probably more important than timetables, even if it is costly. If public sentiment *stops* the canal, timetables don't mean a thing. I cast my lot with Mr. Stewart. I think we can back off from the marshes until later in the season."

"Hear, hear," several others chorused.

Clinton folded his hands and looked at Nathan. "Very well, Stewart. Your point is made. We shall cease work on the Montezuma Marshes until conditions improve." The governor paused, collecting his thoughts. "But don't expect to win them all." He smiled.

Nathan went home to Yvette. He had brought her to a rented house in Syracuse with a view of the canal digs. Her presence had become a warm, constant thing to him, secure and certain in a topsy-turvy world filled with dust and oaths and deadlines. "Darling." She stood on tiptoes to kiss him, her skin milky, her eyes large and softly lashed. She was pregnant.

He nuzzled her neck and placed his hand on the swollen belly. Yvette drew away. "No, you don't. Time for dinner, Mr. Stewart. And first I want you to take a hot bath. You smell like a pig, or something dragged out of a swamp. Which is it?"

He sighed. "Something dragged out of the swamp."

A servant had hot water waiting in the tub. Nathan luxuriated, closing his eyes while the heat soaked weary muscles and bones and mental fatigue. So many things demanded his attention at once, so many problems had to be solved. Sometimes he was certain that they would never, never achieve it all. The Erie Canal was too bold a project, too difficult for mortal man, his puny machines and limited capability. It was crisis upon crisis and the marshes represented only a piece of the whole.

His mind turned from bogtrotters and marshes to hydraulic cement. Technically, he mused, this new problem could be critical. He closed his eyes and made mental pictures. On both ends of the Erie, east and west, they would have to build locks—locks to flood and float the barges up and over hills. Would they build them of wood or of stone? Wood or stone? Wood or stone? He remembered Canvass White's words, as the young engineer defined what they were up against in the locks. "Wood won't last, Nathan. It rots. We'll always be tearing out the rot and rebuilding the locks at heavy cost. Stone? Well and good. But down there under water, we've got to cement that stone. Ordinary mortar won't do; it'll just crumble and wash away. There's hydraulic cement, but it's enormously costly. The only constant source of supply is Europe." Canvass White's young face reflected his worry. "It might not seem like much to you, Nathan, but a little problem like this could make or break the Erie."

One more problem to make or break the canal. He sighed, opened his eyes, looked at his toes. Even the toes, sticking up out of the bathwater, reminded him of what they faced. The toes sloped upward from the little toe to the second toe, which was tallest, and then leveled down across the big toe. And that was just like the Niagara Escarpment...

Yvette knocked at the door. "Darling, are you going to be in that tub all night? I'm starving."

"Coming."

Dinner was his favorite time of the day. Yvette always managed to make it special, always gave it the little extra touches: the white linen, the crystal, the silver, the wine. Even in such a small place as Syracuse, she was able to make the most of local vegetables and meats. Her management of the household was orderly and efficient, and Nathan often wished he could manage his own tumultuous business affairs as well. They kept two servants, a cook and a houseman, but added more when they entertained. When they dined alone, Yvette listened intently to his talk of problems and offered suggestions, always astutely and with practical common sense. "You were quite right, darling," she was saying now. "The marshes can wait for better conditions. It is not fair to the men . . ."

Someone was at the front door. The houseman ushered in Canvass White. The young engineer seemed breathless with excitement. While an extra plate was set for him, he announced joyously: "Trass!"

Nathan was puzzled. "Trass?"

"It's a volcanic pumice and the main ingredient of hydraulic cement. Very unique properties. Put it underwater overnight, and it hardens into solid rock. That's the key to the entire bonding process."

"I see," Nathan murmured, not seeing.

"I've found out that a deposit of trass was discovered in Massachusetts some years ago. I don't know all that much about geology, but it seems likely that we might find it in New York State, too. Isn't the geological development similar?"

"Trass!" Nathan declared, suddenly understanding. "If we can find it, then our problem cementing the lock stones underwater is solved. Do you think you can find it?"

White shrugged. "We'll certainly try."

"Excellent! Excellent! Now have yourself a serving of Yvette's soufflé and some of this marvelous white Bourdeaux wine. You've not had a better meal in your life."

Trass. Nathan chuckled out loud.

He hadn't felt this good in months.

She had heard the whispers soon after they were married, but paid little heed. A man as handsome and as well-known as Nathan Stewart was bound to attract gossip. His involvement with such strong political figures as Robert Livingston and DeWitt Clinton would tend to fuel even more speculation about his private life. It was not lost upon Yvette that the gossip seemed to have been most malicious when DeWitt Clinton first became governor three years ago, shortly after the canal won in the legislature.

The first word had come from old Robert Rosenfoert's female cousin, a fat busybody with a wagging tongue. Politically she was no friend of Clinton's; her husband, a minor functionary caught taking bribes for public contracts with the city of New York, had been fired by Clinton in his last days as mayor. The man had gone over to Tammany Hall and later tried to undermine the Erie Canal project. His wife had then visited Yvette at home.

"My dear, far be it for me to tell tales, but I thought you ought to know." She was overly rouged and had chin wattles that quivered when she talked. "They are saying absolutely *vile* things about your husband, behind his back." The woman looked around as if to make sure they were alone, an habitual gesture done even in private. Her tongue darted reptilelike over thin lips.

"About Nathan?" Yvette was suddenly uncomfortable. "What sort of things?"

"*Well . . .*" It was a breathy expostulation, an audible exclamation point uttered before the sentence. "*Well*, they are saying that he, I mean to say Mr. Stewart, was quite close, very close, to Lucy Durange before he married you."

"They were friends, yes."

"My dear,"—she placed a moist hand upon Yvette's in friendly solicitude—"far be it for me to tell tales, and I certainly don't believe any of this for a minute. But we are such good friends, you and I, and I know you wish only the best for your husband, that I thought—I thought you would want to know. Knowledge is power, I always say." She sighed, placing a hand at her heart. "Those who know not are blind."

"Yes, yes, I'm sure of that."

It pained the woman, did it not? One could see that. Her eyes became great pools of pain and sympathy. The eyes looked deeply and hurtfully into Yvette's. The lips pursed. The mouth opened and closed and opened again. "They are saying that Lucy Durange and Nathan, uh, Mr. Stewart, were having a love affair."

Yvette could not deny the pang of jealousy. It came unexpectedly, under the heart. There was a small, hard knot of hysteria. Intuitively, she said nothing, let her mind do the work. The mind swept down to the hysteria, surrounding it, isolating it, closing off the hurt. She kept her eyes level and let her mouth lift in a small, bright smile.

"Is that all?" she said.

The pain fled from the other's eyes. The mouth made a small "o." The face reflected confusion. "Do you mean you *knew?*"

Yvette smiled more broadly now. The flurry inside was coming under control. Her mind was functioning. She could take the offensive. "That's such an old story, I'm surprised that they're still trying to make something of it. I know that Nathan will be amused when I tell him."

"Amused?"

"Tell me, my dear, how is your husband doing in his business affairs? Did he overcome that—that unpleasantness from before? As you know, Nathan has always spoken so highly of your husband. He just never could believe that such a thing—"

"Yes. Well, really, I must go." She was gathering up her things, rising from the settee, drawing on her gloves. "So many things to attend to, you know."

"It was good of you to come."

"Charming."

"We must have a longer visit next time. There's so much to talk about and so little time, it seems."

Yvette saw her to the door, watched the carriage pull away, closed the door, walked up the stairs to the bedroom, picked up a small china vase, and smashed it against the wall. "Nathan Stewart," she shouted at the empty house, "you *son of a bitch!*"

She never mentioned it, however; not even when Lucy Durange had appeared unexpectedly in the crowded gallery during the Erie Canal legislative debate, nor later at the Clinton dinner and reception when Nathan was made general superintendent of the canal works. But she had seen, on both occasions and in chance meetings later as well, the naked lust that smoldered in Lucy's eyes when they happened to fall on Nathan. Yvette had seen, but carefully masked her own inner fury. Instinct told her that Nathan had this under control, just as he managed to control most things about his life. One did not demean a strong man by direct confrontation. Nathan was hers; she loved him. If Lucy Durange had once possessed him and lost, then so be it. What went on between them was past, done with, gone. Or, at least, so Yvette devoutly hoped.

She kept the knowledge tucked away in a corner of her mind, an unpleasant keepsake that was out of the way and yet available if ever needed. The knowledge was there, certain and irrefutable. The knowledge was power.

Yvette was not prepared, however, for Lucy Durange's arrival in Syracuse.

The woman had come alone and was stopping at the town's

only inn. Yvette would not have known, except that she happened
to see her get off the incoming stagecoach. Discreet inquiry
determined that Madame Durange did not intend to stay long.
Yvette smiled to herself. Fate could play subtle tricks indeed.
For Nathan just happened to be away for a week on a trip with
Canvass White to the Niagara Escarpment. After two days, word
filtered back to her that Madame Durange had been out inspecting
the works in behalf of her husband, Claude, who had been too ill
to make the journey himself. In the company of engineers, Lucy
had looked over a portion of the Long Level and seen the
Montezuma Marshes.

Suddenly, unreasonably, Yvette's anger came surging. It happened
quite by chance. She walked past a full-length mirror in the
hallway and saw her pregnant reflection. In this, the eighth,
month her body seemed a bloated, shapeless mass—so distended
that by polite custom she no longer went out to be seen in public,
but remained in "confinement." Imprisonment would be a better
word. Oh, this damned house! For the first time in her life,
Yvette found herself engulfed in self-pity, unable to control an
unexpected torrent of emotions. She burst into tears and, ignoring
the servant's anxious questions, went up to her room and
slammed the door.

That woman! That woman! That hated woman was here in
Syracuse!

Later, Yvette herself would not understand fully why she did
it, or what precisely she hoped to gain. Impulse overwhelmed
reason. But that very evening, she bathed and put on her best
clothes—a maternity dress was a maternity dress—and took her
carriage to the Syracuse Inn. She rapped smartly on Lucy
Durange's door with her parasol. When the door opened, Yvette
momentarily seemed to lose breath. She had forgotten that her
nemesis was so beautiful; now, in her own pregnancy, the
difference between them was striking. Lucy Durange's soft eyes
widened in recognition, framed in her light blond hair. "Why,
Mrs. Stewart!"

"I've come to have it out with you, Madame Durange." She
pushed past Lucy and into the room. It was a lovely room, with
French windows opening onto the balmy evening and fresh roses
on a glass-topped table. The door closed behind her, and Lucy
stood waiting. "Yes?"

Yvette spun around, her fury rising again. "It's about my
husband. You see, I know about you and Nathan. I've known for

years. And if you've come sneaking up here to see him, I warn you . . ."

The voluptuous mouth upturned slightly, the eyes of Lucy Durange became lynxlike with amusement. Were they mocking her? Yvette suddenly felt uncertain, but she pushed on. "I warn you that I no longer intend to remain silent. We are about to have a child. I'll not let the past interfere with our future. My husband does not need to be bothered . . ."

It was all coming out wrong. The speech that had seemed so right as she rehearsed it on the ride to the inn now came out clumsy and irrational. Yvette felt a touch of nausea. She had made a terrible blunder, placed herself in the hands of this clever woman, let anger override good sense. Why? Why?

Lucy Durange laughed without mirth. "What absolute nonsense, Mrs. Stewart." The eyes, so changeable, so expressive, went flat. "I do see that you're expecting. How touching. And what an odd time for you to seek a confrontation with me. It does put you rather at a disadvantage." She moved across the room, putting her back to Yvette, fingering at the roses as she passed, stopping at the double windows and looking out. She was calm, controlled. It should have been Yvette who was calm, but now Yvette's heart pounded, and her mouth was dry. Her mind fought to grasp control, and reason told her this it was a mistake, a dreadful mistake. Lucy Durange quickly confirmed this.

"Shall I tell you about the man you married, Mrs. Stewart. Yes, why not. Nathan is a marvelous lover, absolutely marvelous. There is no man like him, anywhere; at least none that I've ever known." She laughed lightly, maliciously. "And the wonderful part of it, for me, is that Nathan loves me, absolutely adores me. He wanted for us to marry, of course, for me to leave Claude and marry him. Begged me. But I wouldn't, I couldn't. Claude needs me even more than Nathan does."

Lucy let the lie spin, like a flaxen thread. The little mother had been foolish, stupidly so, and would have to pay the consequences. Besides, the lie was not a lie, really, was it? Over and over she had tried to fathom Nathan's rejection of her, and she had masked it in the fantasy. It came so easily to her mouth now. "As you know, however, it was Claude and I who recommended Nathan to be general superintendent of the canal. He is quite clever, and my husband felt he was the obvious choice. Claude is very astute at recognizing talent." Lucy turned and looked at

Yvette, at the glowing young face and the great swollen body, and hated her. That could have been *her* baby; this lovely little French girl had everything that Lucy Durange wanted, including youth, and was too blind to see it. But she herself was not without error in coming to Syracuse, this grubby little town, on the chance of seeing Nathan. And what an irony: Nathan Stewart was not even here! "As for wanting your husband, however,"— she laughed out loud, as if the notion was all too outrageous, too amusing—"I'm afraid you suffer from delusions, my dear..."

Yvette had had enough. Blindly she turned away, hurried to tne door, rushed out and down the hall. Clumsily she moved along, hearing the laughter at her back. The tears poured now, as if from a broken dam. She lumbered through the lobby, almost falling in her flight. Guests looked up startled.

Yvette climbed into her carriage, gathered the reins, and lashed the horse viciously into a running trot. The thoughts tumbled in her mind. "Oh, Nathan, Nathan. I love you so much. I'm such a fool!" Humiliation wracked her with great, shuddering sobs.

Two days later, Yvette's labor pains began. Nathan had just arrived home with Canvass White. He rushed to bring a midwife. The baby was born shortly after midnight, a fine healthy girl with the warm brown eyes of her mother. They named the baby Francesca.

Nathan knelt by Yvette's side and kissed her lightly. "You're tired," he whispered. "You've had a hard day. Francesca is a beautiful baby. You're beautiful, too. I love you. I love you."

She opened her eyes. "Darling, would you love me even if I was not always clever and self-assured, if I did stupid things?"

Nathan brushed back her hair with his hand. "What stupid things?"

Yvette closed her eyes again, suddenly feeling warm and content. The baby made a small sound at her side. Happiness poured over her like a flowing stream. "Nothing," she murmured. "I'm just prattling."

The work pushed forward well into autumn. Clinton was insatiable for progress to show the public, and thus to best his enemies. The opposition press had made much of the malaria in the Montezuma Marshes and failure of the canal to open new stretches on the dates Clinton promised. In October, however, one could finally take a barge ride along an uninterrupted length of canal from Rome to Utica. The opening was done with typical Clinton showmanship, as he rode in triumph on the gaily painted new barge *Chief Engineer of Rome,* drawn by a single horse plodding along the towpath. Church bells pealed and fireworks boomed. Then cold weather blew down out of Canada, putting an end to the work for the winter. Nathan moved Yvette and the baby to Albany, where they celebrated Christmas with friends, parties, gifts. He had never been happier. And the prospect of a tremendous construction season during the following year promised to open dramatically new reaches of canal.

After Christmas, he had to go to New York. Business of the steamship line demanded his presence there at least for a week. Leaving Yvette and Francesca at Albany, he took the powerful new steam packet *Hudson.* The great river was gray now, as gray as the sunless winter days. Ice crusted along the banks, and the Catskills marched away in unrelieved wilderness of gray and brown. Servants had opened a wing of their New York brownstone mansion on the river, and Nathan arrived there to find cheery warm fires and pleasant surroundings. The mansion was new, a place of rich woods and furnishings with a sweeping view of the river. Yvette had named it Blossom Hill. In time, when the canal work was done, they would return here to live permanently. But it was lonely without her. In the daytime he tended to business and at night went to the theater with friends. Late in the week he did not go out, however. And one night he opened a bottle of bourbon and drank heavily, something he rarely did. The liquor helped to dispel his sense of isolation.

The knock at the door came shortly before midnight. Lucy Durange was there, snow sprinkling her hair and the beautiful face glowing from cold. Behind her, a hansom cab rattled away into the night.

She said: "Are you just going to leave me standing here?"

And then, befuddled, he was closing the door and taking her wrap. He poured her a drink, and they sat together, unspeaking, before the fire. His mind was a confused jumble of delight and guilt and numbness from drink. Finally, he stopped thinking about it and gave way, gratefully, to sensations.

The soft, familiar body slipped naked into his bed. Tiny animallike cries during the night signaled Lucy's pleasure.

He awoke at first light in a torment of guilt. Rolling out of bed, he buried his face in his hands. "What have I done?" he said. "This is wrong. This shouldn't be. I . . . We have no business doing this."

She reached for him, her breasts bare. "You belong to me, Nathan. You want me, I know that. I want you, too. Please, darling, leave her. Actually, you don't even have to leave her. Just don't return to Albany. Stay here with me, darling. Let me love you and make you happy."

Nathan shook the cobwebs from his brain. He felt terrible. His head throbbed. His thoughts were still in disarray. He had betrayed her, betrayed their marriage; and the reality of it struck him like a blow. "No, Lucy," he said. "It was a mistake."

"A mistake!" Her eyes blazed. "It was no mistake. Let me tell you something. The mistake was marrying your little French fancy pants in the first place. Listen, she has known about us all along, darling. She told me. She came angrily to my room in Syracuse last summ—"

"Your room in Syracuse? You went to Syracuse?"

Too late, Lucy saw her gaffe. Her anger flared. "Yes!" she shouted. "Yes, I came to see *you* in Syracuse . . ." It all spilled out. The meeting with Yvette, the quarrel, and Yvette's sudden departure. "I told her everything."

Nathan slapped her.

She came off the bed, a nude tigress, clawing and grappling at him. From the nightstand she snatched up a knife-sharp letter opener and, screaming, plunged it at his throat. Nathan dodged, grabbed her wrist, twisted. The weapon clattered to the floor. She slumped beneath him, panting and sobbing. "You!" she gasped. "You've made me . . . an animal!"

Nathan left New York on board the *Hudson* packet, running the steamer himself. A mate had warned him, "Mr. Stewart, there's ice crusting the river. You won't make it." But with a well-paid engineer and a stoker belowdecks, he drove the *Hudson* upriver anyway, smashing a trail through the thin ice and making full steam. The powerful new vessel made the one hundred and forty miles in record time.

Yvette heard him open the front door. She came running down the stairs, shouting, "Darling! Darling, you're home!" She flung her arms about his neck and covered his face with kisses. He swept her into his arms and carried her back up to their bedroom.

That night, she became pregnant again.

* * *

Canvass White was elated. Triumph wreathed the face of the young engineer. "We've got it, Nathan. We found it! Come with me, and I'll show you." Together they rode horseback to the village of Chittenango. For months during the fall and winter, White had roamed the countryside, asking about soils. Finally, two young men with an interest in geology took him to a deposit that had looked to them like volcanic pumice. Now, the engineer and Nathan knelt excitedly over the soil bed, digging their fingers into it. They took samples back to DeWitt Clinton. The governor shared their joy. "By God," he declared, "nothing will stop us now!"

But Clinton had forgotten about his enemies.

They had worked diligently to block his attempt at reelection, and the best attack was through the Erie Canal. If the canal failed, DeWitt Clinton failed. His old foes, including the powers of Tammany Hall Irish club, held a strong trump: the bogtrotters.

Spring came early to the land, unfolding its gradual and certain beauty. Wagons rumbled westward up the Mohawk Valley bringing more and more settlers. At last they could even travel along segments of the Erie Canal, on barges pulled along by towpath horses at four miles per hour. The Erie was a lure of its own, and tolls were being collected. The growing certainty of the canal also attracted workers of a different kind, bringing unique skills. Farmers, they were; farmers and small artisans, looking for work and possessing Yankee ingenuity with gadgets and machines. Instead of laboring with axes and crosscut saws, such men knew that they could pull down a sixty-foot tree simply by tying a heavy rope to its topmost limbs and winding it down with a windlass. They invented a stump-puller, by means of which a few men and a strong team of horses could yank a dozen stumps a day. For cutting bushes, they bolted sharp steel cutting bars to plowshares. Engineers were astonished at the results.

It was time to attack the Montezuma Marshes again, and the bogtrotters were back, living in hovel shacks at the end of the barge run. With a dry spring and good drainage, chief engineer Ben Wright was confident that fortune was smiling at last. "Nathan, one big push and we'll conquer these swamps once and for all." The day to begin work was set, the crews mustered, equipment gathered . . .

"Mr. Stewart, sor, we got trouble."

"Again?"

"You'd best come and see for yourself."

Nathan and the foreman hurried to the end of the canal run, where the marshes spread westward awaiting the assault. Nothing was happening. Gangs of drunken bogtrotters gathered around a speaker who harangued them from atop an empty barrel on the canal towpath. From a distance something about the man looked familiar to Nathan. As they drew nearer, he recognized the thickset build and features of Michael Ahearn.

"Men, there ain't a one of ye what's got to go into that swamp!" he shouted to the crowd. "All of ye remember what happened last year. How many got sick and how many died, or nearly died, from the fever? Do ye think DeWitt Clinton and his stooges give a damn? O' course, they don't. Nobody gives a damn about a bogtrotter who breaks his back and sweats like a hog for a few dollars and rotten food and a pigsty to live in, least of all Clinton. Ain't that right?"

"Right!" several voices shouted in the crowd. Nathan recognized them as Ahearn's hangers-on. "That's right, Clinton don't care."

"Well, I'll tell ye, lads. Here we sit. Nobody's going back into that stinking muck for the likes of them! Here we are, lads, and here we stay until them engineers figure out a way to drain swamps proper, so's a man can do a day's work like a man and not like a rat..."

"Ahearn, you're holding up the work!" It was Nathan, speaking from the back of the crowd through cupped hands.

Heads turned. Men whispered among themselves. "That's 'im, the general super. That's Stewart."

Ahearn looked across the crowd and smirked. "Well, if it ain't Mr. Big. You come to tell us what to do, Mr. Big?"

"I came to put these men to work so they can earn their pay. Some of them have got to pay you bloodsuckers at Tammany for their passage over, so I'd advise you not to hold us up any longer. Let's go, men..."

The Tammany man held up his burly arms. "He ain't tellin' us what to do no more, men. The bosses' day is over on the Erie. We're goin' to run things the way we see 'em. And we ain't going into that man-killing swamp!"

"There are no mosquitoes now and no malaria," Nathan shouted. "Ahearn knows it's safe. I'll take the first shovel and lead you in there myself..."

Ahearn jumped down from the barrel and pushed through the crowd. "No you won't, Mr. Stewart." He removed his coat and rolled up his shirtsleeves, revealing massive arms rippling with tattoos. The men around Nathan scrambled back, making room. Ahearn swaggered forward and placed himself in front of Nathan, fists on hips, jaw jutting. "You have to get past me, first."

Nathan nodded grimly. "Whatever you say."

He wasn't ready for the attack. Ahearn neither lifted his arms nor squared off, but simply bulled forward and smashed Nathan in the side of the head with a power-driving elbow, knocking him backward and sprawling to the edge of the canal. Nathan's head seemed to explode in a shower of stars. As he shook his head to clear it, someone shouted, "Look out!"

A heavy brogan shoe came rocketing forward, aimed at his face. He rolled, taking a glancing blow on the shoulder, and came to his feet in a rush. Ahearn, a shrewd, free-for-all brawler, locked him in a bear hug with those powerful arms, crushing his ribs. Nathan cupped his hands and smacked them together, hard, over the man's ears. The bear-grip broke, and surprise flicked across the meaty features. Nathan brought up his knee in a short, savage thrust at the man's testicles, but missed. Ahearn spun, drove a fist into Nathan's kidneys. He felt the air rush out of his body and an explosion of pain.

The strength seemed to pour out of him. In a split second, he knew that Ahearn was gathering that powerful body for the killing blow; if he failed to strike back this instant, it was over. Blindly, gasping for air, Nathan drove forward with his full weight and height, fists pumping into the broad rib cage, knees and feet smashing. His fist caught the front of the bullish neck, above the adam's apple; he brought up his right hand, palm first, in a vicious chop to Ahearn's face. He felt the bridge of the nose crunch. He grabbed the face with both hands and gouged at the eyes.

Ahearn bellowed with pain as they locked together, spinning, and plummeted into the canal. Nathan held on grimly. They thrashed in a shower of bubbles. Ducking beneath the floundering Irishman, he circled the heavy neck in a hammerlock and dragged the man under water, flailing. His own lungs were near the bursting point, and the pain of the kidney blow almost caused him to lose consciousness. But by primeval instinct, he tightened his arm in the death lock on that hated neck, immune from the kicks and punches and wild struggles to break free. Tighter went the hammerlock. Tighter.

Something gave way.

The struggles ceased. As he felt himself blacking out, Nathan found the canal bottom with his feet, gave a mighty shove free of Ahearn and shot to the surface, sputtering for air. As the Irishman floated up behind him, the bogtrotters erupted in a deafening cheer. Eager hands pulled Nathan, coughing and wheezing, from the canal and rolled him onto the towpath. Then they dragged the Irishman from the water.

The body was heavy and unresisting, with that curious limpness that caused the cheering to subside. As they flopped him down, the head jerked oddly. The men were hushed, bending over the Tammany man.

"His neck's broken," someone said.

"I seen many a donnybrook in my day, but nothin' like that one."

"The man's dead, mate. Deader'n four o'clock."

"Looks like old Michael tangled with the wrong feller, and once too often."

Two bogtrotters dragged the body off to the side and left it there. The men gathered silently around Nathan as he gradually recovered. Finally, dripping water and swaying, he struggled to his feet.

Nathan looked over at the body of Ahearn. "Nothing can be done for him?"

"No, sor. He's gone to glory, for sure."

Nathan shut his eyes against the pain in his kidney. Then he drew himself up. "Foreman, bring me a shovel, if you please." The shovel was brought. Without another word, Nathan put it over his shoulder and walked painfully away from the canal and into the Montezuma Marsh. He moved into waist-deep muck, sank the shovel and swung it up again to send a heavy gob flying.

"Let's go, men," a foreman said. "We've got us a canal to dig."

They gathered up shovels, barrows, and buckets and sloshed into the marsh after Nathan. Two men stayed behind to bury Michael Ahearn.

Every day for ten weeks, from dawn to darkness, Nathan Stewart led the bogtrotters in their assault on the Montezuma Marshes. Not until the last shovelful of muck was thrown did he stop. They finished the dig a full month ahead of schedule.

At Nathan's insistence, every man drew a bonus with his pay.

* * *

Done. It was done! "A miracle," DeWitt Clinton told the cheering throng at Buffalo. "A miracle of the ages!" And indeed it was. Nathan felt himself buoyed along on the floodtide of triumph. From Lake Erie to the Hudson River at Albany, she was finally open: three hundred and sixty-three miles of engineering marvel. They had dug through soil and marsh and solid rock, conquered more than five hundred feet of rising and falling terrain with eighty-three locks—including the mighty Lockport Fives at the Niagara Escarpment—and built more than a hundred bridges. A great aqueduct with Roman arches spanned the Genesee River to Rochester, another bore the canal for more than a thousand feet at Cohoes, still another skirted Little Falls for seven hundred and fifty feet. It took seven years and more than three thousand bogtrotters to do the job. But done it was.

"Nathan, I can't believe this is happening. It's really happening!" Yvette looked ravishing in a wine-colored gown and shawl, a lighter-colored parasol, and a bonnet with a gay floral bouquet on one side. The little girls, Francesca and Marguerite, were dressed in their Sunday best. Nathan was tall and regal in a gray beaver hat, a double-breasted coat to his ankles in the latest fashion, white neckwear, gray spats, leather gloves, and a walking stick. They clustered with DeWitt Clinton and dignitaries on the flower-bedecked prow of the governor's barge, *Seneca Chief*. In line behind them for the procession came the *Superior, Commodore Perry, Buffalo,* and *Lion of the West*. At Clinton's command, a cannon boomed, the echo of its volley rolling over the hills. On the towpath, Clinton's four matched grays stepped out in tandem, driven by two youthful hoggies. Lake Erie's Black Rock band struck up a martial air, and a thousand spectators cheered.

The cannon shot was picked up by another gun eight miles away. As it fired, still another went off at ten miles distance. In this way, the signal that the Erie Canal was open carried all the way to New York City. The news flashed from Buffalo to the Battery in only eighty minutes! At every village along the canal, DeWitt Clinton stopped to make his triumphant speech. When finally the procession reached the Hudson River basin at Albany, steamboats were waiting to tow the barges downriver to New York.

"Oh, look. Nathan, look at the steamers!"

"Twenty-seven of them, Yvette, here in the harbor."

"They're so beautifully decorated. Children, see all the barges, ships, pilot boats, and those—those are the Whitehall firemen's boats.''

At Sandy Hook, the *Seneca Chief* was brought to a stop. Two cedar kegs were brought on deck. DeWitt Clinton had had them filled with Lake Erie water. These he now poured into the Atlantic. "Nathan," he laughed, "this is our wedding of the waters. What a glorious day for New York."

"A glorious day, Governor, for America."

The ceremony ended, they returned to a city packed with thirty thousand visitors, for a round of banquets and balls in the armories. A monster parade surged down lower Broadway, followed by a massive fireworks display. Nathan and Yvette entertained far into the night, with a lavish party and ball at Blossom Hill. The last guest did not leave until sunup. In their formal evening clothes, Nathan and Yvette strolled the grounds and stood watching the early river traffic cut white wakes on the Hudson. She clutched his arm and leaned her head softly against his shoulder.

"I love you, my darling," she said. "What a glorious time to be alive. And the future—the future is ours."

"Yes," he said. "The future is ours."

But even as he said it, a tiny, unexplained anxiety flicked at the edges of his mind.

A week later, a messenger arrived at Blossom Hill with a note. Claude Durange was on his deathbed. He wished to speak with Nathan. He took his carriage to the Durange townhouse. The old man was propped on pillows in his four-poster bed, with Lucy at his side. As Nathan entered, she withdrew quietly from the room, avoiding his glance.

Durange smiled weakly and beckoned for Nathan to sit beside him on the bed. "It is you, Nathan, second only to DeWitt Clinton, who made the Erie Canal a reality." The voice was a gravelly whisper, and the aristocratic old face had the texture of translucent parchment. "I really don't think Clinton himself could have pulled it off without you, master politician that he is. Well, so much for that."

He gave a gurgling sigh, coughed, caught his breath. "What I really wanted to say to you is a bit out of the ordinary, even for an old reprobate like me. You see, I've known about your relationship with Lucy for years . . ."

Nathan smiled grimly. "It seems that everybody did."

Durange nodded, with a gleam in his eye. "I think," he said, "it was the worst-kept secret in New York. Nevertheless, I am a realist. I considered it a kind of necessary arrangement, and I'm not so blinded by conceit not to accept that. I was simply too old and Lucy too voluptuous, too passionate, to make our marriage work. Because of you, however, Lucy stayed with me. I'm certain of that. So let us part friends." The old man took Nathan's hand and closed his eyes. Nathan sat there, trying to think of something to say. Should he apologize? Should he try to deny it? No. Neither would do justice to a man like Claude Durange. So he said nothing at all. He sat until Claude Durange's breathing indicated that he had fallen asleep. And then he removed his hand, got up softly, and left the room.

Lucy was waiting outside. "Well," she said, "does that surprise you?"

Nathan shook his head. "Nothing surprises me any more."

She turned back to the sickroom. "Claude was a great man, you know," she murmured. "The failure was mine, not his."

And then she was gone.

XV

Nightly they came. It was a quality trade. One knew from the elegant carriages and fine matched pairs, clip-clopping down Bourbon Street on the soft evenings. They drew up at the sign of the red rose. "Whoa!" Liveried black footmen ran out to open doors and fold down steps.The gentlemen alighted with sure step and manner, clothed in suits of broadcloth and silk, beaver hats and soft leather gloves. It bespoke wealth and power. And they made their way to the padded, brass-studded door which admitted them to the delights of Rose Lark's Nocturne.

Out on the dark Mississippi, steamboats churned in a blaze of lights. Along the levy banjos strummed. The nights of New Orleans throbbed. But inside the Nocturne, it was a world apart. Lamplight glowed. Conversation flowed amid rich furnishings and potted plants. Waiters soft-shoed on their constant errands of food and drink. There was the clink of expensive glassware, the soft laughter of expensive women. A string quartet played Mozart. A coal black woman named Missy Lou sang torrid songs of love and life. Sometimes they pushed out a gleaming grand piano of burnished mahogany, brought all the way from Pittsburgh, upon which Rose Lark played songs taught her by Maurice Rambeaux, the aristocratic Frenchman, her lover and partner. There were whispers. Rambeaux had developed a greater passion, said the whispers, for the gaming tables.

"Rambeaux was at the Delta Club last evening. Lost ten thousand at roulette, they say."

"Pity."

"I feel sorry for Rose. Decent sort. She despairs of his excesses."

"Is he badly into debt?"

"There are rumors."

"The fool."

"Ah, here's Rose now."

Her entrances were perfected. One did not barge casually into the Nocturne. One timed herself, saw that the mood was right, the lighting neither too bright nor too dim, the hour appropriate. Rose practiced the art of entertainment. Pleasure, like a good romance or a superb wine, lived on subtlety. Thus, she had brought her decorator from Paris to redo the Nocturne, shopped for furnishings in London, Paris, and Rome, to be crated and sent back by ship. Each piece to its place; each place had a piece. She acquired staff in the same way, so that now the service at Nocturne set standards. As for special delights, her two dozen hostesses were of beauty and delight unsurpassed.

Rose moved, wraithlike, through the beaded curtains into view. Conversation stilled. By a trick of lamplight, the room seemed to brighten around her. Her silken green gown, splotched with roses, caught the light in its irridescent glow, her hair seemingly afire. A murmur of recognition fluttered through the crowd. Applause sprinkled. She smiled, nodded, went to the piano. The faces lifted in the murky light, inspiring within her the old familiar pleasure as a roomful of eyes played over her gown and creamy full bosom. She thought: I am beautiful.

She knew the faces, of course, or most of them. An exiled nobleman here, a slave trader there, a card shark (behind her smile, Rose resolved to speak with Maurice about that), a steamboater, a financier, a gourmand. "Welcome," she said, silky-voiced, "to my Nocturne. If there is anything, gentlemen, that your hearts desire, please let it be known." Her fingers caressed the piano keys. "If you want it, we've got it. If we haven't got it"—a smile played at the corners of her mouth, just so—"it's not worth having." Male laughter rippled around the room. Expertly, then, she played a medley, part classical, part popular, closing with a nocturne that always brought enthusiastic applause.

Afterward, Rose moved to this table and that, greeting her guests. "Senator, we are honored." Even in the dusky light, her eyes caught trouble. The senator was drunk, blinking owlishly, his voice overly loud. He was with two other men, equally drunk. They had gotten that way before coming to the Nocturne, but the problem was hers. The hostess with him was young, pretty, inexperienced, frightened. "It's good of you to grace the Nocturne with your presence," Rose told him. Idly, she twisted a finger ring on her left hand. The signal swept the staff. From across the room, at the office, came a stunning brunette hostess, older and more mature. Smoothly, she moved into the place beside the senator, and the young girl moved out. So artfully was it done that no one noticed. Two other hostesses, equally striking, engaged the senator's two male companions in bantering conversation. Soon, deftly, they were away with them, wafting perfume, brushing breasts to arms, giggling mischievously, isolating them. Finally, the senator himself went along with the brunette, stumbling a bit, speaking aggressively, a wine-soaked boor.

The waiters cleared the vacated table. Rose went to find the young hostess. She found her in a private sitting room, weeping. "You should have let me know earlier," Rose said sternly. "He could have given us trouble, an important man like that. It wouldn't do to let him get drunk and troublesome in here."

The girl sniffed. Her name was Beatrice. "I'm sorry, Miss R-Rose." Her nose was blood red and her eyes brimmed with tears. "I didn't know what to do. I was frightened."

Rose sat down beside her and pulled a hankie from the bosom of her gown. Beatrice's terror suddenly reminded her of another time and another place: St. Louis, and Dove Lovelady's hard but wise lectures on the ways of the world. How long ago had that been? Sixteen years. She resisted an urge to take Beatrice in her arms and calm her, as one would a child.

"How old are you, my dear?"

"I'm sixteen, ma'am."

Sixteen. How young they came to Nocturne. How soon in life they lost home and family and were on their own. It was the way of life in these troubled times. Hundreds of girls, thousands, from poor families had to choose between the harsh respectability of bonded indenture and the uncertain ease of the brothel. The prettiest and the brightest, it seemed, came to Rose's door. They fled from the real world into one of make-believe.

"And your family?"

"My pappy's dead. Trampled by a bull. Momma, she's got seven at home littler than me. So I came to New Orleans. I came to you. I told you all that."

"Uh, yes. You surely did." It was hard to remember. There were so many Beatrices, so many Priscillas, Marys, Mimis, so many faces and names, smiles and tears. "Yes, I remember you telling me that."

Rose took the prettiest and most promising. She taught them how to speak, dress, act, and walk. She put them to work in the Nocturne, entertaining gentlemen in search of diversion after dark. Rose tried to protect them as long as possible from the inevitable, tried to steer young men to their parlors so as to let nature take its course. Just as Dove Lovelady had done.

But she could not protect them forever.

Rose hardened her voice. "If you wish to continue in my employment, Beatrice, I shall expect you to follow the rules. And you'd best make up your mind right now that this is not a church social. This is a business, a profession. Our profession is to entertain gentlemen. In view of your age, I shall permit you to remain a parlor hostess for a while longer. But hereafter, when you're in difficulty, signal for help. I also have a cardinal rule in this house: don't tease. Don't give a customer the notion that you're promising something you don't intend to deliver. Is that clear?"

"Y-Yes'm."

"And don't say 'yes'm.' Say, 'Yes ma'am.' Tomorrow you will begin daily sessions with Miss Pride, the diction coach."

The tears stopped flowing. Beatrice wiped her nose, gave a final sniff and straightened her back. "Yes . . . ma'am."

Rose left the girl, feeling that progress had been made. Progress with Beatrice, that is. The world that brought such children to the Nocturne was the same.

* * *

Maurice had been drinking, and his clothes reeked of cigar smoke. It was dawn. Rose had been waiting since closing the Nocturne two hours earlier. Her rage was volcanic, borne of old slights and miseries. But she held it all in check and kept her voice cold.

"One of your gambling friends was in the club tonight. I've told you that I don't want them there. I won't tolerate it."

The handsome head nodded. The once-black hair was dusted with gray, the small, precise features etched with fine lines. Maurice had lost none of his grace, none of his style; but time and dissolute habits conspired to age him. "Sorry, *Cherie*. But I cannot keep them away, can I? It is a public place."

"A public place indeed. Riffraff from your gaming tables give us a bad name. Regular customers don't like it. It is not wise to mix our customers with common gamblers."

"My, but haven't we become class conscious?"

"You know very well what I mean, Maurice."

Their arguments were commonplace now. For years she had tried to bridle her temper and tongue, if only for the sake of their son, Brack. He was twelve years old and, God knows, had enough unwholesome influence in his life already. Maurice had lost her respect, however, drifted away from the business which by rights he should be managing. Gambling had become his passion and his life. From horses to dice and cards, his days and nights were consumed by chance. What troubled her most deeply were his debts. Deeper and deeper he sank, and more and more frantic were his efforts to recoup. He had borrowed recklessly, from the wrong people. These were reports from Rose's spies, and she knew them to be accurate.

"You are compromising everything we own, everything we've worked for. How can you do that, Maurice?"

"Life," he said wearily, "is full of compromises."

"But the debts. How can you pay? How can *we* pay?"

"A temporary setback, of no consequence."

"No consequence! Maurice, by my accounting you are one hundred and fifty thousand dollars in debt."

He bristled. "How do you know this? You've been spying on me. Who gave you the right to spy?"

"It is my business to find out."

Muttering, he went to the sideboard and poured himself a

whiskey. The hour of the day no longer mattered; Maurice lived in that constant half-light of alcoholic effect: not drunk, exactly, but not wholly sober, either. He used liquor to maintain what he thought was a margin of lucidity.

Rose watched him, thinking: You fool. You poor, dear, misguided fool. How good it could be, and good it has been. You have everything to make life pleasurable—charm, wit, urbanity. But it is not enough. Something, some tiny quirk of the mind, demands the impossible and drives you to self-destruction.

It could not go on. She would have to act. She knew what to do.

"Maurice, I am dissolving our partnership. You go your way, I'll go mine."

He drank off whiskey from a glass, grimaced, poured again. This, too, was unlike him. "Dissolving?" he said. "And how do you propose to do that?"

"The legal papers are drawn for me to assume full ownership of the Nocturne. I'm buying you out." The decision had come hard for her. Even now the words stuck in her throat. Strange, she thought, how we become attached to someone whose life intertwines with ours and remains so, even after the relationship has nothing more to offer. "It's the only thing I can do, Maurice."

He said nothing at first. He sat down and put his face into his hands. The little mantle clock, her mantle clock, chimed the early hour. A sunbeam stole through the blinds. Beyond the window a mockingbird split its throat in song.

"It's too late," he said.

Worry nudged at her. "What are you saying?"

"It's too late." He looked up, avoiding her eyes, and rubbed his hands slowly. He seemed to have aged in a minute. "I have signed over the Nocturne as surety for a note."

She could not move. All she could do was stand there in disbelief. It had been fifteen years since she came to Maurice's saloon, a young woman adrift. In those years they had built the Nocturne, she had built the Nocturne, into the most exclusive nightclub and brothel in America. Their fortunes were assured. And now . . .

"How much of a note, Maurice? How much did you sign over?"

He wiped a hand over his face. "I signed over everything, all of it, for one hundred and fifty thousand dollars." He looked at her squarely for the first time, his eyes beseeching. "They would kill me, Rose. I've known these men for years, longer than I've known you. They would kill me in the bat of an eye."

"You owed them money for gambling debts?"

"I owed them money . . . for gambling debts." He stood up nervously, almost eagerly, and began to pace. "But I can get it back, Rose. I know I can get it back. I can recoup. It's only a setback. I'm confident that with a little luck I can get it all back and more."

Rose turned away from him. She stood looking out onto the terrace in the morning light, listening to the sounds of birds. The center of her being was empty.

They came in the night six weeks later, four heavy men with hard eyes wearing suits and tall beaver hats. They pushed into the Nocturne at show time and took a table in the front. Rose knew who they were without asking, but the alarmed maître d' came to tell her: "Madame, they said to inform you that the new owners are here. What does that mean?"

"A joke, Eduardo. Some of Maurice's friends."

The maître d' bowed, but did not smile.

When the last customer had departed and they were preparing to close, the men still sat at the table, drinking heavily and shouting ribald jokes. Rose signaled the Nocturne's two bouncers to stand by and went over to the table. "Closing time, gentlemen."

"For who?" The speaker was a powerfully built man with silver hair, smoking a cigar. Wide-set, steely eyes looked her up and down. "For you, maybe. Not for us."

Rose beckoned for the two bouncers. The smiling giants ambled quietly across the room. Rose said: "No monkey business."

Another man at the table licked his lips nervously. "Mr. Craven, maybe we ought to . . ."

The silver-haired man motioned him to silence, reached into his belt, and drew out a double-barreled Deringer pistol.

The bouncers stopped walking.

Rose eyed the weapon. "Really, now, Mister . . ."

"Craven," the silver-haired man said. "Thackery Craven."

"This sort of thing is not necessary, Mr. Craven."

"I quite agree." He shoved the pistol back into his belt and pulled a folded paper from his inside coat pocket. "Your partner has sold us the Nocturne. We have come to take possession of the property." He flicked open the paper for Rose to see.

She read it with a sinking feeling. "This merely says that Maurice Rambeaux promises to turn over the property in the event of default. He has not defaulted, to my knowledge . . ."

As she spoke, someone entered the side door. She turned and saw Maurice standing in the lamplight, his face the color of death. "What is it, Rose?" he said.

Rose told him. Maurice rushed across the room and grabbed for the paper. "Craven, you bastard. You promised to give me time!"

"Time?" Craven's eyes opened with frank amusement. "You've had all the time we pledged, and more. Time is a luxury, Maurice, that the moneylender cannot afford."

"It was a gentlemen's agreement."

One of the bouncers said, "Miss Rose—?" She shook her head and motioned for them to leave the room. The two nodded and disappeared. With a scraping of chairs, Craven's men got up from the table.

Craven clapped Maurice on the shoulder. "Business is business, Rambeaux. Besides, we've known each other for a long time. Surely you didn't expect to welsh on the agreement?" He took Maurice's arm and steered him toward the office. "No, I knew you wouldn't welsh."

They went into the office and closed the door. Rose started to follow, but another man grasped her arm. "You stay here." She sat down uncomfortably, and the men settled back into their chairs around her, drinking and smoking in silence.

Angry voices sounded from the office. She could not understand what was being said from behind the heavy door, but Maurice was shouting. It went on for ten minutes. There was a scuffling and the sound of a falling chair. Rose jumped to her feet.

Three shots went off.

Rose and the men were up and running.

Gunsmoke hung in a blue haze in the office lamplight. Craven stood clutching his smoking Deringer. Maurice sprawled on the floor face down, his own pistol fallen from his hand. It, too, was smoking. "He tried to kill me," Craven said. "The son of a bitch tried to kill me!"

One shot from the Deringer had hit Maurice in the chest, the other pierced his left eye. He was quite dead.

For Rose, the days that followed had the bizarre quality of a surrealistic magic lantern show. Years later she would remember it

in fragments and flashes. Standing in the rain with a small group
of mourners, amid odors of crushed flowers, while a priest
chanted Latin and they lay Maurice into a stone vault above
ground. Returning to the empty apartment above the Nocturne
with young Brack at her side, and sitting alone through the
gathering shadows of that dismal afternoon. Giving way, for the
first time in her life, to a grief that bubbled up inside her in a
wailing misery. And, finally, confronting Thackery Craven in
widow's weeds, while the cold gray eyes probed at her body.

"You're ravishing in black, Rose Lark. God's blood, I could
take you right now. But it wouldn't be decent, with the dead not
even cold in the ground." He bit off the end of a cigar and
swung his boots onto the massive desk of carved wood that
Maurice had bought in Paris. "Actually, I'm giving you a choice,
Rose. You can stay here with me and continue to operate the
Nocturne, be my manager, so to speak, or"—he lit the cigar,
puffing up blue smoke, and shook out the match—"you can
move on."

"You did it deliberately," she said. "You goaded him, knowing
he had a gun. You murdered him."

Craven shrugged. "Suit yourself. You're as much of a witness
as anybody else who was there." He chuckled. "It's my word
against Rambeaux, and he is in no position to talk."

She had no money. Brack depended on her. The boy had gone
through all this with no show of feeling. Slender and dark, like
his father, he displayed almost a stoic indifference. If he cared
about the death of Maurice, it was buried deep inside him. There
were others who depended on her, too: the two young hostesses,
Beatrice and Sally.

"What shall we do, Miz Rose?" Sally asked, terrified. She
was a wide-eyed blond with silken skin and a generous bust. "I
couldn't sleep a wink last night, afraid that one of those men
would bust into our room."

"Patience, Sally. You too, Beatrice. We'll come up with
something."

Power is a fickle force. The death of Maurice Rambeaux and
the overnight change in ownership of the Nocturne put Bourbon
Street on edge. But the former friends of Rose Lark, even in the
streets and alleys of New Orleans, did not rush to her support
and succor. The Nocturne was, after all, a high-class brothel;
Rose Lark, or Maybelle, or whatever her real name, was a
madame. That she had been queen of the New Orleans madames

mattered little. That was yesterday, and today was today. And today, she was broke.

"Marsh, all I need is enough money to get back on my feet again, get a business started. You know I can do it."

"I'm sorry, Rose, but there have been a lot of expenses lately. Besides, I'm not sure Craven and his bunch will tolerate your competition. New Orleans is not a big town. No, there's not much good that I can do for you, Rose. But you do have my good wishes."

Good wishes. Good luck.

Then came word that Nathan Stewart was in New Orleans, on business!

She did not wear the rose-printed gown with the matching parasol to see Nathan. Nor did she do her flaming hair in flamboyant style or display lavish cleavage. She was discreet, subdued, quiet-spoken. They drank aperitif on the verandah of his hotel. Nathan's hair was streaked with gray, his sideburns were silver. The years had dug creases in his face, accentuating his maturity. Maybelle was impressed by her brother's sophistication and deep strength. But he did not fulfill the hopes that had brought her to him.

"You look well, Rose. Ravishingly beautiful, in fact. I'm astonished."

"Unfortunately, a woman does not improve with time as so many men do."

"There are exceptions."

"Please God, to be an exception."

He grew thoughtful. "Father disowned you, I suppose you were aware of that."

"No," she said. "I had not heard. It's been so long."

"He disowned you and forbade the mention of your name in the house."

Maybelle bit her lip. "That's his privilege."

"Don't you think you should try to make amends? He is an old man, Maybelle. He cannot live much longer."

"I'll have to think about it," she said.

"Anyway, it's good to see you again, good to know that you're alive and well. You're married, I presume?"

"No. That is, not really. I've been in business, so to speak. But my partner died recently. We had some serious reversals. Nathan, what I came to see you about is . . . I need help."

"Help?"

"I need money. A loan, to get back on my feet. Ten thousand dollars would do it."

Nathan frowned. "Well, I don't know if . . ."

"I'd pay you back, with good interest. Strictly a business arrangement."

His brows knit, and he was quiet for a time. The response was not what she expected. "Maybelle, I can certainly extend you some money. I'd be glad to do it. But not without certain conditions."

"Conditions?"

"I want you to go home and ask Father for forgiveness. It is the only way. You can't go on like this, an exile from the family."

"That's not your concern."

"It is my concern. I'm your older brother. Years ago, I defended you with Father. We had a row. But now, while I still don't agree with him, I understand him better. I have daughters too, now. I'm trying to do what's best for you, what's best for everybody. Believe me, you'd feel better about it."

Maybelle picked up a glass of water, feeling the need for something to occupy her hands. A nervous anxiety seemed to be eating at her. "Nathan," she said, "you don't understand."

"Ah, but I do. I understand quite well. You were a headstrong girl. You had to do things your way. We were all headstrong, except perhaps Burl—God rest his soul. As I say, I don't agree with Father's action; but he thought he was doing what was best, and he felt betrayed. Listen, Maybelle"—he leaned across the table and took her free hand—"I can give you money for passage home. For that matter, you can ride a Fulton-Livingston or a Stewart steamboat free. Once things are patched up with Father, you'll be entitled to share in the family's resources. Then you can find yourself a good, stable husband, settle down . . ."

Maybelle suddenly realized that the anxiety she had felt was not anxiety at all, but a rising anger. Suddenly she wanted to shout at him, to grab him and shake him, make him understand. "Nathan, for God's sake can't you get it into your thick skull? I'm me. I'm myself! Just because I'm a female, I'm no less me and myself than you are you! That's my right, my birthright. You can't take it away from me. Father can't take it away from me. I'm not a child any more, either. I am a full-grown woman, living my own life and making my own decisions." Other guests

on the verandah were staring, but she did not care. "Can't you
understand that, Nathan? Is it so impossible to understand?"

He looked uncomfortable. He smiled at her, a soft, patronizing
smile. It seemed to speak of the past, patronizing and filled with
certainty. "Maybelle, really now, must we go through all that?"

The rage welled up in her and spilled over. Dropping his hand,
she pushed back the chair and came to her feet. "Vanity!" she
shouted. "That's all that you can see, Nathan: your own blind
stupid male vanity. Well, you can keep your pocket change and
keep your lordly advice. I don't need either. And you can tell
Father, for me, to stick it! I'm sorry I came here at all. You're
smug and overbearing and"—grabbing up the glass, she threw
the water into his face—"despicable!" He was sputtering and
mopping his eyes when she walked out.

In the darkness just before dawn, she let herself into the office
of the Nocturne with her own key, opened the cashbox, and
emptied it of eight thousand dollars. Two hours later, accompanied by Brack and the hostesses, Beatrice and Sally, Maybelle
went to the waterfront and boarded the morning steam packet
bound upriver. As the sun came up, she stood on the afterdeck of
the *Heart of Kentucky* watching New Orleans slip away beyond
the flashing paddlewheels. It was September 12, 1831, as good a
day as any to start a new life. But her heart was heavy.
Something nagged at her mind from the talk with Nathan,
something he had said about their brother Burl. "God rest his
soul," Nathan had said. It was as one would speak of the dead.
Could it be that Burl was dead? And what about Stephen? He
had not spoken about Stephen at all. There had been no time.
Emotion, anger, all the old bugaboos about Father had gummed
up their encounter, cluttered the few precious moments together.

Well, so much for family. It didn't matter anyway, Maybelle
told herself. She was leaving New Orleans, leaving the past. And
she hated the Stewarts, hated them with every fiber of her being.

She hated them all.

XVI

From the *Boston Exponent*, June 23, 1832:

> Word has reached here that a serious outbreak of cholera
> has occurred in the vicinity of Toronto, Canada. Public
> health authorities report multiple deaths in outlying villages
> of Ontario Province. Travelers are warned that the scourge
> may be moving toward the northern United States.

"Get out of my way, ye damned canal hog! Move yer scow
over t' the side and let a packet through!"

"Move my eye! Wait yer turn, ye bloody speed demon. Can't
ye see that crowd o' boats ahead? There ain't enough locks to
pull us all through at once, so you ain't goin' nowhere until it's
time."

The loud bickering of the bargemen disturbed Nathan and his
guests. Irritated, he walked forward atop the low, rakish cabin of
his personal barge *Hudson Voyager*. "What is it, Mr. O'Keefe?"

"Ah, 'tis not worth your trouble, Mr. Stewart, sor. The fella
behind us, he's impatient to get into the Fives. Can't say as I
blame him, it's getting so bloody crowded on the Erie."

Nathan smiled and stood with the bargeman. O'Keefe was a
spunky fellow, all bone and muscle and Irish temper, but personable nonetheless and fine company on a drinking spree. He'd
been a bogtrotter during the construction days and followed
Nathan into the Montezuma Marshes. Afterward, like many of
the immigrants, he'd stayed to work the canal, now, in this early
summer of 1832, he was captain of the *Hudson Voyager*.

"A far cry from the old days, eh, Mr. O'Keefe?"

"Indeed it is, sor. Never thought I'd see so much traffic on this here canal. And they're all going to Ohio country and Michigan territory, to settle and open new land.''

"It's exciting times.''

The line of barges moved forward as they talked. They were going into the Lockport Fives, the great stepped system of locks on the western end of the Erie that went over the Niagara Escarpment. Nathan never tired of watching the hydraulic engineering marvel in operation. From the canal bank, a line was finally tossed to O'Keefe on the forward deck of the *Hudson Voyager*. When the bargeman tied off the rope, a youthful hoggy snickered his horse forward along the towpath, taking the strain. Nathan felt the barge slide forward into the yawning mouth of the first lock. As dripping stone walls enclosed them, the great back gates slid shut, the forward gates began to open and water surged into the enclosure from the next lock above. Gradually the barge lifted on the rising flood until it was level with the second lock. O'Keefe whistled for the towhorse to pull them forward again into the second lock. Again the watertight gate closed behind them. The process was repeated five times before they emerged into level canal at last and moved along at a steady four miles per hour with the plodding pace of the big towhorse.

Nathan returned to his guests. There were five men seated on the afterdeck, including old Robert Rosenfoert, the engineer Canvass White, and Nathan's old friend from England, Camden Willoughby, who had arrived on a tour of America. The Earl of Somerset was his ebullient self, having aged gracefully. His presence gave Nathan enormous pleasure.

"I say, Nathan, you Americans are going balmy over canals.''

Nathan laughed. "It's true, Camden. Canals are being dug everywhere. The Erie has started a real trend, with its tremendous success. We're trying to catch up with England.''

"Yes, and Nathan Stewart is general consultant on every project of any significance,'' Robert Rosenfoert chuckled. "Canal builders are almost superstitious about that. A project's got to have the Stewart touch.''

Nathan wagged his head. "Not really, Camden. What they want is the Erie expertise, and that means great engineers the likes of Jim Geddes, David Bates, Nathan Roberts, and Canvass White, here. Talent like that is rare.''

"Geddes and Roberts are working on the Pennsylvania Main Line now,'' Rosenfoert said. "She'll be more than six hundred miles long, from Pittsburgh to the Susquehanna River at Columbia, crossing two thousand feet of Allegheny mountain by portage rails.''

Indeed, they were balmy over canals, Nathan reflected. Raw earth was flying on new waterways that would link navigable rivers and open great expanses of territory virtually inaccessible before. Canals also would be the key to trade and prosperity. At this moment, three thousand men and fifteen hundred teams of horses labored to dig two canals in Ohio. One waterway extended for more than three hundred miles through that impoverished farm state, from the Ohio River to Lake Erie. As a measure of what it would achieve for the poor settlers—who grew wonderful crops and livestock, but had no way to get them to market—a two-dollar barrel of flour could be shipped by canal from southern Ohio to New York city, where it would sell for eight dollars. The cost of shipping: a dollar and eighty cents. When the Ohio canals were completed, a manufacturer would be able to ship his goods from New York state by water all the way to New Orleans . . .

"And how is the lovely Yvette?" Robert Rosenfoert was saying. "We miss her in New York."

"We decided it's more convenient to live in Syracuse during the summer," Nathan said. "This allows me to spend more time with her and the girls."

He begrudged the days and weeks away from Yvette, Francesca, and Marguerite. The girls were pretty, well-mannered children, bilingual in French and English. Yvette selected their governess carefully, as much for tutoring skills as child-rearing ability. Finally, she had insisted on bringing a governess from England. The arrangement was quite satisfactory.

"You're a lucky one, Nathan," Camden Willoughby said.

"Low bridge, everybody!" bawled O'Keefe from the bow. "Duck yer bonnets, gentlemen."

The Earl of Somerset muttered as another low span passed over them. "Dash it all, Nathan, I've lost count of these bloody things. How many bridges did you build over this canal?"

"Hundreds," said old Rosenfoert.

"A tactical necessity," explained Canvass White. The engineer had doffed his tall beaver hat and now dusted it lovingly with the sleeve of his coat. "No landowner was willing to let the canal come through his property unless we built him a bridge for people and cattle to cross over. So that's what we did. The budget, unfortunately, wouldn't allow anything above grade level. So this is what we had to come up with. Every once in a while a passenger gets beaned on the noggin.''

As the men chatted, Nathan found himself thinking again about Maybelle. She was still much on his mind, even after two years. The latest letter from the west was in his pocket. The man he'd hired to search for his sister reported no progress. He wondered if he was really searching at all; probably not. But at least the gesture salved Nathan's conscience a little.

He had failed Maybelle, and the thought tormented him. His sister had needed him badly, swallowed her pride, and come to him for help, and he'd refused to give it; refused on a pompous pretext that was not valid. Maybelle had been right, of course. It was not Nathan's business to force her return to Pittsburgh to beg forgiveness of a father whose stiff-necked attitude had caused her so much misery in the first place. Our parents, despite the Biblical requirement to honor them, were not perfect. The memory of Maybelle's fury came back to haunt him. ''Vanity!'' she had cried. ''That's all you can see!'' And it had been true.

Immediately afterward he had tried to find Maybelle. But it took time, time to discover that she was not Maybelle Stewart in New Orleans but Rose Lark, queen of the Nocturne bordello; time to go there himself and be surprised by the elegance and order of the place. He had never seen a brothel before and walked into this one nervously, sister or no sister. And finally, it took time to piece together the tragic details of her partner's dissolute behavior, his loss of the business and his death at the hands of the man known as Thackery Craven. Nathan had met Craven and disliked him on the spot, especially when he accused Maybelle of stealing eight thousand dollars. ''We'll find her, Mr. Stewart. And I promise you, when we do . . .'' Nathan, in a burst of anger, had slammed the man against the wall and threatened to break him in half if others interfered. Then he wrote out a check for eight thousand and stuffed it into Craven's pocket. ''There. There's your blood money!'' But it all took time. And when he'd scoured the city for Maybelle, it was too late. She was gone on a steamer upriver; and that could mean anywhere. Now, he watched a flock of wild birds wheeling over the last westward mile of the Erie Canal and thought: Take care of yourself, little sister. Wherever you are.

As the town of Buffalo slid past the barge on both sides, a young hoggy driving a mule bedecked with ribbons piped up in a fine Irish tenor:

> *"I got a mule and her name is Sal,*
> *Fifteen miles on the Erie Canal . . ."*

The plague drifted southward out of Canada as silently as the air, invisible, undetectable. Indeed, there were those who insisted that it was a miasma, born of foul zephyrs. Others saw it as a visitation of God's wrath upon a world of lust and sin. Whatever the cause, the spread was virulent, the transmission devastatingly swift. One moment the air was clear and life ordinary; the next . . .

A young fisherman at the town of Black Rock, near Buffalo, complained of a sudden knifelike pain in his stomach. It was a Sunday. He went to church anyway. As the minister opened his sermon, based on the text of Second Timothy, a shriek shattered the morning calm. Shocked mmbers of the congregation saw the fisherman tumble from his pew into the center aisle, doubled over and clutching his stomach. His body began to writhe and twitch. His eyes rolled back in his head. His mouth opened with another shriek. He jerked spasmodically. His mouth erupted in a fountain of black vomit.

By midafternoon the word rippled through the village and surrounding countryside. Cholera.

Nathan Stewart and Camden Willoughby arrived in Buffalo ten days later from the south, after a three-week inspection tour of the Ohio canal diggings. It had been a season of persistent rainfall. The streets of Buffalo were filled with mud and filth. A strong odor of burning tar lay over the town, and smoke from smudge fires curled into a sky the color of slate. Nathan pushed into the Erie Canal office to speak to the manager. "What the hell's happening here, Mr. Fink?"

"Oh, it's dreadful, Mr. Stewart, just dreadful. I'm afraid we've got an outbreak of cholera."

"Cholera!"

"There's half a dozen sick and two dead. It's spreading all along the lakeshore and inland, too. The authorities tried to keep it quiet at first. They said too much publicity would be bad for business and might discourage barge traffic into Buffalo. Finally,

Dr. Burgey put his foot down and made a public announcement. That was two days ago. People are terrified, and the trustees are ready to ride Dr. Burgey out on a rail."

Nathan left Fink and made straight for the office of Dr. Burgey, trailed by Camden Willoughby. The small clinic was packed with anxious people, and the physician was issuing instructions. "Now, folks, try not to panic. Panic doesn't do anybody any good. My advice is to boil your drinking water and make sure that the food you eat is clean. We don't have much in the way of medication . . ."

As Nathan stood in the back of the crowd listening, the door opened and the chairman of the town board of trustees walked in, followed by several leading citizens. The chairman was a hardware merchant and owner of several freight barges on the Erie Canal. Angrily, he interrupted Burgey. "Doctor, this thing has gone far enough. You're spreading fear among these good folks. Do you have any idea what this can do to commerce?"

"At the moment, gentlemen, commerce is not my concern," the doctor retorted. "Saving lives is."

"Merchants are closing their businesses, doctor. There's a terrific rush of people to the canal, getting out of town. If this keeps on, nobody will want to come into Buffalo from the east, and the entire summer season will be ruined. Traffic on the canal will stop. Business will suffer. The reputation of our town will suffer. And it will be your fault!"

Nathan had heard enough. He shouldered through the crowd to the doctor's side. "I quite agree with Dr. Burgey. The important thing right now is to prepare for a possible epidemic. The plague is not something to be trifled with, and even the possibility of it spreading must take priority . . ."

"And who are you, sir?" thundered the merchant.

"Nathan Stewart." He nodded briskly, accepting the murmur of recognition. "And I guarantee you that if need be, we'll shut down the canal."

A ripple of surprise went through the crowd. Someone gasped, "Shut down the canal!" The chairman started to speak again, thought better of it and hedged. "Well, Mr. Stewart, if you really think . . ."

"I really think." Nathan turned to Dr. Burgey. "Now, doctor, what can we do to help?"

The physician's eyes expressed his thanks. "To begin with, Mr. Stewart, we can start getting this town properly organized."

For the next two weeks, Nathan and Camden Willoughby took the lead to organize Buffalo to meet the plague. Supplies of food and medicines had to be gathered. The board of trustees organized a special guard force, designated the almshouse as an emergency hospital, hired nurses, and enlisted volunteers to help Dr. Burgey. Even as they worked, the plague worsened. Nathan dispatched messengers to warn communities inland along the canal. As the number of deaths increased in Buffalo, Black Rock, and other nearby settlements, a bargeman arrived from the east with an urgent message. "Mr. Stewart, sor, there's been a bad outbreak o' the plague east of here, and it's done got clear to Syracuse."

"Syracuse! Yvette and the children are in Syracuse. Camden, I must go!"

"I'll go with you," Camden Willoughby said.

On a normal run he could make Syracuse in four days, including the slow navigation of the Lockport Fives and laying over during the nights. To speed the journey now, Nathan hired a two-horse team. The young hoggy, inspired by the importance of his fare and the generosity of the tip, came out of the Lockport Fives slapping his horses gradually into a trot. The *Hudson Voyager*, a sleek vessel with a sharp prow, raised a forbidden wake as it sliced along at five miles an hour. But the speed did not last. After a scant ten miles, canal traffic ahead of them thickened and slowed. The smell of burning tar pots again was heavy on the air as villages lay in the grip of crisis. More and more barges were tying up along the berm, refusing to venture farther east. At last, even Nathan's hoggy, a strong, blond youth tanned by sun and wind, stopped his horses at the village of Albion.

"Sorry, sor. I can't take ye no farther."

Camden tried to change the boy's mind. "Look, lad, we'll pay you well. Mr. Stewart has got to get to Syracuse." Stubbornly, the hoggy shook his head. "It's the plague, sor. The farther along we go the worse it gets. Bargemen say folks is dyin' like flies up ahead."

Nathan bought the team, paying the hoggy one hundred dollars. The price was exorbitant in normal times, but fair enough now. Then Nathan and Camden took turns on the towpath, driving the horses at a steady walking gait. At Rochester, however, they were stopped at the toll office by a nervous pathmaster carrying a holstered pistol. A crudely lettered sign announced: "Canal Closd to Eastbownd Traffik." Even Nathan's special Letter of Passage failed to budge the man.

"I'm sorry, Mr. Stewart. I got my orders from Albany. There ain't supposed to be no more traffic from the west. People is afraid the boats will bring more cholery."

"That doesn't make sense, man. The plague's worse in the east than it is in the west."

Doggedly, the official stood his ground, even logic failing to shake his stubborn resolve. Nathan moved as if to turn away, but then he stepped swiftly to the pathmaster's side and snatched the pistol from its holster. The weapon was empty and rusty with age. He handed it back to the man, who suddenly had become white with fear. "Please don't hurt me, sor. I'm only doing me duty."

"I'm not going to hurt you. But we are going through. Camden, whip up the horses."

For protection, Nathan always carried a brace of pistols and two rifles in the *Hudson Voyager*. Now he took the weapons from their lockers and loaded them. When he stepped onto the towpath to take his turn with the horses, he carried a rifle and had a pistol stuck into his belt.

Armed men prowled villages and outlying settlements. Berm and towpath were lined with marooned packets, freighters, excursion craft, and penny-a-mile immigrant boats, roped to pegs and trees. Some barges were abandoned, others guarded by nervous men ready to shoot anyone who came near.

"All right, mister, you've come far enough."

Nathan reined in the horses and stared into the muzzles of three rifles. In gathering twilight, the men stepped out from behind a shed at the outskirts of Newark. They wore plumed and sashed uniforms of the local Masonic Lodge.

"Just hitch yer team to the other end o' that there cholera boat and take it back where you come from, mister."

"There's no cholera on this boat," Nathan said, "and we're on official canal business. So stand aside and let us through." He spoke with bravado, but silently cursed himself for being caught unprepared, rifle slung to his shoulder and pistol in its belt.

"You ain't comin' through Newark, mister, we don't care who you are."

"Got any camphor on the boat?" another man asked. "We're all out of camphor here."

"No. We carry no medical supplies of any kind."

The leader, a big-stomached man with triple chins beneath a scraggly growth of whiskers, waved his rifle menacingly. "We told you to turn around and git. So git!"

"I don't think we will." Camden Willoughby spoke coolly from the *Hudson Voyager*. The Englishman's head barely cleared the top of the cabin as he crouched behind it. His rifle was aimed at the bearded man's belly. "Now I say drop your weapons."

There was momentary confusion. Nathan stepped behind the team and brought the pistol out of his belt. A shot went off from the uniformed group, spurting flame in the dusk. Camden's rifle spoke. The fat leader grunted and sagged, clutching his thigh. Nathan lashed the horses forward, straining against the barge. As the leader fell, dropping his weapon, his two companions scattered, firing wildly. Nathan charged the nearest man, caught a fleeting glimpse of a chalk-white face and brought down the barrel of his pistol, hard. The man buckled beneath the blow, streaming blood. The third man pulled the trigger of an ancient horse pistol, but the hammer snapped empty. He flung the weapon aside and took to his heels through the brush. Nathan kicked the fallen weapons into the canal and followed the horses down the towpath. Moments later they were around a bend and out of sight.

Fifty hours after leaving Buffalo, sleepless and bone tired and driving horses that were ready to drop, they pulled into Syracuse.

A sticky heat bore down beneath cloudy skies. Heavy rains had flooded the muddy streets with raw sewage and filth. Columns of smoke rose from the ever-present tarpots. Wagons lurched and rocked along laden with raw wooden coffins and bodies in winding sheets. There was a stench of corruption and death. Nathan almost collided with a walking apparition wearing funereal black and a stovepipe hat. The man intoned in a voice that might have come from the grave, "Repent. Repent. Oh ye of the mortal damned, ye sinners, repent!" He stepped aside and let the man pass. Churchbells tolled. Clots of people prayed in the streets. Wretched human beings sat along curbstones in abject misery: men, women, and children, faces etched in despair or already showing traces of sickness, with pale, pasty skin and staring eyes. A woman slumped over. Profiteers sold quack remedies at curbside stands and from wagon beds, or hawked cheap coffins and winding sheets and burial quicklime. Chloride of lime bubbled in streetcorner vats, giving off noxious fumes.

"Phew!" said Camden, holding a handkerchief to his nose. "What is *that?*" He pointed to a line of shanties which had been newly moved into a flat field. Behind them a narrow two-story frame building brooded on a rise above Fayette Street. The air here was putrid. A sign on the building said, Thompson's Herbalist Institute.

Nathan plucked at the sleeve of a passerby and asked about the building. The man glanced nervously toward it. "That's the Institute. They're bringin' the sick people there. It's the law. And them shacks is for the overflow."

"Overflow? Is it that bad?"

"Mister, it's hell." Quickly the man scuttled away.

Nathan's new house was the most elegant in Syracuse. He had built it in a grove of towering elm and maple trees, commanding a fine view of the canal. Broad stone steps led up to a front porch that swept across the entire front of the house. Now he took the steps two at a time, flung open the front door and shouted, "Yvette! Yvette!"

A woman came hurrying down the great carpeted stairway in a flurry of gray and white. It was the governess, Mrs. Stone. "Oh, Mr. Stewart, thank the Lord you're home!"

He looked expectantly toward the head of the stairs. "Where is Yvette? Where's my wife?"

The governess burst into tears. "She's—she's—Oh, dear me, Mr. Stewart. It's terrible, just terrible."

A small figure in a blue pinafore came down the stairs. Francesca. "Father!" She ran to him with arms outstretched. He gathered her up in a hug.

"Where's your mother, Francesca?"

The child looked at him with doleful eyes. "Mother got sick, and they came and took her away."

Nathan felt a wrenching in his stomach. He turned and found Camden behind him, openmouthed. Mrs. Stone burst into a fresh paroxysm of sobs. Nathan snapped: "Stop it, woman! For God's sake, get hold of yourself and tell me what happened. Where is my wife?"

"She—she's at the Institute, Mr. Stewart. She got ill all of a sudden, chills and fever and vomiting. It was the cholera, they said. I nursed her as best I could and sent for the doctor. But these men came instead and said she had to go to the Institute, that all the sick was being taken there. It was required by the health authorities. I tried to stop 'em, Mr. Stewart. And Mrs.

Yvette, she didn't want to go, but was too sick to protest. They took her day before yesterday.''

"Has anybody been to see her, you or any of our friends?"

The good woman shook her head. "It's not allowed. Nobody's allowed inside the Institute except the doctors and nurses and all. They're afraid to spread the plague."

As she spoke, Nathan was going out the door. "Take care of the children, Mrs. Stone," he shouted. "I'm going to her."

Camden Willoughby fell into step beside him.

At the front door of the Institute, a burly man with a pistol strapped to his middle tried to bar their way. But this was Syracuse, and Nathan Stewart would not be denied. The town's physician, Dr. Clyde Varone, ordered the visitors to be admitted. Varone had often been a guest in Nathan's home and had met Camden Willoughby when the Englishman first arrived. Now the physician showed the ravages of crisis. He was unshaven, his clothing soiled with chemicals and flecks of refuse, his face sagging from fatigue. An assistant had died last week; another was ill. He led them through an outer hallway, seemingly oblivious of the powerful odors—a mixture of putrid stench and camphor.

There came to Nathan's ears a mournful humming sound, like a pervasive orchestrated dirge. His mind tried to identify it, but could not.

"I must warn you, Nathan, that what you're about to see is something beyond your wildest nightmares. We are absolutely and utterly overwhelmed. The few nurses I've managed to find—good women, dedicated—are drooping in their tracks. We don't even have personnel to mop the floors and carry out the dead. I've placed Yvette in a little corner room where there's some privacy, and I look to her needs personally, as much as I can. But frankly"—he paused, as if unable to think clearly for an instant under a crushing onslaught of weariness—"frankly we're losing every other patient, some of them more quickly than others."

"How is my wife?"

"You'll see for yourself shortly."

A strange anxiety seized him. In order to keep it in check, Nathan tried to engage in small talk. "What kind of medicines do you have?"

"Not much, I'm afraid. A friend of mine brought two nitrous oxide machines from Albany." They walked into a hallway. A set of double doors flew open, and a woman hurried out in the gray smocklike garb that identified her as a nursing assistant. Her ears and nostrils were plugged with cotton, and she wore a gauze mask over her mouth. Dr. Varone reached to a shelf and took down a wad of cotton, two masks and two glass vials. "We have camphor for the odors. The nitrous oxide gas seems to be somewhat effective against the cholera miasmas, but we don't really know that. It doesn't cure, but it helps to relieve the suffering in the early stages. We've been able to bleed people and pack their bodies in warm salt. Again, I can't tell you precisely what that does. Many are curable, though, if we can catch them early enough, before the onset of chills. We've got opium for the pain and iodine for treatment of those cases in the throes of collapse. Other than that . . ."

Dr. Varone handed them the cotton and the vials. "The cotton is for plugging your nostrils and ears. This vial contains vinegar. Before you go into the patients' area, wet down your hands and arms with this. Be sure to use it as a wipe if your skin comes into contact with anyone. This other vial contains hartshorn. Breathe its vapor if you think you're about to vomit."

"About to vomit?"

"You'll see what I mean."

Dr. Varone pushed open the double doors, and they walked through.

Nathan winced. The stench struck him like a blow, so powerful that even with cotton wadding in his nostrils he almost gagged. The sound was a cacophony of groans, cries, and shrieks. And the sight . . .

There were bodies everywhere. They lay in large boxlike frames filled with straw, two to a box, with no distinction between old and young, male or female. Most of the straw beds were covered with a coarse fabric or old blankets. Patients lay in their own vomit and excrement. Eyes stared from their sockets, and bodies were wracked with sudden, bone-jarring chills. Even the floor was covered with foul-smelling sludge.

They walked through a cavernous, high-ceilinged area that had been a lecture hall of the Herbal Institute, passing between wall-to-wall rows of the boxlike beds. Some living patients lay with those who were obviously dead. The doctor paused to draw a blanket over the waxen face of a young girl. "I'm sorry, my dear," he murmured. "We did our best for you."

Nurses and volunteers moved about on leaden feet, their eyes glazed with fatigue.

"Who was the young lady, doctor," Camden Willoughby asked.

Dr. Varone sighed. "She was one of our nurses." He opened a side door and led them into a small room containing several cots.

Yvette lay under the window, shivering beneath a blanket. Her eyes were closed. A small stand beside the cot bore a pitcher of water, a vial of brandy, cotton swabs. A shiver passed through her, and she moaned through clenched teeth.

"Nathan," the doctor said softly, "I'm afraid you have arrived just in time."

He knelt clumsily by the cot, cradling her head in his arm. Her eyelids fluttered open. The eyes seemed even larger now, brown and luminous and shining with fever. They blinked in recognition, and she tried to smile. The oval face was drawn and pale, and there was a rattle in her throat.

"Darling," she whispered.

He blinked and looked away, wiping his eyes. Camden was standing behind him, and he was vaguely aware of his presence. A great, insoluble lump formed in his throat, constricting his speech. His mind fought for control, found it. He looked back at her, his face showing no emotion. "You're a bit under the weather," he said. "Dr. Varone says that you . . ."

She shook her head, silencing him. The parched lips opened, and her speech came in a rattle of sound. "I'm dying, my love."

Nathan's head drooped. He put his face upon her chest. One of her hands came up and stroked his hair as lightly as a falling leaf. Her voice strengthened.

"I've loved you so much. I'm the luckiest of women, to love a man this way and have his children. Have I been a good wife, Nathan?"

"You're a wonderful wife. A wonderful, wonderful wife."

She sighed. "That's nice, *Cherie*. I knew that Lucy . . ."

He tried to lift his head, to remonstrate, but she restrained him with the softest of touch.

"No. Let me speak. I knew that Lucy loved you too, and I am sure that other women did. But even that did not matter, as long as I could share your life, be with you. I just thank you, Nathan, for loving me too . . ."

She grew quiet then. The afternoon faded into evening. He held her in his arms, bathed her forehead with the tepid water, gave her sips of it. And finally the window was but a luminous square and her face a pale oval bathed in its dimming light.

He reached under the blanket and touched her feet. They were cold. Her legs were growing cold. He wanted to protest: No. No, stop! It's too soon, too soon! But the cold spread through her limbs, and the dusk deepened.

The brown eyes opened. He could barely see them now. The breath was a soft, gurgling sigh. He heard a whisper in the darkness, so soft that he had to put his ear to her lips to hear.

"I will never leave you," the lips said. "I shall always be with you. I love . . ."

The breathing stopped.

The silence was immense.

The lips grew cold.

And finally, long afterward, a hand touched his shoulder. The voice of Camden Willoughby came to him out of the darkness.

"Come, Nathan. It's time to go home."

He let Camden lead him away, like a child, through the rooms of the dying and the stench and the groans, through the hallway with its staring faces filled with infinite sadness, and out into the night of flickering torches and the odor of smoking tar—the night, with its soft and sheltering darkness.

Only then did the sobs wrack him.

XVII

"All hands stand to to witness punishment!"

A raw wind lashed out of the north over the Liverpool docks. Beneath the glistening hull of the brig *Helen*, the harbor heaved and chopped on a gray wash. The dawn sky was somber and flecked with ragged cloud. Captain Stewart Grant scanned the horizon with a frown. "Dirty weather, Mr. Thorne." He was anxious to put to sea, to be free of the land when the gale struck. "A day, maybe two, I fancy."

The bucko mate, Thorne, sniffed the heavy air. "Aye, sir, every bit o' that."

Running feet pounded on the deck and up companion ladders. "Avast, ye packet rats, get a move on!" bawled Thorne. Sailors in black leather hats and shapeless uniforms with short pea coats mustered into loose ranks. The captain, tall and stern-faced, his black beard streaked with silver, watched them without expression. They were a scurvy lot, not like the proud Cape Codders who'd manned the *Shark,* he mused. But with Mr. Thorne riding their tails and the lash laying on the backs of troublemakers, they functioned well enough, even if most of them did sign on shanghaied. He sensed the eyes flicking at him nervously and knew what they were thinking; he knew what they whispered in the fo'csle. There was no more demanding captain on the Black Ball line than Stewart Grant, quick to punish but also quick to reward. Mutinous mariners had the fight taken out of them soon enough; but when the *Helen* made the Liverpool run from New York in an unbelievable seventeen days, a full week off the average time, the captain had shared his bonus with the packet rats and given them all shore leave to go spend it. Small wonder the *Helen* was the fastest on the line.

"All right, bring him up," Thorne snapped.

A steel-grated hatch cover clanged open. Two men jerked out a sailor roped hand and foot and stood him in front of Thorne. The man's face bore the breaks and scars of many dockside brawls, and his eyes were filled with hatred. For all that, Captain Grant knew him for a hard-working man aboard ship, and none was better at clinging to a spar to bend sail in the teeth of an ice storm.

The bucko mate glared at the miscreant. "Jack Farr, ye been found guilty of fightin' in the fo'csle o' this ship and speakin' disrespectful to a superior officer, namely me. Ye been sentenced to twelve lashes on yer bare back and a dipping."

Thorne stepped back and nodded. They dragged Farr back to the hatch cover, stripped him to the waist, and tied him down. Thorne shook out the lash and rolled up his sleeve. The muscles bulged in his right arm. When ready, the bucko mate looked to Captain Grant.

"Proceed," the captain said.

The lash whistled in the cold air. By the third stroke, blood flecked from the naked back. By the fifth, the lash marks oozed, by the tenth, blood dripped onto the freshly holystoned deck, and by the twelfth, bits of skin were starting to come off. Farr writhed under the strokes, gritting his teeth, but made no outcry.

When it was done, he merely stared like a brute awaiting the next phase of his punishment.

Now they jerked him up by the arms and dragged him to the port gangway. A line hung down from a pulley block lashed to the main yardarm high overhead. Farr's feet were secured to the dangling rope. At Thorne's command, a gang of sailors snatched the man aloft, head down, and he swung over the side. They dropped him from a height of fifteen feet. Headfirst, his bound body plunged into the murky harbor. Then he was hauled aloft again, sputtering, swung back on deck, and taken below, where they sloshed his raw back with brine. His shriek knifed through the ship.

"Punishment concluded, Captain," Thorne announced.

"Very well. Dismiss!"

Captain Grant returned to the quarterdeck. He had a thousand details to attend to in preparation for sailing, and the punishment had been an unwelcome interruption. Its necessity was unquestioned, however, for the Black Ball packets were a harshly demanding service, requiring the utmost in performance of wind, wood, sail, and human spirit. For eighteen years now, in fair weather and foul since 1817, three-masted brigs bearing the great black sphere on their fore-topsails had kept to regularly scheduled service between New York and Liverpool. Emphasis was on speed, speed, and more speed, so that even in the hardest blow, the packet spread as much sail as possible. Men toiled on the yards in weather that on any normal merchant vessel would be regarded only as emergency risk. It was not the sort of duty that sailors took willingly, and so the crews came from waterfront fleshpots and saloons, a teeming riffraff of many tongues recruited largely by professional procurers, the crimps. If a fresh hand was carried aboard ship in an unconscious state, then that was his bad fortune. And the belaying pin laid against the side of the head quieted the most ardent protest.

"Steerage passengers arriving, Captain."

"Very well, Mr. Thorne."

A large crowd of people was gathering on the dock. Men, women, and children carried their worldly goods in boxes, bales, and suitcases. Captain Grant strode to the port side and watched them. As usual, some had relatives and friends who had come to see them off, and there were tearful embraces and farewell hugs. The poor devils didn't know what they were in for, jammed for a month in the dark, airless confines below decks.

They paid twenty dollars a head for the privilege and brought their own food. They'd be wedged into small, hard bunks and subject to every discomfort. And with foul weather likely, this trip would be worse than most.

"How many, Mr. Thorne?"

"Nearly three hundred, sir."

"I was afraid of that. And the first class?"

"Thirty-five, sir."

Three hundred in steerage, thirty-five in the privileged cabin class. What a difference it made to have money! The first class passengers paid a hundred and twenty-four dollars for all amenities, including private cabins, abundant and frequent meals, and plentiful wine.

"Lower the gangway, if you please."

"Aye, sir. Lower the gangway!"

The dock mob moved in a body to the side of the ship. With a final flurry of hugs and tears, they began filing up the sloping gangway onto the deck, some with babes in arms or leading small children by the hand. It took more than an hour for them all to come aboard and descend the steep companionway into the hold. Captain Grant himself followed them down. As usual, there was a great fumbling and bumping in the crowded gloom, amid odors of bilgewater and dampness. Already quarrels had broken out over the selection of bunks and living areas. Thorne bellowed for silence. When the last voice was stilled, except for a few fretting babies, Captain Grant spoke.

"Ladies and gentlemen, you have booked passage in steerage aboard the *Helen*. As you know, this is the fastest, most modern transatlantic service afloat. Black Ball packets have been in service for eighteen years without interruption and have carried tens of thousands of people between Liverpool and New York. Our record for safety is without equal at sea. I must advise you, however, that since you have chosen to make your journey in January, the weather most likely will be severe. The voyage from Liverpool to New York is against prevailing winds, sailing "uphill" we call it. The average sailing time for a packet in that direction is thirty-eight days. Coming from the other direction, from America to Liverpool, the wind is at our backs and we make it in twenty-four days. I intend to land you in New York within the average sailing time, or better..."

He was interrupted by a sprinkle of applause. Looking over

the crowd, he noticed that one young woman was heavily pregnant. He made a mental note of the fact.

"As I told you, the weather may be severe. Storms are quite frequent this time of year. If that occurs, all hatches will be battened down for your safety and the safety of the ship. There will be a lot of seasickness and discomfort. So it is extremely important that you cooperate with one another and try to avoid conflict."

Five minutes later, Captain Grant ascended the companionway and emerged gratefully into the clear air of the deck. He despised the dark confinement of steerage, for it reminded him harshly of another ship and another time. Few captains even bothered to speak to steerage passengers at all. But because of old memories, he had never failed to perform this task in ten years of command. From now on, however, all of his dealings would be with first class passengers, who were now arriving on the dock.

They came to the after-gangway in carriages, many of them attended by liveried footmen and servants who brought expensive luggage aboard. In contrast to the somber humor of the steerage mob, the mood now was gay and festive. The captain changed into a fresh uniform, with gold braid and brass buttons, and went to the gangway to greet each passenger stepping onto the deck. There was a nobleman or two, a doctor, several wealthy merchants, a shipping magnate, an American ironmonger. Last to board was an attractive, shapely woman whose presence caused sailors to pause in their work, staring. She was attended by a retinue of servants who carried aboard an unbelievable amount of luggage from a gleaming coach-and-four bearing a crest. Captain Grant took the soft gloved hand, sensing its warmth, and looked into a pair of violet eyes.

"Lady Kimberly Wyneheath," someone announced.

"Welcome aboard, Lady Kimberly. I'm Captain Stewart Grant."

"Captain."

"Charming."

As Lady Kimberly and a maid moved toward the state-room reserved for most-important passengers, the captain rejected an impulse to turn and look. Such females spelled trouble, and Stewart Grant's warning instincts were aroused. He had not become involved in a romantic entanglement for years. He did not intend to go back to his old ways at this late date.

The *Helen* slipped her moorings with the outgoing tide and

stood out from Liverpool on a spanking cold breeze. By noon she was clear of the headland and laboring, decks aslant, through the deep swells of a restless sea. That evening, Captain Grant joined the first class passengers for the traditional captain's dinner. He was disturbingly aware of Lady Kimberly, who wore a mauve sheath garment that set off the swell of full, firm breasts and rounded thighs beneath a tiny, tucked-in waist. She gave off the scent of costly, musklike perfume. He consciously avoided the violet eyes and kept up a general conversation. The American ironmonger had sailed with him before. "Ladies and gentlemen," he said, "we are fortunate to have in command of our vessel the outstanding captain of the Black Ball line. Captain Stewart Grant"—the ironmonger raised his wineglass—"is a living legend." A lurch of the ship caused the wine to spill, spreading a blood-colored stain on the gleaming white table-cloth.

Even as the meal progressed, Captain Grant was aware of the movements of the vessel. Every creak of timber and slap of sail had meaning for him. Now, the movements of the *Helen* caused his second sense to come alert. Even before dessert was served by a uniformed steward, he murmured his apologies and left the table. Drawing on a heavy rainslicker and boots, he stepped out on deck.

The bucko mate, Thorne, was the officer of the watch. Captain Grant eyed the straining canvas overhead and felt the wallow of the deck beneath his feet.

"Sea's rising," he said.

"Aye, sir, that it is. I think we're in for a blow."

The *Helen* slid off into a steep trough and came up against a large comber, smashing her prow in a shower of spray. Rain pelted the deck, causing Captain Grant to shrug down into the slicker. The cold seemed to be deepening.

"You're right, Mr. Thorne, we're in for a blow."

The storm struck them on the third day at sea.

A watery sunlight came through in the morning hours, but the wind gusted steadily stronger from astern, billowing the sails and slapping ratlines. The following sea was a bilious gray-green capped by froth. As the hours passed, the sun vanished behind thickening cloud masses, and the wind had a cutting edge, lashing the rain as it gradually turned to sleet. The mood of the sea darkened. Swells piled ever higher with scummy, scudding froth. Gusts sharpened. The *Helen* wallowed drunkenly from trough to trough, pitching and rolling. Lookouts aloft clung more grimly to their perches while their mates below crossed themselves, hoping not to be sent into the rigging. Vain hope.

"Take in the fore-topgallants, Mr. Thorne. Reef the mizzen."

"Sir. Hands aloft! Take in fore-topgallants! Lively, lads!"

Into the rain and sleet they climbed, swarming up the ratlines barefoot. The squalls strengthened as a sickly twilight spread across the sea. The *Helen* labored in mountainous swells as the night settled in quickly. Rain swept the decks with wild, lashing blows.

"Strap me into the deck chair, Mr. Thorne."

"Aye, sir. You men, give me a hand with the captain!"

The chair had been bolted permanently to the quarterdeck and was built of solid oak. They lashed him into it using stout lengths of line. The helmsman nearby was also lashed to his wheel.

By midnight the waves roared down upon them with massive force, sweeping the *Helen* onto their crests where she balanced for a sickening instant in time and space before plunging into the next abyss. Frequently, waves broke across the decks in torrents of black water. Men grabbed frantically at stays and ropes to avoid being swept overboard.

Below, all hell broke loose. In pitch darkness, frail souls clung to beams and stanchions, weeping, praying, and vomiting. Chests, drums, barrels, and general cargo broke loose and went flying through the steerage like projectiles. Water cans smashed. The hold became a great welter of people, crockery, plates, spilled sugar, coffee, pottery, tea, wet clothing, sides of salted beef and pork. Women screamed and children cried, their voices engulfed in the groaning, creaking, howling fury of the storm. Seasick and hurled about, suffocating in the fetid air, they were as insects in the grip of a maelstrom.

Abovedecks, the hours wore on in unrelenting misery. Walls of icy water crashed over the decks. The lashed helmsman fought each breasting wave and plunging trough. Stewart Grant remained in his deck chair, monitoring his sails, feeling his ship, noting the changes. Time and again he snapped orders that sent Thorne's voice bellowing into the gale and drenched packet rats swarming into the tops.

"Take in your topgallant studding sails! Haul down and clew up!"

They took in studding sails, furled the main, jib, and mizzen.

The ship eased off, taking the squalls, the decks at thirty-five degree slant. "Clew up the fore and main topgallant sails! Let go topsail halyards!"

Finally, mercifully, it began to ease. The wind gradually abated; the swells and troughs became less precipitous; the rain subsided. But gusts and squalls persisted until the fourth day of storm. At last, in the late afternoon, the *Helen* again rolled rhythmically through moderate seas, and the cloud masses broke apart to let through a magnificent burst of sunlight. Hatches were thrown open, and the miserable masses kicked and fought their way up onto the deck, to lift their arms to the heavens and breath deeply of cold, clear air. The captain ordered men below with mops and buckets to clean as best they could. Then, suddenly remembering, he himself went below.

The stench of vomit and excrement struck him like a blow. Again the old memories surged back. "Mr. Thorne, tell those men to lay on with water and mops. We've got to clean this filth!" He picked his way through shattered cargo and soggy piles of clothing.

She lay on a bunk in the after-section, a stub of candle flickering at her side. An old woman was with her. The old woman looked up as the captain approached.

"The baby?" he said.

The old woman broke into a toothless smile, reached into the bunk, and brought out a wiggling bundle that broke into a lusty squall. The captain looked down at the young mother. Her face was gaunt, but she returned his smile.

"Congratulations, mother. And what have you named your baby?"

"Helen," she whispered. "I'm calling her Helen."

"Good. As soon as you can, then, I want you and the baby to move topside for the remainder of the voyage. We'll find cabin space for you in first class."

An hour later he collapsed on his bunk and slept. He did not awaken until dawn of the following day.

The man had a solitude about him, a deep strength. No captain was more demanding, they said. Men stood in awe of him. And Lady Kimberly Wyneheath knew that a woman's response was much like that, too, but with a powerful physical reaction as well. Her inquiries were discreet, seemingly offhand. She even managed to draw a few words from an elderly, taciturn seaman who'd served for nearly a decade on the packets. "A strange one, Captain Grant," he muttered. "I've heard tales about the man that you wouldn't dare repeat. Sailor talk." What kind of tales? The old mouth snapped shut over a stub of pipe.

But Captain Grant was more than mystery. His superb seamanship consistently set such standards for the Black Ball line that owners of hotly competitive rival packets—the Blue Swallowtail, the Red Star, the Black X—tried to woo him over with offers of a share of profits. He'd declined. As reward, his current vessel was the largest in the fleet, a full eight hundred tons. Rumors were that by next year, 1836, he would be given an even larger vessel of a thousand tons, with capacity for five hundred passengers in both steerage and first class.

Lady Kimberly wondered how any sailing vessel could do any better in providing creature comforts for first class. Her stateroom was elegant and roomy, with gleaming mahogany woodwork and onyx trim. Weather permitting, there was even a warm saltwater bath. She had brought but a single servant along for this trip to the Colonies, as she called them. It had been a whim, of course; an escape from the tedium of English country life with a husband who was more interested in shooting grouse than entertaining with the parties of which Lady Kimberly was so fond. Except for the miseries of the storm, during which she had kept to her pitching bed in the throes of seasickness, the voyage had had its amenities. First class people dined sumptuously off fine dinner plates. They entertained themselves at whist and chess and, for the hardy souls braving the cold airs on deck, shuffleboard. The food was splendid and abundant. She dined on fine boiled ham and mutton cutlets, fried eggs and salted shad fish. There were rolls and cold butter, cognac and Schieldam. But by the third week at sea, the boredom settled in upon her, and she longed for diversion.

The captain was an enigma. At first she was irritated that the man seemed disinterested in her. Unlike other men who devoured her with their eyes—the ironmonger was positively indecent in his leering lechery—Captain Grant gave her barely a glance, and then only in the strictest propriety. His conversation sparkled, nonetheless, and he was excellent company in a social gathering. His uniforms were superbly cut and showed the work of a master tailor. But it was the lean, handsome features and flashing dark eyes that preyed on her mind; the eyes were filled with mystery and boldness and a hint of old hurts. At dinner she leaned across him casually, her breast brushing his arm. At whist, with the captain as a genial fourth, she accidentally dropped a card and placed her hand upon his thigh for support as she bent to retrieve it. If he noticed at all, he gave no sign. A flush of anger rose suddenly to her cheeks, and she snapped irritably, "Captain, it's your turn to bid!" Only then did he look at her squarely; but the eyes were amused and disdainful, as if she were a tavern wench!

He invaded her dreams and thoughts. By the twentieth day at sea, Lady Kimberly found herself constantly aware of the captain. She would lose the thread of conversations, catch herself staring at the sea and wondering if he was near, imagining that he was watching her, shivering at the thought.

Scandalous! She must get hold of herself.

That evening she deliberately avoided another of the captain's dinners, dining alone in her cabin instead. But she was restless and ill at ease, and could not keep her mind on reading. Throwing aside the book, she put on a shawl and went out on deck. The cold air knifed through her thin clothing, but she found it invigorating. The sky was swept free of clouds, and a bright half-moon coasted above the mainmast, its light reflecting on the crests of a surging sea. She walked slowly about the deck, conscious of the helmsman at the wheel, the laboring slant of the deck, the creaking rigging and sighing winds.

A tall, lean figure stood at the after-rail. There was a whiff of cigar smoke. Lady Kimberly shivered again, clutching the shawl about her bosom. The shiver was not, however, from cold. Her tumbling thoughts almost took her breath and put a catch in her voice when she said: "Captain Grant? Is that you?"

She took his arm and pressed it to her breast. "I'm cold," she whispered.

Thirty minutes later, Kimberly Wyneheath trembled violently in the darkness of the captain's cabin as his strong, gentle hands removed her underclothing, and he carried her to his bed. Her bare thighs loosened, and her breath came in great, shuddering pants as his mouth explored the secret wetness of her body.

Then he rose up, all muscle and sinew, his member standing . . .

And he mounted her like a stallion.

* * *

A man cannot live forever in anonimity. Sooner or later it's bound to come: a remembered name, a flash of recognition, a sudden matching of logic.

The *Helen* docked at New York's Battery and disgorged its passengers from Liverpool. True to the captain's word, the trip had been made in thirty-four days despite a massive midwinter storm. Last of the first class passengers to depart was the beautiful Englishwoman, Lady Kimberly Wyneheath, who seemed to linger for an unusual amount of time speaking to the captain and holding his hand. As she left the ship and climbed into a hansom cab, she was seen dabbing at her violet eyes with a hanky.

As the ship prepared to make its next round trip to Liverpool, there came aboard an old sailor who stared at the captain with squint-eyed recognition. Later, in the fo'csle:

"What'd you say the captain's name was, mate?"

"Captain Grant. Stewart Grant. And there ain't no harder man to please."

"Grant, is it? Hah, hah. Well, he might be Stewart Grant nowadays, but he wasn't always. When I knowed him, he was Ward Stewart out of Provincetown, captain of the privateer *Shark*. That was nearly twenty-five years ago, and he's aged and grown a beard and all. But that's Ward Stewart, all right. And if memory serves me, he murdered some important politician in Boston over a woman and is wanted for it to this day."

Word filters rapidly through a ship, especially when she's put to sea. In no time, a packet rat hoping to ingratiate himself whispered to the bucko mate, Mr. Thorne. A short time later, the mate knocked at the door of the captain's cabin. "Beggin' yer pardon, sir, but there's something you might want to know . . ."

Well, he always knew it would happen. Strangly, the knowledge of discovery at last gave him a lifting of spirit. He realized how tired he had become, tired of living under an assumed name, tired of lying and being afraid. A secret burdens a man, and the longer he bears it the heavier it gets. There were options, of course. He could leave the ship at Liverpool, simply walk away and not come back. And he could take another vessel, under another name, and sail to China if he chose. A man without identity. A man without a place to call his own.

But at Liverpool, he stayed on board the *Helen*. The mood of the ship was tense, the crew watchful, expecting him to leave, wanting him to escape. "God knows, I'd do it if it was me. I'd get meself off this ship and get lost." When the *Helen* put to sea again, however, Stewart Grant was still on the quarterdeck, still in command, pacing with his hands behind his back, squinting up at the spreading sails, feeling the movement of the vessel beneath his feet.

Surprisingly, the return voyage to New York was his most pleasurable in memory. Walking that quarterdeck, he sensed keenly the wind in his face, the fresh smell of the sea breeze in his nostrils, the sounds of rigging creaking and the chantey-singing men. The *Helen* docked at the Battery, and he remained on board, roaming the deck and attending to petty details.

Two days later, three black-uniformed constables walked up the gangway. When the captain came forward, the man in charge respectfully doffed his black leather hat and drew out a paper.

"Captain Ward Stewart?"

"That's right."

"I have a warrant for your arrest."

XVIII

The dogs. The dogs bayed in the night, and their sounds struck the running man to the depths of his being. His feet flew faster and faster until the limit was reached, and relentlessly, relentlessly, he began to tire. There was a sharp pain in his chest. His lungs were fit to burst. The muscles of his thighs and calves burned with the pain.

He crashed through brush along the river. Out of the night, branches whipped his face. His feet slid in the muck, and repeatedly he fell. Mud caked his body, his mouth, his nostrils.

Behind him, the dogs drew closer.

He stopped, gasping for air on the riverbank in deep, shuddering gulps. Let them, he thought. Let them come up. As he stood, catching his breath, gathering his senses, he became aware of the glow on the hill. A manor house, it was, glowing on the hill above him; a house filled with light and warmth. He heard a piano, heard laughter, felt a longing—an agonizing longing—in his soul that he could neither fathom nor endure.

Slowly, he turned and walked up the hill.

He came to the back of the house. It was a large, two-story structure of gleaming white, with columns and large open windows. Inside, he could see the men in tuxedos and the women, lovely, laughing creatures, all white and bejeweled and gowned in silks.

He knocked softly at the back door.

It was a black woman who came, a big, soft, warm black woman. She opened the door, and her eyes filled with fear.

"Help me," he said.

She backed away from the door, looking him up and down, her fear so strong he could almost smell it. She had a poker in her hand, from the stove, and she lifted the poker threateningly.

"What you doin' here? You ain't got no right to be here. Look at you, a mess! Mud all over. What you been up to? What you doing, comin' to this house and knockin' on the door?" She hesitated, listening. The dogs. "You're runnin'," she said. "You done escaped, and you is runnin'. Git. Git on!" She waved the poker. "Git on, I say!"

"What is it, Mossy?"

The black woman whirled around. "Nothin', Miss Maybelle. Ain't nothin' but a fella come to the back door. He ain't no account."

"Who came to the back door, Mossy?"

She came into his sight. Red hair, like flame. A scarlet gown, sparkling diamonds at her throat, and skin like cream. She walked to the doorway and saw him, beyond the servant woman called Mossy; she saw him cringing and trembling in the night, covered with mud, the broken shackles still on his wrists.

"You poor thing!" she said. "You poor, poor thing!"

"Don't pay him no mind, Miss Maybelle. He done escaped, a runaway slave. They's after him with the dogs, comin' up the river. It's against the law to help him, Miss Maybelle. We in a slave state now. You could get in a heap o' trouble."

"Nonsense, Mossy." The red-haired woman pushed the servant aside and came out to him. She took his hand and said, again, "You poor, poor thing." She tugged at his hand, pulling him into the house, into the kitchen. His bare feet splashed mud on the floor, the gleaming, spotless floor. He quivered with fright and hunger and longing. The woman's face, a soft and beautiful face with great eyes filled with concern, softened and then abruptly hardened again.

"Take him upstairs, Mossy."

"Miss Maybelle!"

"Take this man upstairs, I say. And don't you come down until I tell you. Put him in my room."

"Miss Maybelle!"

"Do as I say!"

The black woman took him up a flight of back stairs, his feet tracking mud and the iron clanking at his wrists. She led him through a carpeted hallway lit by elegant brass lamps that gave off a golden glow. She led him across wine-red carpeting, past closed doors covering murmuring voices and the laughter of women. She led him into a room with polished wooden floors, lovely carpets, flowers in vases and white, white walls. The black woman stopped him, made him stand and wait, found newspapers to put down on the carpeting, then led him across the newspapers with his dirty feet to a closet. She put him into the closet and closed the door.

"Now stay there, you hear? You stay there."

It was a long time, an eternity of time. He cowered among sweet-smelling dresses and a multitude of shoes and hats; he cowered and did not move, knowing that any moment the door would be snatched open, and the Man would be there to drag him out, shouting: "Nigger, I'll teach you to run! You'll never run again!"

But the door was not snatched open. The door opened slowly. And she was there, the red-haired woman, speaking quietly to him, quietly and confidently. "They're gone now. You don't have to be afraid. They won't come back. You're going to be free now. I'm fixing it so you'll be free. You won't have to run anymore, you won't have to be afraid." She beckoned, and he came out into the huge bedroom. She nodded to the black woman, who led him away again, down the hall and down the back stairs to the kitchen where a large steaming plate of food waited on a table.

He ate voraciously.

And then he went out to a little house in the back, a house full of tools, and bathed at a pump. The black woman brought him fresh clothing, good clothing, and shoes. When he had dressed, she led him back into the kitchen, where the white woman waited, smiling.

"What is your name?" the white woman asked.

"Duke, ma'am. My name is Duke Mankin."

"All right, Duke Mankin. You may stay here, if you like, and work for me. I'll pay you a wage, and you'll have food and a place to sleep in the back house there. How does that sound to you?"

He could not speak. Suddenly there was a knot in his throat, and he could not find his voice. So he went down to his knees instead. He went to his knees and bent low and kissed the toe of her shoe.

It was a fine spring. On the slope, up from the river, the timothy grass was a deep green, and bluebells nodded in dappled shade. The trees had burgeoned into full leaf. Warm, blossom-scented air wafted up from the river and through the tall windows of the manor house with its stately pillars. A small brass plate beside the double mahogany doors was engraved with the words: The Golden Bough. From behind open windows on the second floor, someone ran rapid scales on the piano.

"Bend and stretch. Bend and stretch. That's right, bend and stretch. Maybelle, dear, you must put more into it. Now again, bend and stretch . . ."

Maybelle bent, touching the left toe with the right fingers and then the right toe with the left fingers. She straightened again with both hands aloft, stretched, bent, repeated. She was breathing heavily, and a fine sweat glazed her face. The face was still beautiful, with soft, well-defined Stewart features; but time had etched it with fine lines, too—character lines, Maybelle called them—requiring more time at the makeup table. The body was supple and graceful. Constant exercise kept her flesh firm and waistline trim. It was a body that still attracted male glances and female envy.

"Bend and stretch. Ah, good! We stop now. That's very good for today, eh? You feel good, ja?"

Maybelle toweled herself vigorously. "Very good, Millicent. And thank you. Same time tomorrow?"

"Same time tomorrow."

Maybelle left the exercise room and walked down the hallway, pushed open a door, and stood listening to her son's playing of the piano scales. Brack had turned into a handsome youth with the dark, delicate features of his late father, Maurice. He also had a touch, the long fingers rippling over the keyboard with dazzling ease. Maybelle had hoped he might become a musician, but the boy's mind grasped every subject quickly. His interest ran to mathematics and commerce. Senator Benton urged her to send him to a university back east, preferably Harvard College. "Maybelle, it would be a crime not to educate a mind like that." And, of course, the senator was right. Thomas Hart Benton was usually right, as every would-be opponent discovered to his discomfort.

Maybelle crossed the room quickly and slipped her arms around her son's neck.

The playing stopped. Brack suffered his mother's affections without response. This was his way, unresponsive. She often wondered if Brack was capable of giving and receiving affection. But this did not stop her from demonstrating it.

"Brack, darling, that was lovely."

"Mother . . ." The voice had an edge of impatience. "It's only exercises."

She released him and walked to the window, to stand looking down upon the river. The Mississippi flowed so smoothly here that the water seemed to have no current at all; it lay in that vast muddy bed like a great sheet of greenish-brown glass. "And what do you plan to do this afternoon?" she asked.

"Tutor comes at two-thirty. Later, I shall take a horseback ride."

His fingers picked out a light theme from Mozart. She knew he was waiting for her to leave, but still she lingered. The conversation they'd had at breakfast still weighed upon her mind. She had decided, once and for all, to tell him everything, everything about the past. And so she had unburdened herself. Lately, Maybelle had worried about Brack and about herself. Some sixth sense plucked at her mind, giving her disquiet. It seemed terribly important for him to be aware, to be on his guard. "Those men who killed your father, they can still find us, Brack. I know it has been a long time, but somehow I can't help feeling . . ."

"I hate to see you worry, Mother."

There. He did it again. Brack could be so cold at one moment, and at the next betray his feelings just as any normal boy might do. She thought that she understood him, but knew that she did not.

"And the other thing that we discussed? Have you thought about it?"

"The Stewarts? Yes, I've thought about it. I know that you despise your family. But I must make up my own mind. It isn't altogether fair for you to try to transmit your dislikes to me."

"I wasn't trying to do that, Brack. Not really. I merely wanted you to know."

That was a lie, of course. The old feelings were so much a part of her that Maybelle wanted Brack to share the hatred, share it and nourish it and carry it along. In so doing, perhaps someday he would even avenge her. That's what she wanted in her heart, and why for years she had subtly dripped the poison into his mind. Stewarts are bad. Stewarts treat people with cruel disdain. Stewarts are . . .

"Yes, Mother, I think I understand."

She went out of the room and down the stairs, to prepare for the evening guests. Four of the girls, including Beatrice and Dolly, relaxed on the sun porch doing their hair and nails. It was a constant grooming process each day, and Maybelle knew that the others were in their rooms performing the same task. Grooming was essential for a class house like The Golden Bough: grooming, cleanliness, good health, intelligence. She hired only the brightest young women, paid them well.

The Golden Bough was for the moneyed trade, primarily. Armed bodyguards in tuxedos patrolled the premises each evening. Discretion was the watchword. From the beginning, Maybelle's proposal for a refined operation had been welcomed in St. Louis. The town boomed, fed by steamer travel, the fur trade, and a swelling population in the entire region along the Mississippi. No longer would a rough bordello such as Dove Lovelady's Gown and Slipper suffice. The frontier was giving way to wealth, manners, new ways of living. Rich and powerful men sought more and more to take their pleasures in private. Bankers and businessmen could depend on Maybelle to arrange, say, a small dinner party with attractive hostesses, or diversion for some visiting dignitary free from prying eyes.

Politically, they had been through stormy times. Maybelle made it a rule to leave politics outside the manor house. But it was difficult, if not impossible. The issue of slavery had burned over Missouri, turning friend against friend. As debate raged over whether the state would be admitted to the Union as slave or free, fists flew and dueling pistols cracked. Maybelle's sentiments were passionately antislavery. She had worked in subtle ways, however, to persuade and dissuade while carefully avoiding direct conflict. As a measure of respect for her, even ardent abolitionists accepted The Golden Bough as neutral ground. When Missouri finally was admitted as a slave state, Maybelle took it as a bitter personal defeat, wishing that she had worked harder for the antislavery cause. Instinctively, she dreaded what lay ahead for the country.

St. Louis was restless, expanding. Its broad waterfront teemed with steamboats, many of them bearing the circle-and-triangle mark of the Stewart Line. The town was also a staging area for frontiersmen and adventurers. If the heart of St. Louis was the river, its eyes turned to the west.

"West! That's where the future lies." It was Thomas Hart Benton speaking. The powerful senator and his friends often came for dinner and entertainment, although as always he shrewdly avoided any dalliance with even the prettiest of The Golden Bough hostesses. Like Maybelle herself, Senator Benton saw the wisdom of remaining aloof. On occasion he chided her for her avoidance of men. "Your cold beauty breaks their hearts, Maybelle. You are our Virgin Queen." Maybelle smiled, thinking of her son Brack. "I will admit, Senator, to being a queen."

The West. It was two thousand miles overland to the Pacific, to Oregon territory or California. Maybelle had seen the pioneers, missionaries, and settlers setting out with wagons and oxen and mules, bound for the West, carrying their hopes and dreams in a few boxes and barrels. Strangely, she caught herself envying them. How could a person do that? Simply pick up and go, leave behind all the known, the secure, and trust your fate to the desert and mountains and the Good Lord. Could she do that? Would she have the nerve?

Foolish notion, of course. Maybelle was successful, her business thriving, her hopes for Brack bright. It was the occasional flash of intuition that gave her unease. She hired more armed guards for The Golden Bough, kept an eye out for strangers. Her moodiness was not lost upon Beatrice and Dolly. The former, so childish and naïve when she'd been employed in New Orleans, had developed into a mature woman whose keen business sense made her invaluable to Maybelle in St. Louis. "What is it, Maybelle? You've been so restless lately."

Maybelle started to reply, thought better of it, shrugged. "Nothing, really."

Trouble is a ruthless pursuer. How long could she go on like this? The memory of Thackery Craven nagged at her. He was not the sort of man to surrender to time and distance. She knew how such a man's mind worked. Certainly he was aware that she'd fled to St. Louis, started another business, made a success. He would be the kind to bide his time, let her build it up, then move in to stake his claim, as he had done with the Nocturne.

But it did not happen as Maybelle expected. Thackery Craven and his men did not barge directly into The Golden Bough. If a scoundrel is to be given credit for cleverness, then Craven deserved credit. The assault on The Golden Bough came with a sharp falloff of her most valued customers, the moneyed group. The private dining rooms, usually busy every night and packed on Fridays and Saturdays, began to empty. It did not take Maybelle long to discover the reason. A local banker told her: "I'm sorry, Maybelle, but there is a lot of talk going around. A man came to see me—didn't recognize him; never saw him before—and cautioned me in a friendly way. He asked me for money, to protect my good name. I told him to go to hell. But others . . ."

Blackmail! They were blackmailing selected customers, and these in turn were telling other customers. This applied only to the rich and influential, of course; the run-of-the-evening bordello business went on as usual. The tactic was to cripple Maybelle's carefully developed base of community support but not to jeopardize the bulk of The Golden Bough's income.

Then came a threat against Brack. It was a note, left in Maybelle's private mailbox. "Your boy will not be able to play the piano very well with both hands broken." She insisted that Brack no longer go out with his friends and to remain at home, under guard, at all times.

A week later, one of the younger girls returned from a shopping trip into the city bloodied from a beating that had left her face a mess. "Maybelle," she cried, "somebody threw a sack over my head and dragged me into an alley. Then they just started hitting me. There must have been three men."

She hired more bodyguards. The Golden Bough took on the

mood of an armed camp. Although the guns were hidden, even customers began to notice the number of muscular men stationed about the doors and stairways, from the public parlor with its glittering gilt fountains, velveted walls, and overstuffed furniture to the gambling rooms, dining areas, and upstairs corridors serving the private parlors.

Finally, there came the evening when Thackery Craven walked into the public parlor, trailed by three husky associates. Still tall, lean, and silver-haired, Craven had aged little over the years. His manner was as supercilious as ever, and the restless eyes undressed Maybelle as she advanced coldly to meet him.

"Get the hell out of here, Craven."

"Well, well, if it isn't the lovely Rose Lark. Oh, I beg your pardon. Maybelle Stewart. And how's tricks, Maybelle? You should pardon the pun."

Six guards were on duty. Maybelle looked around to give the distress signal. But suddenly there was not a guard to be seen. Every position in the public parlor was vacant.

"Where are the men, Beatrice?"

"I d-don't know, Maybelle. They just disappeared. All of a sudden, they're gone!"

Craven offered a patronizing smile. "A little sleight of hand, shall we say? I'm afraid your hired hands lack real stomach for their work. There's no loyalty among them. The ones not easily bribed we simply . . . persuaded." Maybelle's dismay caused him to laugh out loud. "Good help these days is hard to find."

He turned, clapped his hands. Twelve more men came in from outside and circulated quietly among the nervous customers. Several of them were Maybelle's former guards.

"And now I'm claiming what's rightfully mine," Craven said. "I'm doing it in the same way that you took eight thousand dollars from me in New Orleans. And I'll thank you not to trouble yourself calling in the constables, because to do so will only mean jail for you, for robbery."

There comes a time when one no longer struggles; when it is prudent to fold the hands, to submit and survive. Maybelle thought of Brack, of jail, of all the advantages that now lay in the hands of Thackery Craven. She had handled it all badly, let him seize the initiative, blindly stumbled into the trap. She was, as always, beyond the law and its protection. Theirs was a game that went by no rules. Maybelle sighed, and gave in.

But she refused to submit herself to Craven, refused to go to his bed. He ordered her to bring him food and to fill a tub of bathwater for his pleasure. In other rooms and parlors, the dozen hostesses were performing similar tasks for Craven's men. When he tried clumsily to kiss her and found his hands pawing over an unyielding statue, he pushed her away and his eyes smoldered. "You're proud now. But we'll find a way to break that."

The contest of wills went on for ten days.

Finally: "Duke? Duke, is that you?"

"Yas'm, Miss Maybelle."

"Oh, thank you for coming, Duke. I—I need help. Can you help me?"

"I'll do anything I can, Miss Maybelle. You know that."

"All right, then here's what I want you to do for me."

As she whispered her instructions, the black man's eyes widened, and a sly grin spread across his face. "Miss Maybelle, you sho' must be mad at that fella. But I'll do it. I'll have 'em here tomorrow night."

Twenty-four hours later, Duke Mankin arrived at Maybelle's back door carrying four squirming sacks. He slipped into the house, made his deliveries to the rooms of several hostesses, and then departed, unseen.

Thackery Craven loosened his cravat and sat down on the bed. It had been a fine evening at cards, and he had also cleaned the fandango table. He looked around the master bedroom with a proprietory pride. Not bad, not bad at all. Now if he could just warm up the Virgin Queen, everything would be to his liking. The woman was beautiful, God knows, but cold as ice. Even a queen, however, can be brought to yield.

There was a soft knock at the door. As he drew his pistol from beneath the pillow, she came in bearing a tray with a bottle and two glasses. Craven felt a warm surge of anticipation. The fiery hair was loosened now, tumbling in soft waves down her back. She wore a gown of shimmering green, the neckline plunging to reveal the twin swellings of snowy breasts. Jesus, what a pair! The eyes had softened in the face somehow, a trick of the light perhaps; the beauty mark seemed to glow, making the eyes seem even larger than usual. The lamplight itself had a warmth that he did not remember before, subtle and sensuous.

"I brought us something to drink, Mr. Craven," she said. "The best in the house."

It was one of those Kentucky bourbons, amber and mellow in the light. There were two glasses on the tray and ice in a pitcher. She unfolded a small collapsible nightstand and drew it up beside the bed. Then she sat down beside him, poured liquor into both glasses. Lightly, as she poured, her hand rested on his knee. The touch sent a thrill through him.

"Well, this is—"

"This is to let bygones be bygones," she said. "What's past is past, Thackery. May I call you Thackery? Let's think about now, and the future."

He gazed into her eyes over the rim of the glass. She was no kid, this one, but spellbinding nonetheless. The eyes enlarged, seeming to draw him in. The woman could cast a spell. He drank. The liquor went smoothly down his throat. Damn, that was good! She refilled his glass, and he drank again. And then she was caressing his chest, running her hand inside his shirt. Her face was close to his, so close, and her nearness was a sudden sweet warmth that filled him, stirred him.

"By God, you're some kind of woman, Maybelle."

The lips came to his, whispering, "Hush." The lips were full and warm and wet, clinging to his, opening.

He felt the electricity of the darting tongue.

"Some kind of woman."

His senses seemed to reel. She opened beneath him, moaning her delights, taking him into her being, thrashing in a rising transport of passion. Consuming, she was; inflaming him, drawing his manhood, taking him in ways he had never experienced before. Between times, he drank of the amber liquor, and the level of the bottle went down and down. He was happy and warm and giggling from the drink. Damn, what a party. His face was numb and his head buzzed with liquor and pleasure and . . . and . . .

"An' ecstacy!" he shouted. "Thash what 'tis, Virgin Queen. Ec-Ecstacy, pure 'n simple."

She giggled, rolling against his nakedness once more, taking him into her hands again, doing things, arousing him again . . .

"Ohh, what a man," she panted. "Where have you been all my life, man?"

He never knew he could do it so many times. How many times? He lost count of the times. And he drank more. And more. And more.

The bed swirled, and he flopped over, exhausted. The bed

swirled and swirled. She rolled away from him and got up. He tried to focus his eyes and mumbled something, but all he could see was the blurry form of her putting on a robe and going away. He let his head fall back. His mind thought: God, what a woman!

Maybelle drew the sack from the closet, gently. It was heavy, heavier than she had expected. The motion caused a stirring inside the sack. She dragged it across the floor, gripping the neck tightly. By the time she got to the bed, the wiggling and squirming was an angry protest. Taking a pair of scissors from the dresser, she snipped the cord that bound the sack at the neck. She lay the scissors aside and lifted the sack gently with both hands. Then she shifted the burden so that one hand supported it from beneath.

Maybelle's heart pounded, and her breath came rapidly. All at once, she told herself. Do it quickly and all at once.

She held the sack above the bed, turned it over, and let the neck fly open.

The two huge rattlesnakes tumbled over the naked body on the bed, buzzing violently.

Thackery Craven opened his eyes and screamed.

Three men had died in the rooms, including Craven. The others took to their heels. For the remainder of the night and for several nights thereafter, Maybelle and the hostesses kept watch with rifles. Duke dragged the bodies, one at a time, down to the river and tossed them in. And finally, on the morning of the fourth day, Maybelle made her decision to leave St. Louis and go west.

"West? You're out of your mind, Maybelle. What's out there for the likes of us?"

"Opportunity. A fresh start. New life. Nobody has to come along. Stay here if you like. I'm signing over The Golden Bough to Beatrice and Dolly anyway. But there's a wagon train making up at Independence in a fortnight, and I plan to be with it."

"And Brack? What about Brack?"

"Brack is staying with friends of Senator Benton's. He will go to Harvard College back east in the fall. It's being arranged."

"But the West . . ."

"California, first, down to Monterey. Nice little town, I hear.

And I've also heard of a place called San Francisco. It isn't much right now, a few shacks and a few hills on a gorgeous big bay, but it intrigues me."

They held a council. The hostesses, still shaken from recent events, argued and pleaded and wept. Maybelle refused to change her mind. Some of the young women shuddered at the thought of attempting such a journey by wagon. "Maybelle, I hear there's folks who die of disease and thirst and Indian attacks, trying to get out west."

"Then go by ship, around the Horn. Anybody who wants to go with me can choose their mode of travel. Take a ship, if you'd rather. Hell, I'm paying the freight."

For nearly a week the debate raged. Maybelle, unyielding, arranged her affairs, bought goods for the trail, packed boxes and bales. From important friends in St. Louis she learned that the constabulary was not interested in the abrupt departure of Craven and his mob. The fact that certain powerful gentlemen of the community were thrilled to see them go further mitigated against official inquiry. Thus, with no questions being asked and no complaints registered—how can there be a crime without a complaint?—the matter quietly slipped into oblivion.

And finally, six hostesses cast their lot with Maybelle, the rest preferring to remain at The Golden Bough. Duke Mankin also felt that he could do better in St. Louis, as a freedman, and Maybelle assured him that his job was secure. The parting from Brack was tearful but quick. On a bright Tuesday morning, Maybelle and her six girls departed for Independence aboard two gaily bedecked wagons, each drawn by plodding oxen with flowers in their harness. Tears poured like the waters of the Mississippi.

Van Harrison was a veteran plainsman, a lean and leathery man accustomed to strange sights and strange people. But in all his years, he had never seen anything quite like this: seven women in gowns and sequins, led by a mature but ravishing redhead, going west in covered wagons painted pink and strung with multicolored ribbons. And the junk crammed into those wagons! Trunks, boxes, bales, a piano, ornate lamps, a full-size mirror. God knows, as trail boss he would have enough trouble leading the twelve wagons already in the train, most of them driven by greenhorn farmers. But now this...

"Begging your pardon, ma'am—"

"Maybelle. Just call me Maybelle."

"—Maybelle, but are you sure you want to go through with this? I mean, you're talking about seven women crossing two thousand miles of plains, deserts, dry waterholes, rattlesnake dens, buffalo herds, Indian hunting grounds, mountains, and dry lake beds burning with the sun, twisters, grizzly bears, and God knows what all. You got folks dropping like flies from mountain fever, dysentery, and cholera..."

Maybelle put on her brightest smile. "Yes, we've heard about all that, Mr. Harrison. Now, do you think we did right by buying oxen? Or would mules do better? Back in St. Louis everybody advised oxen. But the poor things seem so slow and, well, weary."

Harrison sighed. "Oxen, ma'am. That's what I'd use, if it was me. An ox, he's slow and plodding and ain't got much sense, but he can pull you along at a steady four miles an hour farther and longer than either horses or mules. It don't matter to him if it's desert heat or mountain cold."

"Good. I'm glad we made the right choice."

With a whistle and a shout, the Harrison wagon train lurched into motion out of Independence, followed by scampering children and barking dogs. Each of Maybelle's wagons exceeded the three-fourths of a ton cargo which Mr. Harrison insisted was the limit. It had been necessary, then, to acquire an additional four oxen, to provide two pairs for each wagon. Maybelle and the strongest of the girls, a bosomy brunette named Clara Lou, were the main drivers, with each of the others taking a turn to learn how to handle the reins.

"Maybelle, look at my hands!"

"Well, if that don't beat all. Marguerita, you got blisters."

"But it's just the first day!"

"Don't worry, honey. Things will get worse."

They did. And quickly. By the fourth day on the trail, the all-female wagons—which Harrison had assigned to the middle of the train for safety—chorused loud complaints of sunburn, sore muscles, blistered hands, and a pervasive weariness and boredom.

"Look at that big fella on the dappled gray, Clara Lou. I think he's kind of cute."

"Don't you let Maybelle hear you say that."

"I was just thinkin' out loud, that's all."

"Don't think. Don't roll your eyes. Don't do nothing but

concentrate on the rumps of them oxen. Maybelle says she'll horsewhip the first gal that takes a tumble for a man on this wagon train."

"Oh, pooh."

The rigorous rules of chastity, however, merely forestalled the inevitable. On the tenth day out, Van Harrison summoned Maybelle and her girls to an evening meeting of the entire adult population of the wagon train. As they stepped into the circle around the firelight, the silence became intense. Maybelle looked out into a wall of hostility.

"Why didn't you tell us you was prostitutes?" a sunbonneted woman snapped from the crowd.

"Prostitutes. Whores. Imagine, in *our* wagon train!"

"Ladies and gentlemen," Van Harrison said, "I really don't think . . ."

"They got no right to mingle with decent, God-fearin' folks. You just let one of them hussies make goo-goo eyes at my husband, and I'll give her the business end of a Kentucky long rifle."

"Now, Cora—"

"Shut up, you old fool."

Maybelle and the girls stood silently as the harangue went on. Finally, it wound down in sullen muttering. The leading critic, Cora Moran, a gaunt, weather-beaten woman in plain homespun with two small children, a husband, and a brother in tow, decreed what was to be done.

"They move to the rear of the train."

"But Mrs. Moran, it's dangerous for a group of women with no experience on the trail, and little knowledge of weapons, to bring up the rear. We've got our most seasoned wagonmen back there and the volunteer rear guard to boot."

"Glad you mentioned that rear guard. Some of our husbands and older sons make up that group, and they ain't going to shepherd no harlots for two thousand miles neither. Leastways, *my* husband ain't."

"Nor mine!"

"Nor mine!"

Maybelle stepped forward into the firelight at last, her hair blowing in the breeze and defiance in her face. The crowd stilled. She turned to the wagon master. "Mr. Harrison, we have no objections to bringing up the rear and none to being set apart from the main body, either. I can't blame these ladies for the way they feel, and I know none of the girls do. We're trying to learn to be self-sufficient as quickly as we can, and that means driving a team and handling our rifles. Few of us have ever fired a rifle before. But we intend to learn. As for the rear guard, we'll just make do as best we can without it. Thank you." She went back to her group. "Come along, girls." They walked out of the silent circle and into the night.

The ostracizing set in with a vengeance. No longer were Maybelle and her troupe even spoken to, and the men of the train did their best not to steal covetous glances. It was as if they no longer existed to clutter up the lives and fortunes of decent folk. It was up to Van Harrison and his handful of assistants, now, to provide the rearguard protection against surprise encounters, be they Indian, grizzly bear, or natural disaster. The trail boss saw to it that Maybelle was supplied with extra ammunition, and daily the girls became more practiced at shooting, riding and team driving.

"Miss Maybelle, I declare, you all will be the equal of my men, pretty soon." Van Harrison, his features blasted by sun and wind into a craggy mask pierced by pale blue eyes, leaned over in his saddle and spat at the ground. "You're doing fine, just fine."

"Thank you, Mr. Harrison."

"Just let me know when you get tired of haulin' that there piano, and I'll get my men to unload it for you."

"Never you mind about that piano. Where I go, it goes."

The trail boss touched his hat brim and trotted away. Maybelle could not resist a lingering glance at his straight, muscular back and square shoulders.

"Tut, tut, Maybelle," Marguerita said impishly. "Remember what you said."

"Oh, stuff and nonsense, Marguerita. Mind your own business."

The trail followed the Missouri out of Independence to a point near Grand Isle on the River Platte. Then it was due west along level ground in the valley of the Platte to the foothills of the Rockies. The first thousand miles was a test of patience and fortitude. The second quickly became a test of courage and endurance. As the trail grew steeper and rockier, they encountered heat, storm, brackish water and no water at all, Indians prowling the distant ranges, snakes and storms, and the bones of animals. The rocky, sandy terrain wore down the mules of lead wagons and even sapped the strength of the oxen, especially as day followed day of dry, scorching sunshine. Exhaustion drained bodies and shortened tempers. Sickness broke out, with fevers and wracking coughs and chills.

"Do you see them up there, Mr. Harrison? There on the ridge?"

"Yep. They've been shadowing us for six days."

"How long does this go on?"

"Depends on what they want. They know it doesn't get any easier for us, so time's on their side."

Time. Time was not in days, but in weeks. It measured not merely in land crossed—gorges and rivers and boulder-strewn slopes—but also in the steady weakening of the train and the onset of suffering. Sickness broke out in some of the wagons and there was a momentary fear of the dreaded cholera; but it was not cholera, and the main body stopped for prayers to thank God. A young woman died in childbirth, leaving her husband to grieve alone and a baby without a wet nurse. Food ran out. Starvation threatened. There were not enough men to form adequate hunting parties.

"Clara Lou, I want you and Marguerita and Susan to take rifles and go hunt."

"What shall we shoot, Maybelle?"

"Hell, shoot anything that's edible. Birds, jackrabbits, sidewinders, anything. Bring me a coyote's carcass, and I'll boil him."

They came to a rushing mountain stream. As the wagons forded the rocky bed, a big Conestoga tipped over the rapids, and the family and their goods clutched desperately at the wreckage. One of the children, a little girl, lost her grip.

"Cindy! *Cindy!*"

Maybelle's wagons were already in the stream behind the Conestoga. As she watched, fighting the reins of her terrified oxen, Marguerita emerged from the wagon ahead, stripped off her heavy outer clothing, and dived. With three strong strokes, she reached the child and grabbed her around the body. Both were swept downstream and vanished around a rocky point. On the far side, Van Harrison and two other men were after them at a gallop. The horsemen returned yelling in triumph, the water-soaked pair alive and well.

It was Maybelle's custom, whatever the circumstance or the

menu, to have the evening meal properly served. "We're not barbarians, after all. There is no excuse for abandoning manners." And so the girls put on their better gowns for dinner, always, and ate from china plates at Maybelle's folding tables with white tablecloths. On the evening after the rescue, dinner consisted of fried meal mush and rattlesnake meat, with a thimbleful of red wine for each person. As usual, they had their own fire, separate from that of the rest of the wagon train. Halfway through dinner, someone approached from the main camp and stopped just beyond the circle of the fire. The girls' conversation ceased. Maybelle recognized the gaunt figure of Cora Moran.

"Miss Maybelle?" the woman said softly.

"Yes, Mrs. Moran?"

"I—I was wondering if I might borrow a shaker of salt."

The following day, Maybelle's wagons went back into the middle of the train.

The fever worsened. An old woman died. Others were so weakened that travel became difficult. Maybelle's girls volunteered to ride in several wagons, nursing the sick. Where a man had fallen ill, they doubled as drivers. And so Van Harrison's miserable train inched forward across country that became more rugged with each mile. Water ran out. Several mules stumbled and died in harness. Maybelle lent out two of her oxen, her remaining animals straining at their extra loads.

"Miss Maybelle, are you ready to throw out that piano yet?"

"No, Mr. Harrison, I'm not. I'll throw me out first."

"Well, what about those crates over there. What's in them?"

"Gowns, Mr. Harrison. Extra fine gowns for my girls. And that box contains hand mirrors. I've collected mirrors for years, and there's at least a hundred in that box. I'm not throwing them out either."

Van Harrison grinned, leaned over in his saddle and patted her on the knee. "You do it your way then, Miss Maybelle. You do it your way."

Her attraction toward the plainsman grew. Maybelle caught herself watching him, looking forward to his frequent visits to her wagon as they moved, hearing in her dreams the sound of his voice. Van Harrison was so unlike men she'd known in the civilized world. Beneath his rugged strength she sensed a powerful breadth of character, gentleness, and kindness. He had never

been anything but courteous, and his command of the train was
unquestioned. Without him, she suspected that they would all
perish . . .

The shadowing Indians finally made their move.

"They're forming up! Circle the wagons!"

It was bad terrain for defense, a rock-strewn plain circled by
steep hillsides and overhanging bluffs that afforded excellent
cover for attackers but none for defense. Van Harrison surveyed
their situation grimly. "They know what they're doing." When
the wagons were drawn around and the barricades formed, such
as they were, the train settled down to wait. It was a moderate-
size war party of about a hundred braves. They waited until
morning to make their first assault, a test skirmish from the east
with the rising sun at their backs, blinding Harrison's defenders.
The sham attack involved a lot of spear shaking and a few
random shots in the air from old smoothbore fusee rifles. The
wagon defenders did not fire. As the Indians turned away and
regrouped, Maybelle squinted into the blinding sunlight and had
an idea.

She ran to her wagon, climbed in, and dragged out the heavy
box of hand mirrors. Breaking it open, she shouted to the girls to
distribute mirrors to every defender. As her instructions spread
through the wagon train, a ripple of laughter broke out at the
barricades. Then Maybelle removed the canvas cover from her
piano and sat down at the keyboard to wait.

The second attack came with a whooping and yelling, the
ponies at full gallop. Obviously this one was no sham. As the
war party swept over a low rise, Maybelle struck up a fast tune
on the piano, and the defenders flashed their hand mirrors into
the glaring sunlight. Mirror reflection suddenly flecked the harsh
landscape like bursts of starfire, into the eyes of the attackers.
The impact was devastating. Startled braves reined their ponies
so abruptly that several lost their footing and fell. A wild melee
ensued as the assault disintegrated, and Indians went spilling
over the fallen or diverted their charge and swept off to the sides.
Maybelle continued to bang the keyboard, playing a wild bar-
room tune. "Maurice," she whispered, "if only you could hear
me now."

There were no more attacks.

At midday, a group of warriors approached the camp. Van
Harrison, Maybelle, and several of the men went out to meet

them bearing gifts. Maybelle gave them beads, gaudy dresses and several boxes of makeup from her supplies. The Indians painted their faces, draped beads around their necks and wrapped themselves in the colorful fabric, laughing at the result. Van Harrison, in the meantime, conversed earnestly in sign language and scraps of dialect with a man who appeared to be a chief. Finally, he conveyed his message. The Indians stopped their play and drew back, talking among themselves. Abruptly, they threw down the clothing and stalked back to their main body, waiting under a bluff. The party mounted its ponies and rode away.

The wagon train's defenders could not believe their eyes.

"Mr. Harrison, what'd you say to them redskins?"

The plainsman watched the dust cloud of the retreating war party. "I asked 'em for help," he said. "I told them we had cholera."

After that, it was inevitable. Maybelle Stewart had to acknowledge to herself that she was in love with Van Harrison. And it came as no surprise that his feelings were every bit as strong. On the third night after the Indian confrontation, she lay in the plainsman's strong arms under his buffalo robe, her being flooded by a sense of peace beyond anything she had ever known. It was as if fate had intended that they be together; this was right, it was complete, it joined them as one. Maybelle knew that nothing would separate them now. Whatever ordeals awaited them they would face together.

She looked up at a blazing canopy of stars.

"I used to think heaven was up there, Van. As a little girl in Pittsburgh I went to church, you know, and they said that the good things happened to us after we die. But now I know better." She turned her head and kissed his face. "Heaven is right here."

Later, Maybelle would always be convinced that that was the happiest night of her life.

The Sierra range was a misery. It had taken them much longer than Harrison had anticipated. And so a combination of coincidences beset them: the wagon train was behind schedule and an early cold wave swept into the mountain, bringing snow. As they struggled on the steepest pitches of the entire journey thus far, heavy wet flakes fell over the trail. As the snow began to stick, a cloying mist rose out of the deep gorges. By the third day, they

were struggling forward against a howling storm and piling
snowdrifts, battling for every yard.

"We've got to stop, trail boss! We can't go on in weather like
this."

"You can't stop. Nobody stops. Every wagon keeps going and
every animal works until he drops. To stop in these mountains is
disaster."

And so he drove them and hounded them, a mercilous task
master. Only at night did they pause. As the dawns came in
muffled white silences, they cut dead mules from their traces,
pushed useless wagons over the icy cliffs, rearranged surviving
teams and pushed on again. Finally, the day came when Van
Harrison squinted upward to the last high ridgeline and announced: "It's not much farther now, folks. Just over that saddle
and we begin our descent to the coast."

The word gave them fresh energy, born of desperation.

That night, the fever struck Van Harrison. By morning, he
was too sick to climb into the saddle. An assistant was designated to take charge, and the wagon master lay under Maybelle's
buffalo robe in her wagon, wracked with chills, his eyes glazed
and his flesh burning.

Thus, the miserable train crested the last high pass. Behind
them a fresh blizzard darkened the horizon, bearing down on the
mountain peaks. With each mile of descent, however, the weather eased, the snow lessened and finally turned to rain. At last the
warm air of the valley poured into their faces, and the trail
guides went forward at a trot, firing their rifles to attract attention
of ranchers below.

And quietly, without saying a word, Van Harrison died.

Maybelle hovered over him in the wagon. When she saw what
had happened, she began to shout.

"Van, we're there. Van, we've made it. Don't die, Van. You
can't die, my darling! Oh, sweet Jesus, please. Pleeeease! I
haven't got anybody, Van; nobody to love me like you do . . ."

But the lean, weather-ravaged face was waxen, the clear blue
eyes staring and still.

She drew the buffalo robe over them both and lay with him as
darkness fell. All night, she lay with him and did not move.

The following morning they buried Van Harrison beside the
trail, with a few words spoken and the impersonal wind moaning
overhead.

Three weeks later Maybelle Stewart arrived in the village of

San Francisco with two broken-down wagons, four bony oxen, six starved whores, and a piano.

She was pregnant.

XIX

He was not content. Not content at all.

The steamboat empire flourished, yes. Stewart steamboats charged up and down any river wide enough and deep enough to navigate now—the Kanawha, the Tennessee, the Missouri, the Kentucky. The biggest and best, on the Ohio and Mississippi, were floating palaces, dazzling creations of mighty stern wheels, mahogany interiors, mirrored salons, private compartments. Stewart boatyards at Pittsburgh, Cincinnati, Louisville, and St. Louis turned out steamboats at a hectic rate.

It was Catherine who had made this boom; Catherine, with her shrewd business sense and restless energy. She was the blond riverboat queen, pushing and prodding and building. Under her leadership, Stewart steamboats fought for cargo, offering record times and cut-rate prices that were the despair of her competitors. But steamboats, Stephen knew, were not enough, not an end in themselves.

"Overland, that's the logical extension," he told business friends. "Listen, a stagecoach can travel at ten miles an hour on a decent road with a good team. The National Road is nearly through Ohio now reaching for Illinois. Back east, they're building railroads. Somebody told me the other day there's already twenty-five hundred miles of railroad track in this country. Twenty-five hundred miles! That, gentlemen, is the way of the future. Even canals won't be able to compete with that."

"Stephen, Stephen, you're pipe-dreaming. Listen, most of the roads in this country are still mud tracks. So a stagecoach is going to find precious few turnpikes decent enough to allow fast travel. As for railroads, hah, hah. A passing fancy, my friend. A passing fancy. There's just too much opposition to those fire-breathing monsters in this country.''

"But, man, this is 1842! Times are changing..."

They laughed. They wagged their heads. Well, let them. Stephen's mind was aflame with the possibilities. Everywhere he saw a restless country on the move. The river towns were booming but the tide of immigrants and settlers pushed inland as well, and ever toward the west. Stephen moved with them, captivated by the westward expansion. From St. Louis he ventured inland on horseback, accompanied by the boy Thaddeus and the tall Indian Crippled Wolf riding a mule and wearing his stovepipe hat and swallowtail coat with brass buttons.

To mountain men and fur traders, there was nothing repelling about meeting a man with a peg leg, a claw for a left hand, a face half-masked in flesh-tinted silk, and a teenage boy and a lame Indian at his side. If anything, Stephen's marks of suffering gave him a common bond with men accustomed to cruel rigors of mountain and plain, where life was solitary and often unspeakably harsh. Their faces relaxed in friendly grins when Stephen spoke of Lewis and Clark and his experiences with the Omaha tribe more than thirty years ago. From such mountain men, he learned about the gradual opening of the West; of Bill Becknell, the Missouri trader, who'd blazed the Santa Fe Trail to the southwest in 1821, and the Rev. Jason Lee and his mission to the Oregon country, and of the mountain man James Bridger, who'd discovered the Great Salt Lake. By now, of course, the trickle west was rapidly growing, as more and more people dared the arduous trek two thousand miles to Oregon or to the California country, where the Mexican hold was slipping in a wave of public sentiment to join the United States.

Tragedy forms strange bonds. The boy was an example of that. Thaddeus had survived the ultimate calamity of this family, the murder of Burl and Jenny and the baby Mercy. To Catherine, in the aftermath, Stephen had muttered: "Sometimes I think this family is accursed." But Thaddeus, bright and ever-curious Thaddeus, enriched them all. If anything good can come of a terrible event, Thaddeus was that something good. From the beginning, the attachment of Stephen and Catherine to this child was instinctive and full. Even as a toddler Thaddeus always seemed to follow in Stephen's tracks. He would turn around, and the child would be there, arms reaching up to be held. As he grew, the boy was forever making things and tearing things apart. No clock could long endure in the probing of his restless fingers; and by age five, he could take a clock apart and put it together again. His mind for arithmetic was instinctive and sure. And even as Catherine gave birth to twin girls and a son, Thaddeus was no less loved and no less one of their own. So it was still, as he developed into a handsome young man.

Thaddeus' passion for trains had been kindled six years ago, in 1836, when they had all journeyed to England. Stephen always smiled, remembering that trip.

"To England!" exclaimed Martha Stewart, who had grown fussy and dubious with age. "What in the name of heaven for?"

"Thaddeus wants to see a steam train."

They made the voyage by Black Ball packet, Stephen, Catherine, Thaddeus, and Crippled Wolf. Moon Flower had remained in Pittsburgh to care for the other children. On English streets they made a vivid sight, the stunning blond woman, the lad, the grotesquely crippled man, the Indian in his outlandish stovepipe hat and swallowtail coat.

"Who are we looking for, Stephen?"

"A man named George Stephenson."

They found the engineer in Liverpool. He was fifty-six years old, heavy, square-built, as solid as the iron from which he'd built his locomotives. "You came all the way from America to see me?" Stephenson's scraggly tangle of eyebrows lifted in surprise. "Then I'd best be a genial host, and that's a fact."

Stephen took an instant liking for the blunt-spoken man, who started life as a coal miner and hadn't learned to read or write until he was eighteen years old. While Thaddeus listened in rapt attention, the men talked far into the night about overland travel. "Canals is fine, Mr. Stewart. Lord knows, we got canals a'plenty. You got to have roads, too. We're pavin' them now with concrete and a new substance, called asphalt. A stagecoach has got to keep rolling to maintain speed and service, and you can set your clock by some of our fast coaches. But the steam locomotive—ah, that's me pride and joy."

The following morning, they rode Stephenson's train, the *Rocket*, smashing along at thirty miles an hour between Liverpool and Manchester. The little steam engine disgorged acrid smoke and a shower of blazing cinders from its single tall stack, all of which blew back upon the passengers in the open cars. Stephenson shouted a running monologue over the clatter and rush.

"Some scientists in London have warned us against exceeding

this speed, Mr. Stewart. They tell us the human physique cannot stand moving faster than thirty miles an hour. They say we'd suffocate. Do you believe that?''

Stephen laughed. "Absolutely not!"

''The canal owners hate me, of course. They say I'm wrecking their business. Farmers claim that the flying cinders will damage crops. A preacher warned me that females could be stirred to lust by the speeding flow of blood. Do you feel lustful, Mrs. Stewart?—begging you pardon for speaking plain.''

"When I'm near my husband, I always feel that way," Catherine shouted gaily.

To Thaddeus, looking wide-eyed at the green English countryside hurtling past, it was all too much to be real, a wild and ecstatic dream. Thaddeus' rapture was not lost upon the canny George Stephenson.

"''E's catching a glimpse of the future, that lad," shouted the inventor. "In your nephew's lifetime, it would not surprise me to find steam locomotives running clear across that vast American country of yours, from ocean to ocean. No sir, 'twouldn't surprise me in the least.''

Behind them, the dour Indian Crippled Wolf sat like a tall statue, his heavy face devoid of expression, clutching the stovepipe hat with both hands.

They had spent two years in Britain and on the continent of Europe. For their return trip across the Atlantic, they booked passage aboard the *Sirius*, a British steam-powered paddlewheeler on her maiden run. With the weather fine and a sea generally calm, the seven-hundred-ton vessel snorted and clanked along at a steady six and a half knots. She made New York in eighteen days, ten hours, but she had to burn her masts and wooden furnishings to achieve it. When they again set foot on American soil, Stephen heaved a grateful sigh. "I'm glad to be off of that fire-breather. They'd have burned her decks next.''

Before returning to Pittsburgh, he had visited his brother Nathan, who lived in his mansion on the Hudson with two teenage daughters and a brace of hunting dogs. Nathan's wealth, from steamboats, canal packets, and shipping, was even more enormous than Stephen's. And yet he had never married again, still grieved after six years at the huge tomb of carved Italian marble he had built for Yvette at Blossom Hill. He was more and more a recluse, shunning society. The once-handsome face was deeply lined, the hair thinning, the once-powerful body developing a stoop. Stephen could not believe that his brother was only fifty-six years old.

The two collided on an unexpected subject. Trains.

Nathan had grown so accustomed to dining alone that his conversation was halting and strained. They spoke in trite generalities with long pauses. Neither was comfortable. The girls were away at boarding school. Thaddeus sat in silence at his plate. At Nathan's insistence, Crippled Wolf dined in the kitchen.

"There's a lot of railroads being built in this country, Nathan. They've got a hundred and thirty-six miles of track out of Charleston, South Carolina. Longest track route in the world. And up along the Erie Canal . . ."

"I know all about that damned foolishness," Nathan grumbled. "Mohawk and Hudson Railway, they call it. Nothin' but a bunch of stagecoach bodies chained together behind an engine on strap iron tracks. Hah!" Angrily he speared a morsel of beef with his fork. "Monstrous machine. Monstrous."

Stephen was bewildered by his brother's petulant tone, but pushed ahead anyway. "Well, they're in the early stages right now, certainly. There's a lot of room for mechanical improvement. But I've heard talk that other entrepreneurs are thinking about building lines alongside the Erie, to compete with the canal for freight and even passenger business. After all, if a train can go fifteen miles an hour, that's a whole lot faster and more efficient than a canal packet at four, or maybe three."

Nathan muttered something that Stephen did not hear and drank wine noisily from a goblet. A servant quickly refilled the glass. For the first time, Stephen noticed the network of tiny blood vessels in his brother's face and the puffy eyes that indicated a heavy intake of port. The eyes in this light seemed a trifle bloodshot.

"I thought that we might pool our resources, you and I, and get the jump on them. Nathan, we could run a railroad all the way from Schenectady to Buffalo, force the Mohawk and Hudson people to throw in with us, and wind up controlling every ton of cargo that moved between New York city and Lake Erie. We could do it cheaper and faster than canal boats, and eventually run a rail line clear down the Hudson Valley between New York and Albany. Think of it, Nathan! All the way . . ."

His words were interrupted by the sound of Nathan Stewart's

fist crashing down on the table. A water goblet toppled, saturating the white tablecloth and running over the edge onto the carpet. As the servant rushed to clean the mess, Nathan stood up and fixed his brother with a glare.

"Do you know how hard we worked to build that canal? Do you have any idea how much blood and sweat was spilled, how many lives lost? I lost my own Yvette in the process of making that canal a reality." Nathan rocked unsteadily on his feet, his eyes losing focus. Thick gray eyebrows knit angrily as his words spilled out. "When we started building that canal, there weren't two thousand people between Albany and Buffalo. The canal brought in settlers by the tens of thousands, hundreds of thousands. Those that didn't pass all the way through to Ohio country put down roots in towns along the canal. The Erie is the most successful venture of its kind in the world! We got two thousand packets on that waterway—you can stand on a bridge and count packets as far as your eye can see. And now those bloodsuckers with their railroads think they'll cash in on that, jeopardize the canal, grab off its business and its profits."

He stopped speaking momentarily, as if out of breath. He belched and dabbed his lips with a napkin. He was perspiring.

"Well, they aren't going to do it," he said. "Or they'll do it over my dead body. A locomotive is a monstrous machine, the work of the devil. We got a law now that won't even let 'em run on the sabbath. Not only would they absolutely ruin the canal business; if you let this thing go too far, those fire-belching abominations will set fire to barns and fields, kill and maim thousands of people in their wrecks, and absolutely devastate the tranquility of this land with their noise and hooting and clatter. No, sir. We are waterway people. It's waterways that made possible westward expansion clear to the Mississippi and beyond. Cargo simply does not have to move faster than the speed of a towhorse along a canal. People don't either. I shall resist railroads to my dying day!"

Stephen's disappointment was acute. They left the following day, and he was brooding and silent as their stagecoach lurched southward along the rough turnpike into Pennsylvania. It was Thaddeus who spoke first.

"He's wrong, Uncle Stephen. You know he's wrong."

Stephen tousled the boy's hair.

In the years that ensued, all this helped to direct their lives and fortunes.

A man in his fifties, such as Stephen Stewart, could find his enthusiasms tempered by what a brother felt strongly—however impractical those feelings might be. For himself, then, he lost enthusiasm for building railroads. Besides, the West opened other intriguing possibilities. Vast overland distances would have to be linked somehow, for transporting people and goods. He wondered: Could a heavy-duty stagecoach be built to withstand the punishment of such travel, with way stations and depots along the route? And might the day soon come when mail could be rushed across a thousand miles by daring men riding relays of fast horses?

"Darling, now what are you thinking about so deeply?"

"Catherine, I've just had another fantastic idea."

"I'll bet I've got an even better one."

"Hmmmm."

But the restless mind of Thaddeus Stewart, on the verge of nineteen, followed relentlessly along its favorite track. He was tall and lanky now, intense and self-sufficient. The memory of Nathan Stewart's cynicism had only served, over the years, to whet his own interest.

"Uncle Stephen, would you like to go take a ride on the B&O Railway? I hear that they've got a new Baldwin locomotive engine, built in Philadelphia."

"All right, Thaddeus. But can we wait till the weather warms up a little more. I hate to travel in such cold."

"Trains," said Catherine. "Don't you think a boy his age should be thinking about something besides trains?"

"What did you have in mind?"

"Well, the opposite sex."

"All in due time, my dear. All in due time."

XX

The young man was possessed, any fool could see that. A daring rakehell, to be sure, and driven by a passion that ran deep in his soul. But different—subject to moods of introspection as if there was something on his mind that he had to do, and he would find no peace until it was done. This, at any rate, is how they spoke in the cramped fo'csle of the China clipper *Typhoon*. "I'd like to know what eats at the man, that's all." "Caw, it'd eat at you too, if you was a black skipper in a white man's world." "'E's only twenty-five, they say, but a hell of a shipmaster for all that."

Captain Francis Drake Stewart was oblivious to them. Gutter rats, they were, but sailors well enough. Behind his back he knew that they called him the Nigger of the Clippers. It mattered not. He drove the men as he drove himself, completely. The life was cruel aboard clippers under any circumstances. Blood boats, the sailors called them.

"Land ho!" The voice of the lookout came thin and high, down from the rigging.

His eyes swept a gray horizon across the foaming swells of a rising sea. "Where away?"

"Off the port bow!"

He snapped the glass to his eye, scanned, focused. There. A smudge on the point, no more. Sails like pinpoints bracketing the spot. A swirl of birds.

Beside him, the mate said: "A good run, sir. We'll drop anchor by eight bells, best I can figure."

"A fair estimate, Mr. Cochrane."

From habit, he peered aloft at the great sweep of sail soaring above his ship, *Typhoon*. God's blood, he loved this vessel, loved every beam and warp and billow of her. The mighty clipper was his very own now, by command and deed; a great knife-blade of a hull topped by the cloud of sail. Her beauty and grace were, in his mind, almost unearthly of perfection. Her hull was designed to slice through the water, not breast it. Those back-tilted masts formed a mountain of canvas a hundred and sixty feet high, an enormous mass of white catching every zephyr of wind. As the old sea captain, Frank Waters, had written of the clipper ship: "A huge sea bird, with white wings expanded."

Speed. Speed he insisted upon and speed he got. By Francis Drake Stewart's reckoning, she was the fastest thing afloat. *Typhoon* would be making this run from New York to Canton in seventy-two days with a cargo of furs and sandalwood. They'd rounded Cape Horn and crossed the Pacific to Hong Kong, ten thousand miles, in just fifty-one days.

"Steer two points to starboard, Mr. Cochrane."

"Aye, sir. Two points a'starboard."

Cochrane was a chunky Irishman who at first had hated to say the word *sir*. Even a light-skinned mulatto so devilishly personable as Drake Stewart was a Negro nonetheless, and it ate at a man's innards to acknowledge obeisance. But this did not last. In his heart, Cochrane was a fair sort. He came to realize from experience in a score of ports, in brawls and games and pursuit of the ladies, that Francis Drake Stewart was the equal of any white man alive and better than most. The night the captain had rescued him from a Calcutta ginmill, and they'd fought their way out side by side, had clinched it. Cochrane's loyalty was complete

"We'll bear in on the headland, Mr. Cochrane."

"Headland it is, sir."

At nightfall, they dropped anchor in deep water off the crowded harbor of Canton.

"You, Mellican, you buy. Chop, chop! Mellican buy silk? Ah. Nize silk. Mellican, have party? Gotta sister, muchy-muchy!"

The crowd was a living thing, pushing and swirling. Hands reached and clutched from the tumult of market stalls. The sound was a mindless babble. Ahead of him the rickshaw man screamed a torrent of Chinese, at times ducking his head and actually battering a path through the human crush. Smells assailed one from all sides, cooking smells and body smells, fecal smells, and incense smells. The latter marked another house of the forbidden opium, where men whiled away their afternoons in sweet languor, oblivious of life and its torments, heedless of time's urgent flight.

Captain Francis Drake Stewart rode the rickshaw seated ramrod straight in a fine broadcloth tailcoat with velvet collar, a pearl gray vest, a boiled shirt with a starched front, wing collar, and black taffeta bow tie. His top hat was a medium gray beaver with black velvet band. His body rocked to the jerking of the vehicle. He enjoyed the tumult. It was good to be ashore again if only to savor, briefly, the hurly-burly of it all.

Canton. China's entry for foreign traders assaulted the senses. From this crowded waterfront street, Drake could look out over the busy harbor flotilla of sampans, multicolored junks, barges and ferryboats and flower boats. At intervals there stood the hongs, the trading posts flying the flags that signaled they were open for business. Greedy hong merchants connived and haggled with the foreigners, grasping for bribes. One could barter there for silks, fans, porcelain bowls, for shawls of Cantonese crepe and pieces of inlaid furniture. Drake wanted none of these this trip. He was bound for Boston on the return, and the Boston profit would mean tea. A gamble, to be sure, but well worth it. Thus, he had put on his top hat and tailcoat to bargain ashore.

As the street curved, he saw for the first time that another clipper ship also stood in the port. This one, however, rode at anchor in a small cove, as if not wishing to be seen. Those masts, he noticed, could spread as much sail as the *Typhoon*. With his small pocket-glass he could just read her name, *Thundercloud*.

The rickshaw deposited him finally at the tea market. Here, the smells were spicy and sweet, emanating from open wooden casks. A silk-robed merchant bowed him to a table, where Drake sat down in a high-backed chair. The merchant clapped his hands. Barefoot Chinese boys trundled an open cask to the table. The merchant scooped up a handful of tea, which sifted through his fingers. "Velly nice. Excellent grade. You like?" the merchant murmured. "You sniff. You sniff."

Drake sniffed. He pinched some of the tea from the man's open hand. His fingers pressed the leaves delicately, feeling the stems and veins. This was second quality tea. He shook his head. The merchant impatiently clapped his hands again, scowling at the boys as if it was their fault. How dare they bring second grade tea!

The tea was grown in the hills behind Canton and brought to market by river sampans. It was sorted, sifted, fire-dried, packed, and weighed in the warehouse buildings overlooking the marketplace. Drake knew all this. He also knew that to acquire the best grade of tea required patience and exercise of will.

The haggling went on. Again and again, Drake tested the offerings and shook his head. Each time the merchant clapped his hands, and the cask was trundled away. For hours, it went on like that. The merchant grew steadily more impatient, and a crowd gathered to watch. Rarely did they see an American who knew tea and could bargain so fiercely. This American had tan skin and features that were finely formed, but Negroid. They had not seen this before; all American traders and ship captains were pale white men. At one point the tall American stood up and started to walk away, causing the merchant to unleash a volley of urgent instructions to his helpers, accompanied by a few well-placed kicks. As they rushed yet again to the warehouse, the merchant persuaded the American to return to his chair. Then, and only then, was the finest first-grade tea brought out for inspection. The haggling went on for two more hours. But the bargain was finally struck. The event immediately touched off an impromptu celebration.

Dusk was gathering when he started back to the ship. Aboard the junks and sampans the lanterns came on, making their pale glow against the oncoming night. Drake was in a buoyant mood. It had been an excellent purchase, and already the merchant's boats were delivering tea to the *Typhoon*. The crew would work through the night stowing it properly below. As the rickshaw jerked along, Drake lit a thin cigar and let the smoke curl out behind him.

The trouble erupted from a narrow side street. A heavy Chinese man in the robes and hat of a merchant came rushing into view, shouting a wild, terrified babble. There were few people about, and those who could be seen quickly vanished into dark pockets and crevices. Behind the man came three white men in the rough clothing of seamen. They caught up with the fugitive in front of Drake's rickshaw, knocked him to the street, and began kicking him in the back, head, and groin. Drake's rickshaw man dropped his poles and fled. Drake leaped from the vehicle and waded into the melee. A surprised attacker, suddenly jerked up from behind by a tall American, whirled and drove a savage chop into Drake's stomach. Drake felt the wind go out of him, but he kept his feet and momentum. With a short piston stroke of one big fist, he doubled over the first man and smashed a knee into his face. Glimpsing a foot, he stomped down upon it with all his weight and felt the arch break. As those two reeled away, screaming, Drake grabbed the third by the throat and simply rammed him headfirst into a stone wall. The attack disintegrated as rapidly as it had begun.

He helped the intended victim to his feet. The man was profuse in his gratitude, rattling in English so broken that Drake could understand only every fourth word. At the man's insistence, he accompanied him to a handsome walled house overlooking the waterfront, its entrance gate guarded by a pair of stone dragons. As they stepped into a pool of lamplight, Drake saw that his companion was older than he had first surmised. They were greeted at the gate by a much younger man who spoke excellent English. Half an hour later, over tea, they were engaged in easy conversation. Drake learned that the man he had rescued was Bay Ah Wong, a hong trader.

"My father cannot find words to express his thanks," the young Chinese said. "Those men were very angry and would have done him great harm."

"They looked like Americans to me," Drake said. "I've never heard of American seamen robbing people on the street. Usually it's the other way around."

"Oh, they weren't intending to rob. They were angry because my father refused to buy their opium. The emperor, you see, has tightened down on the trade to the point where it is practically nonexistent, on the surface, at least. Once my father was a very important man in such commerce. He owned for years one of the receiving ships that stood off the harbor mouth. But no more. It is not worth the risk. Now, all of the trade is underground."

"What ship did those men come from?"

"The China clipper in the cove. It's called *Thundercloud*. Her owners defy the ban openly, and this puts everybody in a quandary. The emperor does not wish to create an incident by denying them access to the port. Still, the *Thundercloud* is a bad ship. There's trouble every time she hits port. We'll be glad when she hoists anchor and goes back to America."

The Wongs insisted that Drake stay for dinner. He was famished. They dined on succulent snow peas and tiny white onions in a tasty light sauce, fried pigeon wings, and delectable flakes of roast pork. Politely, they ignored his clumsy struggles with the eating sticks, which kept slipping from the grasp of his big fingers. For every bite of food that reached his mouth, two fell back into his plate. He was still hungry when they retired to a terrace, to smoke fine golden tobacco in clay pipes while looking out on the moonlit harbor.

"And your father made it possible for you to own that magnificent clipper ship, Captain? How splendid."

"Yes. I owe him a great debt. I was brought up by his people, you see, on Cape Cod. I worked on a fishing boat by the time I was eight years old. Mr. Throckmorton, who was secretary to my grandfather's firm, saw to it that I studied every subject required of a first-class mariner. Navigation, shipbuilding, mathematics, the quirks of winds and tide—you name it and I studied it. I spent my youth on ships. Sailed here to Canton as a deckhand on a three-master when I was fifteen. I got my first command, a small coastal bark, when I was nineteen. At twenty-one, Mr. Throckmorton handed me the papers for a refitted brig, four hundred and fifty tons, and said I was on my own. With the profits, I finally managed to buy my heart's desire, the *Typhoon*."

"She is a glorious vessel. You must be the envy of every sea captain you meet."

Drake offered a wry smile, remembering the snide remarks, the hostility and veiled threats that were as much a part of his life as breathing. "Not exactly."

"And now your goal is to get your father out of prison?"

"Yes."

"Do you think it can be done?"

"It's possible. Anything is possible, given the right contacts and the right amount of money. American officials are no less pliable than the Chinese. My problem is, I lack contacts. I'm a sailor, not a diplomat."

It was nearly midnight when he took his leave. At the gate, beside the stone dragons, the hong trader spoke volubly to his son, who scribbled something on a slip of paper and handed it to Drake. "My father says that when you get to New York, go to this address. Someone there might be able to help you."

Drake returned to the *Typhoon* and was met at the gangplank by the ever-watchful Cochrane. The mate was visibly distressed.

"We had a visitor this evening, Captain."

"A visitor?"

"A man named Muggeridge, mate of the clipper *Thundercloud*."

"Oh? And what did Mr. Muggeridge have to say?"

"He said he brought a message from his captain, Byron Hatch..." Cochrane faltered.

"Yes? Go on, man."

"Captain Hatch says... He said to tell you..." Cochrane was becoming angry, and the words seemed to stick in his throat. Drake waited. "He said to tell you to keep your damn black nose out of his business, and that if you ever cross his path in an American port, there'll be a score to settle."

"That's all?"

"That's all."

Francis Drake Stewart mounted the deck and watched the sweat gang loading the cargo of tea by lantern light. Overhead.

the moon was a great circle of light that drenched the harbor in silver.

"We'll hoist anchor at daybreak, Mr. Cochrane."

"Aye, sir."

"And see if the cook can fix me up some salt meat and hardtack bread, will you? I'm absolutely starving!"

A rat scuttled in dry rubbish. Deep in the alley two tomcats yowled, nose to nose. A drunk lay unmoving behind a garbage can. The man walked quickly past all this, looking neither to the left nor the right, and up a short flight of stone steps to a green door. He knocked and waited. The door opened. A well-dressed fat man peered into the gloom. "Captain Stewart?" he said.

"Yes."

"Come in. Haurak is expecting you."

The fat man led him through a handsomely furnished parlor with gleaming brass lamps and Chinese furniture of rosewood and teak. Porcelain vases and India hooked rugs were prominent. There was a heavy odor of incense. They passed through a beaded curtain into a low-ceilinged room with a single lamp burning over an alcove where a man reclined. He wore a flowered Chinese robe and a small Mandarin hat. The man was filling a small clay pipe with a brown substance. The pipe had a long stem.

"Please sit down, Captain," the man in the alcove said. "Do you smoke?"

"No, sir."

"Pity. Do you mind if I indulge?"

"Please do."

The man in the alcove smiled. He was Chinese. His name was Haurak. For years he had served the Son of Heaven as supervisor of a receiving ship offshore at the port of Canton. He received opium in bricks from a ragtag fleet of foreign vessels making the opium runs from India and Turkey. He paid in silver. As the emperor's merchant, he'd made a fortune before deciding on clandestine flight to the New World as an alternative to being beheaded for violating the emperor's sudden opium ban. Now he amused himself as an arranger of favors, at a price, sought by individuals from American politicians. One accumulated power by working both sides of the bargain. Such is life.

He was mildly surprised to see this young man standing before him now. A boyish sea captain. But he was clean-cut and obviously of Negro blood. He was decidedly not the type that usually sought Haurak's ear.

"Do you wish to speak freely?" Haurak said.

"It is fine with me. I have nothing to hide."

"I am told you are in command of a clipper ship, a China clipper. This is true?"

"Yes."

"And you have been to Canton."

"I was given this address in Canton."

"And may I ask who gave you this address?"

"Mr. Bay Ah Wong, of the House of Twin Dragons."

The heavy eyebrows of Haurak lifted slightly, but he gave no other sign of recognition. "The harbor," he said, "it is as busy as ever?"

"Not in the same old way."

Haurak made a hissing sound. "The Son of Heaven remains obdurate, then."

"Not entirely. He has relaxed the decree. But not openly. You understand."

"Yes. I understand. And you paid tribute, then?"

"Always there is tribute, even for tea and jade."

Haurak nodded. He finished packing the clay pipe, so that the brown substance filled the tiny bowl. He put a long wooden taper to the lamp flame until it caught fire. This he put to the pipe and drew. After much drawing, a tiny plume of smoke curled from the substance with a sweetish odor. "How can I serve you?" he said.

"I wish to free my father from prison, in the state of Massachusetts."

Haurak's eyebrows lifted again. He peered into the face of the young captain, squinting through smoke. The man's eyes were clear and steady. It was Haurak's business to read men, and he read them in the eyes. "So," he said. "And why is he in prison?"

"He serves a life term for murder. It was over a woman, an actress. The man who died was an important politician, a relative of the governor of Massachusetts. His name was Barnard Hefling. This occurred many years ago."

"And what did Bay Ah Wong tell you that I would do?"

"He said that you know many important people. He said that you would make inquiries, give me a price, and try to free my father. That's all. I am prepared to meet any necessary expenses within reason.''

The almond eyes of Haurak glowed over the bowl of the pipe. The face was waxen, cast in deep shadow. The eyes seemed to drift. Francis Drake Stewart had the impression that Haurak' attention was flagging. The silence in the alcove was intense. Then:

''Very well. Give the details to my assistant, Mr. Kew. W will be in touch with you in a few days.'' Long, tapered finger lifted languidly from the depths of the robe. The fingers were heavily jeweled. They waved dismissal.

Ten minutes later, Drake stepped back into the alley, walked block, hailed a hansom cab, and returned to the dock wher Typhoon tugged at her moorings. Cochrane met him at th gangplank. ''I was beginning to worry,'' the mate said. ''And didn't know where in hell to start looking for you.''

''We will have to wait,'' Drake said.

The message did not come for four days. It was Mr. Kew wh brought it. The fat Chinese mounted the gangplank breathin heavily. ''Captain Stewart? So sorry for the delay. It is a difficul business.''

''Difficult?''

''I am instructed to inform you that the price is sixty thousan dollars.''

''Sixty thousand!''

''Mr. Haurak begs your pardon. It was the gravity of the, uh incident that causes such expense. That is the best we can do.'

''But I've only got ten thousand to my name.''

''There is no hurry. Mr. Haurak is a patient man.''

Drake leaned against the rail looking out over the docks. Sixt thousand. Even by selling the Typhoon he could not rais enough. He became aware that Kew was still waiting for a reply ''All right,'' he said. ''But it will take time.'' The messenge bowed and moved away.

At dawn on the morning tide, the clipper stood out from th harbor under a widening billow of sail. So spectacular was he size and appearance that even at this early hour a crowd gathere on the Battery, watching her departure.

''Beautiful, ain't she?'' said a weathered mariner, hunching i his pea coat against the morning chill.

''Aye, she is that, all right.''

''What vessel?''

"Typhoon. China trade."

The mariner nodded. "That'd be the boy captain, Stewart. Nigger of the Clippers."

"The same."

The mariner spat. "Blood boat."

"A race around the Horn, ye say? God's blood, we'll race the nigger clipper all right, and show 'em what for. Ye can't beat a white man at his own game, and that's a fact."

"He's got a fast vessel, Cap'n Hatch. You've seen her under sail. Her hull's sleek as a knife-blade, and he's got her fitted to carry as much sail as we do."

"Muggeridge, Muggeridge, you're a strange one. What makes ye think a nigger can sail a ship? You can put him in the finest vessel afloat, but"—Captain Hatch tapped the side of his head meaningfully—"it's what's up here that counts. And no nigger's got it up here."

New Orleans was agog with excitement. Nobody knew quite how it had come about, but there was a mortal strain between those two captains, the brutal, wily Hatch and the mulatto, Stewart. Even the mere presence of the two ships in port at the same time was a stroke of fate. Barely had they dropped anchor when a brawl broke out on the docks, with the rival crews going at each other with staves, chains, and marlin spikes. It had taken a dozen constables to break up the melee, and now an uneasy truce, taut with expectancy, kept the city on edge.

It was the black captain who'd goaded Hatch into a race. On a sultry night on Bourbon Street, accompanied by his mate Cochrane, Francis Drake Stewart confronted Hatch and his men in a saloon. But even as chairs scraped and the crowd sank back, Stewart was smiling and taunting his adversary to a race, a race around Cape Horn to San Francisco! "Captain Hatch, we can have our crews brawl from now on, but it isn't going to settle anything. You said in Canton that we had a score to settle? All right, let's settle it scupper to scupper like seafaring men. A race. And fifty thousand dollars bet."

"You ain't got fifty thousand dollars."

"I've got ten thousand, and the *Typhoon,* against your ten and the *Thundercloud.*"

Hatch's face worked in a torment of decision. "I ain't bettin' my ship."

Stewart chuckled. "No guts, Captain?"

Hatch came to his feet, eyes blazing. "I'll show yer who's got guts, nigger. I'll put mine up in cash, on the barrelhead. That'll show you what I think of your scow!"

It was done. The shrewd Stewart, goading and needling, also extracted an agreement to leave the cash, on both sides, in the hands of a neutral banker in New Orleans. Cochrane followed his captain out of the saloon with worry in his eyes. "You're staking *Typhoon* and every nickel you've got in this world."

Drake Stewart grinned. "Keeps things interesting, wouldn't you say?"

The frenzy of preparation began. The two vessels were moored within pistol shot of one another. By day, seamen and carpenters swarmed over each vessel, refitting, repairing, putting on fresh canvas. Within a fortnight, *Thundercloud* gleamed under a fresh coat of black paint. Drake Stewart concentrated, however, on fitting *Typhoon* with all new masts and rigging, adding bracing for the widened yards and mounting an extra oversize mizzen for stability and more speed. Each night the weary crew of *Typhoon* collapsed into their hammocks. But from *Thundercloud* there came the usual sounds of nocturnal roistering, bursts of drunken laughter, and frequent brawls.

One night a disturbance broke out on the deck of the clipper, raising so much noise that Drake came up from his own cabin to pace the deck in irritation. At the height of the tumult, a body plunged over the side with a heavy splash. A short time later Drake's crewmen fished from the murky water a grizzled apparition, all whiskers and stench. The man lay on deck in a pool of his own vomit, begging not to be sent back to the *Thundercloud*.

"What shall we do with him, Captain?" asked Cochrane.

"Send him below. Let him sober up. He can do what he likes in the morning."

The seaman was hauled away, too inebriated to make it under his own power. Drake Stewart promptly forgot about him.

The day of departure dawned clear and fine. A breeze spanked off the river delta, and all New Orleans massed on the docks to see them off. The harbor master, a worthy figure in top hat and swallowtail coat, read a speech that nobody could hear and fired a pistol into the air. A shout went up. "They're off to San Francisco!" Anchors lifted. Men sprang to the rigging. Unfurling sail caught the breeze and billowed. The two great clippers got under way.

"Set all sail, Mr. Cochrane!"

"All sail setting, sir!"

"Hands to the yardarms!"

"All hands aloft. Smartly lads!"

The great clouds of sail billowed above both vessels. Sleek knife prows cut blue water, raising lines of froth. Decks heeled, and the vessels moved toward the far horizon at their slants, flags spanking. Behind them, the din of cheering mobs rolled like volleys of cannonfire.

The weather held fine as they beat southward through the Gulf of Mexico, slicing blue-green swells that rolled in glistening peaks and troughs. Drake paced his deck, feeling the familiar motion underfoot, listening to wind and rigging, eyeing the mountain of sail aloft, so much sail that a man up top seemed the size of a fly. Down the Caribbean moved the clippers, each day a thing of mind-drenching splendor, the sea a dazzling blue and the sky dotted with cloud puffs that turned, at dawn and sunset, to vermillion and gold and blood scarlet. They rounded the mighty hump of Brazil, the air filling with the odor of tropical jungle. As the weather turned cool, they surged down the forbidding coast of Argentina in roughening seas. Finally, the day came when the skies were no longer clear, but gray and loosing cold rain squalls. The sea turned dark, with rising, foaming swells. When finally they veered westward into the straits, it was blowing sleet and snow.

"Captain, we ought to slacken sail. She won't take the strain much longer." It was their third day in the Straits, and Cochrane was a burly hulk encrusted in ice.

Drake peered aloft, his eye working over the rigging and the new masts and spars. He listened to the whistle of wind and felt the slant of deck. Something new had been plucking at his mind; a scrap of warning in New Orleans, from the mouth of a seaman who'd appeared out of nowhere onto the dock. "Haurak has gotten word about Captain Ward Stewart. He says the man is sick from prison life. He fears he cannot much longer survive, locked up. It is not the nature of a free man." And so that was the lie of it now. Suddenly this dash around the Horn had high stakes indeed. "Not just yet, Mr. Cochrane," he said. "All sails full."

A day later, as they beat deeper into the stormy Straits, Drake found himself confronting a gray-haired scarecrow. The man had not a tooth in his head and stood in cast-off clothes two sizes too large. His beak of a nose glowed an angry red from the cold and long drinking ashore. The eyes were rheumy, beneath a wild straggle of brows. "I must warn ye, sir," the man was saying. "They'll try trickery. Captain Hatch does not intend to lose. He's a bad 'un, and so's the entire crew."

Drake's uncomprehending expression finally made its meaning known.

"Oh, I'm Benjamin, sir. The navigator that you fished from the water back in New Orleans."

"A navigator, you say?" Drake shook his head. He did his own navigating and had no need for the likes of this. The man obviously was ill-suited for anything else as well, and could not be expected to climb aloft to bend frozen sail in a gale. "I'm obliged for your advice, Mr. Benjamin. Now if you don't mind . . ."

Three mornings later, off the wild coast of Tierra del Fuego, they caught sight of the *Thundercloud*. She was laboring in heavy seas. The weather was severe, with driving sleet and aching cold. Overhead, the sky was a maelstrom of scudding clouds that threatened any instant to vomit down destruction. Finally, they had to reef more sail and clew up, and still the *Typhoon* was shaking like a terrier in driving seas that could break full over her deck, sweeping and smashing in wild torrents of white water. With the glass, he could see that the *Thundercloud* was having an even rougher time. Cochrane verified his observation. "She's lagging, sir. She looks to be in trouble."

"We can't just run away from her here, Mr. Cochrane."

Drake ordered a change of tack and an approach. As they drew closer, the wind rose to gale force off the distant headland. To the north, he could catch fleeting glimpses of white bursts as mountainous surf exploded onto deadly outcroppings of rock. The wind pushed huge waves and ripped off their tops in flying spray.

"*Thundercloud* looks like she's ready to broach, sir!"

"Stand by the longboats. We might have to try a rescue."

"Not possible, Captain. Not in this . . ."

In a heart-stopping instant, he saw the trap. As visibility lowered, he happened to glance off the port bow in the direction of their drift. Abruptly there loomed into his field of vision a head of semisubmerged rocks, made visible only by an exceptionally violent crashing of surf. They were being drawn into the shoals!

"Hard a'starboard!" Drake bawled into the wind. "All hands aloft!"

"All hands! All hands aloft!"

"Starboard, helmsman! Starboard!"

His mind tumbled. It was a hairbreadth choice. Chop away what sail was still spread or try to reef, keeping steerage way? Men swarmed to the rigging, axes and knives in their teeth. From the corner of his eye, Drake saw *Thundercloud's* seemingly crippled sails begin to billow, driving the vessel froward at full ilt in the storm. His decision was made. "Reef foresails and main and foretops, Mr. Cochrane!"

"Reef main and foretopsails!"

It was risk. But risk it had to be.

"Helmsman, hold her hard a'starboard!"

"Hard a'starboard, sir."

"Steady as she goes..."

Time slowed. Time all but stopped. With paralyzing slowness he watched that deadly splume of tortured sea, nearing and nearing; jagged teeth of stone waited in the boiling frenzy to rip out their hull like paper and send them to the bottom. He was dimly conscious of Cochrane shouting, of the raging wind and the booming sea. But it all came to him as if in a dream, disembodied from time and place. Slowly ... slowly the certain disaster neared. And slipped aside....

And passed them.

Cochrane was pounding him on the back like a madman. From the yards, he could dimly hear men cheering. "We missed her, sir! Twenty yards to port, and we missed her!"

Francis Drake Stewart felt the strength drain out of him.

They lived.

Beyond those mountainous waves, Captain Byron Hatch and the *Thundercloud* now held a commanding lead. Through the straits and into the northward leg they sailed, with no sign ahead of the other clipper. At last the gales were behind, and the weather turned warm again. They beat up the coasts of Chile and Ecuador, past Central America and Mexico, with its perilous currents off the peninsula called Baja. The sun again warmed the decks of *Typhoon*, but the heart of Francis Drake Stewart was cold, his mood as cheerless as the wild coast of Patagonia they'd left so far behind. He paced the afterdeck alone, and even in the fo'csle the atmosphere was bleak. They gave the captain wide berth, and no man could bring himself to speak aloud of what was happening.

It was only the old crackpot, Benjamin, who dared to approach the commander of the *Typhoon*.

"Begging your pardon, sir, but I know these waters quite well."

Drake paused in his pacing, as if jerked back from some dark reverie. "What? What is it?"

"A lot depends on how you make yer approach to San Francisco. It's the currents, you see."

"Oh, it's you, Benjamin. I really don't think . . ."

"Better listen to him, sir." This was Cochrane speaking. The mate had finally been so badgered by Benjamin that he'd heard the man out. "We ain't got a whole lot to lose."

"What is it, then?" Drake snapped.

"Well, sir. What you do is, you take an outward leg, away from the coast. There's tricky currents in here; but farther out, there's strong winds and currents this time of year that can bring you in in much less time. You got forces in your favor, if you know what I mean."

Drake sighed. "Very well, Benjamin. We'll try it. Right now, I'd take advice from the devil himself."

The navigator gave him a toothless grin. "Yes, sir. Thank ye, sir."

As fresh commands were shouted from the quarterdeck, the *Typhoon* turned away from the coast and headed out to open sea.

Three days later, the lookout leaned forward in his perch and cried, "Land ho!" The weather was fine, the sea at their backs. As the mighty cloud of the *Typhoon's* sails billowed, and the helmsman held a steady course into the great bay of San Francisco, a flash of white to the south caught Drake's eye. The *Thundercloud* was still laboring up the coast! All hands raised a cheer as the semaphore dropped on the bald hummock known as Telegraph Hill, signaling their arrival. At last the *Typhoon* struck canvas and coasted to anchorage in the harbor. A crowd gathered among the ramshackle houses and buildings clustered along the waterfront. Behind them, the *Thundercloud* was just clearing the headland.

On shore, an ancient cannon boomed.

"Well, Mr. Cochrane," Francis Drake Stewart said, "I guess we've got ourselves a new navigator."

Old Benjamin bared his gums in a happy smile.

* * *

An icy December wind lashed across the Charles River as
Drake waited outside the fortresslike prison. He had put on a
uniform for the occasion, but suffered from fidgets and nervous
stomach. For an hour he had paced the brick walkway, back and
forth, back and forth. Haurak had warned him that things could
go awry at the last minute, but to be patient. Even with sixty
thousand dollars changing hands, arrangements could not be
made immediately. There had been official parole proceedings to
institute, more hands to grease, suspicions to be allayed. But
finally . . .

There was a sound of steel on steel. He turned and looked up
the long walkway. A solitary man exited from the dark double
gate. The man carried a seaman's duffle and walked painfully,
with a slight rolling gait. He was very tall. He had no hat. The
cold breeze ruffled his long white hair.

Drake's heart beat faster. He wanted to run, but did not. He
wanted to shout, but clenched his teeth instead. His hands were
sweating. He kept them in his coat pockets.

A cold sunbeam shot through the cloud cover, to play over the
dead grass, the drab hulk of prison facade, the long brick
walkway, and the limping, white-haired man.

Ward Stewart was halfway down the walkway before his son
moved forward to meet him.

XXI

'They are trying to destroy everything we built, Yvette.''

He was alone as always, speaking to her, sensing her nearness.
He sat on the bench, slouched, hands clasped, and directed his
thoughts to the silent marble with its cold, rich veins. It dominated the river here, this tomb, and it had cost him one million
dollars to build. The brooding structure could be seen for miles.

And to complete the great monolith, he had had it surrounded with a formal garden that swept down to the Hudson. The whole was incorporated with Blossom Hill mansion itself, which rose in its gothic splendor behind where he held his vigil.

A chill wind off the river brought down another shower of leaves from the giant maple trees and ruffled his white hair, but he paid it no heed. The sweater that he always wore was old and moth-eaten. She had knitted it for him years ago, and he could not conceive of wearing any other. In his sixty-sixth year, Nathan Stewart could find no warmth anyway.

"They want to grab off the Erie's business, as I said they would. You know, I told Stephen that when he came here with all that talk about railroads. Now some men want to build a line straight down the Hudson Valley between Albany and New York. We've got to put a stop to such foolishness as that."

Up at the mansion, someone had come out onto the front porch and was looking down at him. Francesca.

"Father," she called, "are you all right?"

He ignored her. "Francesca's a good girl, Yvette. A proper girl. Not as flighty as Marguerite. I'm afraid Marguerite's a bit of a scamp. But Francesca has decided to live here all the time now, and look after me. She doesn't know I'm going up to the canal. I haven't told her. I haven't told anybody. Just you."

"You'll catch your death of cold, Father. Don't sit there in that old thin sweater. Come back to the house."

Francesca came down the sloping lawn. She helped him to his feet. He shook off her hand querulously and walked by himself, using the cane. "Dinner is almost ready," she said.

He left the mansion the following morning before dawn, still wearing the tattered sweater. He went to the street and hailed a hansom cab, which took him to the offices of Stewart Steamship Co. He caught the morning steamer to Albany, spent the night in a hotel, and then boarded an early westbound Erie Canal packet that made its way slowly through the multiple locks. No one recognized him on the crowded boat or paid any attention to him. He found it difficult to sleep in the cramped, stuffy cabin. The food was hard for him to chew. They reached Schenectady, and it took them two more days to get to Syracuse. At last he got off the packet at a point near the new railroad. Stiff and sore, he walked to the railroad and sat down wearily on the track.

Nathan sat in silence, listening to the distant sounds of the canal, the youthful hoggies singing to their mules and dray horses, the signal horns of the packet boats. He was thinking about Yvette.

They had not been given much time together, not nearly enough. She was taken too soon, without even a chance to enjoy the full life. He had never been a religious man, but the death of Yvette had driven him even farther away from the church. God would not be that cruel; not if he were a merciful and loving God. The preachers had come to the house, making somber faces and praying for her final rest. Somebody told him that God often took the young and the beautiful as His way of reminding us of our mortality. Somebody else said that God needed a beautiful flower in His heavenly garden, and Yvette was that flower. Nathan did not believe either of them.

In the years afterward, as time did its work on his mortal being, Nathan would never have another woman. That, he felt, would defile her memory. He had built her great tomb, that showplace of the Hudson. But it mocked him in its silences. His wealth and power were of such magnitude that they called it a dynasty; but of what worth was wealth that could not save her, could not return her to life? He had spent a fortune on spiritual readers and charlatans in an attempt to communicate with her in the Great Beyond. He'd whispered in the solitude of his dark nights, "You said you'd never leave me." But none of it mattered any longer . . .

He must have dozed. It was late afternoon. A cold breeze rustled the dry leaves. A brown mongrel dog came loping down the railroad track, shivering. The mongrel approached the seated man, sniffed, tentatively wagged its mangy tail and moved on.

"The bogtrotters would have made a stew out of you, dog," he said.

He had been waiting five hours when the monster came. He heard it at first, out of the west, chuffing and clanking and ringing its bell. It came into view at last around a bend, all black iron and gleaming brass dominated by a single tall smokestack, grinding its iron wheels and hissing steam. He thought of Robert Fulton, nearly half a century ago, riding that infernal steam machine in the streets of Birmingham, and of old James Watt venting his wrath at railroad trains. He could see in his mind's eye the professor's mouth repeating, over and over and over, "Infernal machines. Infernal machines. Infernal machines infernalmachinesinfernalmach . . ."

The whistle split the twilight.

"Curse you, monster!" He stood up, waving his cane. This one had an eye, gleaming in the middle of its snout; a dimly lighted eye, but an eye nonetheless, growing larger. "Spawn of Satan, destroying a man's work and his life, disrupting his peace and tranquility. Damn you, train!"

The eye enlarged. Steam blew. A whistle screeched.

"Damn you, train!"

He swung his cane to strike the hated eye...

They could not conceive of him dying. It was too much, too much. The fact of Nathan Stewart ceasing to exist, as do mortal men—of being transformed in one blinding instant from a colossus who was still the talk of salons and society suppers, which he no longer attended, into Nathan Stewart, corpse—was all too irrational.

Onlookers gathered early in the whispering rain beneath clusters of umbrellas, straining against police barricades to gaze up the winding driveway at the front of the mansion known as Blossom Hill. For hours they contented themselves to watch, spellbound, as if the great multistoried brownstone would suddenly spring to life from its sweeping porte cochere to its steep slate roof bristling with chimneys. There was that mood of hushed intensity reserved for the dead.

Shortly after noon the mourners came, the favored and invited, the important and the rich. They came in closed carriages and surreys, drawn by trotting horses whose flanks steamed in the wet. As each vehicle drew up under the porte cochere, the occupants alighted in black clothing to move with stately grace up the broad stairway to the huge double doors framed in leaded windows.

Among the street bystanders, newcomers mingled with the old under the umbrellas, white face to white face, meeting acquaintances, gossiping in breathless whispers.

"A train. Imagine! What was he doing on a railroad track, of all things? At Syracuse, of all places!"

"He drank, you know."

"The newspapers said—"

"Bother the newspapers. You don't believe newspapers, do you? There's more to it, I say. Nathan Stewart would never, never stand up in the middle of a railroad track and try to strike down a train with his cane! My word!"

"Where is she? Has she come yet?"

"There she is, getting out of that carriage. There, in the black veil, see? You can just see the white hair poking out from beneath the hat. That's her. That's Lucy Durange."

"But she looks . . . old. I thought she would be younger."

"My dear, do you realize it's been years? But let me assure you, in her day . . ."

"Always loved him, they say. Never married again, after Claude Durange died. Never had another man, even though he'd been a heller. It was Nathan Stewart, always Nathan Stewart. I have a friend whose cousin was her upstairs maid. Knew all about it."

"The daughters. There they are, coming in that carriage now. Marguerite and Francesca. Poor things. Aren't they pretty? Poor, poor dears."

"Heavens. There's an Indian. I really do see an Indian. He looks like an Indian. And the man with him, that tall man with the peg leg beside the blonde woman. I believe his face is masked. Yes, half of his face is masked. How odd."

"Very odd."

"Don't you think that's odd?"

"It's very odd . . ."

Even in the house there was a dampness, a sense of cold, a heavy odor of flowers. The people poured in through the foyer and beyond, to the great formal rooms where so many of them had once been entertained as guests at Blossom Hill. They brought odors of damp woolens and wet furs. The double doors of the dining room were thrown open, and there were folding chairs in every available space. Mourners filled the chairs and stood along the walls. The noise of movement and murmured conversation subsided into creakings and coughing. There was a busy surreptitious glancing about at the famous personages present. The Vice President was present, the governor, the mayor, many councilmen and members of official boards. Among the bereaved were presidents of banks and presidents of steamship lines, owners of freight companies and commercial establishments. There were many legislators and members of Congress. There were plain men, rivermen, bargemen. There were relatives, near and distant.

The Stewarts of Pittsburgh occupied an area unto themselves. Isaiah Stewart, white-haired and palsied at the age of ninety, stared at the closed bronze coffin in which the body of his son had lain for ten days in ice. Nathan's mother, Martha, occupied a wheelchair, her face heavily veiled. The brother Stephen, gray, tall, impeccably tailored, his face partly concealed by the flesh-tinted silken mask, sat rigidly at the head of a row of chairs filled with his personal retinue: Catherine, the three teenage children, the tall and scholarly nephew Thaddeus, the Indians Crippled Wolf and Moon Flower. Several people saw Catherine slip her hand softly into Stephen's and hold it.

The Rev. Merwin R. Brookshield, pastor of the Second Congregational Church, had never met Nathan Stewart in person. He would have loved to enroll a man of such substance into the flock, God knows. But Stewart, it was rumored, had no formal religion and was uncomfortable in the presence of the clergy. It had to do, some said, with the untimely death of his young wife Yvette in the cholera epidemic. Well, that was sixteen years ago, but there was no accounting for grief. The Rev. Mr. Brookshield would have welcomed the opportunity to speak frankly to the man. He would have informed him that God needed a lovely flower for His heavenly garden, and that this undoubtedly was His purpose in taking Mrs. Stewart. Yes. Invariably this thought brought comfort to the bereaved. It was with gratification, however, that the Rev. Mr. Brookshield could perform this sacred duty today, at the invitation of the deceased's lovely daughter Francesca, who was a member of Second Congregational. Well, the poor thing actually wasn't all that lovely, in fact, she was rather plain, but plain in a proper and religious way. Now, attired in his black cassock with the purple surplice trimmed in gold and carrying his Holy Bible, the Rev. Mr. Brookshield stepped to the lectern facing the mourners and took a deep and pious breath.

"In my father's house," he intoned, "there are many mansions . . ."

The Rev. Mr. Brookshield had never preached a more eloquent funeral. As his measured cadences rolled through the rooms of the great house, he noted with satisfaction the intent expressions of the governor and the mayor. He sensed that his words were striking the proper balance with the legislators as well. Carefully he praised Nathan Stewart's part in building the Erie Canal and expanding the steamships, but deftly he avoided any breath of the bitter controversies such efforts also had ignited. "His name will go down with those of the great men of vision who saw the future with an inner light and answered its call!" He gave this phrase an extra measure of volume, and then quickly lowered his voice to just above a whisper. "Nathan Stewart *believed*." Pause. Closing of the Good Book. "Let us pray."

When it was done, the mourners filed past the closed coffin paying their respects. The bronze repository of Nathan Stewart's mortal remains was banked with a vast array of floral tributes. But the flowers also had a twofold purpose. Beside the bier stood a nervous mortician whose sensitive nostrils told him that the warmth of the room was having its effect. And then the coffin was borne by eight pallbearers, dignitaries all, to the waiting horse-drawn hearse—a magnificent conveyance, all black oak and silver and cut glass, drawn by black-tassled horses. Thus were the remains of Nathan Stewart taken down the slope to the great marble tomb, where the granite-lined vault—beside the tomb of Yvette—gaped open to receive it.

There was a sound of weeping. It was Francesca, looking even taller and plainer in black. As they closed the vault and sealed it, she sat down on the stone bench, his bench, and wrung her hands in the rain.

Two mornings later, Stephen Stewart and his nephew Thaddeus leaned at the railing of a steam packet chugging through the mist off the coast of New Jersey, southbound for Baltimore. They planned to board the B&O Railway and ride it as far as it went inland. Then they would take a stagecoach across the Alleghenies to Pittsburgh. The Jersey coast was a dark smudge passing in the distance.

"Was Uncle Nathan really that unhappy, Stephen?"

"I'm afraid so, Thaddeus. In his last years he was a very unhappy man."

"It was a tragedy to lose his wife like that."

Stephen turned up his collar against the morning chill. "Yes, I suppose it was. But she died a long time ago. My brother's problems went deeper than that."

"Deeper?"

"He was inflexible in many ways, Thaddeus. Nathan Stewart was unable to adapt himself to new ways, new attitudes. He could not accept change."

"But why would he have such unreasoned hatred for railroads? They posed no personal threat to him. He certainly didn't stand to lose financially."

"Nathan didn't see it that way, Thaddeus. Trains threatened Nathan's concept of order, speed, distance. Like so many people who build empires, he was locked into his own point of view and could not deviate from it. The steam engine was a means of moving ships; to travel overland, you built a road or dug a canal. The idea of putting down iron rails and running a steam-powered engine over that, at speed, was simply too much of an extension for Nathan. The prospect was too daring, too complex, too vast. And so instead of adapting, he resisted; instead of rationalizing, he went by instinct."

The conversation lapsed. Thaddeus, deep in thought, watched the dark coastline flow past. The rhythmic labor of the packet's engine intensified their silence. Then:

"I can't wait to finish college, Stephen."

"I envy you, Thaddeus. I wish I had gone to college. Nathan had all the education in this family."

"Do you know what I intend to do after I've graduated?"

Stephen chuckled. "No. What do you intend to do?"

"I intend to build a railroad. But not just any railroad. A transcontinental railroad, from the Mississippi River all the way to the Pacific Coast. Do you think I'm crazy, Stephen?"

"No, I don't think you're crazy."

"I have a powerful feeling that this country is at the brink of great change. There's a restlessness everywhere that—that astonishes me. A great pressure has been building. In a little over two more years it will be eighteen and fifty . . ."

The whistle of the steam packet blasted across the slate-colored sea, warning dorymen of its approach.

"This is just the beginning," Thaddeus said.

Stephen wished that he could share such bright optimism. But he was growing old now. He had lived for more than six decades. The years tumble in a turgid stream, eroding at one's trust in the future. The nation was restless, all right. It was also torn with sectionalism. Men fought duels over politics. Slavery ate at America's vitals like a cancer. For reasons that he could not fully define, Stephen Stewart could not shake a nagging sense of dread.

"Yes," he said. "It's just the beginning."

XXII

San Francisco had accepted her freely and openly and without guile, as it accepted the morning fog and the afternoon sunlight, as it accepted the odd mix of people who came and went or the scrubby chaparral that clung to the sandy slope of Telegraph Hill. It was less than nine hundred souls, for God's sake, dwelling in a cluster of shacks and tents and ramshackle buildings crowding a crescent-shaped cove commanding a stunning view of the great bay. But San Francisco gave Maybelle a feeling, for the first time in her life, of belonging. It took a tolerant view of all who came, of sombreroed Mexicans and Yankee soldiers, down from the hills for a drink and a carouse; of settlers and drifters, sailors and drunks, New England traders, Mormons, the Kanaka from the Sandwich Islands, and even three Chinese from Canton. There was no telling what would come wandering next down the dirt main street, the *embarcadaro*. There was room for all, including six whores and their aging red-haired madame. The changeover from Mexican to American government two years before had taken place peacefully.

One could not survive by bordello alone in a town of under nine hundred souls. And so Maybelle had opened a saloon, one of numerous saloons, with a cafe adjoining. Two of her girls had gone down to Monterey, and the remaining ones served as waitresses and saloon hostesses. The piano gave Maybelle's Bayside a special atmosphere. In a short time it became the most popular place in town. They were so busy ushering in the new year, 1848, that she had to hire extra help.

"Maybelle, it ain't much now, but let me tell you this town has got potential." The speaker was Jim Lick, a newcomer who'd sailed into the bay from Lima, Peru, with an iron safe filled with golden doubloons. Barely had he stepped off the boat when he began buying up lots at sixteen dollars apiece. Now he was sharing his hunch, with a grin and a wink. "It's a natural."

Always, it seemed to be this way. Maybelle had accumulated her years gracefully and, despite the trials of the past, retained good humor. The little girl, Vanessa, was five years old now and the light of her life. Vanessa had the quiet ways and stunning blue eyes of her father, Van Harrison. Instinct told Maybelle the girl would be a beauty. A pity Van had not lived to see her. Other men were drawn to Maybelle, but she would have none of them. She preferred to bring up the child alone. And so the men who frequented Bayside exchanged confidences and gave advice and, more frequently than not, borrowed a few dollars from the generous redhead. She never expected to get any of it back.

"Well, I might not be the smartest woman in the world, Jim," she said, "but I'm not a fool, either. I'll take your advice."

Maybelle Stewart, like Jim Lick, began to buy up land in and around San Francisco at sixteen dollars a lot. On occasion she paid as high as twenty-two dollars. Owners of such property, including the thrifty and canny Mormons, were only too willing to sell. Heads wagged. "A fool and her money," said a businessman, "are soon parted."

Thus, fortune began to take its subtle turn. The sudden decision to acquire land, however, was not the only break that would make Maybelle Stewart the richest woman in California. The real bonanza would be the unexpected reward for an act of generosity.

In the middle of February, a backcountry drifter named Charlie Prime wandered into Maybelle's Bayside looking for a free meal. He was dirty and stank and had not shaved in a month. One of the hostesses came into Maybelle's office with the word. "Charlie's here again. Remember, he hit you for a loan six months ago. Want me to throw him out?"

Maybelle shook her head. "No. How does he look?"

"Terrible. He stinks and he's half-starved."

"Give him a drink and something to eat. I'll come out directly."

"Maybelle, you don't have to..."

"Do as I say."

When Maybelle went out to see Charlie Prime, the drifter was polishing off the last of a blue plate special, meat loaf and fried potatoes. While other customers stared, she sat down at the table.

"Charlie."

"How'd do, Miss Maybelle."

"Ain't seen you in a while."

"Been up in the Sierra Nevada."

They made small talk. Charlie Prime seemed restless and excited, as if something inside him was ready to burst. Finally:

"Have you heard the news, Miss Maybelle?"

"What news, Charlie?"

He looked around cautiously and licked his lips. "Gold. They found gold up at a sawmill that John Sutter's buildin' on the American River. Fella name of Jim Marshall and some carpenters, they found it. The word's spreading like brushfire."

Maybelle looked into the glittering eyes and smiled to herself. Gold, eh? There were always stories of gold strikes and coal strikes. They came as frequently as the rain and never amounted to anything. The Mexicans even talked of a great vein of gold beneath the foothills, running for more than a hundred miles from Coloma south to Mariposa. *La veta madre*, they called it. Legend. Pure legend.

"That's what I really come to see you about, Miss Maybelle," Charlie Prime said. "You been good to me, and I figured maybe I could do you some good too. I—I need me a stake. Nothing big, mind you. Enough to get me a mule and a few diggin' tools. I know them foothills like the back of my hand; I been over every yard of 'em. I know the run of the rivers out there, the Yuba and the Bear and the Sacramento. I figured, well, I figured you and me could go partners, fifty-fifty. You stake me, Miss Maybelle, and I'll split with you, all the gold I find. You got my word on it, but I'll put it in writin'."

Maybelle laughed and patted his hand. "Charlie, I'll be glad to stake you. Hell, what's a friend for? You don't need to put anything in writing, though. Your word's good for me."

"No," Charlie Prime said stubbornly, "I want it in writing. Half of everything I get is yore'n."

"All right, Charlie." She stood up. "But right now, I want you to go out back and get yourself a bath. I don't think even a self-respecting mule could stand a whiff of you."

Charlie Prime left the Bayside the following morning with Maybelle's stake in his pocket. The hostesses were loud in their disapproval.

"How much was it this time?"

"Two hundred dollars," Maybelle said.

"You're a damn fool."

"Well, Charlie needed it. I figure if a person needs a little help . . ."

"You can just kiss it good-bye. These fellas never pay you back, Maybelle. When are you going to learn that?"

"But I'm Charlie's partner!"

The hostesses burst out laughing. They laughed until the tears streamed down their faces. They laughed for half an hour. Nobody had heard such a huge joke before in the Bayside.

Seven months later, in the rugged, isolated country at the headwaters of the Tuolumne River, the solitary Charlie Prime drove his pick into the Mother Lode.

ABOUT THE AUTHOR

CHARLES WHITED was born in West Virginia, attended the University of Virginia and was a paratrooper sergeant during the Korean War. He has been a journalist for twenty-five years and now writes a daily commentary column for the *Miami Herald*.

He ghostwrote Mrs. Elliott Roosevelt's autobiography *I Love a Roosevelt* for Doubleday. He later collaborated with treasure hunter Martin Meylach to write *Diving to a Flash of Gold*. His book about the true adventures of Dan Chiodo as a NYC decoy cop, *The Decoy Man*, was published in hard and soft cover by Playboy Press. He has published several paperback novels.

Charles Whited is now working on the third volume in the SPIRIT OF AMERICA series.

Read this preview
of the thrilling second book in
THE SPIRIT OF AMERICA

DESTINY

BY CHARLES WHITED

On sale July 15, 1982

From a thousand pulpits the warnings came. "I tell you, my brethren, the railroad is an abomination in the sight of God. Man was not made to go at such terrific speeds. The heart will stop, the blood be caused to boil. I shudder at the moral consequences for young females. Danger to life and limb will be devastating, maiming and killing, showering sparks across this land. You farmers, your hens will refuse to lay, your cows will go dry. Woe betide us. And what's more, it is against our democratic principles to place such economic power in the hands of the few greedy men who shall own railroads . . ."

Thaddeus Stewart, fidgeted. He was nine years old. His skin prickled. His starched white collar was hot. He stared at the angel in the stained glass window. He waited until the service was finished. And then he dutifully followed his Uncle Stephen as the crowd flowed up the aisle. Women murmured down to him, smelling of eau de cologne. A line formed at the double doors, where the sunlight streamed through. He ached to be outside. Slowly, slowly, they approached the sunlight. The parson was shaking everybody's hand. "Mighty fine sermon, Parson," Uncle Stephen said. Thaddeus gravely shook the parson's hand. The parson was a cadaverous man with a nose like a rooster's beak. He patted Thaddeus on the head and said, "Good lad."

Two weeks went by. They joined a crowd of laughing yokels on the outskirts of Baltimore, watching the steam engine *Tom Thumb* race a big gray mare belonging to a rival stagecoach company. The tiny locomotive belched and chuffed. "Hah, hah, teakettle on a track!" jeered the crowd. Engine and horse went the full thirteen miles of track. The horse won. Red-faced officials of the B&O departed in a huff. Later, it was said that they gave *Tom Thumb* back to its inventor, a man named Peter Cooper.

"Uncle Stephen, I hear there's a new railroad out of Charleston, in South Carolina. Can we go? Can we go?"

The Charleston and Hamburg Line was experimenting with faster methods of moving their small, open, carriage cars along the track; faster methods, that is, than mule power. It was a breezy spring day. The conductor was resplendent in a dark coat with brass buttons. "Ladies and gentlemen, please take your seats. We are about to raise the sail." They climbed aboard, Stephen and Thaddeus in a front seat, their friend Crippled Wolf in the back. The Omaha Indian wore his favorite costume, a gray stovepipe hat, green split-tail morning coat, beads, braids, and buckskin trousers. ("Upon my word, Maude, do you see that Indian?")

The seats filled at last, the sail billowed, the cars began to move. Faster and faster they went. "My heavens, Thaddeus, we must be doing seventeen miles an hour!" They came to a curve, got halfway around, and the train blew off the track.

Two years passed. Again the scene was Charleston. A stubby engine huffed clouds of live steam. The engine was named, happily, *The Best Friend of Charleston*. An engineer stood on the platform behind the boiler, stoking wood into the firebox. A steam safety valve hissed at his elbow. The locomotive snorted, chuffed, jerked into motion. Gathering speed, the steam valve hissed louder. And louder. And louder. The engineer, irritated, shut it down. "Uncle Steph . . ." *The Best Friend of Charleston* blew up. The engineer was dead in the wreckage.

Thaddeus became the thoughtful teenager, ever

doodling, ever scribbling in his diary. "Uncle, what a shame that trains can run only in daytime. With proper lights, they could operate at night, too." Reflectorized candles didn't work, for the wind blew them out. Thaddeus doodled and pondered. "I've got it, Uncle! We'll let the engine push a flatcar carrying a bonfire built on sand."

Trainmen were skeptical. "Well, I don't know, Mr. Stewart." A gold piece dropped into the hand of the reluctant engineer. The good man became more flexible. "What the hell, we'll let the boy try."

A pinewood bonfire was lit on a flatcar. The train chuffed off into the night. A feeble light was cast for a short distance down the track but only when the fire was at its height. Thaddeus wearied of throwing on wood. He ran out of logs and pine knots. The disgruntled train crew, unable to light their way back home, spent the night in the forest. Uncle Stephen shrugged. "Nothing ventured, Thaddeus, nothing gained."

In the year 1842, Thaddeus was thirteen years old. The state of Illinois had great plans for building more than a thousand miles of railroad. Fifty-nine miles were completed. A mighty steam locomotive the *Northern Cross* chugged the entire distance at eighteen miles an hour. But the line was doomed. Prairie grass, silent and swift, grew over the tracks faster than it could be cut away. Portions of the trip were unbearably slow as passengers were constantly getting off the train to form bucket brigades for water. Within seven years the Illinois Railroad gave up and shut down. The once-mighty *Northern Cross* gathered rust in a barnyard, a dead leviathan. Thaddeus and Uncle Stephen made the trip between Meredosia and Springfield behind a plodding mule. Illinois was left millions of dollars in debt.

There were those who saw the demise of the *Northern Cross* as the handiwork of God Almighty and the Iron Horse itself as an instrument of Satan. The Illinois Railroad, they declared, was dead for all time, and good riddance.

"Do you believe that, Uncle?"

"Of course not, Thaddeus."

"Neither do I."

So begins DESTINY, book two in THE SPIRIT OF AMERICA, the towering, passionate saga of one family who carved an empire from America's limitless riches.

The year is now 1848. The Stewart fortune has grown immeasurably, but the ceaseless pursuit of their country's vast wealth has splintered the family in internal competition. During dinner on a night when most of the Stewarts have gathered to see ailing patriarch Isaiah Stewart for perhaps the last time, the simmering conflict between members of this proud family builds up a furious head of steam . . .

Thaddeus sat at one end of the great mahogany table surveying a scene of faces, above expansive white cloth, gleaming silver settings, formal plates, steaming bowls and tureens of food. The servants worked with quiet efficiency tending to plates, water goblets, wine.

"They are planning to extend the railroad clear to Pittsburgh," Thaddeus said. "Probably in three years, we'll get on the train here and ride it all the way to Philadelphia."

"That's going to make a tremendous difference in shipping time, too. Not to mention costs," the visiting ironmonger said. "Railroads are really cutting costs on freight."

"But isn't that going to hurt your business, Stephen?" asked one of the merchants. "Why ship by wagon if you can send it cheaper and faster by rail?"

Stephen cut into a wedge of roast beef, forked a morsel into his mouth and chewed thoughtfully. "It would hurt if we were unwilling to change, Hiram. The point is, we can be flexible. There's plenty of freight business for all. The way I see it, railroads have their limits, just as riverboats and canal barges have theirs. Trains can carry the goods from city to city and from state to state, but somebody's got to haul the goods from the train depot to the inland town and from the town to the farm. And then there are vast areas of this country that aren't served by railroads, and may never be served by them. This means there will always be a profitable business in overland freight wagons. The Stewart Freight Line isn't going out of business. Riverboats aren't in any danger either, as far as I can see. It will be a long time before there's a direct rail link from, say, Pittsburgh to New Orleans, touching the major cities in between. Besides, slow-moving bulk cargo, like coal and crushed stone, cotton, farm commodities, even a lot of industrial goods, will always be shipped cheaper by water."

"What Uncle Stephen's saying," interjected Thaddeus, "is that we're going to need every means of transportation to meet the demand. This country is growing at a fantastic pace. Why, the National Road is open now all the way to Illinois, and crowded every mile of the way during the warm weather months. But for fast, cheap transportation, the railroad is the most dramatic development in history. Why, a transcontinental railroad would—"

Someone guffawed. "A transcontinental railroad to where?"

"Why, to the far west, of course," Thaddeus said. "To the Pacific coast. To California!"

"What on earth for? Who could possibly want to go to California?"

Laughter rippled around the table. Unaccountably, the talk was growing boisterous. Thaddeus, like all true believers in a cause, was unabashed by the ridicule of others.

Finally, a female voice sliced coldly through the tumult. "Young Thaddeus suffers from the empty-headedness of inexperience. What he is suggesting, of course, is absolute balderdash. The railroad will not survive in this country, because good Americans simply will not tolerate it!"

Heads swiveled. Thaddeus looked down the table into the eyes of his cousin Francesca Stewart. They were twin steel chips in a face of fury. His mouth worked at protest, but a warning frown from Uncle Stephen caused the words to die on his lips. The table talked hushed.

"I'm appalled," Francesca said, "to hear Stewarts speak openly in favor of this monstrous creation. Have you no loyalty, no indignation? Must I remind you, all of you, that my own father, Nathan Stewart—he was your brother, Uncle Stephen, and Isaiah Stewart's eldest son—was killed by a locomotive? Run down like a dog!"

"Francesca!" Marguerite protested.

Thaddeus felt his temper rising. Francesca lectured about the ruination railroads would wreak upon America, their direct competition to Stewart financial interests, their noise, their pollution, and the corruption which their enormous economic power threatened to foist upon the nation's body politic. Finally Thaddeus could take no more. He stood up abruptly, knocking over his chair.

"That's enough!"

Francesca, startled, fell silent.

Thaddeus fought to bring his anger under control.

White-faced, he glared at Francesca and whispered, "This is insane."

He picked up his chair and sat down again.

This will not be the final clash between Thaddeus and Francesca. Embittered by the death of her father Nathan, Francesca despises all Stewarts—even her own sister Marguerite. Now Francesca will use the wealth gained from her shrewd business dealings to become Thaddeus' most powerful enemy.

But between Thaddeus and the beautiful Marguerite, a very different flame burns ...

The coal smoke of Pittsburgh wafted up from the valley.

Marguerite wrinkled her nose.

"What's wrong?"

"That smell. Is it always so strong?"

Thaddeus laughed. "Worse. This is a clear night. But that's Pittsburgh. We don't mind actually. Coal smoke means prosperity. It comes from the works. We make nearly everything in Pittsburgh, y'know. Even glass."

He was comfortable. Here was a subject he could discuss without shyness. Aware of the light pressure of her hand on his arm, Thaddeus talked on about the glories of Pittsburgh. "I didn't realize anyone really had strong feelings about this town," Marguerite said.

"I was born here, grew up here," Thaddeus said. "I'm not exactly unbiased."

The confrontation at dinner nagged at Thaddeus' mind. He felt a powerful need to make amends. This seemed as good a time as any. "I'm sorry for the way I acted with your sister. I should have been more tactful. She does have reason to feel strongly. After all, your father was..."

"Killed by a train?" Marguerite sighed. "Well, that's certainly true enough. But it wasn't the train's fault. Trains can't think, after all. Even you've got to admit that."

He caught the teasing inflection in her voice and smiled in spite of himself. "True enough."

"Besides, Francesca can be terribly assertive. I honestly think sometimes she wishes she were born a man instead of a woman."

"Are you not happy with your sister?"

Marguerite shrugged.

"Francesca's all right in her way. After father died, she felt responsible for me. We're only two years apart in age, but two years between sisters can make a tremendous difference. Francesca had a need to be dominant. It's her nature. But I suspect that she's awfully lonely deep inside."

"I understand she's done amazingly well in business."

"True. When it comes to business, Francesca is a match for any man."

Marguerite seemed to welcome a chance to talk, to unburden herself to someone who would listen, who cared. The sisters had inherited the fruits of their father's steamship and freight empire, notably on the Hudson River and the Erie Canal. Their wealth was reckoned in millions. When Francesca reached age twenty-one, she filed a law suit to take personal charge of the business—the river steamers, the canal packet boats, the freight warehouses. Her father's former business associates cringed. The all-male management threatened revolt. "A woman," they declared, "has no head for commerce. She'll ruin us."

Francesca won her suit. Her first act was to fire all the men who had opposed her takeover and replace them with people of unquestioned loyalty. She raided rival companies for management talent, then viciously undercut competitors for freight business to build volume business. Within a year, the voices of derision were stilled along New York's docks and wharfs. Francesca Stewart, just turned twenty-three, was a competitor to be reckoned with.

But among the sisters, things did not run smoothly. Marguerite had an independent nature, refused to be bossed like a hireling. Clashes were frequent and bitter, and all the more so because Marguerite attracted males as strongly as Francesca repelled them. The sisters drifted apart.

Thaddeus thought of his own strained relations with his cousin, John Colby. The two had been brought up as brothers, and yet John Colby's animosity at times became open, naked hatred. Thaddeus started to speak of it, and then changed his mind. A more compelling mood possessed him. "But you're so different," he said, "so beautiful and"—he caught himself, flustered, but stumbled on—"and desirable."

Her face turned to him. In the dim light, he could not tell if she was smiling or teasing. Thaddeus suffered another flash of embarrassment. Damn his clumsiness!

"Desirable?" she asked. The face of Marguerite Stewart was a light oval in the shadows, almost translucent. Her beauty, at this closeness, seemed ethereal. They had stopped walking and she turned, her breast lightly brushing his arm.

"What?" he said.

"You use the word 'desirable.' Do you find me so, Thaddeus?" Her voice dropped almost to a whisper. He had the distinct impression that Marguerite was trembling. His mind must be playing tricks! He drew back from her slightly.

"I . . . mean to say that you're a young woman of charm and, uh, personality. Not at all like your sister."

"I see."

They walked on, not touching now. But his mind was in turmoil, his heart hammering. Were his senses deceiving him?

They walked in silence, deep in thought. Finally, he realized that they had walked off the hill and were now on the river road. A cold breeze came off the Monongahela. A half-moon stood high over the Pennsylvania hills, outlining the woodlands in ghostly silhouette. Marguerite shivered and took his arm again. It was such a natural act, taking his arm, and the pleasurable sensation poured through him with a molten warmth. The rest happened as an automatic response for both. At one instant they were apart, two separate lives in the night; at the next, he had folded her into his arms and their mouths met. Her lips were soft and afire. As he drew her to him, she moaned and tightened her arms around his neck. The fire of it inflamed his mind, his chest, his loins.

"Marguerite," he said. "Marguerite."

Abruptly, they separated. The flush of joy and embarrassment was in his face. Her eyes glowed in the darkness from dark orbs. A trick, he thought. A trick of the light.

"What are we doing?" she whispered. "I don't know what's come over me."

They locked hands, turned and walked back up the road. Moonlight sifted through the trees. The empty road fell away before their feet, and they seemed to float. His mind was a mad swirl, his chest seemed on fire.

"This is unbelievable," she said.

"Yes. How do you feel? What do you feel?"

"I feel . . . I feel lighter than air, like a thistle. I have wonderful pains, like needles, running all through me. I want . . ."

His arms encircled her again. Again, they came together. Their mouths met hungrily. They strained against each other and felt a joyful, moonstruck, spectacular madness. Around them all nature held its breath. The damp hollows of the night waited expectantly. The moon rode high, sliding in and out of fleecy clouds. Then . . .

"Please. Thaddeus, no." She pushed away, gasping for breath.

He backed away from her again. They linked hands, staring at each other. They turned and walked once more. The road steepened, winding through the night. At last the white pillars of Stewart House rose into view, and behind them the windows glowed with lamplight.

They were separate once more, climbing the porch side by side, hands apart, communing in their shared silence. At the door, he whispered, "I shall never forget this evening."

"Nor I," she said.

DESTINY continues the surging saga of the Stewarts—men and women who conquered every challenge their country offered and forged an empire as great and as vast as the land they loved:

Stephen—The new leader of this bold family. Blessed with the ambition his father emblazoned into his soul, he fired the lifeblood of a raw nation's industrial power.

Thaddeus—The nephew Stephen raised like a son. At an early age he displayed the unyielding ambition that drove the Stewarts to greatness, and his friendship with Abraham Lincoln revolutionized Western expansion.

Marguerite—Her all-consuming love and determination spurred one man to glory and another to tragedy.

DESTINY

Ruth—*Thaddeus' wife. Torn by desires she could not control, she stood to lose the man she fought so desperately to win.*

John—*Stephen's son. His scandalous actions were an embarrassment to the family and his insane jealousy plunged Thaddeus into grave danger.*

*The irresistible power of **CHALLENGE** continues in **DESTINY** as the Stewarts rise up and embrace **THE SPIRIT OF AMERICA.***

**A stirring new novel by the World's
Bestselling Frontier Storyteller**

THE CHEROKEE TRAIL
LOUIS L'AMOUR

Our foremost storyteller of the authentic West
with over 120 million copies of his books in
print around the world, Louis L'Amour has
thrilled a nation by bringing to vivid life
the bold men and women who settled the
American frontier. Now L'Amour introduces
us to Mary Breydon, a brave woman suddenly widowed and isolated with her young
daughter on the Colorado frontier. Though
everyone tells her that it is no work for a
woman, Mary takes a job managing a run-
down stagecoach station on the Cherokee
Trail. With the support of a spirited Irish
woman, a fearless orphan boy and, most of
all, the mysterious gunman Temple Boone,
Mary finds the courage to face down the
constant danger of attacks by outlaws and
marauding Indians and shape Cherokee
Station into a vital stop on America's westward journey . . . Until the vicious murderer
whose bloody rampages stained her past
stalks Mary once again.

(#20846-2 • $2.95)

*Read THE CHEROKEE TRAIL, on sale July 15, 1982
wherever Bantam paperbacks are sold. Or order directly
from Bantam by including $1.00 for postage and
handling and sending a check to Bantam Books, Dept.
CT, 414 East Golf Road, Des Plaines, Illinois 60016.
Allow 4-6 weeks for delivery. This offer expires 2/83.*

THE LATEST BOOKS IN THE BANTAM BESTSELLING TRADITION